Pandit Madan Mohan Malaviya and the Formative Years of Indian Nationalism

Pandit Madan Mohan Malaviya and the Formative Years of Indian Nationalism

Vishwanath Pandey

LG PUBLISHERS DISTRIBUTORS

First Published 2015

ISBN 978-93-83723-06-5

Published by
LG PUBLISHERS DISTRIBUTORS
49, Gali No. 14, Pratap Nagar
Mayur Vihar Phase I, Delhi 110 091
Tel : 011 2279 5641 email: lgpdist@gmail.com

Printed at
Mudrak, 30 A, Patparganj, Delhi 110 091

Dedicated to

My Uncle and Parents

Contents

Foreword by Mushirul Hasan ix

1. INTRODUCTION AND LIFE SKETCH 1

   Mahamana Pandit Madan Mohan Malaviya: The Colossus 1

2. LEGISLATIVE WORK 14

   The Abolition of Indentured Labour 14

   The Indian Councils 32

   The Press Bill 36

   The Seditious Meetings Act 51

   Gokhale' S Education Bill 62

   The Simultaneous Examination 74

3. SPEECHES, NOTE AND PRESIDENTIAL ADDRESS OF THE INDIAN NATIONAL CONGRESS 90

   The Reform of The Legislative Councils 90

   A Federal System of Government for India 96

   Lahore Congress Presidential Address 104

   Congress and the Political Reforms 164

   Indian Demands 168

   Self-government for India 187

   Delhi (33rd Session) Presidential Address 189

   Calcutta (47th Session) Presidential Address 233

   Appendix No. 1 242

   Appendix No. 2 248

4. DISSENT NOTE IN THE INDIAN INDUSTRIAL COMMISSION 251

Note on Report of Indian Industrial Commission 251

5. THE MORLEY-MINTO REFORMS AND THE MONTAGU-CHELMSFORD REFORMS 355

The Morley-Minto Reforms 355

The Montagu-chelmsford Reforms 365

6. SPEECH ON THE HINDU UNIVERSITY BILLS 421

Speech on The Introduction of BHU Bill 421

Speech While Passing BHU Bill by the Legislative Council 425

7. CONVOCATION ADDRESS (1929) OF BHU 434

Pandit Madan Mohan Malaviya's Address 434

8. OTHER IMPORTANT SPEECHES 465

Gaya Presidential Address Hindu Mahasabha: 1923 465

MALAVIYAJI'S LAST MESSAGE (EXCERPTS) NOVEMBER 1, 1946 471

Index 473

Foreword

The 20s of the twentieth century was one of the most creative periods of our history. Led by Mahatma Gandhi, men of outstanding calibre dominated the political scene. Poets and writers surfaced giving creative expression to the fears and aspirations of the people. What is more, reformers thought of the future in terms of regenerating the nation. For this reason, scores of education blueprint were prepared, discussed and debated, and then placed before the colonial government. One such blueprint was prepared by Pandit Madan Mohan Malaviya.

The Pandit was a key figure in local, regional and national politics. In Allahabad, he was widely respected for his learning and admired for his reforming zeal. He was associated with scores of local bodies for the promotion of, for example, Hindi. Slowly but steadily, he spearheaded the All-Hindu Mahasabha and the *sangathan* (consolidation) campaign.

Pandit Madan Mohan Malaviya was a fervent nationalist, who joined the Congress quite early in public life. He had differences with the party on many issues, but he did not sever his links with its policies or its leaders. As a matter of fact, he held Gandhiji in high esteem; the mahatma, too, thought of him as a patriot.

As a man of vision, Malaviyaji took the momentous decision to set up an educational centre in Banaras. Implementing this decision, more so in the presence of the colonial government, was not easy. But Malaviyaji worked tirelessly to achieve his goals. He showed great skills in mobilising people to his cause.

Today, the Banaras Hindu University stands out as a tribute to its founder.

I am glad that a thoughtful analyst like Vishwanath Pandey has found time for this scholarly intervention. He has been closely associated with the Banaras Hindu University and seen it grow. The text of this book makes it clear that he and his associates are proud inheritors of Malaviyaji's legacy.

The book puts together a great deal of information on Malaviyaji and on the development of his educational ideas. It is compulsory reading.

Legacies are meant to be interpreted differently. What is important is how the students and teachers reflect on their inheritance and communicate their academic and intellectual experiences to the next generation.

Mushirul Hasan

1

Introduction and Life Sketch

MAHAMANA PANDIT MADAN MOHAN MALAVIYA: THE COLOSSUS

Mahamana Pandit Madan Mohan Malaviya, the great founder of the Banaras Hindu University, was among the most eminent makers of the modern India. Except for Mahatma Gandhi, probably no man in India is so much loved and respected and had such a wide following among its people as had Pandit Malaviya. Mahatma Gandhi regarded him as his elder brother. The well-known editor of the *Leader*, C.Y. Chintamani treated Pandit Madan Mohan Malaviya as the only man fit to be bracketed with the sage of Sabarmati. Annie Besant referred to Malaviya as the symbol of the Indian unity among diversity of opinions.

He had a good deal to say about education, the neglect of which in his opinion largely accounted for the backwardness of India. Before 1770, neither India nor Britain had a national education system. Since the British rose to the pinnacle of power and prosperity by virtue of measures, which had transformed its education system, India remained neglected, even the British did not agree to the modest Primary Education Bill sponsored by Gopal Krishna Gokhale and supported by Malaviya himself. But Malaviya's unbending belief that without education, India could not have its social transformation paved the way for the fulfilling agenda, gradually in the subsequent decades.

He advocated provision of agricultural, mechanical and commercial education at all levels from the primary to the university. He considered it necessary that primary education should be made compulsory if not free. The Indian Industrial Commission of which he was a member, recommended mechanical training to be imparted in schools attached to the railway workshops. Malaviya feared that if such trainings were confined to railway workshops alone, it would not benefit the Indians to any appreciable extent. He suggested the introduction of mechanical training in ordinary schools and recommended introduction of courses of mechanical and electrical engineering in schools and colleges leading to an examination of the London B.Sc. standard. He expressed the hope that Calcutta and other universities would start such courses (as he himself did at the Benares Hindu University), and practical training be made available in railway and other workshops. He considered it essential that the government should give adequate financial aid to the institutions providing such training and naval engineering and stressed the immediate need for starting commercial education in all the universities.

While welcoming the commission's recommendation for the establishment of an industrial development department at the centre and also in each of the provinces, he strongly opposed the creation of an Imperial Industrial Service and of a cadre of scientists styled "Imperial Chemical Service" for carrying on scientific research in aid of industries. Such steps, he argued, would place the future of Indian industries in the hands of the bureaucrats recruited in England, like the existing imperial services, who would be both costly to this country and indifferent to its interests. He referred, indignantly, to the services and working of departments such as agriculture, veterinary, meteorological and geological surveys, which were intended to be manned by the Indians, but having been initially recruited abroad by reason that the Indians with requisite qualifications not being available at the time, continued to be manned by Europeans even after the Indians with degrees in the European universities became available. He cited the glaring example of the "Indian Education Service" to which such eminent scientists as Sir Profulla Chandra Roy had not been admitted.

Intensive Efforts for Banaras Hindu University (BHU)

Malaviya's most notable achievement in the sphere of constructive activities is the establishment of the Hindu University at Banaras for which he worked ceaselessly for over 25 years. Such important institutions are usually built-up by the benefactions of super-rich men, or by the high officials taking the lead with the backing of government, or by means of public subscriptions raised to commemorate a great name. But in the present case, the University was brought into existence by the devoted exertions of a private citizen, mainly through the trust reposed by the public in his devotion, character and high moral purpose.

Advocate of the Industrial Development

Malaviya's interests were nation-wide and not confined to merely politics or education. Every good public cause had his sympathy and support. He was a strong supporter of the compulsory primary education from the time the late Mr Gopal Krishna Gokhale introduced his bill in the Imperial Legislative Council in 1911. He was also one of the principal organisers of the Hindu Mahasabha Movement, the object of which was to promote the co-operative efforts for all good purposes among the Hindus so that the community might not fall below other nationalities, either within or outside the country, in energy and virile power for defence or self-improvement.

Malaviya was a vigorous advocate of the policy of industrial development in the country. The minutes he wrote for the report of the Indian Industrial Commission (1916-18) has often been quoted as the true Indian view of the industrial needs of the country. In the minutes he pointed out how Indian industries have suffered in the past by discouragement and neglect and how vital it is to foster industries on modern lines for the economic upliftment of the country. If a genuine movement for this purpose were set on foot, he hoped to be able to carry on a campaign and collect a very large sum within the country itself to provide the capital needed for organised industries.

Need for the Scientific and Technical Education

India cannot regain her prosperity till the study and application of the modern sciences becomes, so to speak, naturalised in the country. The patriotic endeavours which are being made to send students to foreign countries for technical education, in his opinion, are most praiseworthy. But they are no doubt meant to serve, as a small beginning. Technical education cannot be expected to make any real progress till there is at least one well-appointed polytechnic institution in the country capable of giving efficient instruction in the principles and practice of the technical arts, which help the production of the principal necessities of life of the Indian population.

But mere industrial advancement cannot restore India to the position which she once occupied among the civilised countries of the world. And even the industrial prosperity cannot be attained amongst all the concerned, and these can only prevail and endure amongst those who are fair in all their dealings, strict in the observance of good faith and steadfast in their loyalty to truth. Such men cannot be found in sufficiently large numbers to keep a society in an organised, efficient and healthy condition, when the society to which they belong is not under the abiding influence of a great religion, acting as a living force. The foregoing considerations point to the need for bringing the Hindu community under a system of education which will qualify its members for the pursuit of the great aims of life (*trivarga*) as laid down in the scripture:

1. Discharge of the religious duties (*Dharma*)
2. Attainment of material prosperity (*Artha*), and
3. Enjoyment of lawful pleasures (*Kama*).

The fourth great aim, salvation (*moksha*) must be pursued by each individual by his own efforts under the guidance of his spiritual preceptor and in accordance with the methods of his own particular creed or denomination.

"Believing that observance of the religious duties provided the foundation for a peaceful and well functioning society, Malaviya wanted to see India guided by the religious principles of both the Muslims and Hindus. Pandit Malaviya believed that under the colonial rule, many Indians remained uneducated concerning the highest attainments of their own culture and religious practice was subsequently declining in the face of the dominance of the western pattern of living."[1] Believing in the values of culture and the religious practice, it was a challenge for him to create a genuine Indian nationalism.

"Strong in their religion, unified by a new awareness of their own national identity, and equipped with modern knowledge, the Indians would be prepared to assume responsibility for their nation."[2] At the Punjab Hindu Sammelan in 1923, Malaviya said that only a religiously oriented society would unite the Indians as a nation and allow them to make progress. In order to achieve unity, Muslim and Hindu communities alike needed to be more religious."[3]

"He is said to be a supporter of Santanan Dharma. What is Sanatana Dharma? Not the rites and ceremony, not the different things which have changed from centuries but there are certain qualities which are of a universal character which have got an appeal in vitality even today. *Abhaya, Ahimsa, Asanga*. These are the qualities which are the characteristics of the Indian culture. *Abhaya* is a freedom from fear, integrity of spirit. Look at the world and you find everything is subject to the law of times, to rotation, to death, to annihilation. You ask whether this death, whether this annihilation is all."[4]

"If that is *Abhaya* it remains to be followed that it must result in action of love and friendship, *Ahimsa*. You find the *Dhammapada* saying, "Victory breeds hatred". The conquered live in sorrow. The Yogasutra tells us when *Ahimsa* is established, there is (*Vairatyaga*). There is a complete aspect of renunciation, so to say, of hatred."

"And when Malaviya took up this problem of raising our country from slavery to freedom, from spiritual ignorance to some kind of spiritual enlightenment, he tried to remove all these technical difficulties and defects from which we suffer. He tried to throw himself into the work of the world. He tried to do what one man can do and he has done a great deal to remove the suffering in this world, to raise the country to a higher level. Religion is a supreme effort to improve the human condition."[5]

"There are four distinct strands to the debate on secularism in India. First, the liberal left position holds that religion and politics belong in different realms. This position saw the rise of Hindutva in the 1980s as a failure of the secular state and of modernisation."[6] Some have argued that secularism is not a Western concept but has a long history in India. This is the secularism-as-tolerance argument which asserts that the ancient history of India demonstrates the inherent secularity of its culture. "India, the argument goes, 'has since ancient times accommodated many different peoples: Aryans, Huns, Turks, Bactrians, Scythians, Persians, and all the rest. Hindu *dharma*, with its loose, accommodative structure, was able to draw into its ambit the more of these different people, for it held within it an indigenous concept of secularism, *sarva dharma samabhava*, the idea that all religions are true. Gandhi, most famously, argued that tolerance and the accommodation difference was a core characteristics of the Indian culture."[7]

"Prof. T.N. Madan suggests that advocates of secularism in India ignored the fact that the religion itself could be a powerful resource in the struggle against religious extremism.[8] Similarly, Prof. Ashis Nandy sees the project of secularism in India as an attempt to impose from above a model of social behaviour incompatible with the particularities of a traditional society such as India."[9] The attempt represents, he argues, "An imperialism of categories." Madan and Nandy, both maintain that the Indians have practices of tolerance that they can draw on from their own religions. However, in their search for the indigenous answers to the problems of sectarianism, they see the Indian traditions of tolerance as stemming from what can broadly be called Hindu civilisation.

"Political philosopher, Prof. Rajeev Bhargava, argues that the discussion of secularism in India has to move beyond the opposition with religion in which it is mired. He reflects that the divide between the "secular" and the "religious" is somewhat of an institution in our country and asks if it is not possible to take the spiritual and ethical elements common to all religions and transpose them into a secular, non-doctrinal framework for behaviour. More specifically, Prof. Rajeev

Bhargava asks if there cannot be a "spiritualised, humanist secularism", at least there has to be encapsulate of incorporate values shared by many religions into the public life of India in a way that could be embraced by all as a sort of secular religion. Interestingly, this suggestion is not very different from that of George Jacob Holyoake, who first coined the term secularism in England in 1851. George Jacob Holyoake also wanted to create an ethics for everyday life that was not irreligious or hostile to religion but was not bound by any particular religious tradition. In this sense, it was a secular, namely worldly, ethic."[10]

"The apparent anti-modernism of Prof. Madan and Prof. Nandy, the *dharmic* universalism of the Hindu right, and the spiritual humanism of Prof. Bhargava are all primarily responses to the failure of the liberal ideal that posed secularism as an answer to the problem of communalism. The incongruence between a normative model of secularism and the reality of the Indian society prompted either a wholesale rejection of the idea, as with Prof. Madan and Prof. Nandy, or an adoption of the term by qualifying its meanings. The latter approach has been more common. As the normative model did not appear to correspond with the Indian society, India developed its own version of the idea: 'Indian secularism'. According to the Hindu right, by pandering to minorities liberals had not properly applied the institutional rules required of a secular state and were therefore 'pseudo-secularists'. For Prof. Rajeev Bhargava the doctrinal intransigence towards religion implied by the term should be forsaken in favour of an ethics of tolerance."[11]

"A fresh outlook on these lines has helped to sort out the earlier confusion amongst some historians regarding Malaviya's role in conflicts such as secular vs non-secular, communal vs Hindu politics, conflict vs harmony. There now seems to be a consensus amongst the recent historians that Pandit Madan Mohan Malaviya's contributions were not in conflict with the existing theorisations of the secular polity. His work in organising, promoting and motivating the Hindus to progress in the historical process by following the dictates of the Sanatan Dharma, as a way of life, fully supports the true secular way of working."[12]

Malaviya was the first leader to announce: "India belongs to the Hindus, the Mohammedans, the Sikhs, the Parsis and the others alike. No single community can rub over the rest... Act in such a way that all may unite... Let there be mutual trust." It was exactly in this spirit of brotherhood that he opposed the Communal Award, and even had to oppose Congress, which was maintaining a neutral position on the subject. He toured the northern part of the country and explained to the nation about the danger of the Communal Award, which according to him was dividing the nation. Ultimately, the Congress could see his point and rejected the Communal Award in 1936. The Constitution of India also endorsed Malaviya's views."[13]

"Malaviya had declared: 'If the Communal Award stands, every class and creed in the country will be organised under it as a separate political community to scramble for its own interests in the legislature in disregard of the people as a whole.' The truth of Malaviya's visionary prophesies can be seen in light of the danger which looms large over the country.[14] A wide diffusion of science in India as a means of rescuing the people from the abject poverty into which they have fallen is not possible until science, both theoretical and practical, can be learnt by the Indians in their own country, noted the first prospectus of the BHU."[15]

"Malaviya was a man of deep convictions although he was always able to see the other person's point of view. This exceptional quality commended him as a friend and guide to the groups and parties holding different views and not unfolding conflicting ideas. He had in him a store of sympathy and equanimity of temperament which always cut across the political differences and religious distinctions. There is little wonder, therefore, if with the leadership of the masses he managed to combine successfully the respect of many a ruling princes, dedications to learning and western education and his own orthodox view of life. The gamut of his activities was wide enough embracing the political, economical, social, education and religious aspects which enabled him to influence all these spheres with equal felicity.

Malaviya was born on December 25, 1861 and died on November 12, 1946. He got his BA degree in 1884, LLB in 1891, and practiced in the High Court of Allahabad. He was the editor of various newspapers and journals. viz. *The Hindusthan* (a daily Hindi newspaper), *The Indian Union, Abhudaya, Maryada* and *The Leader* and Chairman of the *Hindustan Times Group* till his last breath. Malaviya was one of the earliest protagonists of the Indian National Congress and since 1886 he had been associated with it. Four times, he was bestowed the presidentship of the Indian National Congress, a unique distinction of the political maturity and respect which he commanded. In 1903, Malaviya was elected to the provincial legislative council. There he delivered the important speeches on the annual financial statement, the Excise, Rowlatt and the Bundelkhand Land Alienation Bills. He was subsequently elected to the imperial legislative council in 1910 and continued to be its member till 1930. His enthusiastic support to Gopal Krishna Gokhale's Elementary Education Bill was well known.

Malaviya's vision of the modern India envisaged rapid industrial and agricultural development of the country and for that he advocated education in the field of sciences and technology. At his behest the Indian Industrial Conference at Banaras (1905) and UP Industrial Conference at Allahabad (1907) were organised. His dissent to the report of the Indian Industrial Commission (1916-1918), as its member, is a brilliant exposure of the economic and industrial problems of India and at the same time an indictment of the British economic policy towards the country.

"At the Calcutta Congress of 1920, Malaviya opposed the adoption of the Gandhian programme of Non-Cooperation. In 1932, he presided over the "All India Unity Conference" at Allahabad. The Communal Award of Ramsay Macdonald was severely critised by him at the Congress Nationalist Party Conference in August 1934 at Calcutta.

"Malaviya was the principal figure behind the meeting of the Sanatan Dharma Mahasabha at Allahabad in January 1906.

He did tremendous work in solidification and rehabilitation of the Hindu community in northern India. The establishment of the Banaras Hindu University may be deemed as part of his efforts in this direction.

"Malaviya's services to the socio-political life of India and its economic regeneration have indeed been great. But greater still and more enduring has been his selfless devotion to the cause of education through the establishment of the Hindu University at Banaras. He wished to make it an ideal centre of learning, and gave up his lucrative practice at the bar for his ideal. Many people had greeted his scheme with ridicule, regarding it as utopian and impracticable. Obviously, there was a grave problem of financial support. But by dint of his personal charm, integrity and sincerity, Malaviya was able to collect the large sum of money required to establish the university of his dream. It will not be an exaggeration to record that Malaviya was the heart and soul of the Banaras Hindu University, a living monument of his untiring energy and endeavour and supposed to be one of the greatest achievements of the twentieth century in the country. One of the major objectives behind this university was to create manpower for the reconstruction of India after attainment of its freedom. It is noteworthy to record here, that the mandate has been fulfilled by the alumni of the university in laying down the infrastructure and developmental projects. It may also be noted here that the engineering and science education in the Banaras Hindu University had been the backbone of creating an institutional network in the country and that includes prestigious institutions like the Indian Institute of Techonology, Management, Medicine and a number of the scientific laboratories and institutions. Infact steel, coal, power and such other mining industries are flourishing because of the labour of the alumni of the BHU.

"He worked ceaselessly to put the university on a firmer footing and guided its destiny as its Vice-Chancellor (1919-39) and Rector (1939-46). He exhorted the Indian youths to be men of character. In his famous convocation address (1929) he observed that the education they had received was required to plant an ardent desire in their minds to see their country free and self-governing. He cherished the desire to prepare the youths to discharge every obligation which may be cast upon them for the early fulfilment of it. He reminded them that the highest duty of a citizen was to offer the final sacrifice of his life when the honour of the motherland required it. Conclusively, he wished them to act with a full sense of responsibility and to work in the right spirit and under proper guidance for the freedom of the country.

"To sum up Malaviya's colossal personality, it may be relevant to quote Mahatma Gandhi, who wrote:

> I found him (Tilak) as Himalaya, I thought that it was not possible for me to climb that an unscalabel height. I then went to Shri Gokhale. He appeared to me like a deep ocean. I found that it was not possible for me to enter so deep. Lastly, I approached Malaviyaji. He seemed to be as crystal like as the stream and I decided to have ablutions in the sacred stream.

"The Malaviya Bhawan itself is a monument of national importance along with the Banaras Hindu University to commemorate the memory of the relentless freedom fighter, an outstanding cultural giant, a great champion of the economic and social reforms, who devoted himself to ameliorate poverty wherever he saw it, and worked for social and economic transformation. A memorial befitting the born leader endowed with a striking personality, sterling character, deep scholarship, sincere devotion to the public cause is the need of the hour. In fact, everything which goes to make a man accepted, adored, loved, respected and enthusiastically followed by the nation has to be inbuilt in a suitable memorial to the one who "wore the white flower of a blameless life", always presenting a radiant smile, exuding energy, vigour and kindness, a shining example of plain living and high thinking, selfless service, an example of single-minded devotion to the cause of the Indian freedom and nation building. A memorial to the one who was steadfast in his conviction that what is needed to reorganise the national life is to reorganise education and in order to ensure a better future for the nation to produce leaders of the future. A memorial to the one who visualised and brought to fruition, by establishing the BHU a combination of the best in the Western scientific thought and the eastern classical wisdom.

"It is with this end in view that the Mahamana Malaviya Heritage Complex has been announced. This complex will be a national and international centre for grappling with the issues and problems, challenges and perspectives, horizons and heights for the new millennium. It shall be a forum for focussing on the rich cultural heritage of India and the entire humanity and transmit the message for the peaceful development of the mankind on the basic principle of truth and non-violence. The message of our ancient thinkers, saints and seers, and particularly Mahatma Gandhi in the twentieth century, who inspired the freedom fighters of India all over the world has to be extended to all the frontiers of the world which are facing the danger of complete and partial annihilation from the nuclear holocaust on the one hand and the technological and scientific disaster on the other. The Malaviya Complex and all its encompassing activities shall serve as a centre of light to encourage the stewards of the Banaras Hindu University and provide constantly innovative thoughts and ideas to inspire the entire community to aspire to reach the heights of learning and the human resource development that makes a better being.

"In order to project greater clarity in relation to the heritage complex the intended focus and thrust of the complex is:

i. Malaviya and His Times
ii. The National Movement
iii. Towards the National Reconstruction

"On the solid foundation of the moral, philosophical and cultural heritage of India, Malaviya reconstructed and built the scientific, technological and educational edifice in which the students will take a dip in the holy waters of the ancient knowledge on the one hand and the best in techno-scientific knowledge of the west on the other, to be fully equipped for the new challenges which an independent India will usher in.

"The Complex is proposed to be the pilgrim centre for the sons and grandsons of the alumni, fortunate to have heard from their fathers or grandfathers about their nostalgic reminiscences of their stay under Malaviya's benign influence and partake the best in terms of education from the great masters, attracted by Malaviya whose spirit and personality inspired the *kul* of the *gurukul* to drink deep of the fountain of knowledge and the ambassadors of the Malaviya and his creation, the Banaras Hindu University."[16]

NOTES

1. Renold, Leah, 2005, *A Hindu Education: Early Years of the Banaras Hindu University*, Oxford University Press, New Delhi, p. 27.
2. Ibid.
3. Madan Mohan Malaviya, 'Punjab Hindu Sammelan, Lahore, February 23, 1924', in *Mahamana Pandit Madan Mohan Malaviya*, Vol. 1, Sitaram Chaturvedi, ed., (Banaras: Sitaram Chaturvedi, 1936), p. 119.
4. Dar, S.L. and Somaskandan, S. 2007, *History of the Banaras Hindu University*, Banaras Hindu University Press, Banaras. Reprint of original ed. 1966; quoted from Dr. S. Radhakrishnan Speech (Malaviya Centenary and After), p. 850.
5. Ibid.
6. Tejani, Shabnum, 2007, *Indian Secularism: A Social and Intellectual History, 1890-1950*, Permanent Black, Ranikhet, p. 7.
7. Ibid., p. 8.
8. See T.N. Madan, 'Secularism in its Place' *JAS*, 46, 4, 1987; and Ashis Nandy, 'The Politics of Secularism and the Recovery of Religious Tolerance', *Alternatives*, XII, 1988, both reprinted in Rajeev Bhargava (ed.), *Secularism and its Critics*, Delhi, 1998.
9. Ibid.
10. Bhargava, Rajeev, 'Religious and Secular Identities', in U. Baxi and B. Parekh (eds), *Crisis and Change in Contemporary India*, Delhi, 1995, p. 341.
11. See, Tejani, Shabnum, pp. 10-11.
12. Maini, S.K., Pandey, Vishwanath and Chandramouli, K., (2011), *Visionary of Modern India: Madan Mohan Malviya*, Roli Books, New Delhi (from Preface-xi).
13. Ibid.
14. Ibid.
15. See the article of Vishwanath Pandey published in *Hindu* (Chennai) December 28, 2008 with the title 'Malaviya: Visionary with Selfless Devotion to Education'.
16. BHU website http://internet.bhu.ac.in/malviyaheritage/index.html

2

Legislative Work

THE ABOLITION OF INDENTURED LABOUR

At the meeting of the Imperial Council held on March 20, 1916, Malaviya spoke:

"My Lord, I beg to move the following resolution:

"That this council recommend to the Governor-General-in-Council that early steps be taken for the abolition of the system of the Indian Indentured Labour.

It is now nearly eighty years since the system of the indentured labour was first introduced in India. It followed in the wake of the abolition of slavery by the British Parliament in the British colonies. That happened in 1834, and at that time the planters in the British colonies, who severely suffered from the total abolition of slavery, tried to get labour from India in order to carry on their work. They could not reconcile themselves to the loss of slave labour, and the object that they had in view was to get persons who would work for them under conditions as favourable to them as they could establish. The Sanderson Committee, which was appointed a few years ago, said that the object of these planters was to re-establish the conditions of labour, so far as they could, which existed when slavery had not been abolished. 'The aim of the planters who had suffered so severely from the entire discontinuance of the slave labour', said 'The Committee was too often to acquire complete control over the labour market by the means of regulations and administrative measures which aimed at compelling the coolie to re-engage himself on the expiry of his indenture rather than encouraging the free settlers.' In consequence of this feeling, the laws relating to the Indian immigrants, introduced into several colonies, gradually assumed a complexion less and less favourable to freedom, and, as the report of the subsequent commissions show, they were framed and administered in a spirit of substantial injustice to the Indian immigrants.

"Various serious abuses naturally cropped up under this system in the different colonies, and commissions were appointed in Mauritius, the British Guiana and Natal, and some of the most flagrant abuses were remedied. In the meantime, the establishment of the recruiting depots in India at various centres gave rise to the complaints of kidnapping and other objectionable practices, and the question of revising the existing enactments relating to emigration was taken up for consideration in 1882, and an Act was passed in 1883. The aim of the new Emigration Act, Act XXI of 1883, was to ensure prompt and careful registration of the emigrants, so as to enable them to be easily traced, and to provide for the magisterial supervision of the up-country depots. But as the Resolution of the Government of India, issued in 1883, and the speech of Mr Ilbert showed the object also was to make recruitment more popular. In his evidence before the Sanderson Committee, Sir Edward Buck, who was the Secretary to the Government of India for fifteen years in the Department of Revenue and Agriculture, said that the legislation of 1883 did make recruitment much easier.

"In 1908, the Emigration Acts were consolidated, and up to that time the Government of India was not much perturbed in mind as to the treatment which the Indians received in the colonies. In 1909, Lord Crewe appointed a committee to consider (l) the general question of emigration from India to the Crown Colonies; (2) the particular colonies in which the Indian immigration may be most usefully encouraged; and (3) the general advantages to be reaped by India itself and each colony.

"During all this time the Government of India put her trust exclusively in the colonial governments and laws for the fair treatment of the Indians during the period of indenture there.

As the Hon'ble Mr Ilbert stated, in presenting the Report of the Select Committee on the Indian Emigration Bill, in 1883, 'Every precaution had been taken which our law could enforce that the emigrant should be properly treated from the time when he leaves the place where he is recruited to the time when he lands in the colony for which he is bound. Further than this, our law cannot follow him, and after this point we can only provide for his welfare by such influence as we can bring to bear on the government of the country in which he has established himself.'

"In 1909, Lord Crewe appointed a Committee, as I have said, to go into various questions relating to the Indian emigration, but the main object of that Committee was also to find into which particular colonies the Indian immigration could be most usefully encouraged. Evidently, up to that time, the government did not realise that the treatment meted out to the Indians in the colonies by those under whom they were placed was such that it called for a very serious consideration.

The Indian public was in a state of ignorance about the conditions to which the Indians under indenture were subjected until the nineties, when Mahatma Gandhi began to expose its evils. But both the public and the government realised the seriousness of the problem when the subject was forced upon their attention by the anti-Indian policy of the Transvaal Government. Since then, the condition of the Indians in all parts of the world has been a matter for anxious consideration, and it would be no exaggeration to say that, since it was brought to the force, no question has exercised the public mind more or given rise to the greater bitterness of feeling than the ill-treatment of the Indians outside their country. I do not propose, my Lord, to refer here to the general question of the status of the Indians in the British Empire, though it is a matter of deep and keen concern to all the Indians. It may be that the question can best be settled when the war is over. But the question of indentured labour stands on quite a different footing and can be solved without extra delay.

"The council will remember that, in 1910, our late lamented

friend, Mr Gopal Krishna Gokhale, moved a resolution urging the prohibition of the recruitment of indentured labour for the colony of Natal. He was convinced even then, as he said, that the system should be done away with altogether. But he was content with urging, at the time, as a prudential measure, the prohibition of the indentured labour to Natal, and the Government of India was pleased to accept that recommendation, and prohibited the supply of indentured labour so far as Natal was concerned. Two years later, he brought forward another resolution urging the total abolition of the system, the evils of which he graphically described, and which he rightly characterised as a monstrous system, iniquitous in itself, based on fraud and maintained by force, a system so wholly opposed to the modern sentiments of justice and humanity as to be a grave blot on the civilisation of any country that tolerates it. It was a matter of deep disappointment to the public that the Government of India was not convinced till then that the system was one which must be ended. They still hoped that it might be mended, and in that hope that they appointed a Committee to visit the colonies and to report on the actual working of the system. The report of Messrs. McNeill and Chimman Lal was submitted to the government more than a year ago, and I regret to say that the report was received by the public with great dissatisfaction and disappointment, as it unmistakably showed a tendency to underrate the evils of the system and even to apologise for it. The facts, however, which the Committee have recorded tell their own plain tale, and supply abundant evidence to enable every impartial man to form his own judgment. That judgment is entirely against the system. For what in essence is the system? It is one under which simple, illiterate, ignorant village people, belonging largely to the poorest classes, are inveigled into entering into a very solemn agreement which compels them to leave their homes, to leave their kith and kin, and to go to a distant country of the conditions of existence in which they are entirely ignorant, to work in circumstances in which they are practically at the mercy of their employers, for a continuous period of five years, to work under men who do not understand their language, custom and manners, who have no sympathy with them under conditions in settling which they have no voice without being informed that they will be liable to be punished criminally, the punishment extending sometimes to two or three months' hard labour, if they fail to perform the tasks which are assigned to them, tasks, in the fixing of which they have no voice and in making complaints against which they find but little support.

"A system like that, my Lord, is an utterly unfair system. It ought not to be called by the name of a contract as the word is known to the legal minds and the legislative codes of the Government of India. Under this system, these simple village people go out to distant lands, and are tied down to work there for five years. They cannot buy their freedom, because they have no means to do so. My Lord, in order to show how injuriously this system has worked, I would invite attention to some of its principal features. I will take up the question where the Emigration Act of 1908 left it. When the Bill of 1883 was under discussion in the council, it was proposed by the late Mr Kristo Das Pal that the nature of the agreement into which the emigrant was asked to enter ought to be explained to him in a written statement with a copy of which he should be supplied. The Hon'ble Mr Kristo Das Pal urged that it was highly desirable that, in the initial stage of the engagement, the emigrant should have a clear idea of the agreement he was about to enter upon. The Hon'ble Member said:

> It is well known to the Hon'ble Members that the emigrant is often an ignorant and illiterate person unable to read the statement before him and would often ask the recruiter to read it. The recruiter, if he was inclined to deceive him, could quite easily do so. The emigrant was often entirely or almost entirely in the dark as to the nature of the life he would be called upon to live. It was at this stage that it was of the utmost importance that every facility should be given to him to understand the nature of his agreement, and that a statement should be given to him so as to enable him to take it home to show to the villagers and the village headmen and to consult them about it before making up his mind.

"This amendment, my Lord, was carried by the casting vote of the then Viceroy Lord Ripon and a provision was inserted, in the act as follows:

> The recruiter shall give a true copy of the statement to every person whom he invites to emigrate, and shall produce the statement for the information of any magistrate or officer-in-charge of a police station, when called upon to do so by the magistrate or officer.

"It is in consequence of this amendment, my Lord, that in the form of agreement now supplied to those whom it is sought to emigrate, a clause is put in stating that the period of service would be five years and the nature of the labour expected of him, and yet unfortunately all the information that is given to the man who is to be engaged, of the nature of the labour which he is to be engaged on is, that it will be work in connection with the cultivation of the soil or the manufacture of produce at a plantation or domestic service. My Lord, nothing is said in the agreement as to the conditions under which he would have to live and work. He was never informed that the moment he would set foot to board the steamer all his cherished ideas and beliefs about caste and religion would have to be abandoned under sheer compulsion; that he would have to sit and dine in conditions under which he would never have consented to dine if he was a free man. My Lord, this has led to grave results.

"In the admirable report which Mr Andrews and Mr Pearson have published on the indentured labour in Fiji, they say,

> We found, further, on examination that the agreement, which the coolie signs before going out, does not truly represent the faces of coolie life in Fiji. It is a misleading document. Not a word, for instance, is said concerning the penalties which await the coolie, if, for any reason (which he may regard as valid) he refuses to work. Another serious omission from the agreement (seeing that those who sign it are for the most part ignorant and illiterate people) is the failure to record the fact that food rates in Fiji differ materially from those in India. The coolie is told in the agreement, that he will be paid at the minimum rate of 12 *annas* a day. But

> he is not told that the purchasing power of 12 *annas* in Fiji is scarcely equal to that of 5 *annas* in India. He is not told, also, that more is required in the way of clothing and other necessities of life in Fiji than in India. So that the bare living expenses are nearly three times as high in Fiji as in India itself.

I should add, that he is also not told, that the 12 *annas* which is promised will not be paid to him unless he is able to finish the full task that will be set to him. He is also not told that he will be liable to lose in the shape of fines a good portion of the 12 *annas*. And, as I have said before, he is also not told that there will be any interference with his religion. Apart from all other considerations I am certain that if he was informed that there would be a violent interference with his religion, few of the recruits, however humble their caste, would consent to go to the colonies.

"Let us, my Lord, now consider the nature of the service which the emigrant is to render. That service is described in the printed form of agreement as agricultural work or domestic service. But Messrs. Andrews and Pearson state it as a fact that some of these coolies, as they are called, have been compelled to perform the hateful task of cutting up meat in a butchery. My Lord, it would be utterly repugnant to all sense of fairness to suggest that the domestic service can include the cutting up of meat in a butchery, and yet this has been forced upon our people. The results have been very sad.

Mr Andrews says:

> A low caste Hindu, who was brought out under indenture for agricultural work was set to cut up meat in a butchery. When asked by us how he, a Hindu, could engage in such a work, he replied that he could not help it, as he was ordered to do it. A *Kabir Panthi*, now out of indenture, had been originally obliged to do the same kind of work. He told us that he had continually refused and had been imprisoned. We looked up his record on the estate and found he had been given 692 days imprisonment while under indenture.

"My Lord, the *Kabir Panthis* are a sect who have a deep-rooted belief of not injuring life. That a man like that should be forced to cut up meat under compulsion in a place where he is utterly helpless is a matter which is very sad to reflect upon.

"My Lord, let us now see who the recruiters are and what are the devices that they resort to in dealing with the emigrants? In his evidence before the Sanderson Committee, Mr J.A.C. Brown, GSI, a Commissioner of my province, stated as follows:

> My impression is that the recruiting staff is very bad, the recruiters are the worst kind of men they could possibly have. They are generally very low-class men, and as far as I understand, they are paid by the results, by the number of emigrants that they get. The consequence is that they very often try to entice married women away from their husbands and try to get anybody they can.

"In the western districts of the United Provinces the recruiter gets ₹ 45 per head for every male and ₹ 55 per head for every female whom he can induce to emigrate. In the eastern districts, he gets less and so also in Madras. My Lord, the temptation is strong enough to induce the low-class people to practise every fraud and deception they can for their selfish gain. The Sanderson Committee admits that a fair proportion of the emigrants leave India without having any clear idea of the duties they have to perform. They are uncomfortable and welcome any change of circumstances, or they have quarrelled with their families, with their parents and leave their home in search of work and have not been able to find it. But that is not all. Several of them are actually deceived and most unscrupulously so. Say Mr Andrews and Mr Pearson:

> In a very large number of cases the coolie's own home people knew nothing about his recruitment. Very possibly many such coolies were escaping from justice, or running away from some family quarrel at the time. But others were clearly quite simple village people, involved in no such trouble. They had perhaps lost their relations in a crowded railway station. They were on a pilgrimage and did not know the way. They were merely going from one village to another, when the recruiting agent came along and tempted them with his story. It was noticeable among the women how many were recruited at the pilgrim centres. The common narrative was that the recruiting agent came up, offering

> to take the woman to her relations, or to show her some sacred shrine, and then took her to the depot instead. The evidence given of such practices was far too circumstantial in detail, and far too frequently given with fresh details and fresh names of places, to allow any doubt concerning its substantial accuracy.

"My Lord, time will not permit my mentioning all the cases of deception which have been referred to by Messrs. Andrews and Pearson, and which are mentioned in the memorial of the Marwari Association. But there are just one or two which, I think, I should mention,

After speaking of other cases, Mr Andrews goes on to say:

> We then went to see a Gaur Brahmin who had gone mad on account of his wife being taken away by the recruiting agent. The whole neighbourhood collected, showing their sympathy and pity. The madman was a pathetic sight to witness. Then a respectable Jat came up to us. His brother was blind and had an only son who was taken by the recruiters. A Hindu, by caste a Bania, spoke to us concerning his wife. She had been taken by the recruiters, and he was very bitter against them. We asked him if he had made any attempt to get her back. He said he could not.

"My Lord, I have personal knowledge of several cases of deception practised by the recruiters which have happened during the last few years in my Province. Often, have I, or some of my friends tried to get a woman rescued from the depots. No one but a magistrate or a person who has obtained a permit from a magistrate can enter any such depots. When we enter them, we ask for the woman who, we have been informed, has been induced by false pretences to go there. Either she is not produced, or she is produced after being tutored to say exactly what the recruiter wishes her to say. If she says anything different, she knows she will be dealt with harshly by the recruiters. Mr Andrews truly observes that the recruiting agent is able to stupefy these victims of his fraud with fear; he is able to coach them in the questions they will have to answer, and they very rarely refuse to reply according to his directions when the time comes.

"When the emigrant has embarked on board the steamer,

he is confronted with the state of things which I have already mentioned. In addition to that there is absolutely no privacy for the modesty of women. Altogether the conditions in which the emigrants find themselves are so hard that, as Mr Andrews points out, there have been lamentable and tragic cases of the Indians, both men and women, who have thrown themselves into the Hughli in order to escape from the emigrant ships, and also of the actual suicides occurring on the high seas.

"When the emigrants get to the colonies, they are confronted with the trouble of different characters. The hours of work fixed are about 7 hours in British and Dutch Guiana, and 9 hours in the remaining three colonies. Including intervals for meals, the labourers have to be out for about 10 hours. This, my Lord, is too long, and in the case of women, it is harder still. They have to wake up between 3 and 4 in the morning to cook their food, and to be at the farm at about 5 and to remain there the whole day. What is worse, in the case of those who have children, they have to leave their children behind in order that work should not be interfered with. This is cruel enough. But to show that it is worse still in practice, we have a case mentioned by Mr Andrews in which an overseer actually whipped a woman who was taking her child with her because the child was ill, and compelled her to leave the child behind.

"In every colony an adult male is paid, roughly speaking, at the rate of 12 *annas* per day, while the women receive 8 or 9 *annas* a day. But it would be a great mistake to think that their daily earnings amount to 12 or 9 *annas*. On the contrary their average earnings are very much less. As the subject is a very important one, it having been frequently asserted in favour of the indentured emigration that it benefits the labourer financially it is necessary to go into details.

"In Trinidad, the daily wages of an able-bodied adult male and an adult female are 12.5 and 8 *annas*, respectively. But the average weekly earnings on the estates visited by the members of the Committee of 1913 amounted to 4s. 3d. or ₹ 3-3 As. only. The food of an active, industrious man, says the report of the Committee of 1913, costs about ₹ 2-4 As. and that other wants may increase the expenditure to be ₹ 2-10 As. This is the minimum expenditure. Thus the savings cannot amount to more than 9 *annas* per week. But so far, no account has been taken of the labourer's family responsibilities. If these be taken into consideration the margin will appear to be more nominal than real. That this is the correct view to take is abundantly clear from the fact that the Committee appointed by the Government of India recommends that an average of 5s. 6d. or ₹ 4-2 As. should be aimed at. And if this result cannot be secured in any other way, it proposes that the wage unit should be raised or a bonus given to the steady workers.

"Women earn from 1/2 to 2/3rds of what men do, and their wants cost from 2s. 6d. upwards. Thus they hardly earn enough to maintain themselves. It is worth mentioning that while the Committee of 1913 states that the wages per adult male averaged 4s. 3d. per week, it was stated before the Sanderson Committee that the labourers had long ceased to receive the 5s. 21/2 l d. solemnly promised in India as a minimum, their present earnings being in the neighbourhood of 3 shillings per week. It was contended that this was nothing short of deliberate misrepresentation. The immigrants, it was said, 'Were not promised 5s. 2 extra 1/2d. per week but 25 cents (12½ *annas*) per day for every day they worked. This they have never failed to receive,' Were the labourers made to understand these subtleties when they were tempted to leave their country?

"My Lord, according to the figures supplied to the Sanderson Committee, the average weekly earnings in the British Guiana in 1906, 1907 and 1908 amounted roughly to ₹ 3. The average has apparently risen, as it is stated to have been ₹ 3.10 As. for 1910, 1911 and 1913. The cost of living being much the same as in Trinidad, it is clear that there is no margin for the savings here. In Jamaica, the loss of working days owing to sickness is excessive, and it appears from the figures given by the Committee of 1913 that the average earnings are below 9 annas per day or less than ₹ 3.6 As. per week. The cost of living being slightly higher than in Trinidad, it is quite clear that the wages are insufficient. In Fiji, the wages are the same as elsewhere, while the cost of food and clothing is higher.

"There is therefore, even a smaller chance of saving anything here than elsewhere. The daily wages of an adult male are 13 *annas* in the Dutch Guiana. But the average number of working days in 1909, 1910 and 1911 was 187, 187 and 177, respectively. Roughly speaking, the average number of working days is about 180. The annual earnings therefore, come to about ₹ 150. As the cost of food and clothing is about 4 shillings per week, the annual expenditure too is about ₹ 150. And yet the Committee of 1913 felt no compunction in saying, 'The proportion of annual remittances to India or deposits in the Savings Bank contributed by the indentured immigrants is not known, but the habits of remitting or saving are almost always formed during the indentured service.'

"The observations of the Sanderson Committee confirm the accuracy of the facts mentioned above. It states that during the first one or two years the labourers can hardly be expected to save anything. That they are unable to lay by or save anything even in the subsequent years is also clear from the facts mentioned by it. In the British Guiana an attempt was made to introduce the ex-indentured labourers to settle in the colony by enabling them to commute the right to a return passage for a grant of land. But the attempt proved unsuccessful, and in Sir Charles Bruce's opinion, 'The cause of failure was that the immigrants, when they became entitled to the return passage, were hardly yet in a sufficiently independent position to make their living entirely by the produce of their own land.'

"And it may be noted here, adds the committee, 'That later experiments of the same nature in the other colonies have been equally unsuccessful.' Can there be a more convincing proof of the poverty of the Indian immigrant?

"The economic condition of the labourers may be tested in another way. In 1911-12, 469 statute adults, excluding those rejected or sent back as unfit, returned to India and brought back with them from Trinidad about 9,150 pounds. This gives an average of less than 20 pounds per head after a stay of at least ten years. In 1912-13, 608 the statute adults returned to India from the British Guiana with the savings amounting to about ₹ 1,45,000, which gives an average of ₹ 240 per head after a stay of at least ten years. From Fiji, 414 men brought back savings amounting to 13,800 pounds which gives an average of 33 pounds per head after a stay of at least ten years. From the Dutch Guiana, 603 men returned in 1911-12 bringing with them savings amounting to about 5,70 pounds, or about 9 pounds per head after a stay of at least five years. With the exception of Fiji, the savings do not amount to much in the case of any colony. Besides, it has to be remembered that the savings include the earnings of immigrants for at least five years in the case of the British colonies as free men. There is nothing to show that any appreciable portion of the savings was accumulated during that period of indenture.

"Then, my Lord, as to the nature of the tasks imposed and the hardships of the conditions under which these immigrants work, the number of the prosecutions gives very remarkable evidence. This is the cruellest part of the story. That the number is excessive has been admitted by the Sanderson Committee and the committee appointed by the Government of India, and both have referred pointedly to it in their reports. It reveals the true nature of the indenture system, and shows that it is perilously akin to slavery. Men can be prosecuted not only for desertion or criminal conduct, but even for using insulting words or gestures. The entire evidence before the Committees of 1909 and 1913 was to the effect that the Indians are very docile and law-abiding and very easy to manage. Why should there be such a large number of prosecutions then? Obviously, the system places too much power in the hands of the overseers who seem to regard everything but silent and unquestioning obedience as a crime. In order to give an adequate idea of the extent of the evil, it is necessary to mention a few figures. There has been some improvement in the recent years, but the position is still intolerable. In 1911-12, the indentured population in Trinidad was about 9,600, and of the number of prosecutions about 2,000. The percentage of prosecutions to the indentured population was, therefore, 21. The committee appointed by the Government of India recommends that the prosecutions should be reduced by the direct interference of the Immigration Department, and remarks that reliance on the courts seems to have become a habit of mind with the majority of the managers. In British Guiana, the number of indentured-labourers was about 9,600 in 1912-13, and the percentage of prosecutions, which was much higher in the previous years, was the 18.3. On large estates the percentage varied from 0 to 32 per cent. The Committee of 1913 explain this in their own characteristic manner by saying:

'Though the managers are very far indeed from being harsh towards their labourers, the majority have developed a wrong sense of proportion.'

"In Jamaica, with an indentured population of about 4,200, the percentage of the prosecutions was 12 in 1912-13. Formerly it was much higher, but it has fallen very recently. For Fiji, the corresponding figures are 15,400 and 7.4 per cent. This figure is the lowest when compared with the percentages of the other colonies; nevertheless, it will be admitted that it is high enough. But for the percent employers, says the Committee of 1913 in their cynical style, 'The palliating circumstance may be noted that they have been taught in a school which shows very little consideration for neglect or incompetence, and the impatience which they manifest towards the Indians is exactly the same as they manifest to all the others.'

"In the Dutch Guiana, with its indentured population of 5,800, the percentage of the complaints was 16. 6 in 1911. It is thus seen that the position everywhere is highly unsatisfactory. The labourer's life is practically made intolerable. He is in a country where his language is not understood, and the Inspectors and Magistrates belong as a rule to the class from which the planters come. Knowing human nature as we do, it is idle to expect justice under such circumstances. Yet, the Committee of 1913, in reviewing the whole subject, has the heart to say that:

> If too many labourers were judicially punished, all but the most worthless were gainers in skill, enterprise and self-respect.

"Can cynicism go further? One may be pardoned for asking what faith can be placed in the impartiality of men imbued with such extraordinary sentiments?

"My Lord, the most degrading feature of the indenture system is the immorality associated with it. The law requires that the number of the female immigrants must be 40 per cent of that of the male immigrants, and the women need not be the relatives of the male labourers. The consequent paucity of women and the character of the women recruited have been a fruitful source of immorality. With the exception of Trinidad, the number of adult males in every colony is about twice that of the adult females. In Fiji and Dutch Guiana, the males are almost exactly twice as numerous as the females. In Jamaica, the number of men is 2½ times that of the women. In Guiana, the proportion in the population over 15 years of age is as 3 to 2, and in the population above 20 years of age it is as 5 to 3. In Trinidad, the proportion of males to females in the total population is 7 to 5. If the adult population only were considered it would perhaps be appreciably higher. As to the character of the women recruited, the Sanderson Committee states that, 'The Government of India wrote long ago to the Secretary of State that they largely consisted of prostitutes, or women of the lowest classes in whom habits of honesty and decency are non-existent.' "

"And the Committee of 1913 states that, 'The women who come out consist, as to one-third, of the married women who accompany their husbands, the remainder being mostly widows and women who have run away from their husbands or been put away by them. A small percentage are ordinary prostitutes.'

"The evil results of this outrageous system are too easily discernible in the lives of the people. We have fuller material to judge of them in the case of Fiji than in the case of other colonies. It will therefore be more profitable to discuss the state of things in Fiji. Mr J.W. Burton denounced the immorality prevalent in the estate population some years ago in scathing terms, and Messrs. Andrews and Pearson's experience confirms the accuracy of his statements.

"We cannot forget, they write, our first sight of the coolie lines in Fiji. The looks on the faces of the men and the women alike told one unmistakable tale of vice. The sight of young children in such surroundings was unbearable. And again and again, as we went from one plantation to another, we saw the same unmistakable look. It told us of a moral disease which was eating into the heart and life of the people ....Though we were no novices to conditions such as these, yet what we met with in Fiji was far worse than we had ever anticipated. There seemed to be some new and undefinable factor added, some strange unaccountable epidemic of vice. The sanctity of the marriage tie is utterly disregarded and bestiality reigns supreme. Women exchange their husbands as often as they like, and girls are practically bought and sold. And the marriage law has made things worse. Religious marriages have no validity, and the children of the unregistered unions are regarded as illegitimate. As the majority of the Indian marriages are unregistered, one has not even to take the trouble of applying to the courts for dissolving a union.

" 'Sexual jealousy has inevitably led to a great increase in the suicides and murders. A substantial proportion of the suicides must be attributed to the conditions of life on plantations, but the disproportion between the sexes is also partly responsible for it. The rate of suicide during 1908-1912 among the indentured Indians stood at the appallingly high figure of 926 per million and among the non-indentured population at 117, while the rates for Madras and the United Provinces the provinces from which the immigrants largely come are only forty five and sixty three, respectively.

As for murder, Messrs. Andrews and Pearson state that, 'There has been one conviction for murder each year in every 300 persons, or 333 per million per annum. While the corresponding proportion for Madras and the United Provinces is only four.

" 'It is noticeable', they add, 'that the greater portion of the people murdered are women. On the other hand, almost all the suicides in Fiji are those of men. In India, what few suicides exist are generally those of women.'

"My Lord, what a horrifying record of shame and crime is unfolded here? One hopes that the other colonies are not subject to the same curse; but one fears that they are unfortunately no better.

" 'There is no doubt,' wrote the Committee of 1913, 'that the morality of an estate population compares very unfavourably with that of an Indian village, and that the trouble originates in the class of women who emigrate.'

" 'While as to the suicides in Jamaica the mean suicide rate among indentured labourer during the decade 1903- 04 to 1912-1913, was 396 per million; among the indentured population in Trinidad during the same period the rates were 400 and 134 for the indentured and the free immigrants, respectively. In the British Guiana, the corresponding figures are 100 and 52, and for the Dutch Guiana, 91 and 49. These figures conclusively demonstrate the difference between the conditions of life of the indentured and the free labourers, and show the appalling state of things existing in Fiji, Trinidad and Jamaica.'

"If anything were wanting to complete this picture of human degradation and misery, it might be stated that 90 per cent, of the violent crime in Fiji is committed by the Indians, according to an Indian doctor of the British Guiana, the last census showed that 90 per cent of the beggars and 78 per cent of the lunatics were the Indians.

"Even if all that is said about the financial prosperity of the indentured labourers is true, it is a matter of no consideration, when we reflect on the broken hearts and the blasted lives that are the outcome of the indenture system. Can any amount of wealth ever compensate for the utter loss of character that it necessarily entails? Of what use can such moral wrecks be to themselves or to their fellow-men? What shall it profit a man if he gains the whole world but loses his own soul?

"My Lord, it has been shown that the indenture system is thoroughly indefensible. It begins, as Mr Gopal Krishna Gokhale observed, in fraud and is maintained by force. It does not benefit the labourer. He can earn as much at home as abroad. On the contrary, it is a curse to him. And it lowers the status and wages of the free population and brings the name of India into contempt. It is a source of advantage to the capitalist only who uses the labourer as a tool, and the sooner a system like this, which permits such heartless exploitation of the human beings, is put an end to the better will it be for the all concerned.

"My Lord, no reforms will prove sufficient; tinkering will not do; the system must be abolished root and branch. During the last three-quarters of a century a policy of tinkering has been tried and has failed. Commissions have been appointed to inquire into abuses, deputations have been sent to the other countries, and changes have been made in the law to safeguard the interests of the labourers, but they have failed to combat the evil. On the contrary, the complaints are growing louder and louder and its victims are crying to us for deliverance. Nothing short of a complete abolition of the system will meet the requirements of the case, and it is the duty of the Government of India to take that step unhesitatingly.

"My Lord, wherever the indenture system has been tried it has failed. It was tried in Natal, the period of indenture being five years, and we know how miserably it failed there. The introduction of the Chinese labour under contract for five years led in the Transvaal to equally undesirable results, and it had to be abandoned. In the Straits Settlements and the Federated Malay States, the agreement is for 600 days only, but the indentured labour is being steadily replaced by free labour, and the change has been attended with beneficial results.

"My Lord, the European labour is employed all over the world, but nowhere are such degrading restrictions attached to it as those that attach to the Indian labour. And although the European labourer is far more capable of judging of his own interests than the Indian labourer, the greatest care is taken to ensure that he has understood the exact terms of his contract. And then the contract, which is always for a very short period, is a purely-civil contract, and can be cancelled if the labourer can prove in a Court of Justice before a magistrate of his own race that unfair advantage was taken of his ignorance.

"My Lord, human reason and experience alike show that the indentured labour is an unmitigated curse, and greater the inequality among the contracting parties and longer the period of contract, greater is the extent of the evil. And both humanitarian and political considerations, humanitarian far more than political demand that it should be abolished as early as possible and replaced by free labour, which is, after all, the most efficient form of labour. The Indian indentured labourers have too long been denied their birthright as human beings, and it is high time that the yoke of slavery was removed from their necks.

"My Lord, I shall now conclude. I feel I have sufficiently pointed out the evils which are inseparable from the system of the indentured labour. It is a system which cannot be mended; it is therefore necessary that it should be ended. My Lord, since it was announced that the Government of India had recommended the abolition of this system to the Secretary of State, there has been a great feeling of relief and thankfulness. The system has worked enough moral havoc during 75 years. We cannot think, my Lord, without intense pain and humiliation of the blasted lives of its victims, of the anguish of soul to which our numerous brothers and sisters have been subjected by this system. It is high time that this should be abolished. My Lord, the British Government abolished slavery and paid down 25 million for emancipating the slaves. The Government of India has sacrificed their opium revenue in order to save the Chinese people from its demoralising effects. It is to such a government that we appeal against the utterly degrading and immoral system of the indentured labour, and, I am sure, we do not appeal in vain. I feel confident that Your Excellency's government will be pleased, as we humbly beg to recommend, to put an end to this system at as early a date as possible."

THE INDIAN COUNCILS

Speaking on the Budget debate in the imperial legislative council on March 23, 1917, Malaviya said, "I mean no disrespect to your Excellency or your colleagues in the Government of India, but I am sorry to say that not you but His Majesty's Secretary of State is the Government of India, because it is an open secret, we all know it to our regret, that every matter of importance relating to the revenues of India must be decided by the Secretary of State for India. A few minutes ago my honourable friend, Mr Wacha, asked whether we were not a self-governing body, I honestly wish we were, but I regret to say we are not because in all the matters of importance the fiscal policy of the Government of India is laid down by the Secretary of State. The influences to which he is subjected decide for the time being what particular course is to be taken on any question. Today it may be those who denounce the evil of supplying opium to China, tomorrow it may be the Lancashire merchants who do not want to lose any of their profits; the day after, it may be the War Office which thinks that certain burdens should be cast upon India. The Government of India may protest, I gratefully recognise that they have protested on many occasions, but their protests have gone in vain on too many occasions. Now, this is as unsatisfactory as anything could be, and I hope after the war is over this will be one of the most important questions that will be taken up, and that the Government of India will be really established in India and removed from London.

"The second point is the constitutional position of this Council. I have already entered my protest against the manner in which the offer of 100,000,000 was settled. I do not mean any disrespect to the Government of India, but I feel it my duty to them and to His Majesty's Government and also to my country, to say that while the Council was in existence it was entirely wrong on the part of the executive Government to decide to make such a contribution without the consent of the Council. It shows as if this Council exists in name only and has really no fiscal powers except to legalise taxation. This again is highly unsatisfactory. Lastly, as regards the general position of the members of this council, while we feel grateful that His Majesty's Government have invited representatives from India to assist the Secretary of State at the War Conference, we cannot conceal the feeling that, as it was on our recommendation that His Majesty's Government agreed to invite the Indians to represent India at the Conference, it was due to us that we should have been consulted before the nominations were made. The government would have lost nothing if that courtesy had been shown to the council; on the contrary, there would have been a real feeling of satisfaction throughout the country. We feel that we, who offer our humble services free to the government and who have a recognised status as the chosen representatives of the people, should not be passed over when a question like that, in which we have shown an interest, is to be decided.

"These considerations lead me naturally to the larger question raised by my Hon. friend, Mr Sastri, and other members on the Post-War Reforms. We have been advised by some gentlemen that we should not refer to that question at present. Those who offer such advice do not realise the position. They seem to forget or fail to appreciate what Your Excellency was pleased to tell us in the opening speech of this session, that from May to October last that is for six months before the session of the legislative council which produced the Memorandum submitted by nineteen of the elected members to Your Excellency, to which also you were pleased to refer, the Government of India was engaged in considering the Despatch on the question of the Post-War Reforms which you addressed to the Secretary of State for India in the autumn of last year. With that statement of your Excellency before us, I feel I am bound to refer to the matter. I do so particularly because as the Hon'ble Mr Basu has said, this council will not meet again till September. We are hoping that this war, the accursed war, will have come to an end and that His Majesty the King-Emperor will have been able to proclaim a glorious peace before that time. In that view it is not improbable that this question of Post-War Reforms will be taken up for consideration before we meet again. Your Excellency's Government has spent six months over the Despatch you have sent to the Secretary of State and we the elected additional members of your Council, have submitted to you a Memorandum over which we spend a good deal of time and thought.

"The Indian National Congresss and the Muslim League have also put forward a carefully-considered scheme of reforms. There is, thus no doubt, much material that is before the government to help it to come to a decision on the reforms. But, my Lord, we do not know what proposals Your Excellency's Government has made on the subject, and we request that you may be pleased in fairness to be the members of this Council, to publish these proposals, in order that we may submit our criticism on them with a view to help the government to arrive at a correct conclusion. I need hardly say that the question of reforms is a much larger one now than it was before the War. As Mr Lloyd George said the other day, the War has changed us very much. It has changed the angle of vision in India as well in England. I venture to say that the War has put the clock of time fifty years forward, and I hope and trust that India will achieve in the next few years what she might not have done in the fifty years. Some persons are frightened at the use of certain expressions; some dislike the use of the term 'Home Rule'; some cannot bear to hear even of 'Self-Government on the colonial lines'. But all will have to recognise that the reforms after the War will have to be such as will meet the requirements of the India of today and of tomorrow, such as will satisfy the aspirations of her people to take their legitimate part in the administration of their own country.

"My Lord, among these reforms, one of the most important forcibly suggested by the discussion on the budget today is that India should enjoy fiscal autonomy and that its legislative council, which is constituted by law, should have the sole power to determine what taxes should be raised and how the money raised should be spent. The action that has recently been taken by the Lancashire party in England with reference to the increase made in the import duties on cotton goods throws a lucid light on the need of having fiscal autonomy conferred on India. As regards the general question the claim of us Indians to have a real voice in the administration of our domestic affairs is unanswerable.

"Justice is on our side. The forces of time are on our side. We rejoice to think that His Majesty's Government is engaged in a righteous war, in the cause of liberty and justice, and the freedom of nations, small and great. It is in no small measure due to this knowledge that from the beginning of the war we have heartily offered our humble services and have earnestly prayed for the success of His Majesty's arms. Before this War we congratulated England because she loved liberty and had helped other nations to acquire freedom."

THE PRESS BILL

At the meeting of the Imperial Legislative Council on April 4, 1910, the Hon'ble Sir Herbert Eisley moved for the introduction of a bill to provide for the better control of the Indian press. The Hon'ble Pandit made the following speech, in connection with the bill:

"My Lord, it is perhaps an advantage that I rise to lay such views as I have on this Bill before the council, after having had the benefit of listening to the many able speeches which have been delivered in connection with it. I regret, however, to say, my Lord, that having heard all those speeches, I am still unconvinced as to the necessity of this Bill or of dealing with it in the manner in which it is being dealt with. A great deal of regret has been expressed both in this council and outside it that a measure of the extraordinary importance of this Bill should be dealt with in the hurry in which it is being dealt with. Reference has been made to the hurry in which the Vernacular Press Act was passed in 1878. My Lord, one mistake does not justify another. In the present instance, neither in the long and lucid speech of the Hon'ble Mover of the Bill nor in the subsequent speeches that have been made has any explanation been offered as to why it is necessary to rush this measure as it is being rushed. My Lord, the great advantage which the government has thought it necessary to secure to the public in connection with measures which are brought before the legislative council in giving publicity to them is that those who are interested in the measures should have the fullest opportunity of expressing their opinions regarding them and of submitting them to your Excellency's Council in order that those opinions may be considered before deciding the final shape which the measures should take. As soon as this measure was introduced, it was referred to a select committee. The select committee have no doubt considered the Bill; but if there had been a general discussion in the Council of the principle of the Bill and the general lines of criticism had been known to the Committee, I am certain, my Lord, that it would have been a great advantage to the select committee in doing their work. I have received telegrams from my own province, from the President of the United Provinces Congress Committee, from the president of the People's Association at Lucknow and from the secretaries of the Mahajana Sabha at Madras asking me to lay them before the select committee and Your Excellency, and to urge that more time should be given for consideration of the Bill. My Lord, it is not enough to say that the Bill has been published and that it has been before the public for three or four days. The measure being of the importance which it is, I submit, that a great deal more time should have been given to the press and the public to consider and to criticise the Bill, particularly as no circumstance has been mentioned which could justify its being hurried through the Council. Now, my Lord, coming to the Bill itself, we are no doubt confronted by the outstanding fact, the unfortunate outstanding fact, that there have been certain anarchical crimes and outrages committed in this country. Every good man must deplore and detest these crimes. They are hateful in the sight of God and men, and they have been condemned all over the country in unmistakable language. If it were shown that any particular measure was necessary to extirpate the germs of anarchical crimes, I am sure the whole country would rise as one man to support the measure, and to thank your Lordship's Government for introducing it. But it is evident from all the remarks that have been made both by the official and non-official members that there is very little expectation entertained that this measure will really have any substantial effect upon the anarchical crimes. I do not deny that it may check the distribution of the poisonous literature which some newspapers have been indulging in; but that it will have any effect upon those men who have gone into the wicked camp of the anarchists or terrorists, I do not think any member to entertain even the hope that it will achieve that result. That being so, my Lord, we have to consider what are the circumstances which justify the passing of such a measure as the one before us. The whole country, as I say, all decent people, are united, are of one mind with the Government in desiring that whatever measure may be necessary for the purpose of putting down the anarchical crime should be adopted. But it must be shown that a particular measure is calculated to secure that object. The Hon'ble Mover of the Bill said in his opening speech that he had to justify the bill before the council and to show why and how the laws which exist already are not sufficient to deal with the situation. My Lord, he referred to the murderous conspiracy which has come into existence, and he said that the outrages which that conspiracy had committed or attempted to commit were the direct result of the teachings of certain journals. The Hon'ble the Advocate-General also, in the speech with which he has just now favoured us, spoke of the stream of poisonous sedition which has been passing through several of these journals. My Lord, the picture which the Hon'ble Mover of the bill has drawn of the existing situation would suggest a question in many minds as to whether there was any law in the land which could deal effectively or at all with the poison of the seditious literature which was passing through the papers. One would imagine that there was no law which could deal with the abuse of the liberty of the Press as it was described in the speech of the Hon'ble Mover of the Bill. But, my Lord, as the Council knows, there is already a great deal of legislation existing in our Statute book which seeks to deal and which does deal with all the abuses of that liberty.

"The Hon'ble Member began by saying that it was his duty to show why the government could not be content to rely on the ordinary criminal law. He ended by merely asserting, not proving, that the law was insufficient, I am sorry I did not find any explanation in the speech of the Hon'ble Member as to why these provisions had been found to be not sufficient or wherein they had been found to be insufficient. The Hon'ble Sir Harold Stuart has tried to make up for the omission and has said that Section 108 of the Criminal Procedure Code has been found to be a useless weapon. He said that there had been three papers which had been convicted twice, two papers which had been convicted three times, and one which had been convicted six times. My Lord, a repetition of an offence by six papers out of a total of, I believe, nearly 800 papers in the country, does not show that there is not sufficient provision in the existing law to deal with the cases of sedition or attempts to promote sedition. The situation therefore demands that before we give our assent to a new and stringent measure being placed on the Statute book, the existing provisions of the law should be dispassionately examined.

"Now, my Lord, there are two matters to which I would especially invite attention. The present bill, as the Council has noted, defines what would be regarded as the prohibited matter, and the publication of which would expose a man to the penalties or to the consequences which are described in the Bill. Among the matters so prohibited, as the Hon'ble Mover of the Bill pointed out in his speech, are certain offences which are already provided for in the existing Codes. Take, for instance, those mentioned in the clause (a) of Section 4 of the Bill, to incite to murder or to any offence under the Explosive Substances Act, 1908, or to any act of violence, these are fully provided for by the Act VII of 1908, an Act for the prevention of incitements to murder and to other offences in the newspapers.

"The Hon'ble Mover said that it was thought advisable to include them in this bill in order that the government may, if necessary, take action of a less severe kind than that prescribed by the Act of 1908. I submit, my Lord, that the outrages that have been committed of late, would make one think that this was not the time when the government would seek milder methods to deal with cases which fell within the purview of that Act. Clause (b) relates to the offence of seducing any officer, soldier or sailor in the Army or Navy of His Majesty from his allegiance or his duty. Section 131 of the Indian Penal Code already provides that any person who attempts to do any of these acts shall be punished with transportation for life or with imprisonment which may extend to ten years and shall be liable to fine. Then, my Lord, the third clause incorporates the provisions of Section 124A and 153A with the addition of an offence against the Native Princes or Chiefs. And the clause which seeks to protect the judicial officers serving His Majesty from being maligned or unjustly attacked. These, my Lord, are the most important provisions of the bill. And I beg to invite the council's attention now to the provisions of section 108 of the Criminal Procedure Code. Under that section any person who disseminates either orally or in writing or attempts to disseminate or in any wise abets the dissemination of any seditious matter, that is to say, any matter, the publication of which is punishable under Section 124A of the Penal Code, or any matter, the publication of which is punishable under Section 153 of the Indian Penal Code, or any matter concerning a Judge which amounts to criminal intimidation or defamation under the Indian Penal Code, that section provides that if any editor or printer or publisher or proprietor of a newspaper shall be guilty of any of the offences specified there, the District Magistrate or the Chief Presidency Magistrate shall have the power, with the previous sanction of the Governor-General or of the Local Government, to call upon the person so offending to show the cause why he should not be bound down with or without the sureties to be of good behaviour for a certain period. I submit, my Lord, that this is a provision which should enable the government to deal with the cases of persons who disseminate seditious or other objectionable matter who, that is to say, publish the prohibited matter or such matter as the present Bill says will be the prohibited matter. Then, again as I have said before, there is the Newspapers (Incitements to Offences) Act. That Act was passed in 1903 after the writings of certain journals, to which the Hon'ble Mover of the Bill I think referred, had led to the commission of some outrages. Now, my Lord, Section 3 of that Act provides that where upon an application made by the order of or under authority from the local government, a magistrate is of the opinion that a newspaper contains any incitement to murder or to any offence under the Explosive Substances Act, 1908, or to any act of violence, such magistrate may make a conditional order declaring the printing press used, or intended to be used, for the purpose of printing or publishing such a newspaper or found in or upon the premises where such a newspaper is or at the time of the printing of the matter complained of was printed to be forfeited, and to make such a conditional order of forfeiture absolute unless the person concerned appears and shows good cause against it. These two sections, my Lord, give ample power under the existing law to the government to deal effectively and speedily too with the persons who abuse the liberty of the press. It has not been shown in what respects these provisions are insufficient, and I submit that justification for introducing a new measure has not been established, It may be said, my Lord, that the procedure and punishment provided by Section 108 are insufficient to deal with cases of persons who repeatedly commit the same offence. I am unable to understand why in such cases also a repeated application of the provisions of that section should not put an end to the evil activities of such persons. But assuming that it would not, I submit, that the proper course would have been to ask for an amendment of that section in order to incorporate more penal provisions to effect the end which the government has in view and not to introduce a new measure.

"If, my Lord, the necessity of a new act has not been established, then I submit that the matter should end here. Assuming, however, that a real necessity has been felt for giving greater power to the courts, assuming also that the course of amending the existing acts has for any valid reason not commended itself to the government, and the government feel in all the circumstances of the case that a new act should be passed, I should like then to hear some explanation as to why a great, a novel and, I submit with great respect, a dangerous departure has been introduced into this bill against the principle of all the existing enactments, which the Government has passed during the last fifty years and more. My Lord, under the Criminal Procedure Code once the sanction of the Governor-General or of the Local Government is obtained to proceed against any editor, printer, publisher or proprietor of a newspaper to require him to give security for good behaviour, the whole procedure which is regulated by the provisions of that act is judicial, and the whole matter is left to be dealt with judicially by the Magistrate. So also in the case of the Newspapers Offences Act which deals with offence of a far more grave character. The government passed that enactment less than two years ago and they considered it both just and wise to adhere to the principle of leaving it to the Magistrate and the courts established by the government to decide what matter fell within the definition of sedition and what did not. I do not understand, my Lord, why this new departure should have been made in the present bill by which, instead of leaving it to the Magistrate to decide what matter came within the definition of the prohibited matter and what did not, the Local Government is empowered to take upon itself to decide what matter is seditious without giving an opportunity for hearing to the person against whom it may so decide. I submit, my Lord, that this is a departure which is not justified by the existing circumstances of the country. The crimes at the prevention of which the Newspapers Offences Act aims are, my Lord, more serious and certainly not less serious, than the crimes which it may be hoped that the present bill may tend to prevent. That being so, I submit, that if the legislature has thought it right to leave it to the Magistrate to decide whether a newspaper contained incriminating matter within the meaning of that act, it should have been left also to the Magistrate to decide what matter came within the definition of the prohibited matter under the proposed law. My Lord, the bill raises a political question, to quote the weighty words of Mr Gladstone uttered in the House of Commons in connection with the Vernacular Press Act of 1878, of great importance, of the utmost delicacy, namely, whether it is wise for the government to take into its own hands and out of the hands of the established legal jurisdiction the power of determining what writing is seditious and what is not. In the course of the same debate, Mr Gladstone observed that the most unfortunate feature which the measure presents is the removal of Press prosecutions from the jurisdiction of the judicial establishments of the country in order that they may be dealt with as matters of executive discretion. The bill before us seeks to revive that feature of the Vernacular Press Act which was so justly condemned by Mr Gladstone, My Lord, the argument that in taking proceedings against the offending printers or publishers under the ordinary criminal law there would be a great deal of publicity given to the offence and that would be a public disadvantage, is not a new one. It had been urged to support the Press Act of 1878. Speaking in reference to that argument, Mr Gladstone said, 'The argument that is made for the abstraction of these matters from the Courts of Justice is the one which strikes at the root of our policy, and the best part of our policy, in India.' It is said, 'Oh no, we will not prosecute in one court, for if we do that the prosecution will bring these men into popularity, and the mischief of the prosecution will be greater than that of submission to the evil.'

My Lord, this argument has no greater force today than it had in 1878; and, I submit, it is not an argument which is worth considering in the face of the great danger involved in the departure which it is sought to make from the principle upon which the entire system of the administration of justice is built, and which the government has followed throughout in enacting all its laws that being so, I respectfully submit that if the government fees that a new measure must be passed, this novel principle which has been introduced into the bill should be eliminated, and power should be left to the Magistrate as in other enactments to deal according to law with what may be regarded as the prohibited matter. There can be no possibility, my Lord, of the effect of this measure being weakened by adhering to the right principle: it will still be quite as potent for preventing mischief as the present measure can be. The sanction of the Local Government will yet be necessary before any action is initiated but once the proceedings have been initiated the matter will be left to be dealt with by the Magistrate acting as a Judge, and any order that he may pass will rightly and properly go up to the High Court for revision or in appeal. I may say here that I do not see why an appeal should not be allowed from an order asking for a deposit of security as well as from an order for forfeiture of that security.

If an order is made by the Magistrate of the district or the Chief Presidency Magistrate and it is taken up in revision or appeal before a High Court, there will be a greater assurance in the public mind that the merits of the order will receive due consideration, then my Lord, human nature being what it is, and the circumstances of the country being what they are, there would be when an order passed by the local covernment on the executive side will be brought up for revision before the High Court. So far then with regard to the necessity of the new measure and in regard to the new change of principle which it introduces. I submit, my Lord, that the necessity of it has not been proved, the justification not established.'

"Let us now consider some other aspects of the bill. The Hon'ble Mover of the bill has stated the objects of the bill to be larger. He has stated that the object of the bill is 'to provide for the better control of the press or to confine the press the whole press, European and Indian, the English and Vernacular within the limits of legitimate discussion. 'My Lord, that clear statement of the object clears the ground to a great extent for discussion. It naturally gives rise to the question whether the condition of our press, the European and Indian, the English and Vernacular, in this country is such as to justify any legislation to keep it within the limits of legitimate discussion. My Lord, the Hon'ble Mover of the bill has given us a history, of the liberty of the press in this country. He has told us that during the last seventy years, with the exception of the two short periods of one and three years respectively, the press in India has been free: he has told us that these two periods were, one the short period in the dark days of the Mutiny, and the other the period of the Vernacular Press Act. My Lord, the Vernacular Press Act was repealed within three years and action was taken under it only once. We can take it then that there was no necessity for the Government to restrain the liberty of the press in actual practice. Up to the year 1907, the Hon'ble Mover of the bill has said that there had been only sixteen press prosecutions. My Lord, I ask the Hon'ble Member to say if in Austria to which he referred, or in any other country to which he might refer, the press has as a whole behaved better or been conducted more respectably than in India during the last seventy years. The remarks of the Hon'ble Member would lead one to think that the press had been offending for a long time; he has spoken of the great forbearance which the government exercised in dealing with the press: he spoke of that forbearance as extreme: he said that some people thought that it was excessive; and he complained that in spite of that much forbearance being shown, the press did not mend its ways but went from bad to worse. My Lord, if the picture drawn by the Hon'ble Member were true, it would have cast a most serious reflection upon the administration. If it were true, it would show that while the administration saw that the press was going steadily from bad to worse, it did not take any steps to check the evil course. But happily for the press and for the government we have in the remarks quoted by my Hon'ble friend Mr Dadabhoy the testimony of more than one very high official of the government that the press of this country has as a whole behaved respectably and honourably and that it has given little ground for complaint. I will not quote, my Lord, what the Hon'ble Member may regard as the ancient history. Sir Herbert Rislay gave us the history of the press up to the year 1907, and he then drew attention to the resolution which your Excellency's Government was pleased to issue in that year for the better control of the newspapers. In that resolution it was stated that the Governor-General in Council has no desire whatever to restrain the legitimate liberty of the press to criticise the action of the government, and he would be most reluctant to curtail the freedom of the many well-conducted papers because of the misbehaviour of a few disloyal journals. My Lord, barely two years have passed since your Lordship was pleased to graciously acknowledge that the many papers in this country were well-conducted and that the journals which were disloyal were a few. I venture to say, my Lord, that that is the position even today. With the regrettable exception of a few papers in some parts of the country, the great bulk of them are still well-conducted. If this is so, the case which my friend sought; to make against a general restriction of the liberty which the press has enjoyed, the case which he sought to make for taking legislative action to confine the whole press within the limits of the legitimate discusssion, has not, I submit, been made out Your Lordship will be pleased to remember that the last two years and a half have been a period of exception. Up to the beginning of the year 1907 or I will go back a little earlier, up to nearly the end of the year 1905, the press generally behaved in an excellent manner, even in the Province of Bengal. I do not think that there were many papers till then the conduct of which could be much complained of. My Lord, we all know then the unfortunate but momentous event which occurred about the end of 1905. We all know the act of violence, as many millions of people believe it, which was committed by Lord Curzon's government; in partitioning Bengal against the prayers and protests of the people. And it is from that time, my Lord, that the evils which we are now deploring, and which have led to several deplorable results, largely date their origin.

"My Lord, it was in 1906 that a certain portion of the press assumed a tone of bitterness and even hostility which continued to grow also in 1907, but, I submit, my Lord, that that evidenced abnormal condition. The causes of the change in the tone of press were discernible by everybody who cared to think about it. We regret them, but we cannot overlook them. It was due to the cause to which I have referred and to the bad feelings which were excited in the year 1905 and in the succeeding year by certain official acts and utterances. I am sorry to say therefore that the regime of your Lordship's predecessor was largely responsible for diverting a section of the press from its honourable course into a course which has caused immense pain to all the lovers of the country, to all the lovers of the peaceful progress and good administration. My Lord, the evil is there, but in dealing with it, in taking steps to extirpate it, let us remember the causes which have brought it about, so that our judgment may be tempered as the circumstances of the case may require. Let us remember also that since the time these newspapers began to abuse the liberty which they enjoyed, the government has not been sitting idle. At no stage during the last three years could it be said that the government failed to do its duty in regard to the suppression of all expressions of seditious opinions. We are bold that the government has been mild, the impression among the people generally is that the Government has been unduly severe: but, my Lord, there is another class of opinion which holds that the government has been firmly mild and sympathetically severe as it thought the occasion required it to be. As soon as it felt that there was a necessity for doing so, it passed the Newspapers Offences Act in 1908, which can by no means be described as a mild measure. That act has led to the suppression of certain journals which offended most severely; either have been tamed down or have died out If there is any journal existing which still offends against the law, there is provision enough in the existing code to stamp it out of existence. There is not a single member in this council who would desire that any mercy should be shown to such journals, no one who desires that they should be allowed with impunity to abuse the liberty of publication which they enjoy. But I submit that unless the existing enactments are shown to be insufficient, that unless it is shown to be necessary to introduce new legislation, the government should not place one more repressive measure on the Statute book. I am sure your Excellency would be most unwilling to place one such other measure on the Statute book. There is no doubt that this bill, if passed, will become a new source of discontent. This is evident from what I have seen of the comments that have already been made in some papers and from the many communications to which I have referred. Your Lordship was pleased in the noble and gracious speech with which you opened this expanded council, to point out that, deplorable as were the outrages which the anarchists had committed, they were mere passing shadows. Your Lordship will allow me to quote your Lordship's words. You were pleased to say:

> Though I have no wish to disguise from you the anxieties of the moment, I do not for an instant admit that the necessity of ruthlessly eradicating a great evil from our midst should throw more than a passing shadow over the general political situation in India. I believe that situation to be better than it was five years

> ago. We must not allow immediate dangers to blind us to the evidences of future promise. I believe that the broadening of political representation has saved India from far greater troubles than those we have now to face.

"My Lord, that being the situation, that being the correct reading of the situation, there is very little justification for introducing and passing the measure that is now before the council. If it cannot be abandoned, my Lord, I submit, that there should be at any rate time allowed for further consideration of this measure. There is a real danger felt that the provisions of the bill as it stands will seriously affect the legitimate liberty of the press. Those provisions are unnecessarily wide and drastic. I will not take up the time of the council by dwelling on them in detail. By way of illustration, I beg to invite attention to the fact that the bill has discarded even the very reasonable provision which existed in the Vernacular Press Act of 1878, whereby the Local government was required to give notice in the first instance to an offending newspaper, a warning so that the publisher might avoid offending again. Section 6 of that act required that such a warning should be given, and Section 7 laid down that if the warning was not heeded certain consequences were to follow. I submit, my Lord, that such a provision at least should have been included in this bill. Secondly, there is danger from the bill not only to the new presses but also to the existing presses. In the case of new presses there is no reason shown for requiring everybody who wants to start a press to deposit a security. The fact that there are certain persons in the community who abuse their liberty does not justify action being taken against persons who have not so misconducted themselves. To require every newspaper which may now come into existence to deposit a security is, I submit, placing an unnecessary barrier in the path of journalism and casting an undeserved slur upon the good conduct of the person who may wish to start a paper. If, however, the government insists that some security must be deposited, it is nothing but reasonable to suggest that the Magistrate should only require it from a person in whose case he considers that there are grounds for believing that he might make use of the press for evil or seditious purposes. My Lord, considering that the liberty of the Press has not generally been abused during the long course of seventy years, I submit, it is fair to ask that this change at least should be made in the Bill. I do not wish that an offender should be saved from the consequences of his evil action. I am only anxious that persons who are not guilty, who have never allowed any idea of disloyalty or sedition to enter their minds, should not be punished because some other person or persons have offended. Then, my Lord, in the case of existing presses, the bill says that whenever any person goes to register himself as a publisher of a paper, the Magistrate shall demand a security from him. I submit that will mean that if the publisher of a paper which has existed for thirty years and which has never offended dies and a new publisher goes to make an application to have himself registered as such, or if the owner of a paper or a press which has existed for fifty years dies and the son or the heir goes to make an application that he should be registered as the keeper of a press or the publisher of the paper, he will be called upon to give a security. I submit that this is extremely hard and unjust. The bill does not give the protection which it was thought at the first reading of the bill was given to the existing presses.

"My Lord, I will not take up further time of the council. I am only anxious that the provisions of the bill which have created an apprehension in the minds of the people that the liberty of legitimate discussion which is highly beneficial to the people and the government will be curtailed, should be given up or recasted. My Lord, when the press is left at the mercy of the local government, when it is left to the local government by merely issuing a notice to demand a security, I submit the freedom with which the newspapers have expressed their criticisms of the acts and omissions of the government is very much likely to suffer. After all, local governments are composed of human beings who are liable to err; and we have had instances of local governments committing mistakes which sometimes the Government of India have had to correct. If it should happen, my Lord, that a paper has been writing a little more outspokenly than it should have done, if a paper has offended by a series of criticisms passed upon the local government, any incautious or careless expression in it might much sooner be construed as falling within the definition of prohibited matter than might be the case if the paper had not been so criticising the government. A notice issued to the keeper of the press or the publisher to deposit a security will, I fear, in many instances, at least in some instances, lead to the extinction of the paper. The paper might be owned by an individual who may not be in a position to lose the little property he has. It may be owned by a company, and they may wish at the first indication of danger to close the business to avoid the threatened loss. In that way, my Lord, I submit, papers generally will be constrained to write under a greater sense of restraint than is needed for the purposes of good administration or of fair discussion. For these reasons, I submit, that the further consideration of this Bill should be postponed. And in support of this submission I would remind the council of what Mr Gladstone said in connection with the Vernacular Press Act. He said, 'I think, if one thing is more obvious than another, it is that, whatever we do give, we should not retract, and that when we have communicated to India the benefit which is perhaps the greatest of all those that we enjoy under our own institutions, viz. the publicity of proceedings in which the nation is interested, and the allowance of sufficient time to consider them at their several stages, to afford securities against wrong and error it is deplorable in a case like this in India that the utmost haste... should have been observed, not in amending or altering, but in completely overturning, so far as the press was concerned, a cardinal part of the legislation of the country.' I have omitted the word "Native" because the present Bill affects the whole Press, the European and Indian, the English and Vernacular. My Lord, I submit, that those weighty observations give us very sound guidance as to the lines which this Council should pursue. We should not expose ourselves to a similar criticism by passing this bill today. No possible injury can happen if the further consideration of this Bill is postponed in order that the public should have further time for consideration. Members of the council should have a further opportunity of weighing the Bill, and the government of reconsidering its decision as to the necessity of a new measure, or at least of introducing the new principle, viz. that of substituting executive discretion for judicial decision in determining whether a man has been guilty of some of the most serious offences of which any man can be guilty."

THE SEDITIOUS MEETINGS ACT

At a meeting of the Imperial Legislative Council held on Saturday, the August 6, 1910, the Hon. Mr Jenkins introduced the bill to provide for the continuance of the Seditious Meetings Act, 1907. The Hon'ble Pandit Madan Mohan Malaviya opposed the motion and spoke as follows:

"My Lord, the measure before the Council is of exceptional importance, and perhaps it is due both to the government and to the public, a portion of whom at least I claim to represent, to state the reasons why I think it my duty to oppose the motion that the act for the Prevention of the Seditious Meetings should be continued for another five months. My Lord, after the many able and elaborate speeches that have been made against the motion, it will not be necessary for me to take up much of the time of the council. But I must complain at the outset of the action of the Hon'ble Member who has moved for leave to introduce the bill in having thrown the burden of making out a case for not continuing this act upon the non-official Members. My Lord, I understand that it has been the rule in respect of all the legislative business which comes before the Government of India, that the Hon'ble Member who introduces a bill should state clearly the reasons upon which his motion is based, and should set out before the Council the facts and circumstances which would enable the members, non-official as well as official, to decide whether to vote in favour of the Bill or against it. The Hon'ble Member has told us very briefly than all that the Bill aimed at was the continuance of the Seditious Meetings Act for only five months. He has also told us that the local governments have unanimously demanded it. So far as he was concerned, he was no doubt; free, as he was willing to surrender his judgment to the judgments of the local governments, particularly of one which is presided over by a gentleman of the experience and large views of Sir Edward Baker. But he seemed to forget that there were other members in the council who were not in the confidence of these Local Governments as he evidently happens to be, who did not know what the circumstances were which had led Sir Edward Baker and other Local Governors to ask for a continuance of this Act. My Lord, there is a certain responsibility resting upon the non-official members of this council as well as upon the official members. It is also given to us to think, and we have to satisfy the still small voice that even we feel within us that there is some justification for supporting a motion to saddle the Statute book of the country with a measure which was described by Sir Harvey Adamson, as many speakers have reminded the council, as a repressive measure of considerable potency. This exceptional measure, intended for exceptional times and exceptional places, has now been on the Statute book for nearly three years. The Government of India when they passed it almost offered apologies for introducing it, and for asking that it should be continued for three years, such was the state of the country at the time. Sir Harvey Adamson repeatedly said that the measure was intended for exceptional times and exceptional circumstances only, and he took the greatest care to point out that in order that the measure might lack the element of permanency, the life of every notification which was to be issued by a local government to declare an area to be a proclaimed area was confined to a period of six months.

"My Lord, the assurances given by Sir Harvey Adamson and the remarks which fell from Your Excellency in concluding the debate, had led the people to believe that unless some very special circumstances which would justify the continuance of that measure were shown to exist, it would be dead on the October 31, 1910. It was with much surprise and regret therefore that we learnt that, while the Government was at Shimla, a Bill would be introduced to give a new life to this repressive measure even before it is dead. I submit, my Lord, that in the circumstances of the case it lay heavily upon the Hon'ble the

Home Member to place before the council facts and circumstances which would enable the non-official Members to decide whether they should give their support to the measure or oppose it. I may be permitted to say, and I am sure Your Excellency will accept the statement, that it is not a pleasure to the non-official members to oppose the government measures. We feel the very reverse of pleasure in opposing them. But we feel, my Lord, that we are here to express the opinions which we can justify first to ourselves and then to the public. We feel that we are to be judged not by this Council only but also by the much larger and far more important body of our countrymen who are keenly watching the conduct of non-official members as well as that of the members of the government in dealing with any legislation which affects them.

"Now, my Lord, we might all of us agree in the view that when the circumstances which gave rise to this legislation ceased to exist, this measure should have been allowed to die a natural death. Let us see therefore what those circumstances were and whether they exist in the country today. When the Regulation of the Meetings Ordinance of 1907, which was a prototype of the Act which is now under consideration, was issued, it was stated in the Statement of Objects and Reasons which accompanied it that the 'acute disorder' which prevailed in the Punjab and the parts of Eastern Bengal had led to the passing of the Ordinance. My Lord, that acute disorder had almost died before that Ordinance was issued; it certainly did not exist when in November, 1907, the government decided to pass the present Act. But even assuming that there were circumstances in 1907 which justified the passing of the Act, or at any rate satisfied the members of the government that it was necessary in the interests of the good government, in the interests of the preservation of the public peace, that a strong measure like that should be continued or be placed on the statute-book, the Hon'ble member who has put forward the motion under consideration before the Council was bound to satisfy this Council that these circumstances or conditions similar to them exist today when he seeks to give a new life to the measure. When piloting the measure through the Council the Hon'ble Sir Harvey Adamson said that he had no desire to disguise the fact that the measure was one of considerable potency. He justified, it however on the ground that in his opinion in the then condition of India such a measure was necessary. My Lord, what are the conditions which exist now? Do they make even the faintest approach to the conditions which existed in 1907? Sir Harvey Adamson complained at that time that the scheme of the constitutional reforms which the government had formulated had not brought about such a change in the public mind as had been expected, and that the government felt that they had to deal with a section of irreconcilables. But we know that the scheme of reforms originally put forward has, after undergoing many important changes, been carried out since; and notwithstanding the fact that there have been some serious complaints about the regulations framed under the new Councils Act, no one can deny that the reforms as a whole have been received with a feeling of gratitude and have greatly improved the political situation. I believe that there has been a consensus of official and non-official opinion that the reforms carried out have brought about a marked change for the better in the attitude of the general public towards the Government. Is that change to count for nothing in determining whether a repressive measure should be allowed to die its natural death or should be kept alive by the fresh legislation?

"We have been told that the local governments have asked for the Act. With due respect to the local governments we cannot blindly substitute the judgments of the local governments for our own. My Lord, it is difficult for us to understand why, while all that is open and visible to the public eye indicates an absence of those conditions in the country which should justify the reenacting of a repressive measure like the one before us while it is undeniable that there is a world of difference between the conditions which obtain in some provinces and those which prevail in the others, all the Local Governments are unanimous in recommending that such a measure should be brought on the Statute book for the whole of this vast Indian Empire.

"My Lord, the political situation in India was carefully summed up not long ago in the letter which the Government of India addressed on the 14th March last to the Government of Bengal and to the other local governments. In that letter Your Lordship in council was pleased to recognise that nowhere in India was any considerable proportion of the population imbued with the spirit of disaffection towards the British rule; that there was a party, small in numbers, though of considerable influence, in the opinion of the government, which was opposed to the continuance of the British rule; that among this small party also there was a class which was opposed to a resort to violence; that the other class which advocated and practised fine methods of terrorism consisted for the most part of youths who are still at school or College, and of young men who have not long passed that period of their life. The letter went on to say that these active revolutionaries were most prominent in parts of Bengal and Eastern Bengal and Bombay; that their movement had spread to the Central Provinces and Behar and to the Punjab; but that it had made little headway in Madras and in the United Provinces; and that the Government of India had received no information of its existence in Burma and in the North-West Frontier Province. That being so, I appeal to Your Lordship, I appeal to every Member of the Council, to judge what change has been brought about since March last which should justify the saddling of my province, the United Provinces, or of Madras, or of Burma or the North-West Frontier Province with this repressive measure. My Lord, one event has no doubt happened, and that a very sad one too, namely, the death of our beloved King Emperor. But the demonstrations of grief which that event called forth should have satisfied even the most sceptical mind that the heart of the people is sound; that they mourned the loss of the King-Emperor with as much sincerity as their fellow-subjects in any other parts of the Empire; that they would not have done so if they did not appreciate the British connection and did not want the British rule to continue. What else, my Lord, could be the meaning of the great demonstration that took place in Calcutta, where a hundred thousand Hindus walked a long distance in burning sun, bare-headed and bare-footed, in order to give united and public expression to their grief? My Lord, there have been manifestations of similar grief all over the country and there are movements going on at present in all the provinces to raise suitable memorials to the revered memory of Edward the Peacemaker. With these evidences of a strengthening of the feeling of loyal allegiance to the Crown that has long existed in the minds of the people, is this the time for the Government of India and for the local governments to ask for a continuance of a repressive measure, the life of which is to expire by the efflux of time in the October next? One should have thought, my Lord, that the government would at such a time have welcomed the removal by natural death of a measure which it has seldom, if ever, found it necessary to use, but which must always be a source of irritation and complaint to the great body of the loyal and law-abiding population of the country, particularly as there is nothing special in the existing circumstances which would justify an opposite course.

"It may be said, my Lord, that the government cannot ignore the existence of the hand of terrorists and anarchists. Your Lordship was pleased, in that same letter to which I have referred, to deal also with the case of these misguided enemies of their country and of its Government. I need not repeat what several other members have said before me, that every sensible man who has the interests of this country at heart must deeply deplore all the anarchical outrages and all unconstitutional action. But it cannot be said with any reason that the prevention of public meetings of twenty persons and more will exercise any restraining influence upon the evil conspiracies, on the action of those who hatch their plots in secret, and who must, by the very nature of things, always endeavour to carry out their diabolical designs without all avoidable publicity. It is important to remember in this connection that the existence of the Act in question has not evidently hampered the terrorists in their action during the last three years. This Act cannot therefore be claimed to be a remedy for that disease.

"Your Lordship's Government was pleased in the letter of

March last not only to analyse the political situation but also to suggest some suitable remedies, if I may say so, with the eye of a statesman. The government expressed its belief that the seditious movement is in the main due to ignorance and misapprehension of the natural consequences of the British rule in India; that though there existed in the ranks of those who were hostile to that rule a residue of implacable hatred of all the alien intrusion, all the information which has been placed before the Governor-General-in-Council supports the view that the majority of the advocates of nationalism have been misled by shallow arguments and prejudiced statements. The obvious remedy for this state of things was that the other side of the case should be put before these young men. Your Excellency therefore wisely called upon all the officers of government, and indeed all the supporters of law and order, to do his best, each in his own sphere, to combat misrepresentation and to remove misapprehension regarding the character and results of British rule. The officers of the Education Department were rightly asked to check the spread of seditious views among their wards by sympathetic discussion and kindly guidance; the attention of all the District officers as directed to the necessity of taking leading men in each district into their confidence, and of cultivating a courteous and considerate demeanour towards all with whom they are brought in contact. The concluding portion of the letter stated:

> The Governor-General-in-Council believes that there is every reason to expect success for a policy on the lines described in the foregoing paragraphs. There is much ignorance and misunderstanding on the subject of British rule in India, and thence has arisen a spirit of disaffection. That spirit has not spread far, and the wrong impressions on which it rests are capable of removal by conciliatory discussion and earnest remonstrance. Many supporters of this so-called nationalist programme have taken alarm at the development of what they regarded as a permissible political movement into the fanatical outrages of the terrorist section. The moment is favourable for detaching them from the party of disaffection and for convincing all but the most extreme of the danger to the general welfare of the persistent attacks upon the foundations of the established

> Government. The great body of the people are entirely loyal and prepared to join with the officers of Government in this mission against disaffection.

"I submit, my Lord, that that was a clear and statesmanlike pronouncement on the policy which the government should pursue at the present time. It supplied the true remedy for the disease from which the country has in parts suffered and is unfortunately still suffering. But these methods of conciliation require that a free and public discussion of grievances and views should be encouraged rather than discouraged, cases of any serious abuse of the liberty of speech or meeting being left to be punished by the ordinary laws of the land. At any rate the policy of sympathetic guidance and conciliation which the Government of India deliberately decided upon but a few months ago will be to a large extent stultified if this fetter on the freedom of speech and action is continued, if this repressive measure is given a fresh lease of life. This being my view of the situation, I submit, with great respect, that the government should not go on with the proposed legislation. I fully realise how vain it would be to hope that the Hon'ble Member in charge of the Bill will drop the motion. But, my Lord, I consider it my duty to say that it is very unfortunate that he should not be able to do so. There is nothing more important at this juncture for the good government of this country than that there should be a feeling abroad among the people that the government is willing more than ever to listen with sympathy to the representations of the Indians, to give due consideration to the wishes and opinions of the representative Indians, who are quite as much anxious to uphold the law and order, as being the *sine qua non* of the peaceful progress, as any official member can be. Your Lordship has seen that there is a large body of the unofficial opinion almost begging that the government should not proceed with this measure. In these circumstances, unless the Hon'ble Member can lay before the Council the opinions of the Local Governments that he has received and relied on, unless he can disclose facts and circumstances which show that there is a danger that, if the meetings are allowed to be held freely as they used to be held before this Act was passed, this circumstance will tend to disturb the public tranquillity or lead to some other crime which cannot be dealt with by the existing enactments, I submit, it cannot but be deplored that the Bill should be proceeded with and passed.

"I do not wish to dwell at length upon the existence of other provisions in the Law which place ample power in the hands of the government to suppress meetings which are likely to promote sedition or to lead to a disturbance of the public tranquillity. Some speakers who have spoken before me, including the Hon'ble Mr Madge, have said that the existing law is not sufficient. My Lord, it is not necessary for me to enter into a discussion with these gentlemen as to whether that is so or otherwise. My lawyer friends have presented the correct view of the situation. Besides, an ounce of fact is better than a ton of argument. The Council has had a few such facts placed before it, facts which go to show that meetings of 50,000 persons and more in Calcutta, and other large meetings in Nagpur and Eastern Bengal, have been dispersed quietly under the Section 144 of the Criminal Procedure Code. It may be said that if it is a fact that both in that section and in the section relating to the unlawful assemblies there is ample power given to the Executive to disperse any assembly which it considers to be objectionable, then why should we object to a measure of this character, which merely gives the same power to the government which it already possesses under the other Acts? The reason for it is this. We submit that while the powers which the Government possesses under the other acts are amply sufficient to deal with every individual case or cases of the abuse of the right of meeting that may arise, the conferring of this general power of proclaiming an area, by which the voice of the whole population there may be silenced, is most dangerous and unjust. My Lord, what is it that may happen under such an act? As some of my friends have pointed out, some mischievous miscreant or some misguided young men talk a little nonsense in a place, the police send up long, reports of danger to the state or to the public peace, and the whole district is proclaimed. I do not say that the Lieutenant-

Governors and Governors of the Provinces do not fully weigh the situation; but they are after all human, and therefore liable to err. They have to act upon the reports of the man on the spot, who in his turn must act upon the reports of the Police or of the Criminal Investigation Department. And we have had sufficient instances of the abuse of the powers given under the act.

"We have seen how far the faults, more imaginary than real, of a few men or a small coterie of men, the population of a whole district, the great bulk of whom must, as the letter quoted before has told us, be regarded as undoubtedly loyal to the government, have been deprived of the right, which they enjoy under the British Government, of free public meeting and of giving free expression to their opinions and their sentiments, to their grievances and desires in relation to the public questions which affect or interest them. It cannot but be regarded as a serious public grievance that, for the misconduct of a few individuals, the whole oommunitiy in a locality should be prevented from freely exercising a privilege which they have never abused.

"My Lord, not only has no necessity been shown for the measure before us, but there is also the fear, as my friend Hon'ble Mr Gopal Krishna Gokhale has pointed out, that a repressive measure may itself, by being abused in its working, lead to promoting the evil which it was intended to cure. The Seditious Meetings Act and the Press Act have both already given illustrations of the truth of the old adage that the sight of means to do ill-deeds often makes ill-deeds done. Look for instance at the action of the authorities in Eastern Bengal in suppressing three District Conferences and the meeting which sought to help the depressed classes. I venture to doubt if the said Conferences or the said meeting would have been stopped if the Seditious Meetings Act had not been in existence. Look again at the action taken in several places under the Press Act in contravention of the pledge given by the government when it was going through the council, and think of the irritation which the abuse of its provisions must cause in the public mind. So long as the government will keep these two measures on the statute book, I regret to say, but I feel it my duty to say it, so long will all the efforts to conciliate the public opinion generally be beset with unnecessary difficulties, will continue to be unnecessarily difficult of accomplishment.

"I do not wish to detain the council any longer. But I cannot help referring in this connection to the action taken under the Press Act with regard to Mr Mackarness' pamphlet. I know that several Local Governments have thought it wise to suppress that pamphlet. I have no doubt that they believe that they have acted rightly in the matter. But with due deference to these Governments, I venture to think that if the new Press Act had not given them the indefinitely wide powers which it has given them, not one of them would have ever thought of suppressing the pamphlet. None of them perhaps would even now think of prosecuting Mr Mackarness for it. The pamphlet might not have done full justice to the efforts of the Government to improve the Police. But what did it aim at except a suppression of the evil practice which it exposed? It has been said, My Lord, that the Government of India has been denouncing the practice of torturing accused persons with a view to extort confessions from them at least ever since they enacted the Indian Penal Code, which has laid down that any person who would so put people to torture would be liable to be punished with imprisonment which may extend to seven years. But the existence of such a provision has not evidently proved to be a sufficient deterrent, and in view of the facts brought to light in some of the recent cases, it was clearly necessary in the public interests to draw the public attention to the evil with a view to have special measures taken to effectually discourage it.

His Excellency the President, "I am afraid that I must interrupt the Hon'ble Member. Mr Mackarness' pamphlet has got nothing whatever to do with the present discussion."

The Hon'ble Pandit Madan Mohan Malaviya, "I bow to your Lordship's ruling. I wished to point out how easily a repressive measure may be abused, and may give rise to great irritation, when the object of the government is that cause for irritation should not be given.

"I will now conclude. I think I have said enough to show that no justification has been made for proposing an extension of the life of the Seditious Meetings Act; that the powers which the government possess under the existing provision of the law are amply sufficient to effectively prevent as well as to punish any attempt to promote sedition or to disturb the public tranquillity, which might be made by persons who are hostile to the government and whose number is small; that the great bulk of the people are loyal to the core, and are more than ever inclined to co-operate with the government in maintaining law and order; that the policy of conciliation is in these circumstances the only safe and wise policy; that it should be steadily and earnestly pursued; that unless some overpowering causes intervene, nothing should be done which is likely to interfere with the success of that policy. I believe that no such causes demand a continuation of an act of an abnormal character, which must operate against the return of the normal relations between the government and the people. For these reasons, I beg humbly to oppose the motion which is now before the council."

GOKHALE' S EDUCATION BILL

At the meeting of the imperial legislative council held on the March 19, 1912, in supporting Mr Gopal Krishna Gokhale's motion that the Elementary Education Bill be referred to a select committee, Malaviya spoke as follows:

"I beg to support the motion that the Elementary Education Bill be referred to a select committee. I will briefly explain my reasons for this view. In the first place, I must express the gratification with which the remarks of the Hon'ble Member for Education have been listened to by this council. They will be read with much satisfaction throughout the country. We fully recognise that the government has done a great deal in the past to promote education. In fact, the present public system of education is one of the greatest gifts which the government has conferred upon the people, and the people feel deeply grateful for it. The fact that we ask for more does not in any way detract from our appreciation of what we have received. On the contrary, it is the greatest proof of such appreciation. We desire to secure to all our people what is at present enjoyed by only a few of them. And we regard a measure like, the bill before us essential to the attainment of this object. What has been said by previous speakers and particularly by the Hon'ble Member for Education already disposed of many of the objections raised to the bill, and therefore my task is an easy one. Briefly, those who oppose the bill may be divided info three classes. First, there are those who are opposed to universal education and therefore opposed to the bill because it introduces the principle of compulsion which will lead to the universal education. In this class, I am sorry to find, are some prominent members of the landed aristocracy, among them my friends the Hon'ble Nawab Abdul Majid and the Hon'ble Sir Gangadhar Rao Chitnavis. They seemed to speak in blissful ignorance of the fact that the Government of India has long been committed to the principle of universal education. They have put forward rather late in the day objections of a social, political and miscellaneous character against the introduction of universal education. Several of these objections have been so well answered by my friend Hon'ble Mr Jinnah that I will not go over the same ground. But, apart from the social objections and the political objections which he has disposed of, there are some miscellaneous objections which remain to be answered. One of these has been put forward by Hon'ble Nawab Abdul Majid in the name of the language difficulty. He has said there are many languages current in this country, and he has thus apprehended, speaking with special reference to the United Provinces, that if the bill was passed into law an attempt might be made to injure the Urdu language and to compel the Mohammedan students to study Hindi. Now, Sir, I will not take up the time of the council by going into a historical dissertation as to the respective ages and characters, the merits and demerits of the Hindi and Urdu languages. I shall content myself with saying that so great a scholar as Sir William Hunter has said that Hindi stands at the head of all the vernaculars of India. For the rest my friend is entirely mistaken in entertaining the fears which he has expressed. For the last seventy years the government of the United Provinces have been utilising both Hindi and Urdu in imparting education among the masses, and if the bill is passed there will be no change in that direction and no cause for offence or complaint given to any Mohammedan or non-Mohammedan.

"Then objections have been urged against the bill on the ground of there being numerous castes and numerous creeds in this country. I submit, Sir, that the existence of numerous castes and creeds has not proved to be an insuperable obstacle in the way of extending education among the masses. The British Government have for the last seventy years been extending education among the masses, including the most backward classes, notwithstanding the existence of different creeds, notwithstanding the existence of numerous castes in the country. The lines which they have followed are sound lines, which need not be departed from in the slightest degree, but which will enable the government if the bill is passed into law to bring the blessings of education home to every caste and to every creed in the country.

"These are what I call the miscellaneous objections, which do not affect the principle of the bill. It is sufficient to say that, if the bill ever comes to be examined in the Select Committee, ample provision can be made to safeguard every possible interest which requires to be safeguarded.

"Then, in the second class of those who are opposed to the bill come those who accept the principle of universal education but think that the principle of compulsion should not be introduced into the educational system of this country. They want education to be universal but they have a mortal fear of the principle of compulsion, because they urge that compulsion will mean an unnecessary interference with the liberties of the people.

"They forget that the principle of compulsion has necessarily to be introduced in some departments of every civilised administration. In the very first place, to establish, and maintain order and to repress crime, a certain amount of compulsion of restraint has to be exercised on the wills and actions of the individuals. In the second place, in a higher atmosphere in promoting the social well-being also, compulsion does come into play. The government introduced the system of vaccination many years ago. Under that system, whether they will it or not, people have to subject themselves to the provisions of the Vaccination Act. There are penal clauses in it, there are prosecutions under it, the act is in force over vast areas in the country, and yet nobody has heard that the people have strongly resented it, much less that it has led to riots or disorder. The introduction of water works and drainage has not been brought about in many places, at least with the consent of the general public. They have had to submit to it for the general good, and have had to pay taxes, to undergo hardships, prosecutions and so on. So also in the matter of other improvements. I submit that the principle of compulsion has to be introduced where it is clearly for the benefit of the people at large that it should be. If the great bulk of the community appreciate its introduction, the difficulties of the situation are lightened. If the bulk of the community have not been prepared to appreciate it, it only casts an additional duty upon us to educate them to do so, and that education can easily be given where the object is so patently good, as in this case, of securing this blessing of education to all classes and sections of the community. The theoretical objection to the principle of compulsion does not stand in the way of any real beneficial improvement being brought about, and ought not to stand in the way of the proposed humanitarian measure. Then, Sir, there is the third class of opponents to the bill. This consists of those who are entirely and whole-heartedly for universal education, and who are also in favour of the principle of compulsion, but who think that the time is not yet for introducing that principle. In this third category are many local governments. The Bengal government says that it sees no objection *per se* to the principle of compulsory elementary education, but urges that the conditions essential to its success have yet to be created. The Madras government says: 'It is an axiom that the universal education of the masses is the goal to be aimed at, and all who have the interests of the country at heart are equally interested in bringing about this consummation, but that His Excellency the Governor-in-Council cannot recommend the adoption of the bill for sometime to come.' Even the government of the United Provinces, which I regret to note has put forward some very unreasonable and unjustifiable apprehensions regarding the effect of the measure if it is introduced, even that the government says that when a desire has been created in the majority of parents that their children should obtain some form of elementary education, compulsion may be adopted as the statesmanlike measure to bring laggards and malcontents within the fold. So that, I submit, the majority of the local governments are not opposed to the principle of compulsion *per se*. They only argue that the time has not yet come when that principle should be introduced in India. But I need not take up the time of the council by laying these opinions in detail before it. The statement made by the Hon'ble Member for Education makes the position quite clear. The Government of India is clearly not afraid of introducing the principle of compulsion in the matter of elementary education.

"The statement made by the Hon'ble Member, which will be read with great hope and satisfaction throughout the country, makes this very clear. 'All of us are working for the same object,' said the Hon'ble Sir Harcourt Butler, 'I should rejoice as much as they (Gokhale and those who support this motion) to see a condition of things in which the elementary vernacular education could be compulsory and free in India. The Government of India is deeply concerned to bring about such a condition of things. The statement is worthy of the Government of India. It is entirely in keeping with their numerous previous pronouncements on the subject of the education of the masses. It is also what we should have expected from a government which is presided over by our present Viceroy. I may remind the council here of the words which were uttered by His Excellency in replying to a deputation at Lahore. After reviewing the progress of education in the Punjab, His Excellency there said:

The past has had its triumph, the present may have its successes;

> but it is in the horizon of the future that our watchful eyes should be fixed, and it is for that reason that the future needs of the students and youth of this country will always receive from me sympathetic consideration and attention.

"In another place His Excellency said: 'But the goal is still far distant when every boy and girl and every young man and maiden shall have an education, in what is best calculated to qualify them for their own part in life and for the good of the community as a whole. This is an ideal we must all put before us.'

"Clearer language could not be used to indicate the high aim, the noble goal, which the Government of India has placed before itself. But the question that awaits an answer is, how is that goal to be reached? Sir Harcourt Butler has shown that the government has been steadily and systematically endeavouring to improve education and to the extent is that there has been real progress under the existing systems. We know it, and we feel deeply thankful for it. But he has also said at the same time that the progress has not been satisfactory. 'I grant you', said the Hon'ble Member, 'that we are not satisfied'– we are profoundly dissatisfied with the general rate of progress, and Gokhale has shown that it would take 115 years, if we continue to proceed at the rate we are proceeding, for India to see every boy of school-going age at school, and 665 years to see every girl of school-going age at school. That period may be absolutely correct, or it may not be. But it cannot be denied that it would take a very very long time to see primary education universally diffused among the people if only the voluntary method which obtains at present is adhered to. Sir Harcourt Butler has said that the Government is advised by all their experts that the present rate of progress can be enormously accelerated by the provision of funds to finance the schemes of advancement. No one can doubt this. He has also said that the government hopes to finance these schemes with liberal grants from the Imperial revenues. This is a matter for much satisfaction and thankfulness. But it may still be permissible to doubt whether the future of the elementary education of the masses can be placed on a secure basis, whether the supply of the efficient funds needed to spread it among all the classes of the people, can be ensured without recourse to legislation, whether on the lines suggested or on the different lines. In this connection it may perhaps be useful to remind the council that the question of the universal extension of the primary education has had the attention of the Government of India for many decades past. In 1882 Lord Ripon appointed an Education Commission, and the report of that commission dealt largely with that question. The commission reviewed the progress, which had been made upon the basis of voluntary effort, and expressed themselves very much dissatisfied with it. They made several recommendations to ensure greater progress in the future. They re-affirmed the policy upon which the British Government had acted since 1871, and said, 'We therefore express our conviction that while every branch of education can justly claim the fostering care of the state, it is desirable, in the present circumstances of the country, to declare the elementary education of the masses, its provision, extension and improvement to be that part of the educational system, to which the strenuous efforts of the state should now be directed in a still larger measure than heretofore.' They felt satisfied that this object could not be gained without legislation. They, therefore, recommended that 'An attempt be made to secure the fullest possible provision for an extension of primary education by legislation suited to the circumstances of each Province.' Now, Sir, it will be useful to quote to the Council the grounds of their decision. The commission stated them as follows, 'Hitherto the State has mainly relied for the extension of education upon departmental effort or upon voluntary effort. But the former is obviously limited by financial considerations, and is therefore inadequate to the need, while it moreover tends to discourage local effort and self-reliance. The latter is necessarily partial and uncertain, and is least likely to be forthcoming where it is most wanted. What is now required seems to be some measure that will not only meet present necessities in each province but be capable of expansion with future necessities. It is not thereby intended that any one large measure should regulate the details of education throughout all India. On the contrary the recommendation cited is carefully guarded in its reference to the circumstances of each province.'

"Then, after pointing out that there were legislative councils in only three provinces at that time, and that therefore for each of the other province some or more acts would have to be passed by the Supreme government, the commission went on to say, 'In the case of all the provinces alike, it is right that the central authority, being most conversant with principles, should supply principles, while the local authorities should embody those principles in the acts suited to the circumstances of each province. A declaration of the general principles by the supreme council will be no bar to the exercise of free scope and discretion by the local authorities in the matters of detail; still less will the one province be bound by provisions primarily designed for another. In this way it is hoped that in the course of time, by a process of gradual expansion on well-considered lines, each province may be furnished with sufficient and efficient primary schools.'

"The commission went on to discuss the question whether the object desired could not be attained by the executive orders without legislation, and they pronounced themselves in favour of legislation as against the executive action. The commission said: 'On the equally important question whether the executive orders would not ensure the desired end without legislation, it was argued that the history and statistics given in our report show that the executive orders of clear import and general application issued from 1854 to the present time have failed more or less in all the provinces to ensure uniform attention to the broad principles prescribed for general guidance.'

"They went on also to point out that 'In all the countries where education has been most successful, it has been based on law of ordinance which has laid down the broad outlines of a general policy. Even in England where there is so much jealousy of any central action that can be avoided, it was never advanced, in the prolonged discussions which resulted in the Acts passed between 1870 and 1880, that if a national and adequate system of primary education was at last to be established it would be established otherwise than by the legislation.'

"And the last argument which they urged was that, 'Legislation is the only way in which all or any of the recommendations of the commission, after approval by the government, can be made to live and last'."

"It is much to be regretted that the legislation recommended was not undertaken. It is true that in the Municipal Acts which have been passed in the different provinces since that time some provision has been made regarding education, but the measures recommended by the commission were not adopted so far as legislation concerning the country as a whole was concerned and the want of such legislation accounts in a large measure for the unsatisfactory progress of the elementary education. The council will be interested to hear what some of these recommendations were, as they afford a great deal, of support; to the bill which is now before it. Among other recommendations the education commission urged that the duties of the municipal and local boards in controlling or assisting schools under their supervision should be regulated by the local enactments suited to the circumstances of each province. They recommended the creation of school districts, or rather the declaration that the area of any municipal or rural unit of local Self-Government may be declared to be a school district. They recommended the creation of school boards for the management and control of schools placed under their jurisdiction in each such district. They further recommended that every school board should be required to submit to the local government through the department an annual report of its administration together with its accounts of income and expenditure in such form and on such date as shall be prescribed by the local government. And this is the most important part of the recommendation to which I would draw attention.

" 'And,' said the commission, 'the local government should declare whether the existing supply of schools of any class of which the supervision has been entrusted to such board is sufficient to secure adequate proportionate provision for the education of all the classes of the community, and in the event of the said government declaring that the supply is insufficient, to determine from what sources and in what manner the necessary provision of the schools shall be made.' "

"The commission made other necessary recommendations regarding the creation of a school fund in every school district, and the rights and duties of the school boards. Can it be disputed that if their recommendations had been carried out, the history of the progress of primary education would have been written very differenly to what it has been?

"Now, Sir, my Hon'ble friend Gokhale has already said that he is not particular that the bill should be accepted in the particular form in which he has drafted it. He has appealed to the Hon'ble Member for Education and I humbly join in that appeal to bring in a measure which he and the government consider to be suitable in the circumstances of the country to ensure a more satisfactory progress of primary education. I submit that whether legislation may be partly imperial and partly provincial, legislation there should be in order to give reasonable uniformity to the education department and in order to provide that sufficient funds, both imperial and local, shall be regularly forthcoming to ensure that every part of the country should have a sufficient number of schools provided within a reasonable period of time. In the absence of such legislation, the progress of education will not be equable. No doubt the government is providing some funds at present, and these funds are being devoted to creating some schools. But what is the principle on which these schools are being created? It is a principle which exposes the government in a greater degree to a charge, which has been brought against the bill before us, of involving injustice to the areas where schools are not created. This must happen when you, arbitrarily create schools in certain localities and led other localities go without any school. But if you will create school districts and school boards and lay down a definite principle that imperial funds should be distributed in some proportion to the amount which may be raised by the people of each district, which will of course include all the local funds raised in the district, you will take away all the just causes of complaint, and ensure that in every school district there will be some provision made for the education of the children within the district. This can only be done by legislation, and, if it is, more funds will necessarily be found for education, whether the funds be partly contributed by the district boards or municipal boards and partly by the provincial government and partly by the imperial government. It may be said, Sir, that even conceding that it is desirable to introduce some legislation on the lines indicated by the Education Commission, there is no need yet for introducing the principle of compelling parents or guardians to send their boys to school, because boys of school-going age are rushing to school without any such compulsion. Assuming that it is so, this argument overlooks a very important point. The question is whether it is the duty of the government to see that every child of school-going age shall receive the benefit of education, or whether it is not. I submit, Sir, that it is in the interests of the community and of the state that every child, both boy and girl, should receive education; and if that object is to be secured, it will not do to leave it to the option of parents or guardians to send their boys to school or not as they like. In the case of girls there should of course be no compulsion for the present. But if you proceed on the voluntary system in the case of boys also, education will never become universal. A certain number will, no doubt, receive education; but a large number will not. Every civilised country has found that compulsion is the only means by which universal education can be secured. No country has succeeded without it, and we cannot expect to succeed without it. The case for compulsion has been admirably summarised in a paragraph which occurs in the very able minute of Mr Maynard, the Officiating Financial Commissoner of the Punjab, which I take the liberty of quoting here. Says Mr Maynard:

> But the true justification for the adoption of compulsion lies in the assumption that elementary instruction ought not merely to be vigorously extended, but, ultimately, to be made universal, and that this is impossible without compulsion. That there will

> always be a proportion of parents, weak or apathetic or shortsighted or greedy, who will neglect their duty, except under pressure, is implied in the legislation of all the western countries. This country is full of conservative elements, non-official as well as official, which will decline to accept the theory that elementary instruction ought ultimately to become universal; but responsible opinion appears to be committed to that conclusion, and considering what is being done elsewhere in the world, we do not see what else is possible without the gravest economic and other risks. We stand then, ultimately committed to the necessity of compulsion, and the present is a proposal for the cautious and tentative introduction of the new principle in specially favourable localities, in order to feel the way towards a further plunge, when the right time comes for it.

I submit, Sir, that the case for compulsion for the principle of the bill, could not be better or more clearly put than it has been put in that one paragraph. If then compulsion shall have to be our ultimate resort, the question is whether we should wait and wait until we think the time is come to introduce, is all at once all over the country, or whether we should make a beginning now with the measure which has been proposed and introduced it tentatively in the select areas. As has been observed by Hon'ble Sir Harcourt Butler, the bill is a modest measure. It is full of safeguards, which are regarded by some people as too many. But it is undeniable that it is a very cautious measure. If it is passed, it will only enable and not compel a municipal or a district board, with the previous sanction of the local government and subject to such rules as the Governor General-in-Council may make in this behalf, to declare that the Act shall apply to the whole or any specified part of the area within the local limits of its authority, and thereby to render it obligatory upon parents or guardians residing within that area to send their boys, and in certain circumstances and in certain areas their girls also, to the school provided that a recognised school is in existence within a mile of the home of the boy or the girl. It is important to note the safeguards which the bill provides against hasty or ill-considered action. The ultimate declaration which will determine the extension of the Act to any area can only be made with the previous sanction of the local government. That the government will not be bound to sanction such a declaration; and it may reasonably be presumed that it will refuse to do so when and where any class or community or a large section of it is opposed to it. All the fears and apprehensions which have been expressed by some Hon'ble Members who have preceded me, that the principle of compulsion might be introduced in any area against the wishes of the community or the people, fall to the ground when it is remembered that the local government alone will have the power to sanction whether the act shall or shall not be applied in any area. In addition to this, power has also been specially reserved to the local government to exempt particular classes or communities from the operation of the act. Secondly, the local government cannot take action of its own motion; it can sanction the extension of the act to any area only at the instance of the municipal or the district board of the locality. This is to ensure that the act shall not be applied to any area where the majority of the people are opposed to it. Further provision can be made in the bill to ensure this result."

THE SIMULTANEOUS EXAMINATION

The following is the full content of the speech delivered by Hon'ble Pandit Madan Mohan Malaviya at the meeting of the Imperial Legislative Council held on September, 1917, on the question of the simultaneous examinations: Sir, I beg to move that:

> This Council recommends to the Governor-General-in-Council that the Government of India should move the Secretary of State to arrange that the examination for the Indian Civil Service should henceforth be held simultaneously in India and in England, successful candidates being classified in the list according to merit.

"As we all know, Sir, this question is an old one. In 1793 the East India Company Act was passed while appointments under the East India Company were limited to certain members who had the sole right of conferring employments in the higher civil appointments in the service of the Company. But when the Charter Act of 1833 came to be framed, a clause was introduced, recognising the natural right of the Indians to employment in the higher services of their country. The clause was described by Macaulay as 'that wise, that benevolent, that noble clause.' It recognised that though India had come under the dominion of England, it was the natural birth-right of the Indians, that if they were qualified by education and character they should be employed in all the higher offices under the crown. In the course of the discussion that arose on the bill which subsequently became law, many excellent sentiments were expressed; but I will invite the attention of the Council to only one utterance, viz., that by Sir Charles Grant, in which he said: 'If one circumstance more than another could give me satisfaction, it was that the main principle of this bill had the approbation of the House and that the House was now legislating for India and the people of India on the great and just principle that in doing so the interests of the people of India should be principally consulted and that the other interest of wealth, of commerce and of revenue should depend upon the legislature promoting the welfare and prosperity of that great Empire which the Providence has placed in our hands.'

"When this great and first principle was recognised that the interest of the people of India should be principally consulted in all the arrangements for the administration of this country, it was to be hoped that employment of Indians in higher services would come about, but not a single Indian had been appointed. When, in 1853, a renewal of the Charter of the Company came to be discussed in the parliament, Mr Bright, Lord Stanley and the other gentlemen drew prominent attention to the fact, and it was hoped some remedy would be forthcoming; it was not however until 1854, that the system of the competitive examinations was introduced for civil service. Hailbury College was abolished in 1855, competitive examinations were held in 1855; Indians were still not able to compete after the Mutiny, after the Crown took the direct control of the Government of India, the pledge of 1833 was repeated and reaffirmed by the Proclamation of the Queen and in the House of Commons, that the Indian subjects of Her Majesty would be entitled to hold any post if they were qualified; we all know the gracious words of the Proclamation on which I need not dwell. It was hoped after the Proclamation that at any rate the claims of the Indians would not be ignored but nothing came of it. In 1860, a committee was appointed by the Secretary of State to suggest the best means for admitting the Indians into the service. The committee considered two proposals. The first was to allot a certain portion of the total number of posts declared in each year to be competed for by the Indians in India, and the second was to hold simultaneously two examinations for the Indian civil service, one in India and one in England, candidates sitting for either examination having to answer the same papers to be examined by the same examiners, and to be classified in one list in order of merit. It is important to draw attention to the report of this committee which consisted of Sir J. Willoughby, Mr Mangles, Mr Arbuohnot, Mr Macnaughten and Sir E. Perry, all of whom were all well acquainted with India, They reported as follows: " 'Two modes have been suggested by which the object in view might be attained. The first is by allotting a certain portion of the total number of appointments declared in each year to be competed for in India by the natives, and by all the other natural-born subjects of His Majesty resident in India. The second is to hold simultaneously two examinations, one in England and one in India, both being, as far as practicable, identical in their nature and those who compete in both countries being finally classified on one list, according to merit, by the Civil Service Commissioners. The committee have no hesitation in giving the preference to the second scheme as being the fairest, and the most in accordance with the principles of a general competition for a common object. In order to aid them in carrying out a scheme of this nature, the committee have consulted the Civil Service Commissioners. The Civil Service Commissioners do not anticipate much difficulty in arranging for this.' This report was unfortunately not acted upon; it was not even made public so far as I am aware, until 1876. In the meantime, in 1867, Mr Dadabhai

Naoroji took up the question, and with the help of the East India Association agitated the question in the parliament. Mr Fawcett moved a resolution in the House of Commons, urging that examinations should be held simultaneously in London, in Calcutta, Madras and Bombay. He urged that unless this was done the people of India would not have a fair chance of competing for these appointments; that if some scheme like that he urged was not carried out the promise held out in the Charter Act of 1833, and in the Proclamation of 1858, would not be faithfully fulfilled. 'It was no doubt true,' said he, 'that the natives of India might compete in these examinations, but as they could only do so by coming to London, at great expense, and then might be unsuccesful, to say that the examinations were practically open to them was an idle mockery.'

"His proposal was that there should be examinations at Calcutta, Madras and Bombay; there should be the same papers and the same tests as in London, and that the successful candidates, whether English or native, should spend two years in England. There would be no difficulty in carrying out the plan, for the examination papers might be sent under seal to India, and the examination being fixed for the same day as in London, the candidate's papers might be sent to England under seal and inspected by the same examiners, the name of the successful candidates at all four examinations being arranged in the order of merit, The then Secretary of State, expressed sympathy with the object of the resolution, as has often been done in the case of questions affecting the Indians, but he did not approve of the idea of holding simultaneous examinations; he stated that he was going to introduce a bill by which a certain number of posts would be secured to the Indians. Mr Fawcett pointed out that that would not satisfy the aspirations of the Indians and would not do full justice to them, but he agreed that the course proposed might be tried and withdrew his resolution. After that the Act of 1870 was passed which empowered the Government of India to frame rules to admit the Indians to a certain number of appointments in the civil service that proved unsatisfactory. In 1886 the Public Service

Commission was appointed, and it went into the question of the simultaneous examinations. A lot of evidence was given in favour of such examinations being held in India and in England but the commission reported against it. In 1893 in co-operation with Mr Dadabbai Naoroji, who was then a Member of the House of Commons, Mr Herbert Paul brought forward a motion urging the holding of simultaneous examinations in England and India. The resolution was carried, but unfortunately the Secretary of State was not in sympathy with it. He sent it to the Government of India. Excepting the government of Madras all the local governments reported against it and the Government of India did not give effect to it.

"Thus, though we have the Statute of 1833 in our favour, though we have the Proclamation of 1858 in our favour, though the committee appointed by the Secretary of State reported in favour of the simultaneous examinations, and though the House of Commons resolved in 1893, that such examinations should be held in the two countries, the proposal has never yet been accepted by the government. The question of the larger employment of the Indians was taken up in 1911 in this council by my friend Mr Subba Rao, who moved a resolution on the subject. In consequence of that, the Royal Commission on the public services was appointed in 1912. Unfortunately the commission have reported against it and one more unfortunate circumstance to be mentioned in this connection is that while before the commission of 1886, a number of European gentlemen, forty-nine of them were disposed in favour of simultaneous examinations, before the commission of 1913 no European witness except one spoke in favour of it.

"What is worse, and has pained us most is that a number of the European witnesses, both official and nonofficial, seemed to delight in giving as bad a character to Indians as they could. The result is that the majority of the commission have reported against the proposal. But, Sir, our conviction is that justice will not be done to the claims of the Indians unless the examinations for the civil service are held simultaneously in India and in England. The result of the examinations being held only in England has been that up to 1910 only eighty Indians had succeeded in entering the service by the door of examination as against over 2,600 Europeans. And out of 1,478 officers, who on the April 1, 1917, held posts ordinarily reserved for the members of the Indian Civil Service including 72 Statutory Civilians and the officers of the Provincial Civil Service holding listed posts only 146, or about 10 per cent, appeared to be the statutory natives of India. Surely this is not a state of things which is consistent with or carries out the spirit of the Act of 1833 or the Proclamation of 1858. I think it was in the debate of 1853 that one speaker had asked how many Englishmen would send their sons to India to compete for the civil service examination on the off-chance of getting admission into it. Speaking in London about 1878, Mr Bright said that to hold the examination in England alone and to tell the people of India that they had equal opportunities with Englishmen was akin to telling them that they must be eight feet six inches in height before they could be admitted into the civil service. In view of all that has been said above, the question is whether this recommendation of the commission is one which the government ought to accept. I submit most respectfully that it ought not to.

"In addition to our natural claim to which I have already referred and which has been repeatedly supported by many high-minded Englishmen, we have now a different state of things. The Government of India, as it is constituted at present, has been described by a member of the Indian Civil Service in a manner which brings out the disadvantages of the present system in very clear words. Sir Frederick Lely wrote in 1906 as follows: 'Perhaps the position may most vividly be brought home to our minds by imagining the same in England. Suppose that in England foreigners were ruling, say the Japanese who committed the province to one of their statesman who had never been in Europe before and surrounded him with a group of men of his own race, who got their knowledge of the country chiefly from books and papers at Whitehall, who for the most part could not talk the English language, whose unreserved intercourse with Englishmen was limited to a few Japanese-speaking callers in London, and who, when not in London, divided their time between the Scotch Highlands and the Riviera. What sort of government would it be? It might seem admirable to the people of Tokyo but would it be to the men of Yorkshire and Cornwall?' "

"I submit, Sir, that this is the result of practically refusing admission to His Majesty's Indian subjects into the Indian civil service. If the examination had been held in India, since 1855, I think it is not unreasonable to think that though our English fellow-subjects have very great advantages in the way of educational facilities, and facilities for coaching, and in the fact that the examination is held through their own mother-tongue, I think it is not unreasonable to think that there would have been a far larger proportion of the Indians in the Indian civil service than we have at present. When in 1833 the claims of the Indians to the higher ranks of the services were recognised, education had made but little progress. The famous minute of Lord Macaulay had not been written, there were no colleges, no universities but a few schools. Inspite of that fact the government of the day recognised that it was only fair that those Indians who could show that, by their education, integrity and character they were qualified for admission, ought to be admitted into the higher ranks of the services. Since that time we have had universities established in the several parts of India and they have turned out thousands of graduates. They have competed very successfully with their English fellow-subjects in all he walks of life to which they have been admitted. In the judicial line, Indian Judges have shown how high they stand both in point of character and ability; they have proved themselves to be the equals of their English brother judges. In other sphere also the Indians have proved their capacity in the high offices, under the British Government, in the Native States, as heads of Districts, as Commissioners, as members of Executive councils, as Dewans of Indian States, those Indians who have had opportunities afforded to them or those who have been able to force admission into the service have shown that if they are given an equal chance they are able to render a very good account of themselves. All that we have asked for in this connection from the beginning is not that we should be put on a favoured footing but that we should be put on a footing of equality We say that if two young men are to run a race, all fair rules of the game require that we should start both of them from the same centre, and not compel one to start several miles behind the other and yet expect the man who started several miles behind the other to succeed in the competition. We want that Indian youths should be subjected to the same test to which English youths are subjected. We do not want any differentiation in that respect. What we do say is that if the English men are allowed to sit for the examination in their own country, the Indians should also be allowed to sit in their own country for the same examination. One might very well say that the more natural, the more reasonable, the more just course would be that the examinations for admission into the civil services of India should be held in India alone, but the time for it is not yet. In view of the present circumstances of the country, remembering how we are situated at present, in view of the difficulties that have hitherto lain in our path, and of the desire we all have that we, Indian and European fellow-subjects, should move together in brotherly co-operation, and with as little dislocation as possible our prayer at present is, as it has been for the last fifty years, that the examination for the admission into the Indian civil service should be held simultaneously in India and in England.

"Sir, the not holding of this examination in India has exposed us to the great disadvantages, political, economic and administrative. The political disadvantages are obvious. Here we are discussing the question of the Self-Government, and of the larger admission of the Indians into the higher services. We are told we have not held charge of the high offices, we have not been dealing with the large problems and it is not right that we should ask to be entrusted with these problems at once. Well, if we have been shut out from these advantages, from the exercise of these high functions the fault is not ours. I submit, Sir, that it is an unreasonable proposition that because we have so long been kept out of these advantages, therefore we should be kept out of them in the future as well.

"I need not refer again to the remarks of Gokhale to which my Hon'ble friend Mr Sarma referred yesterday in which he pointed out that the moral evil of the present system was even greater and more serious than the political and economic disadvantages. The people of this country desire that they should be able to feel that they stand on a footing of perfect equality with their fellow-subjects in England and the United Kingdom. That is practically denied to them by the refusal to hold the examinations simultaneously which leads to the inevitable result that but few can enter through the door in London.

"So far as the economic evils are concerned, they were again and again pointed out by the late Mr Dadabbai Naoroji. I do not want to detain the council by dealing with them at length, but I will refer to a few facts to show how serious the economic evil is. According to a return presented to the House of Commons, in 1892, excluding the rank and file of the British Army, the total of the salaries, pensions and allowances received in 1889-90 by the public servants and the retired Government officials drawing salaries of ₹ 1,000 and over annually, amounted to about 18.5 crores, while the real revenue was about 61.5 crores. Of this, only about 3 crores was received by the 17,000 Indians, while the remaining 15.5 crores went to the pockets of 28,000 Europeans and Eurasians.

"That the lot of the Indians has not improved materially since then is evident, as my friend Pandit Hirday Nath Kunzru points out in his valuable pamphlet on the public services in India from the statistics published by the Government of India in 1912, which shows that out of 5390 posts to which monthly salaries of ₹ 500 and upwards were attached, no less than 83 per cent, were held by the Europeans and Eurasians.

"Long ago, Sir William Hunter pointed out that the salaries paid in India are very high and that India cannot afford to pay at the high rate at which the services are remunerated at present. In his pamphlet 'England's Work in India' he wrote, 'The truth is that we have suddenly applied our own English ideas of what a good government should do to an Asiatic country where the people pay not one-tenth per head of the

English rate of taxation. I myself believe that if we are to give a really efficient administration to India many services must be paid for at lower rates even than at present. For those rates are regulated in the higher branches of the administration by the cost of officers brought from England. You cannot work with imported labour as cheaply as you can with the native labour, and I regard the more extended employment of the natives not only was an act of justice but as a financial necessity...The salaries of the covenanted services are regulated, not by the rates of the local labour, but by the cost of the imported officials. If we are to govern the Indian people efficiently and cheaply, we must govern them by the means of themselves and pay for the administration at the market rates for the native labour.'

"You must recognise the fact that if you want to carry on the administration of India efficiently and cheaply, you must employ a larger number of Indians than have been employed hitherto; so that from the economic point of view it is obviously necessary that a larger number of the Indians should be admitted into the civil service. Then, Sir, there is the advantage of the administrative experience which can only be acquired if the Indians are admitted into the higher ranks of the service. Mr Dadabhai Naoroji summed up the whole situation in his own inimitable manner in a few words. He pleaded for a beginning for the Self-Government being made by the institution of the simultaneous examinations in India and in England, and he urged that that beginning will be the key, the most effective remedy for the chief economic and basic evils of the present system.

" 'A three-fold wrong is inflicted,' said he, 'upon us, i.e., of depriving us of wealth, work and wisdom, of everything, in short worth living for, and this beginning will begin to strike at the root of the muddle. The reform of the alteration of the services from the European to the Indian is the keynote of the whole.' "

"Of course Mr Dadabhai Naoroji did not mean that there should be an immediate or an early replacement of the Europeans by the Indians as a whole; what he urged was that a beginning should be made in order that the Indians should be able to obtain an increasingly large share in the higher services of their country.

"This, Sir, was the state of affairs before the War. What is the position of the affairs now? The War, as Mr Lloyd George has said, "has changed things enormously; as one of the members of the commission has observed, centuries of progress have been effected by this War. Naturally in consequence of it, things have begun to be looked at from a changed angle of vision; and we have been looking forward that our claims, which are based on justice, based on right claims, which were solid and strong before the War and without any reference to the War, will now be regarded as much stronger by reason of the part which the Indians have had the privilege of playing in this great world War. I would like to quote here a few remarks from a speech of the Marquis of Crewe. In his speech at the Guildhall in London, he said: 'It is perhaps even more striking certainly no less gratifying, that those representing the various races in India, races representing a civilisation of almost untold antiquity, races which have been remarkable in arms, and the science of government that should in so whole-hearted a manner rally round the British Government, most of all round the King-Emperor at such a moment as this and I am certain that the House will desire to express through those who are entitled to speak for it, its appreciation of their attitude and its recognition of the part they have played.' And Lord Haldane said: 'Indian soldiers are fighting for the liberties of humanity as much as we ourselves. India has freely given her lives and treasure in humanity's greater cause; hence things cannot be left as they are. We have been thrown together in this mighty struggle and made to realise our oneness, so producing relations, between India and England which did not exist before.'

"Now, Sir, in view of this momentous event, I submit the problem should be looked at in a much more sympathetic spirit than it has been heretofore. Our claim to have the simultaneous examinations for admission into the Indian civil service held in India as well as in England, was quite strong before the War, and without reference to the War; but the attitude of India during the War has given added strength to that claim. His Majesty's Government have recently announced the goal of British policy in India. In that announcement we have been told that,

> The policy of His Majesty's Government, with which the Government of India is in complete accord, is that of increasing the association of the Indians in every branch of administration and the gradual development of the self-governing institutions with a view to the progressive realisation of the responsible government in India as an integral part of the British Empire.

"His Excellency the Viceroy also in the memorable speech, to which it was our privilege to listen on the 5th of this month, told us that the increased association of the Indians in the higher services was one of the matters which was close to his heart and to that of the government.

"We also have the statement of Mr Montagu in the speech which he delivered a short time before he was appointed as the Secretary of State, and which he reaffirmed after he had been appointed the Secretary of State, in which he pointed out how necessary it is that the Government of India should be radically altered. I will not take up the time of the council by reading the large extracts from that important speech, but I will draw attention to only one important passage in it where he says:

> Your executive system in India has broken down because it is not constituted for the complicated duties of the modern government. But you cannot reorganise the Executive Government of India, remodel the Viceroyalty and give the executive government more freedom from this House of Commons and the Secretary of State unless you make it more responsible to the people of India.

"Now that is the position that the executive government has to be made more responsible to the people of India. With the altered state of things which the War has brought about, the recognition of the comradeship of the Indians and Europeans in arms, the recognition of the free contributions and the loyal services rendered during the War, and above all with a full recognition of the fact that the present system has outgrown itself and must be altered, so that the government shall be made responsible to the people of India, we have to approach this problem for solution. And I submit, Sir, that of all the questions relating to the constitutional reforms there is none which is more important, which lies at the root of the problem, more than this question of instituting examinations for admission into the civil service simultaneously in India and in England.

"There is one other aspect of the question which I think I ought to ask the council to bear in mind in this connection. Things have changed, they have changed greatly. The prayer for simple justice which we have gone on repeating and, I say it with regret, repeating vainly for fifty years, cannot be disregarded. Indians feel that, in being excluded from the higher appointments of the services of their own country, they are being very unjustly dealt with. They find that the people of many other countries have made and are making great progress in all the directions, that in many of them the systems of government has undergone a change to the great benefit of the people. They find that a new life has come over Japan.

"In the last fifty years Japan has reorganised itself and has won a place amongst the foremost nations of the world. When they contrast the condition of Japan with what it was in the last fifty years, with the progress made in the condition of India during the last sixty years, since the Proclamation of 1858, they cannot help drawing inferences and making comments which are unfavourable to the present system of government, Indians clearly want to feel, they want to realise that in India, as the subjects of His Majesty the King-Emperor George V and his successors, they can and they shall rise to the same height in their own country to which the Japanese have risen under the Mikado. They feel that other countries, even Asiatic countries, have been making great progress and they find a difference in the treatment given to the youth of this country. The British Government has established colleges and universities in our midst and have given us good education. We feel grateful for it. But the governments of other countries have done one thing more, which the government of this country has not done to the same extent. After having educated the youths of those countries, they have opened all the portals of higher service to those youths. In this country these higher portals have been practically closed against us, and as has again and again been pointed out by several English writers, if you will not allow the advantages which ought to flow from the acquisition of higher knowledge to come to those who have received that knowledge, you will necessarily create dissatisfaction and discontent. Having regard therefore to the justice of our claim, to the entirety of the circumstances and considerations which have come into existence because of the War, having regard to the circumstances of surrounding countries, and of the civilised world generally, the government ought not to hesitate any longer in instituting simultaneous examinations for admission into the Indian civil service in India and in England.

The Hon'ble vice-president: "I have to remind Pandit Madan Mohan Malaviya that he has already exceeded the time limit.'

The Hon'ble Pandit Madan Mohan Malaviya: "I am sorry, Sir, I was not conscious of it. The subject is one which touches the hearts of us all, and I hope you will kindly allow me just a few minutes more to bring my remarks to a close.

The Hon'ble Vice-President: "I hope you will be as brief as possible.

Hon'ble Pandit Madan Mohan Malaviya: "I was going to deal with the question of the character of the Indians which has largely, it seems, influenced the decision of the majority of the commission, but I will reserve it, if it should become necessary for me to do so, for my reply. But before concluding, Sir, I wish to make an earnest appeal to the government to take up this question in an earnest spirit and to solve it. There ought to be no necessity for discussing it at any great length. We have got the authoritative opinion of the parliamentary committee of 1860, we have got the authority of the House of Commons of 1893, we have got the opinions of many gentlemen who appeared before the public service commission in 1886 and of many more who appeared before the Royal Commission of

1912, in favour of the simultaneous examinations. We remember that the Committee of 1860 pointed out that there could be no better way of honourably fulfilling the pledges which had been given then by instituting such examinations. I wish also to make an appeal to my friends, the members of the Indian civil service. My friend the Hon'ble Mr Sastriar made an appeal to them yesterday. I wish, if I may, to support it, I would earnestly ask them to look at the question from the point of view that the honour of the English Sovereign, the honour of the English parliament, the honour of the English nation, is involved in fulfilment of the pledges which have been given to us during the last eighty years. Many of your own statesmen have said that those pledges have not been faithfully fulfilled. Lord Lytton once said that they had been made a dead letter and Lord Salisbury cynically urged that there was no good in keeping up an hypocrisy. But I am sure the documents containing the pledges will not be treated by the great English nation as a mere "scrap of paper". I am sure they realise that the honour of every Englishman, the honour of every Britisher, is involved in the honourable fulfillment of those pledges and that those pledges can only be faithfully fulfilled by the holding of the examinations for admission into the Indian civil service simultaneously in England and in India. One of the members of the bureaucracy has appealed to the members of the Indian civil service to decide their duty with reference to this question. I feel that it lies with them more than with any other body of men to help us to realise what we believe to be our birthright. In concluding his book on Bureaucracy, Mr Bernard Houghton says:

The Hon'ble Vice-President: "The Hon'ble member must not read quotations at this period of his speech. He has already exceeded the time limit.

The Hon'ble Pandit Madan Mohan Malaviya: "I will take only a minute, Sir.

The Hon'ble Vice-President: "Very well, I will give you a minute more."

The Hon'ble Pandit Madan Mohan Malaviya: "Mr Bernard Houghton says: 'And the members of the Indian civil service, easily the finest in the world, I am sure this will gratify the hearts of my friends, may recall with pride, even when handing over the sceptre of the supreme control they have wielded so long, that their dominion in India has not been without its glories. To have replaced turbulence and disorder by peace, to have established the courts of impartial justice, to have cast over the country a close network of roads and railways all these are the achievements which will ever rebound to the honour of themselves and of England. But perhaps the greatest of boons, although an indirect one, which India has received at their hands, has been the birth of a genuine spirit of patriotism. It is a patriotism which seeks its ideals, not in military glory or the apotheosis of a king but in the advancement of the people. Informed by this spirit, and strong in the material benefits flowing from the British rule, India now knocks at the portal of democracy. Bureaucracy has served its purpose. Though the Indian civil service were manned by angels from heaven, the incurable defects of a bureaucratic government must pervert their best intentions and make them foes to the political progress.'

"Not all of them, I am sure, Sir. It must now stand aside, and, in the interest of that country it has served so long and so truly, make over the dominion to the other hands. Not in dishonour, but in honour, proudly, as the shipbuilders who deliver sixty seamen the completed ship may they now yield up to the direction of India. For it the inherent defects of the system which nobody of men, however devoted, can remove, which render inevitable change to a new polity. By a frank recognition of those defects the service can furnish a supreme instance alike of loyalty to these land of their adoption and of a true and self-denying statesmanship.

"I earnestly hope, Sir, that my friends of the Indian civil service will approach this question before us in the spirit in which this appeal has been made to them by one of the former members of their service, and I trust that, approaching in that spirit, they will help us to obtain such a solution for which we ask of this very important problem which concerns our welfare."

3

Speeches, Note and Presidential Address of the Indian National Congress

THE REFORM OF THE LEGISLATIVE COUNCILS

The following speech was delivered in support of the following resolution of the Sixth Indian National Congress held at Calcutta in 1890:

> That this Congress, having considered the Draft Bill recently introduced into the Parliament by Mr Charles Brad, entitled, 'An Act to amend the Indian Councils Act of 1861' approves the same as calculated to secure a substantial instalment of that reform, in the administration of India, for which it has been agitating, and humbly prays the Houses of Parliament of the United Kingdom of Great Britain and Ireland to pass the same into law; and further that its President, Mr Pherozeshah Mehta, is hereby empowered to draw up and sign, on behalf of this assembly, a petition to the House of Commons to the foregoing effect and to transmit the same to Mr Charles Bradlaugh for presentation thereto in due course.

"I am happy to find that we are discussing today the leading features of the scheme for the reform and expansion of the legislative councils. You know since we met last, our position has somewhat improved in this matter, and the difference between us and the government is not now quite so great as it was a year ago. The four principal points which the Congress has been urging on the government in relation to the reform of the councils have been, firstly, that the number of members on the council should be increased; secondly, that the privilege of electing at least half of these members should be given to the people: thirdly that the budget should be laid every year before the council; fourthly, that the members should have the right to interpellate the executive on the questions of public concern. Of these, gentleman, His Excellency the Viceroy assured us in his speech on the occasion of the last discussion of the budget in his council, that Her Majesty's Government had decided to grant us three, viz., the enlargement of the council; the presentation to them of the budget every year, whether there be any new tax to be imposed or not; and the right to interpellate the government in regard to any branch of the administration. Of course there are some limitations to be put upon the exercise of this latter right; but His Excellency's words made it perfectly clear that the right itself will be conceded.

"The only vital point of difference between us and the government now, therefore, is with regard to the manner of appointing members to the council. The government wishes to nominate all the members, and we ask for the privilege of electing half of them. How evidently simple and just our prayer and how utterly indefensible the unwillingness of the government to grant it! You know, gentlemen, that in the reformed councils the government will be exactly what they now are the final arbiter of all the questions that may be brought before the Council. Even in the cases where the majority of the members are opposed to any measure and vote against it, the government will still possess the power to veto their decision, and carry things entirely according to their own will and pleasure. In other words, they will occupy the position of a judge in deciding all the questions affecting our purses, our character, in fact our whole well-being. The sole privilege which we are praying for is to be allowed to choose our own counsels to represent our cause and condition fully before them. And the government seems unwilling to allow us even that ! They will appoint counsels of their own choice to plead our cause. Now, gentlemen, we thank them for this overflow of kindness towards us, but we feel, and we have good reasons to feel, that, we should be much better off if they allowed us to exercise our own discretion in the choice of the counsels, who are to plead our cause, defend our rights, and protect our interests. The legislative council is the great tribunal before which measures of the greatest possible moment, affecting not only ourselves, but even our posterity, are continually coming up for decision, and justice requires that before the council passes its final judgment upon them, we should be allowed to have our say with regard to them, through our chosen and accredited representatives. We do feel, gentlemen, and feel strongly that we should no longer be debarred from exercising this simple and rightful privilege. The privilege of selecting one's own counsel is not denied even to the most abandoned of criminals under the British rule. Why, then, should it be denied to the loyal and intelligent subjects of Her Gracious Majesty?

"When a jury is being empanelled, the judge asks the person whose fate is to be decided by that jury, to say if he has any objection to any person composing it, and in case he has any such objection that person is removed from the panel. But the Government of India and our Secretary of State if the reports published in the newspapers represent their views faithfully seem unwilling to allow the vast millions of Her Majesty's subjects in this country any voice whatever in the appointment of persons who decide questions which, concern not merely any one man or any set of men amongst them, but the entire nation of them and their posterity. Could there be anything more in conflict with reason and justice?

"If, gentlemen, the choice of government in the selection of non-official members had, even generally, been exercised in a manner tending to promote the interests of the people who might not have been so anxious to burden ourselves with the responsibility of electing our representatives ourselves. But, unhappily, as you know, in a large majority of cases their choice has been exercised in favour of persons, who have proved to be the least qualified or willing to advocate the interests, and plead fearlessly for the rights of the people, nay, not unfrequently, in favour of persons whose presence in the council has helped to contribute to the miseries of the people. We would much rather that there were no non-official members at all on the councils than that there should be members who are not in the least in touch with the people and who being ignorant of their true conditions and requirements, betray a cruel want of sympathy with them, in headlessly supporting measures which tend to increase suffering and discontent among them.

"I will recall to your mind only two instances to illustrate what I have said. A couple of years ago, you remember, the government was driven by reason of its excessive and, as we think, wasteful military expenditure to find some fresh means of increasing its revenue, and it resolved upon drawing the required money from the poor, the class least able to offer any resistance or protest. The question came up before the legislative Council and unofficial honourable members, the so-called representatives of our people, so far from protesting against the proposal, gave their ready consent to it. Some of these gentlemen even went upto the length of declaring that the enhancement of the duty on salt would not inflict any hardship on the poorer classes of the people. Now, gentlemen, these big honourable gentlemen, enjoying private incomes and drawing huge salaries, may find it hard to believe that the addition of a few *annas* every year to the burdens of the poor can cause any serious hardship to them. But those who know in what abject misery and pinching poverty our poorer classes generally exist, know how painfully the slightest increase in their burdens presses upon them. But these honourable members were pleased to say—'The people will not feel the increase in the tax.' "

"I will remind you of only one more case. You remember a few months ago the government again found itself badly in want of money. Those who regulate their income by their expenditure, and not their expenditure by their income, must frequently find themselves in that unhappy position. It became necessary to raise more revenue, and after misappropriating the Famine Insurance Fund, and mulcting the provincial governments (thereby starving education and arresting progress in all the directions), the government then resolved again on squeezing something more out of the poor. It resolved to re-impose the *Patwari* Cess on the *ryots* of the North-Western Provinces and Oudh. Now you may know that when the Government of our good Lord Ripon had by a cessation of war and warlike operations, effected a saving in the public expenditure, and desired to give relief to those who most needed it, they found after inquiry that the *ryots* of the North-Western Provinces and Oudh stood most especially in need of some- relief, and they remitted the *Patwari* Cess to the extent of 20 lakhs. But the Government of Lord Lansdowne has this year reimposed the same cess upon them! See, I beseech you, gentlemen, what gross injustice has been perpetrated in the re-imposition of this *Patwari* Cess? The *Patwari* Cess was remitted seven years ago but the poor *ryots* have had to pay it, it seems all the same, year after year. It was said that the cess had been amalgamated with other taxes and could be separated from them. If the money had had to go to the cofferes of the Government, such a plea would never have been listened to for a moment. But it was the poor *ryot* who was concerned, the plea was allowed to hold good, the *Talukdars* and *Zamindars* were thus allowed to enjoy the entire benefit of the measure which the Government of Lord Ripon had passed in the interests of *ryots*; and it is now on this very plea that the remission of the Cess did not benefit the *ryot*, that the *Patwari* Cess has been re-imposed, not on the *Zamindars* but on the poor *ryot*, whereby he is now compelled to pay the Cess, twice over for no other fault of his than that he is poor and helpless.

"The Hon'ble Mr Quinton who represented the Government of Sir Auckland Colvin at the Viceroy's Council, said in his speech on the subject that the consent of the *Talukdars* of Ouadh had been obtained to the measure. Fancy, gentleman, the justice of adding to the burdens of the *ryot* on the strength of the consent of the *Zamindar*! But that was not all. There were other honorable members present in the Council, who said that the re-imposition of the cess would not add much more than about 12 *annas* a year to the load of taxation on the *ryot*, and they said it was so slight a sum that the *ryot;* would not feel the pressure at all. Well, gentlemen, it is sinful to desire unhappines to any one. But when I hear these honorable members assert with cruelity of heart that the addition of a few *annas* a year to the burthens of the insufficiently fed and clothed poor, whether it be in the shape of the Salt Tax or the *Patwari* Cess will not increase their wretchedness and misery, I feel tempted to exclaim with old Lear: 'Take physic pomp, Expose thyself to feel what wretches feel That thou may 'st shake the superflux to them And show the heavens more just.'

"If these gentlemen had to live even for a day or two on that coarse unpalatable diet which is the best our poor, often starving, can command in the brightest times, and if they had to brave the cold of our up-country winters without all those warm and soft clothings they themselves luxuriate in, they would understand what hardship the enhancement of the Salt Tax and the re-imposition of the *Patwari* Cess entails upon the people. There are hundreds of thousands of *ryots* at this moment in the North-Western Provinces and Oudh who cannot buy sufficient cloth to cover even the upper half of their bodies properly to protect themselves and their children from the piercing chill and cold of our northern winter nights; and remember, you gentlemen of the south, that the times are far more relentlessly severe with us there than with you here. These miserable people cover themselves, their wives and children, when the season becomes very severe, with grass at night and when the intensity of the cold drives away sleep, they warm themselves by burning some of the very grass. And even that is now and than taken away from them for feeding the cattle of officials on tour. Such is the condition of the people to whom the honorable members of the Viceroy's Council said that an increase of 12 *annas* a year in their burdens would not mean any serious hardship! Do you think, gentlemen, such members would be appointed to the Council if the people were allowed any voice in their selection? And even if they were by some mistake, once appointed, would they not be scornfully rejected at the next election?

"But such men are appointed at present, to the great

disgust of the people and the people are forced to submit to their legislatorship.

"I fear, gentlemen, I have taken up too much of your time, and I won't detain you any longer. I hope I have made it clear why we pray the government to allow the people the privilege of electing at least half of the members of the councilmen whom the people esteem and confide in by reason of their loving sympathy with them in all their sorrows and joys. And I earnestly hope the government will no longer delay granting us this simple rightful privilege, which while conducing greatly to our happiness, will not fall to add to the strength and glory of the British rule in India. Gentlemen, I heartily support this resolution."

A FEDERAL SYSTEM OF GOVERNMENT FOR INDIA

The excerpts from a note prepared for the decentralisation commission early in 1908:

"There are eight major provinces in British India which are administered by the separate Provincial Governments. The administration of the Presidencies of Madras and Bombay is vested in a Governor-in-Council, whose powers and duties are regulated by the Act of Parliament. Bengal, the United Provinces, Eastern Bengal and Assam, the Punjab and Burma are administered by the Lieutenant-Governors. The Central Provinces are still under the charge of a Chief Commissioner.

"The Governor-General in Council is the final authority responsible for the finances and administration of the country. But the actual work of the administration is divided between the Government of India and the local governments. The Government of India, that is to say the Governor-General in Council, retains in its own hands all matters relating to foreign the relations, the defences of the country, general taxation, currency, debts and tariffs, post, telegraphs and railways. Ordinary internal administration, the assessment and collection of the revenues, education, medical and sanitary arrangements, and irrigation, building and roads fall to the share of the provincial governments. But in all these matters the Government of India exercises a general and constant control.

It lays down lines of general policy and tests their application from the administration reports, which are, as a rule, annually submitted to it, of the main departments under the Local Governments. Besides the controlling officers for departments which it directly administers, such as Railways, Post Office, Telegraphs, the Survey of India, Geology, it employs a number of inspecting or advisory officer for those departments which are primarily left to the local governments, including Agriculture, Irrigation, Forests, Medical, Education and Archaeology. Not only does it receive, and, when necessary, modifies, the annual budgets of the local governments, but every new appointment of importance, every large addition even to minor establishments has to receive its specific the sanction, with the practical result that no new departure in administration can be undertaken without its preliminary approval. Outside Madras and Bombay the approval of the Governor-General is necessary to the appointment of some of the most important officers of the provincial administration. In all the provinces, questions of policy or of special importance are submitted for the orders of the Governor-General in Council, and the financial powers of the local governments are limited by definite and strict rules. That is to say the local governments are merely delegates of the supreme government, and exercise financial and other functions subject to its approval and control.

"The Government of India considers itself the master of the entire revenues of the whole of British India. Up to the year 1870, each of the local governments used to present to the Governor-General in Council, its estimates of expenditure during the coming twelve months. The Governor-General in Council, after comparing these collected estimates with the expected revenue from all India, granted to each local government such sums as could be spared for its local services. The evils and disadvantages of this system led Lord Mayo to introduce a system of financial decentralisation. After undergoing several modifications, this has now developed into the system of quasi-permanent settlements introduced in 1904. Certain heads of revenue have been declared to be wholly imperial, certain others to be wholly Provincial, the revenues of other heads are to be shared between the Imperial and the provincial governments in certain proportions. These settlements are to be permanent only in the sense that they shall not be subject to revision at the end of the fixed periods. But the Government of India has reserved to itself the power to revise the settlement of any or all the provinces at any time whenever necessity may demand it. The Government of India will be the sole judge of such a necessity. The Local Governments will have no voice in the matter, nor have the Local Governments any potential voice in determining the terms of these settlements. These are based on no just or equitable principle. The Government of India laid down certain rules, and applying them to the actual figures, it was found that the aggregate Provincial expenditure represented rather less than one-fourth of the whole, while the Imperial expenditure, which includes the army and the home charges, was in excess of three-fourths. These proportions have accordingly been taken as the basis of the division of revenue between Imperial and Provincial, though numerous adjustments have been made to meet certain difficulties. This fairly represents the present position of the Provincial Governments both as regards the general administrative and financial power which they enjoy under the Supreme Government.

"The system described above has served to establish political unity and uniformity of administration throughout the Indian Empire. It has contributed to the expansion and the development of that Empire. The Government of India has commanded the financial resources of the whole country, and has used those resources a great deal too liberally for Imperial purposes. It has not devoted an adequate share of these resources to promote the moral and material progress of the people. The result has been that the condition of the people as a whole contrasts very unfavourably with the splendour of the Empire. The injustice of the existing arrangement is patent from the fact that while for many years the Government of India has been revilling surpluses some of the provinces which have contributed largely to those surpluses, have been living on subsistence allowances. The very fact that the aggregate provincial expenditure which has to provide for the whole of the ordinary internal administration, the assessment and collection of revenue, for education, medical and sanitary arrangements, buildings and roads, in all provinces of India, represents rather less than one-fourth of the whole, while Imperial expenditure, which includes the Army and the Home Charges, is in excess of three-fourths, makes it sufficiently clear that unless the existing arrangements are radically changed, sufficient provision cannot be made for promoting the most vital interests of the people.

"The eight major provinces of India are equal in extent of area and population to several large countries of Europe. Burma is about the size of Sweden, with nearly twice its population; Bengal (undivided), though slightly smaller in size than Burma, contains nearly eight times as many inhabitants, and about twice as many as France; Madras has nearly as large a population as the United Kingdom; Bombay approximates in area to the United Kingdom, though its population is much smaller; the United Provinces contain many more souls than Austria-Hungary; the Central Provinces including Berar, cover almost as large an area as the United Provinces with thirteen millions of people: and the Punjab, only a slightly smaller area with twenty million. His Majesty's Government in England and the Government of India have recognised that each of these provinces is large and important enough to require a separate Provincial Government. With the exception of the Central Provinces, each has been given its separate legislative Council; each has its independent system of administration, of civil and criminal justice, its separate departments of education, of medical and sanitary arrangements, and of public works. It is high time that each of these Governments which are responsible for the weal or woe of the many millions committed to the care, should be given a larger measure of both administrative and financial power.

A More Responsible Government

"To bring this about the unitary form of government which

prevails at present should be converted into the federal system. The provincial governments should cease to be mere delegates of the supreme government, but should be made semi-independent governments. A similar proposal was, I believe, put forward before the government about the time when Lord Mayo determined to invest provincial governments with a share of financial responsibility in order to minimise the evils of over-centralization.

" 'More than one of his predecessors,' says Sir William Hunter, had arrived at a similar conclusion, and indeed one school of the Indian statesmen had gone so far as to advocate the almost complete financial independence of the local governments. This school would surrender to each separate administration the revenue raised within its territories, on the single condition of a rateable contribution for the expenditure common to the Empire, such as the army and the public debt. Unfortunately their scheme was not adopted. I venture to think that if it had been adopted, provincial governments would have been able to devote vastly greater sums to promote the moral and material progress of the people entrusted to their care, then they have actually been able to do. However, the progress in administration which has been achieved during the last thirty-seven years, makes it easier to adopt the scheme now, and the necessity for doing so has become greater. This will not in any way impair or injuriously affect the unity of the Empire. The Government of India should retain in its hands, as at present, all matters relating to foreign relations, the defences of the country, currency, debt, tariffs, post, telegraphs and railways. It should continue to receive all the revenue and receipts derived from heads which are at present called "Imperial". To meet the ordinary imperial expenditure which will not be met by these receipts, it should require the various provincial governments to make a rateable contribution based on a definite and reasonable principle. Having secured this, the Government of India should leave the provincial governments perfect freedom in levying and spending their revenues as they may consider best in the interests of the people. It should exercise its power of imposing additional general taxation in any province, only when it has to meet any extraordinary expenditure, and when the province or provinces concerned have refused to give the assistance required. This will impose a very much-needed and healthy check upon the spending tendencies of the Government of India, and make it possible for the provincial governments to retain in their hands, and to devote a fair proportion of their revenues to promote the well-being of the people.

"The expenditure of the Government of India is terribly overgrown, particularly in the military department, and it is devoutly to be hoped that there will be a reasonable reduction made in it. Until this is done the provinces may have to contribute almost the same amount that they have to do at present. But it is not unreasonable to hope that that expenditure may be somewhat curtailed in the near future, in view of the convention made with Russia and the alliance made with Japan.

Constitution of the Provincial Governments

"If the increased administration and financial powers are to be given to the provincial governments and the general control which the Government of India exercises over them even in matters which have been entrusted to them, is to be removed, it is highly desirable that their character and constitution should be improved. Bombay and Madras are governed by a Governor in Council, which consists of two members. It is desirable that two more members should be added to that Council of the Secretary of State for India, and it has been recently stated that the Secretary of State and His Excellency the Viceroy have expressed their willingness to appoint an Indian as a member of the executive council of the Governor General. The recommendation, therefore, to have two Indians as Members of the Executive Council of the Governor in Council in Madras and Bombay has both reason and a kind of precedent in support of it and will, I hope, be accepted.

A Governor in Council for the United Provinces

"The United Provinces are the second of the larger provinces of India. Though they cover a smaller area than Madras or Bombay, they have a population of 48 millions, whereas Madras and Bombay have a population of only 38 millions and 19 millions, respectively. So far back as 1883, the Charter Act of that year directed that the Presidency of Fort William in Bengal should be divided into two distinct presidencies, one to be styled the Presidency of Fort William in Bengal, and the other, the Presidency of Agra. The same Act provided that the Executive Government of each of the several Presidencies of Fort William in Bengal, Fort Saint George, Bombay, and Agra shall be administered by a Governor and three Councillors. But the new Presidency of Agra was never fully constituted, chiefly because of the financial difficulties; and two years later an amending Act empowered the Governor-General to appoint a Lieutenant-Governor instead for the North-Western Provinces, and to declare and limit his authority.

"The financial position of the government is however, ever so much better now than it was in 1833. And taking into account the vast changes that have occurred during the three-quarters of a century that have since elapsed, it seems to me that these provinces should no longer be kept out of the benefit of being governed by a Governor in Council who should be a statesman of rank and experience, and should, as a general rule, be appointed fresh from England. The Indian Civil Service has no doubt produced some Governors of great ability and power, like Sir Antony MacDonnell, who have attained greater success and distinction as rulers of men than has fallen to the lot of many Governors. The door of appointment should be open to men of such exceptional ability in the service. But, as I have said before, the appointment should, as a rule, be made from among statesmen of rank and experience in England. If the selection is properly made, a gentleman coming fresh from the free atmosphere of England is likely to infuse something more of that sympathy which his Royal Highness the Prince of Wales graciously wished to see more largely diffused in the Indian Administration, than is generally to be seen at present.

"If a Governor in Council is appointed, the Board of Revenue should be abolished, and two senior members of the civil service, who are at present appointed members of the Board of Revenue, should be appointed as the Councillors of the Governor. It would be desirable that one of the two councillors should, as is the case in Bombay, be taken from the judicial branch of the service, and the other from the executive branch. In addition to these, there should be two Indian councillors in the executive council. The advantages of having Indians of ability and experience in the executive councils of the different provinces will be very great. The executive government composed of Europeans only, whether they be the members of the civil service or not, is not always able to correctly understand or appreciate the feelings and wishes of the Indians, and is thus led to commit mistakes which could, and would be easily avoided if it had timely and trustworthy advice. As the people of India are awakening to a new consciousness of their rights and privileges, and will endeavour more and more to realise them, the importance of the presence in the executive council of the Indians of ability and integrity who may be able to correctly interpret their views and actions to the Government, cannot be exaggerated.

The Legislative Councils

"In order that the increased administrative and financial power should be exercised by the provincial governments to the greatest benefit of the people, it is necessary that the number of the representatives of the people in the Legislative Council should be increased and that they should have the power to propose amendments to the budget, and to divide the Council upon such amendments, as also upon any motions which they may think it fit to bring forward. Half the members of the Council should be elected, one-fourth nominated by the Government, and one-fourth officials. The Governor should have the right of vetoing any resolution arrived at by a majority of the Council. This will secure a better administration, financial and general, than is possible without it. Too much emphasis cannot be laid on the fact that good finance cannot be attained without intelligent care on the part of the citizens. The rules of the budgetary legislation are serviceable in keeping administration within limits; but prudent expenditure, productive and equitable taxation, and due equilibrium between income and outlay will only be found when responsibility is enforced by the public opinion of an active and enlightened community. Provision should, therefore, be made for the adequate representation of such public opinion in the legislative council, and in order to make that opinion effective for good, the representatives should be given a real voice in the discussion of the budget.

"The proposals I have made above apply to all the eight major provinces of India. It may be said that the Central Provinces and Berar, which are under a Chief Commissioner now, should not be given the same kind of Government as is proposed for the large regulation provinces. But the population of the Central Provinces is larger than that of Burma, which is placed under a Lieutenant-Governor and, in my opinion, the smallest of these eight provinces is large enough to require the kind of government that I have proposed for the largest of them.

The Cost

"As regards the cost of my proposals, official salaries range excessively high in India, and there ought to be a curtailment of them. At any rate, in making the new appointments that will have to be made if my proposals are accepted, a reasonably lower scale of salaries ought to be prescribed. But even if that is not done, I believe that the improvement in administration which will result will more than compensate for any increase in expenditure."

LAHORE CONGRESS PRESIDENTIAL ADDRESS

The following is the full text of the presidential address delivered at the Indian National Congress held at Lahore in 1909:

"Brother-Delegates, Ladies and Gentlemen, When I received intimation in a rather out-of-the-way place in the mofussil where I was engaged in professional work, that some Congress committees had very kindly nominated me for election as the president of the Congress, I wired, as there was no time to be lost in the matter, to my honoured friend Mr Wacha, the General Secretary of the Congress, to inform him that I was too weak from the effects of a recent illness, as I am sorry to say I still am, to be able to undertake the duties and responsibilities of the high office of the president of the Congress. I need hardly say, ladies and gentlemen, that it was not that I did not fully appreciate the high honour which was proposed to confer upon me. The presidentship of the Congress, as has often been said, is the highest honour that can come to any Indian. But, I am sorry to confess, I was not cheered up by the prospect of receiving it, because I really believed that I did not deserve it. I knew how unworthy I was to occupy the chair which had been filled in the past by a succession of eminently able and distinguished men who had established their title to the esteem and confidence of their countrymen long before they were called on to preside over this great national assembly of India. Besides this general consideration, I had present to my mind the special fact that I would be required to fill the chair which Congressmen all over the country and the public at large had been expecting would be graced by that distinguished countryman of ours who towers above others by his commanding ability and influence, I need hardly name Sir Pherozeshah Mehta; and I felt that the election of a humble soldier from the ranks as I am, to step into the breach created by the retirement of such a veteran leader, could but deepen the already deep disappointment and regret which has been felt all over the country by his resignation of this office. In addition to all this, I could not forget that with the exception of a single short speech, I had never in my life been able to write out a speech, and I could not expect, especially when there were hardly six days left before me to do it, to liable to write out anything like an address which is expected from the presidential chair of the Congress. But, ladies and gentlemen, all my objections expressed and implied, were over-ruled, and such as 1 am, I am here, in obedience to the mandate issued under your authority, to serve you and our motherland as best I may, relying on the grace of God and the support of all my brother-Congressmen. This fact cannot however diminish, it rather deepens, the gratitude which I feel for you for the signal honour you have conferred upon me in electing me your president at this juncture. Words fail me to express what I feel. I thank you for it from the bottom of my heart. You will agree with me when I say that no predecessor of mine ever stood in need of greater indulgence and more unstinted support from the Congress than I do. I trust you will extend it to me with the same generosity and kindly feeling with which you have voted me to this exalted office.

Messrs Lalmohan Ghose and Romesh Chandra Dutt

"Before I proceed to deal with other matters, it is my painful but sacred duty to offer a tribute of respect to the memory of two of the former presidents of the Congress and of the one distinguished benefactor of the country whom the hand of death has removed from our midst. In the death of Mr Lalmohan Ghose we mourn the loss of one of the greatest orators that India has produced. Of his matchless eloquence it is not necessary for me to speak. He combined with it a wonderful grasp of great political questions, and long before the Congress was born, he employed his great gifts in pleading the cause of his country before the tribunal of English public opinion. The effect which his eloquent advocacy produced on the minds of our fellow-subjects in England was testified to by no less eminent a man than John Bright, the great tribune of the English people. To Mr Lalmohan Ghose will always belong the credit of having been the first Indian who made a strenuous endeavour to get admission into the great Parliament of England. It is sad to think that his voice will not be heard any more either in asserting the rights of his countrymen to equality of treatment with their European fellow-subjects or in chastening those who insult them, after the manner of his memorable Dacca speech.

"Even more poignant; and profound has been the regret with which the news of the death of Mr Romesh Chandra Dutt has been received throughout the country Dutt has had the glory of dying in harness in the service of his motherland. It is not for me to dwell here on varied and high attainments and of the various activities of a life which was so richly distinguished by both. Time would not permit of my referring to Dutt's work on the Decentralisation Commission or in Baroda, or to his numerous contributions to literature, history and economics. But I cannot omit to mention his contribution for the vernacular literature of Bengal. Dutt recognised with the true insight of a statasman that to build up a nation it was necessary to create a national literature, and he made rich and copious contributions to the vernacular of his province. An able administrator, a sagacious statesman, a distinguished scholar, a gifted poet, a charming novelist, a deep student of the Indian history and economics, and, above all, a passionate lover of his country who united to a noble pride and deep reverence for its glorious past, a boundless faith in the possibilities of its future, and laboured incessantly for its realisation up to the last moments of his life, Dutt was a man of whom any country might be proud. It was no small tribute to his work and worth that the patriot-prince, the Gaekwar, chose him for his adviser, and found in him a man after his heart. Grievous would have been the loss of such a man at any time; it is a national calamity that he should have been taken away from us at a time when his country stood so much in need of his sober counsel and wise guidance.

Death of Lord Ripon

"The last but not the least do we mourn the loss of the greatest and the beloved viceroy whom India has known—I need hardly name the noble Marquis of Ripon. He was loved and respected by the educated Indians as I believe no Englishman who has ever been connected with India, excepting the father of the Indian National Congress, Mr Allan Octavian Hume, and Sir William Wedderburn, has been loved and respected. Lord Ripon was loved because he inaugurated the noble scheme of Local Self-Government which, though it has never yet had a fair trial, was intended by his Lordship to train the Indians for the very best form of government, namely, a government of the people by the people, which it has been the proudest privilege of Englishmen to establish in their own land and to teach all the other civilised nations to adopt. He was loved because he made the most courageous attempt to act up to the spirit of the noble Proclamation of 1858, to obliterate race distinctions and to treat his Indian fellow-subjects as standing on a footing of equality with their European fellow-subjects. He was respected because he was statesman, yet friend to truth, of soul sincere, In action faithful, and in honour clear.

"He was respected because he was a God-fearing man, and showed by his conduct in the exalted office he filled as the Viceroy of India, that he believed in the truth of the teaching that righteousness exalteth a nation. He was loved because he was a type of the noblest of Englishmen who have an innate love of justice, and who wish to see the blessings of liberty which they themselves enjoy extended to all their fellow-men. The educated Indians were deeply touched by the last instance of his Lordship's desire to befriend the people of India, when he went down to the House of Lords from his bed of illness in the closing days of his life, to support Lord Morley's noble scheme of Reform and to bid the noble Lords who were opposing some of its beneficent provisions to be just to the people of India. It is a matter of profound grief that such a noble Englishman is no more. And yet the Marquis of Ripon lives, and will ever live in the grateful memory of the generations of the Indians yet to come.

Truly has the poet said:

'But strew his ashes to the wind
Whose voice or sword has served mankind,
And is he dead whose noble mind
Lifts thence on high? To live in minds we leave behind
Is not to die.'

The Morley–Minto Reforms

"Ladies and gentlemen, among the many subjects of importance which have occupied attention during the year, the foremost place must be given to the regulations which have been promulgated under the scheme of constitutional reform for which the country is indebted to Lord Morley and Lord

Minto. That scheme was published a few days before the Congress met the last year in Madras. It was hailed throughout the country with deep gratitude and delight. And nowhere did this feeling find warmer expression than at the Congress. The regulations, on the other hand, which were published nearly five weeks ago, have, I am sorry to say, created widespread disappointment and dissatisfaction, except in the limited circle of a section of our Muslim friends. The fact is of course deplorable. But no good will be gained and much evil is likely to result from ignoring or belittling it, or trying to throw the blame for it on the wrong shoulders. The interests of the country and of the good government will be best served by trying to understand and to explain the reason for this great change which twelve months have brought about in the attitude of the educated Indians. The question is, are they to blame for not hailing the regulations with the same feelings of thankfulness and satisfaction with which they welcomed the main outlines of the scheme, or have the regulations so far deviated from the liberal spirit of Lord Morley's despatch as to give the educated classes a just cause for dissatisfaction? To obtain a full and satisfactory answer to this question it is necessary to recall to mind the history of these reforms. And this I propose to do as briefly as I can.

"Ladies and gentlemen, it was the educated class in India who first felt the desire for the introduction of the Self-Government the government of the people through the elected representatives of the people in India. This desire was the direct outcome of the study of that noble literature of England which is instinct with the love of freedom and eloquent of the truth that the Self-Government is the best form of government. To my honoured friend Babu Surendranath Banerjee, whom we are so pleased to find here today, growing older and older in years but yet full of the enthusiasm of youth for the service of the motherland, to Babu Surendranath Banerjee will ever belong the credit of having been among the very first of Indians who gave audible expression to that desire. It was he and our dear departed brother Mr Ananda Mohan Bose who established the Indian Association of Calcutta in 1876, with the object, among others, of agitating for the introduction of a system of the representative government in India. This desire was greatly strengthened by the deplorable acts of omission and commission of Lord Lytton's administration, to which, by the way, the administration of Lord Curzon bore in many respects a striking family resemblance. The discontent that prevailed in India towards the end of Lord Lytton's Viceroyalty was but slightly exceeded by that which prevailed at the close of Lord Curzon's regime. The overthrow of the Conservative ministry and the great Liberal victory of 1880 was consequently hailed with joy by the educated Indians, as they read in it; an assurance of relief from the effects of Lord Lytton's maladministration and a promise of the introduction of the liberal measures in India. Public expression was given to this feeling at a great meeting held in Calcutta at which in the course of an eloquent speech our friend Babu Surendranath Banerjee uttered the following pregnant words:

> The question of the representative government looms not in the far-off distance. Educated India is beginning to feel that the time has come when some measure of Self-Government might be conceded to the people. Canada governs itself. Australia governs itself. And surely it is anomalous that the grandest dependency of England should continue to be governed upon wholly different principles. The great question of the representative government will probably have to be settled by the Liberal party, and I am sure it will be settled by them in a way which will add to the credit and honour of that illustrious party and will be worthy of their noble traditions.

"This feeling was not confined to Bengal. About the same time a remarkable paper was published in my own province, the then North-Western Provinces, by the late Pandit Lakshmi Narayan Dhar in which he strongly advocated the introduction of the representative government in India. The Liberal party did not disappoint India, and it could not, as it was then under the noble guidance of that greatest Englishman of his age, William Ewart Gladstone, who was one of the greatest apostles of liberty that the world has known. Mr Gladstone never rendered a grater service to this country then when he sent out

Lord Ripon as Viceroy and Governor-General of India. His Lordship's advent at the end of Lord Lytton's Viceroyalty proved like the return of a bright day after a dark and chilly night. His benign influence was soon felt. Discontent died out, and a new hope, a new joy soon pervaded the land. India rejoiced to find that her destinies were entrusted to the care of a Viceroy who regarded her children as his equal fellow-subjects and was righteously determined to deal with them in the spirit of Queen Victoria's gracious Proclamation of 1858. Lord Ripon studied the wants and requirements of India. It is not unreasonable to suppose that his Lordship had taken note of the desire of the educated Indians for the introduction of the principle of Self-Government in India, holding evidently with Macaulay and a whole race of the liberal-minded Englishmen that 'no nation can be perfectly well-governed till it is competent to govern itself.' Lord Ripon inaugurated his noble scheme of the local Self-Government, not primary as he was careful to point out in his Resolution, with a view to an immediate improvement in administration, but chiefly as an instrument of political and popular education which was to lead in course of time to the Self-Government in the administration of the provinces and eventually of the whole of the Indian Empire. Lord Ripon also tried to disregard distinctions of race, colour and creed and appointed the Indians to some of the highest posts in the country. His measures were intensely disliked by a large body of the Europeans and Anglo-Indians, official and non-official. And when he endeavoured subsequently, by means of what is known as the Ilbert Bill, to place the Indians and Europeans on a footing of equality in the eye of the law, the storm of opposition which had long been brewing in Anglo-India burst against him in full force. It was not an opposition to the Ilbert Bill alone, but, as his Lordship himself told Mr Stead not long ago, to the scheme of Local self-Government and to his whole policy of treating the Indians and Europeans as equal fellow-subjects. Barring of course the honourable exceptions, our European and Anglo-Indian fellow-subjects arrayed themselves in a body not against Hindus alone, nor yet against the the educated classes alone, but against the Hindus, Mohammedans, Christians, Parsis, and all the Indians alike, making no exception in favour of either the Mohammedans or the landed aristocracy. It was the educated class then, who organised the Indian National Congress with a view to promote, not the interests of any class or creed, but the common interests of all the Indians irrespective of any considerations of race, creed or colour. Not even the worst enemy of the Congress can point to even a single Resolution passed by it which is opposed to this basic principle of its existence, to this guiding motive of its action. Indeed no such resolution could be passed by it an eradication of all possible race, creed or provincial prejudices and the development and consolidation of a sentiment of national unity among all the sections of the Indian people was one of the essential features of the programme of the Congress. This Congress of the educated Indians put forward a Reform of the legislative councils in the forefront of its programme, because it was not only good in itself but it has the additional virtue as the late Mr Yule happily put it, of being the best of all the instruments for obtaining other Reforms that further experience and our growing wants might lead us to desire. I respectfully drew the attention of the Government to the poverty of the vast numbers of the population and urged that the introduction of the representative institutions would prove one of the most important practical steps towards the amelioration of their condition. The Congress also pressed for many other Reforms, among them being the employment of Indians in the higher branches of the public services and holding of the simultaneous examinations in India and England to facilitate the admission of the Indians into the Indian civil service. Instead of welcoming the Congress as a most useful and loyal helpmate to the government, the Anglo-Indian bureaucracy unfortunately regarded it as hostile to the government. The Anglo-Indian Press, with some honourable exceptions, railed at it as if its object was to overthrow the British Government. Owing to this hostility of the Anglo-Indian bureaucracy and of the Anglo-Indian press, which is generally regarded as the mouth-piece of that bureaucracy, the bulk of our

Mohammedans fellow-subjects held themselves aloof from the Congress: I say the bulk, we have always had the benefit of the co-operation of a number of the patriotic men from amongst them. And for fear of offending the same body of the Anglo-Indian officials, the landed aristocracy also as a body kept itself at a safe distance from the Congress.

"It is sad to recall that as the Congress continued to grow in strength and influence, some of our Mohammedan fellow-subjects of the Aligarh school and some members of the landed aristocracy came forward openly to oppose it. Notwithstanding, however, all the opposition of the Anglo-Indian bureaucracy, notwithstanding also opposition of our Mohammedan fellow-subjects and the indifference of the landed aristocracy, the educated middle class continued to carry on the good work they had begun. They soon found a powerful champion in the late Mr Bradlaugh, and achieved the first victory of the Congress when, as the direct result of its agitation, the Indian Councils Act was passed in 1892 and the Legislative Councils were reformed and expanded. The attitude of the bureaucracy towards the educated class did not, however, show any change for the better. In fact their dislike of them seemed to grow as they continued to agitate for the further reforms. And lest they might displease the officials, our Mohammedan fellow-subjects, as a body, continued to hold themselves aloof from the Congress and never asked for any Reform in the constitution of the government. So also the landed classes. The educated middle class, the men of intellect, character, and public spirit, who devoted their time to the study of public questions and their energies to the promotion of the public good, felt however that the Reforms which had been effected under the Act of 1892 still left them without any real voice in the administration of their country. They found that that administration was not being conducted in the best interests of the people of the country They found that it continued to be conducted on extravagantly costly lines; they found that the level of taxation was maintained much higher than was necessary for the purposes of good administration; they found that the military expenditure of the government was far beyond the capacity of the country to bear, and they were alarmed that there was a heavy and continuous increase going on year after year in that expenditure; they found that an excessively large portion of the revenues raised from the people was being spent on what we may call Imperial purposes and a very inadequate portion on purposes which directly benefit the people, such as the promotion of the general, scientific, agricultural, industrial and technical education, the provision of medical relief and sanitation; they found that the most earnest and well-reasoned representations of the Congress fell flat upon the ears of the bureaucracy which was in power; and the conviction grew in them that their country could never be well or justly governed until the scheme of the constitutional reform which the Congress had suggested at its very first session was carried out in its entirety.

"At this stage came Lord Curzon to India. On almost every question of importance he adopted a policy the very reverse of that for which the educated Indians had for years been praying. He showed unmistakable hostility to the educated class in India, and he is responsible for having greatly fostered it among some of his countrymen whom he has left behind in power. His attempt to lightly explain away the pledges solemnly given by the Sovereign and Parliament in the Proclamation of 1858 and in the Act of 1833, his officialising Universities Act, his overt attack upon the Local Self-Government, and last, but not the least, his high-handed partition of Bengal in the teeth of the opposition of the people of that province, filled the cup of discontent to the brim, and deepened the conviction in the minds of the educated men that India could never be well or justly governed, nor could her people be prosperous or contented until they obtained through their representatives a real and potential voice in the administration of their affairs.

"This conviction found the clearest and most emphatic expression in the Congress which met in Calcutta in 1906. Mr Dadabhai Naoroji, the revered patriarch of the educated community, speaking with the knowledge and experience born of a life-long study of the defects and shortcomings of the existing system of the administration and the oppressed with the thought of the political and economic evils from which India has been suffering, declared in words of the burning conviction that, 'Self-Government is the only and chief remedy. In Self-Government lies our hope, strength and greatness.' Mr Dadabhai did not urge that the full-fledged representative institutions should at once be introduced into India. But he did urge, and the whole of the educated India urged through him, that it was high time that a good beginning was made such a systematic beginning as that it may naturally in no long time develop itself into full legislatures of Self-Government like those of the self-governing colonies.

"Happily for India, just as had happened at the end of Lord Lytton's administration, there was a change at the close of Lord Curzon's reign, of the ministry in England and the Liberal Government came into power. The faith of a large body of the educated Indians in the efficacy of the constitutional agitation had been undermined by the failure of all the efforts of the people of Bengal, made by prayer and petition, to avert the evil of the partition. But Mr John Morley, who had long been admired and adored by the educated Indians as a great lover of liberty and justice, happily became the Secretary of State for India, and the hearts of the educated Indians began to beat with the hope that their agitation for a real measure of Self-Government might succeed during the period of his office. Our esteemed brother Gokhale was appointed its trusted delegate to England by the Congress which met at Benares and over which he so worthily presided, to urge the more pressing proposals of reform on the attention of the authorities there. What excellent work our friend did in England, how he pressed the urgent necessity and the entire reasonableness of the reforms suggested by the Congress and prepared the minds of the men in power there to give a favourable consideration to our proposals, it is not for me here to tell. In the meantime, gentleman, our liberal-minded Viceroy, Lord Minto, who found himself face to face with the legacy of a deep and widespread discontent which his brilliant but unwise predecessor had left to him, had taken a statesmanlike note of the signs of the times and the needs of the country, and had appointed a Committee of his Council to consider and report what changes should be introduced in the existing system of administration to make it suitable to altered conditions.

"Ladies and gentlemen, up to this time, up to the beginning of October 1906, our Mohammedan fellow-subjects did not trouble themselves with any questions of reforms in the system of administration. But there were some members of the Indian bureaucracy who were troubled with the thought that the liberal-minded Viceroy seriously contemplated important constitutional changes in that system, and they knew that the statesman who was at the helm of the Indian affairs in England was the high priest of liberalism. They saw that there was every danger, from their point of view, that the prayer of the educated class for the reform and expansion of the legislative councils on a liberal basis, might be granted. They frankly did not like it. And it was at this time that our Mohammedan fellow-subjects of the Aligarh school were roused from their apathy and Indifference. They suddenly developed an interest and an excessive interests too in politics. A Mohammedan deputation was soon got up and waited on Lord Minto. It claimed that Mohammedans were politically a more important community than other communities in India, and that they were therefore entitled to special consideration and even preferential treatment. I regret to say it, gentlemen, but it is my duty to say it, that the concession which His Excellency the Viceroy was persuaded to make to this utterly unjustifiable claim in his reply to that deputation, has been the root of much of the trouble which has arisen in connection with these reforms. The bureaucracy had however gained a point. The proposals for reform which were formulated in the letter of Sir Harold Stuart dated August 24, 1907, gave abundant evidence of the bias of that body against those who had agitated for reform. The proposals for the special representation of Mohammedans contained in it, tended clearly to set one religion against another and to counterpoise the influence of the educated middle class. The proposals for the special representation of landholders, who had never asked to be treated as a separate class, also had their origin evidently in the same kind of feeling. So also the proposals for creating the Imperial and Provincial Advisory Councils. Those proposals met with a general condemnation from the thoughtful men all over the country, excepting, of course, some among the landholders and the Mohammedans. They could not meet with a welcome because they did not deserve it. Later on the Government of India revised their provisional scheme in the light of the criticisms passed upon it, and with some important modifications submitted it to the Secretary of State for India. Lord Morley did not share the bias of the bureaucracy against the educated class, it would have been as strange and sad if he did. He recognised that they were an important factor, if not the most important factor, who deserved consideration. In his speech on the Indian Budget in 1907, his Lordship observed: 'You often hear men talk of the educated sections of India as a mere handful, an infinitesimal fraction. So they are in numbers. But it is idle, totally idle to say that this infinitesimal fraction does not count. This educated section makes all the difference, is making and will make all the difference.' His Lordship appointed a committee of his own council to consider the scheme which the Government of India had submitted to him, and after receiving its report framed his own proposals which were published in the now famous *Despatch of the 27th November, 1908*. His Lordship had indeed accepted the substantial part of his Excellency the Viceroy's scheme, but he had liberalised it by the important changes he had made in it into a practically new scheme. The proposals for the imperial and the Advisory Councils which had been condemned by the educated India were brushed ceremoniously aside. The provincial legislative councils were to have a majority of the non-official members, who were to be, with very few exceptions, elected and not the nominated members. His Lordship had already appointed two distinguished Indians as the members of his own council. The Indians were to be appointed to the executive council of the Governor General of India and of the Governors of Madras and Bombay. Similar executive councils were to be established, with one or more

Indian members in them, in the other large provinces, which were still ruled by the Lieutenant-Governors. Under a scheme of decentralisation, municipal and district Boards were to be vested with increased powers and responsibilities and to be freed from the official control. The cause of the local Self-Government was to receive an effectual advance. Its roots were to be extended deep down into the villages. Taking full note of the various interests for which the representation had to be provided in the enlarged councils, Lord Morley suggested a scheme of the electoral colleges which, as was rightly claimed, was as simple as any scheme for the representation of the minorities can be. It was built upon a system of a single vote, and fully avoided the evils of double and plural voting. It was equally free from the other objection to which the original proposals were open, viz., that they would set one class against the another. It gave the power to each section of the population to return a member in the proportion corresponding to its own proportion to the total population. This scheme, as we all know, was received throughout the country with feelings of great gratitude and gratification. An influential deputation composed of the representatives of all the classes of the people waited upon His Excellency the Viceroy to personally tender their thanks for it to him, and through him, to Lord Morley. Did the educated class lag behind any other classes in welcoming the scheme? Did the feelings of grateful satisfaction find a warmer expression anywhere than in the speech of my honoured predecessor in office, who speaking in reference to it exclaimed that, 'The time of the singing of birds is come and the voice of the turtle is heard in our land?' The Congress unanimously passed a resolution giving expression to the deep and general satisfaction with which the reform proposals formulated in Lord Morley's despatch had been received throughout the country, and it tendered its most sincere and grateful thanks to his Lordship and to Lord Minto for those proposals. It expressed the confident hope at the same time that the details of the proposed scheme would be worked out in the same liberal spirit in which its main outlines had been conceived. This unfortunately has not been done, and a very important part of the scheme has been so modified as to give just grounds of complaint in a large portion of the country.

Indians in the Executive Councils

"Now, gentlemen, the feature of the reforms which most appealed to the minds of the educated Indians was the proposal to appoint Indians to the executive councils of the Governor-General of India and of the Governors of Madras and Bombay, and the proposal to create similar councils in the other large provinces of India, which were placed under Lieutenant-Governors. The most unmistakable proof of this fact was found in the thrill of grateful satisfaction which passed all over the country when the announcement was made of the appointment of Mr Satyendra Prasad Sinha as a member of the Viceroy's Council. And I take this opportunity of tendering our most cordial thanks for that appointment both to Lord Minto and to Lord Morley. That appointment has afforded the best proof of the desire of both their Lordships to obliterate distinctions of race, creed and colour, and to admit Indians to the highest offices under the Crown for which they may be qualified and it has been most sincerely and warmly appreciated as such by thoughtful Indians throughout the country. Our friends in Bombay and Madras will soon have the satisfaction of finding an Indian appointed to the executive councils of the Governors of their respective provinces. And thanks to the large-hearted and liberal support given to the proposal by Sir Edward Baker, our brethren in Bengal too, will shortly have the satisfaction of seeing an executive council established in their province with an Indian as one of its members. But, gentlemen, the people of my own provinces the United Provinces, and of the Punjab, of Eastern Bengal and Assam, and of Burma have been kept out of the benefit of the undoubted advantages which would result by the judgment of the Lieutenant Governor being "fortified and enlarged" in the weighty words of Lord Morley's despatch, 'By two or more competent advisers, with an official and responsible share in his deliberations.' We in the United Provinces had looked eagerly forward to having an executive council created there at the same time that one would be established in Bengal. Hindus and Mohammedans, the landed aristocracy and the educated classes, were unanimous in their desire to see such councils established. Bombay with a population of only 19 millions, Madras of only 38 millions, have each long enjoyed the advantage of being governed by the Governor in Council. The United Provinces which have a population of 48 millions have been ruled all these many years and must yet continue to be ruled by the Lieutenant-Governor. Bengal, the population of which exceeds the population of the United Provinces by barely 3 millions, will have the benefit of an executive council. Not so the United Provinces nor yet Eastern Bengal and Assam which have a population of 31 millions, nor the Punjab which has a population somewhat larger than that of the Presidency of Bombay. This is unclearly unjust, and the injustice of it has nowhere been more keenly felt than in my own Provinces.'

The Provincial Executive Councils

"The people of the United Provinces have special reasons to feel aggrieved at this decision. So far back as 1833, Section 56 of the Charter Act of that year enacted that the Presidencies of Fort William in Bengal, Fort St. George, Bombay and Agra shall be administered by a Governor and three Councillors. But this provision was suspended by an act passed two years later mainly on the ground that the same would be attended with a large increase of charge. The Act provided that during such time as the execution of the Act of 1833 should remain suspended, it would be lawful for the Governor-General of India in council to appoint any servant of the East India Company of ten years standing to the office of the Lieutenant-Governor of the North-Western Provinces. When the Charter Acts of 1853 was passed it still contemplated the creation of the Presidency of Agra under the Act of 1833. Those enactments have never been repealed. In the long period that has elapsed since 1833, the provinces have largely grown in size and population by the annexation of Oudh and the normal growth of population. The revenues of the provinces have also largely increased. If the objection that the creation of an executive council would be attended with a large increase of charge was at any time a valid one, it has long ceased to be so. The Provinces are not so poor that they cannot afford to bear the small increase in expenditure which the new arrangement will involve. They have for years been making larger contributions to the Imperial exchequer than the sister Provinces of Bombay, Madras and Bengal. On the other hand, the arguments for the creation of such a council have been growing stronger and stronger every year. The question was taken up by the Government of India in 1867-68 but unfortunately the discussion did not lead to any change in the system. The eminent author of Indian Polity, whose views on the questions of Indian administration are entitled to great respect, strongly urged the introduction of the change fifteen years ago. Wrote General George Chesney: 'In regard to administration, the charge (the North-Western Provinces) is as important as Bengal. It comprises 49 districts as against 47 in the latter, nearly twice as many as in Bombay, and more than thrice the number of districts in Madras, and every consideration which makes for styling the head of the Bengal Government a Governor, applies equally to this great province. (This was said when Bengal had not been partitioned.) Here also, as in Bengal, the Governor should be aided by a Council.

Sir George Chesney went on to say,

> The amount of business to be transacted here is beyond the capacity of a single administrator to deal with properly, while the province has arrived at a condition when the vigour and impulse to progress which the rule of one man can impart, may be fitly replaced by the greater continuity of policy which would be secured under the administration of a Governor aided by a Council. So far from the head of the administration losing by the change not to mention the relief from the pressure of work now imposed on a single man, and that a great deal of business which has now to be disposed of in his name by irresponsible Secretaries would then fall to be dealt with by members of the government with recognised authority it would be of great advantage to the Governor if all appointments and promotions in the public service of this province, a much larger body than that in Madras and Bombay, were made in consultation with and

on the joint responsibility of colleagues instead of at his sole pleasure.

"The work of administration has very much increased since this was written and we have it now on the unimpeachable testimony of the Royal Commission on decentralisation, who submitted their report early this year, that "With the development of the administration in all its branches, the growth of the important industrial interests, the spread of education and political aspirations, and the growing tendency of the public to criticise the administration and to appeal to the highest Executive tribunals, the Lieutenant-Governors of the larger provinces are clearly over-burdened.' Sir Antony MacDonnell who ruled over the United Provinces not many years ago, could not bear the strain of the work continuously for more than four years, and had to take six months leave during the period of his Lieutenant-Governorship. The present Lieutenant-Governor of the United Provinces also has, I regret to learn, found it necessary to take six months leave at the end of only three years of his administration. And we have been surprised and grieved to learn that both Lord Mac-Donnell and Sir John Hewett have opposed the creation of an Executive Council for the United Provinces. The Decentralisation Commission did not however rest the case for a change in the existing system on the sole ground that the head of the province was over-burdened with work. They rested it on a much higher ground. They rightly urged that, 'Even if a Lieutenant-Governor could dispose of all the work demanding consideration at the hands of a Provincial Government, we think that such powers are too wide to be expediently entrusted to one man, however able or zealous.' And they unanimously recommended the establishment in the larger provinces of India, of a regular Council Government such as obtains in Bombay and Madras, improved with the addition of an Indian member to them. Lord Morley was pleased to accept this recommendation with the important modification that the head of the provinces should continue to be a member of the Indian civil service; and though we did not approve of this modification, we were content and thankful that a council government should be introduced even in this modified form. But even that has been withheld from us, and the high hopes that it had been raised have naturally given place to a correspondingly deep disappointment. There is a widespread belief in my provinces that if our Lieutenant-Governor had not been opposed to the proposal in question, the provinces would have had an executive council just as Bengal will soon have. And the fact has furnished a striking instance of the disadvantages of leaving vital questions which affect the well-being of the 48 millions of people to be decided by the judgment of a single individual, however able and well-meaning he may be.

"Gentlemen, this is not a mere sentimental grievance with us. We find that the Presidencies of Madras and Bombay which have had the benefit of being governed by a Governor-in-Council have made for greater progress in every matter which affects the happiness of the people than my own provinces. And a conviction has gained ground in the minds of all thoughtful men that the Provinces will have no chance of coming abreast even of Bombay and Madras until they have a Government similar to that of those provinces, so that there may be a reasonable continuity of policy in the administration and the proposals of the Provincial Government may receive greater consideration than they do at present from the Government of India and the Secretary of State. Gentlemen, the noble Lords and the members of the Anglo-Indian bureaucracy both those who have retired and those who are still in service, who opposed the creation of an executive council for the United Provinces have I regret to say done a great disservice to the cause of good government by opposing this important portion of the scheme of reform. That opposition has caused deep dissatisfaction among the educated classes and has greatly chilled the enthusiasm which was aroused among them when the proposals of Lord Morley were first published. I would strongly urge upon the government the wisdom of taking steps to give an executive council at as early a date as may be practicable, not only to the United Provinces but also to the Punjab, to Eastern Bengal and Assam, and to Burma. The creation of such councils with one or two Indian members in them will be a distinct gain to the cause of good administration. It will afford an effectual safeguard against serious administrative blunders being committed, particularly in these days of repressive measures and deportations without trial. England is just now on the eve of a general election. But the elections will soon be over. Let us hope for the good of this country that it will result in bringing the Liberal Government again into power. Let us hope that in the result the House of Lords will become somewhat liberal. Let us hope that soon after parliament has been constituted again the Secretary of State for India, who let us also hope will be Lord Morley again, and the Governor-General of India in Council will be pleased to take the earliest opportunity to create Executive Councils in the United Provinces, the Punjab, and Eastern Bengal and Assam, by either getting the Indian Councils Act modified, or by obtaining the assent of both the Houses of Parliament to the creation of such councils under the provisions of the existing Act. Ladies and gentlemen, I wish to make it clear here that we have no complaint whatsoever in this connection either against Lord Morley or Lord Minto. We know and we acknowledge it with sincere gratitude that both the noble Lords did all that they could to get the original clause (3) of the Bill passed as it had been framed. We know that we owe our discomfiture to the action of Lord Curzon, who seems unfortunately for us to be afflicted with the desire of swelling the record of his ill services to India, and to the opposition of Lord Mac Donnell, from whom we of the United Provinces had hoped for support to our cause, and lastly, to the regrettable attitude adopted towards the proposal contained in that clause by the present Lieutenant-Governor of our provinces. I still venture to hope, however, that Sir John Hewett will be pleased to reconsider his position, particularly in view of the important fact that our sister province of Bengal also is shortly going to have an executive council, and that is Honour will earn the lasting gratitude of the people over whom Providence has placed him, and whose destinies it is in his power to mar or make, by moving the Government of India to take early steps to secure to them the benefit of Government by a council before he retires form his exalted office.

The Regulations

"Gentlemen, the question of the creation of the executive councils affects, however, only particular provinces of India; but the regulations that have been promulgated under the scheme of reform have given rise to even more widespread and general dissatisfaction. I will therefore now ask you to turn your attention to these regulations. We all remember that Lord Morley had put forward a most carefully considered scheme of proportional representation on the basis of population. We therefore regretted to find that in the debate which took place on the bill, his Lordship accepted the view that the Mohammedan community was entitled on the ground of the political importance which it claimed, to a larger representation than would be justified by its proportion to the total population. His Lordship was pleased, however, to indicate the extent of the larger representation which he was prepared to ensure to the Mohammedans after taking into account even their alleged political importance; and, though the educated non-Muslim public generally, and many far-seeing men among our Mohammedan fellow-subjects also, were and still are opposed to any representation in the Legislatures of the country on the basis of religion, yet there were several amongst us who recognised the difficulty that had been created by Lord Minto's reply to the Mohammedan deputation at Shimla, and were prepared not to demur to the larger representation of Mohammedans to the extent suggested by Lord Morley. We were prepared to agree that a certain amount of representation should be guaranteed to them; that they should try to secure it through the general electorates, and that if they failed to obtain the number of representatives fixed for them, they should be allowed to make up the number by election by special Mohammedan electorates formed for the purpose. The regulations which have been published, however, not only provide that they shall elect the number of representatives which has been fixed for them on a consideration not only of their proportion to the total population but also of their alleged political importance, by special electorates created for the purpose but they also permit them to take part in elections by mixed electorates, and thereby enable them to secure an excessive and undue representation of their particular community to the exclusion to a corresponding extent of the representatives of other communities. The system of single votes which was an essential feature of Lord Morley's Scheme has been cast to the winds; the injustice of double and plural voting which Lord Morley tried to avoid has been given the fullest play, In my provinces, and I believe in other provinces also, some of my Mohammedan fellow-subjects have voted in three places. So long as there was still a chance of getting the government to increase the number of seats which were to be specially reserved to them, our astute friends of the Muslim League swore that none of them would seek an election to the councils by the votes of non-Muslims. When the regulations were passed, they lost no time in cancelling the Resolution of their League, and put forward candidates to contest almost every seat for which elections were to be made by mixed electorates. Members of Municipal and District Boards to whom the general franchise has been confined were elected or appointed at a time when the Muslim League had not preached the gospel of separation. The electors did not then accept or reject a candidate on the ground of his religion. Mohammedans therefore filled a far larger number of Seats on Municipal and District Boards than their proportion to the total population or their stake in the country would entitle them to hold. The result has been that in addition to the four seats specially reserved to the Mohammedans, they have won two more seats in the United Provinces in the general elections, and these with the nominations made by the government have given them eight seats out of a total of 26 non-official seats in the legislature of the province, where they form but one-sixth of the population . This is protecting the interests of a minority with a vengeance. It looks more like a case of allowing the majority to be driven to a corner by a minority. What makes the matter worse, however, is that this advantage has been reserved only to the favoured minority of our Mohammedan fellow-subjects. No such protection has been extended to the Hindu minorities in the Punjab and Eastern Bengal and Assam. The Hindu minorities in the said two provinces have been left out severely in the cold. And yet they are founding fault with for not waxing warm with enthusiasm over the reforms.

"Gentlemen, let us now turn to the question of the franchise. Direct representation has been given to the Mohammedans. It has been refused to the non-Mohammedans. All the Mohammedans who pay an income-tax on an income of three thousand rupees or land revenue in the same sum, and all the Mohammedan graduates of five years standing, have been given the power to vote. Now I am not only not sorry but am sincerely glad that direct representation has been given to our Mohammedan fellow-subjects and that the franchise extended to them is fairly liberal. Indeed, no taxation without representation being the cardinal article of faith in the political creed of Englishmen, it would have been a matter for greater satisfaction if the franchise had been extended to all payers of income-tax. The point of our complaint is that the franchise has not similarly been extended to the non-Mohammedan subjects of His Majesty. A Parsi, Hindu or Christian who may be paying an income-tax on three lakhs or land revenue in the sum of three times three lakhs a year, is not entitled to a vote, to which his Mohammedan fellow-subject, who pays an income-tax on only three thousand a year or land revenue in the same sum, is entitled. Hindu, Parsi and Christian graduates of thirty years standing, men like Sir Gurudas Banerji, Dr Bhandarkar, Sir Subramania Iyer and Dr Rash Behari Ghosh, have not been given a vote, which has been given to every Mohammedan graduate of five years standing. People whose sensitiveness has been too much sobered down by age may not resent this. But can it be doubted for a moment that tens of thousands of non-Mohammedan graduates in the country deeply resent being kept out of a privilege which has been extended to the Mohammedan graduates? It is to my mind exceedingly deplorable that when the Government decided to give direct representation and a fairly liberal franchise to the

Mohammedans, it did not also decide to extend them to the non-Mohammedans as well.

"Let us next consider the restrictions that have been placed on the choice of the electors in choosing the candidates. In the regulations for Bombay and Madras, and in those for Bengal also, eligibility to a membership of a provincial council has been confined to the members of the Municipal and District Boards only. This is a novel departure from the practice which obtained for the last seventeen years under the Indian councils Act of 1892, and I regret to think that it is a departure taken without a full consideration of its result. That result is most unfortunate. It is acknowledged that the scheme of Local self-Government which Lord Ripon introduced into the country, has not yet had a fair trial. Lord Morley in his Despatch of the last year took note of the fact that the expectations formed of it had not been realised and in explanation thereof his Lordship was pleased to say, adopting the language of the Resolution of 1832, that 'There appears to be great force in the argument that so long as the chief Executive officers are, as a matter of course, Chairmen of Municipal and District Committees, there is little chance of these Committees, affording any effective training to their members in the management of the local affairs or of the non-official members taking any real interest in the local business.' Further on, His Lordship truly observed that the Non-official members have not been induced to such an extent as was hoped to take real interest in the local business, because their powers and their responsibilities were not real. Owing to this fact the Municipal and District Boards have with a few exceptions here and there not attracted many able and independent members. The result of confusing eligibility as a member of council to the members of the municipal and district boards has therefore necessarily been to exclude a number of men of light and leading in every province, excepting in my own where, I am thankful to say, no such restriction has been made from being eligible for election. Under the operation of this short-visioned rule, in Bengal a number of the public men of the province were found to be not eligible for election; and Sir Edward Baker had to modify the regulations within barely three weeks of their having been published, to make it possible for some at least of the public men of his province to enter the provincial council. In Madras Sir Arthur Lawley had to resort to the expedient of nominating some of the ex-members of the Legislative Council, as members of the Municipal and District or *Taluq* Boards in order to make them eligible as the members of the provincial council under the new regulations. In Bombay two ex-members of the Council had to enter Municipal Boards, which they were only enabled to do by the courtesy of obliging the friends who resigned their seats to make room for them, in order to qualify themselves for the election to the Council.

"This does not, I regret to say, exhaust the grounds of our objections to the regulations. A property qualification has for the first time been laid down in the case of candidates for membership of the Provincial Councils. No such qualification is required of Members of Parliament in England. None such was required in India under the regulations which were in force for nearly seventeen years under the Indian Councils Act of 1892. No complaint was ever made that the absence of any such restriction on the choice of the electors, had led to the admission of any undesirable person into any of the councils. The possession of property or an income does not necessarily predicate ability, much less character, and does not, by itself, secure to any man the esteem or confidence of his fellowmen. No more does the absence of property necessarily indicate want of capability to acquire it. It certainly does not indicate wand of respectability. The ancient law-giver Manu mentions five qualifications which earn for a man the respect of others Says he:

'वित्तं बन्धुर्वयः कर्म विद्या भवति पञ्चमी।
एतानि मान्यस्थानानि गरीयो यद्यदुत्तरम्।।

[Wealth, relations, age, good deeds and learning are the five titles to respect; of these each succeeding qualification is of greater weight than each preceding one.]

"According to this time-honoured teaching, education is the highest qualification and the possession of wealth the lowest. The regulations have not merely reversed the order but have excluded education from the category of qualifications required to make a man eligible as a member of the legislative councils. The framers of the regulations have taken no note of the fact that in this ancient land thousands of men of bright intelligence and pure character have voluntarily wedded themselves to poverty and consecrated their lives to the pursuit or promotion of learning or religion or other philanthropic objects. The result is that so far as the Provincial Councils are concerned, in several provinces selfless patriots like Mr Dadabhai Naoroji or Mr Gokhale would not be eligible as members of those Councils. Regulations which led to such results stand self-condemned.

"Again, the clause relating to disqualifications for membership has been made unnecessarily stringent and exclusive. A person who has been dismissed from the government service is to be disqualified for ever for a membership of the councils. Whether he was dismissed for anything which indicated any hostility to the Government or any moral turpitude, or whether he was dismissed merely for disobeying for not carrying out any trumpery order, or merely for failing to attend at a place and time when or at which he might have been required he must never be permitted to serve the government and the people again even in an honorary capacity. It does not matter whether his case was rightly or wrongly decided, his having been dismissed constitutes an offence of such gravity that it cannot be condoned. So also does a sentence of imprisonment, however short it may be, for any offence which is punishable with imprisonment for more than six mouths. Here again, no account is taken of the fact whether the offence for which the punishment was inflicted, implied any moral defect in the man. No such disqualification exists in the case of a membership of Parliament. Mr John Burns was once sentenced eighteen months imprisonment; he is now a cabinet minister. Mr Lynch actually fought against the British Government in the Boer War; he was sentenced to death, but the sentence was mitigated later on, and eventually entirely commuted, and he has since been elected a member of the parliament. What then can be the reason or justification for laying down such a severe and sweeping disqualification in a country where the judicial and executive functions are still combined in one officer, and where the administration of justice is not as impartial and pure as it is in England?

"More objectionable still is clause (i) of the disqualifying section which lays down that a man shall not be eligible as a member of the council if he has been declared by the local government to be of such reputation and antecedents that his election would in the opinion of the head of the local government be contrary to the public interest. Now, gentlemen, you will remember that in the debates in the parliament the question was raised whether the deportation of a man under Regulation III of 1818 and similar regulations would by itself disqualify him for sitting in a legislative council. Bearing probably in mind that a man might be deported without any just or reasonable cause, as it is believed happened in the case of Lala Lajpat Rai, Lord Morley could not perhaps bring himself to agree to a deportation being by itself made a ground of disqualification. We may take it that His Lordship gave his assent to clause (i) being enacted in the belief that it was less open to objection. But with due respect to His Lordship, I venture to submit that this clause is open to even greater objection than the disqualification of deportees as such would have been. In the case of a deportation the local government has to satisfy the Government of India what action should be taken under any of the drastic regulations relating thereto. This new clause empowers the local government on its own authority to declare a man to be not eligible, and thereby to do irreparable injury to his character. The judgment of the local government may be entirely unjust, but there can be no appeal from it. How seriously liable to abuse this clause is, is demonstrated by the case of Mr Kelkar, editor of the *Mahratta*. Mr Kelkar offered himself as a candidate for election to the Bombay Council. Thereupon His Excellency the Governor of Bombay made a declaration under the clause in question that in His Excellency's opinion Mr Kelkar's antecedents and reputation were such that his election would be contrary to the public interest. Now, gentlemen, the knowledge which His

Excellency the Governor has of Mr Kelkar's reputation and antecedents, is presumably not his own personal knowledge, but must have largely been derived from the reports. There happens to be another man, however, in the Bombay Presidency, in Poona itself, where Mr Kelkar has lived and worked whose solicitude for the public interest is it will perhaps be conceded, not less keen, and whose opinion, as to what would be contrary to the public interest, is not entitled to less weights than that of even Sir George Clarke or his colleagues, and that is my esteemed brother Mr Gokhale. He has one great advantage in this respect over Sir George Clarke, that he has a personal knowledge, borne of many years of personal contact in public work, of Mr Kelkar's character. When the declaration in question was made Mr Gokhale felt it to be his duty to protest against the action of the Governor of Bombay and to publicly bear testimony to the good character of Mr Kelkar. Mr Kelkar appealed to the Governor, but his appeal has been rejected, and he remains condemned unheard.

Non-official Majority

"One of the most important features of the reforms which created widespread satisfaction was the promise of a non-official majority in the provincial councils. The Congress had, in the scheme which it put forward so far back as 1886, urged that at least half the members of both the Imperial and the provincial legislative councils should be elected and not more than one-fourth should be officials. Congressmen regarded this as the *sine qua non* for securing to the representatives of the people a real voice in the administration of their country's affairs. Lord Morley did not think it fit, however, to give us yet a non-official majority in the Imperial Legislative Council. We regretted the decision. But Lord Morley had been pleased to accept the recommendation for a non-official majority in the provincial legislative councils, and we decided to accept it with gratitude, in the confidence that after the provincial legislative councils have worked satisfactorily for a few years under the new scheme, the more important concession of a non-official majority in the imperial council was certain to come.

"We are glad and thankful to find that a real non-official majority has been provided in the case of Bengal. And I take this opportunity of expressing our high appreciation of the large-hearted and liberal support which Sir Edward Baker has given to Lord Morley's proposals of Reform. It is due to that support that Bengal will shortly have the advantage of a council government. To Sir Edward Baker alone, among all the Governors and Lieutenant-Governors of the different provinces, belongs the credit of having secured a non-official majority of the elected members in the Legislative Council of the great province over which he rules. The regulations for Bengal lay down that out of a total of the 49 members of the council, 26, i.e., more than half shall be elected, and that the members nominated by the Lieutenant-Governor shall not exceed 22, not more than 17 of whom may be officials, and 2 of whom shall be non-officials to be selected one from the Indian commercial community and one from the planting community. But in sad contrast to this stands the case of the second largest province of India, viz., the United Provinces. The provision for non-official majority has there been reduced to a practical nullity. Sir John Hawett had warmly supported the proposals for the creation of the Imperial and Provincial Advisory Councils. Those proposals, as we know, were rejected by the Secretary of State for India. But His Honour seems to have been so much fascinated by them that he has done a good deal to make his legislative council approach the ideal of what were proposed to be advisory councils. Out of the tolal number of the 46 members of the council, only 20 are to be elected, and 26 to be nominated, of whom as many as 20 may be officials. Sir John Hewett has nominated the maximum number of 20 official members, and His Honour has shown great promptitude nominating six non-official members. Two of these are independent Chiefs, viz., His Highness the Nawab of Rampur and His Highness the Raja of Tehri, and the third is His Highness the Maharaja of Banaras who is practically regarded as an independent chief. No subject of the British Government has any voice in the administration of the affairs of these Chiefs. What justification can there be then for giving them a voice in the discussion of any legislation or other public questions which affect the weal or woe of the subjects of the British Indian Government? I mean no disrespect to these chiefs when I say that they do not study the wants of the latter. They cannot be expected to do so. And even when they have formed an opinion about any matter that may come up for discussion, they cannot always afford to express it, except when it should happen to coincide with that of the government. It is thus obvious that they cannot be useful members of the council which they are to adorn. Why then have they been nominated, if it be not to act as a counterpoise to the influence of the educated class? Of the three other nominees of Sir John Hewett, one is a Mohammedan Nawab who is innocent of English, and one a European indigo planter. The sixth nominee is a representative of the non-official Indian commercial community, which the regulations required him to be, but he too is innocent of English.

"Some of the other objections to which the regulations are open have also been most forcibly illustrated in the case of my unlucky province. Our Mohammedan fellow-subjects constitute only 14 per cent of the population there. But four seats have been allotted to them out of the total of 20 seats which are to be filled up by election in consideration of their proportion to the total population plus their alleged political importance. In addition to this they have been allowed to participate in the elections by mixed electorates, and they have won two seats there. The government has, besides, nominated two Mohammedans as the non-official members. Thus out of the 26 non-official members 8 are Mohammedans. Among the elected members as many as 8 are the representatives of the landed aristocracy, and only five of the educated classes. The non-official majority has thus been reduced to a farce.

"Time will not permit me to deal at length with the case of the other provinces. But I cannot pass over the case of the Punjab, the grievances of which are very real. Having regard to its position, its population, and the educational, social, and industrial progress made by it, the number of the members fixed for its legislative council is quite inadequate, and the number of the elected members is extremely meager, being only 5 in a total of 25. Besides this the franchise for the general electorates through which alone the non-Muslim population can take any part in the election of any member for the council, has been limited to an extremely small number of persons. The number of Municipalities in the Punjab is larger than in any other province of India. In more than one hundred of them, the elected representatives of the people have been serving for a long time past. Yet the privilege of voting for the election of the members of the council, has, I regret to find, been confined to only nine of these bodies. Can there be any justification for narrowing the franchise in this manner? The people of the Punjab would seem to be entitled to as much consideration as the people of any other province in the Empire, and if a large number of the member of Municipal and District Boards in other provinces were considered to be fit to exercise the franchise usefully and beneficially, the privilege should have been extended in at least an equal degree to the people of the Punjab. I do not wish to dwell upon the resentment which has been caused in the province by its being so unjustly dealt with, I trust the Government will be pleased to consider whether the exclusion on the face of it an unreasonable and unjustifiable exclusion of the vast numbers of the educated men in a progressive province like the Punjab from a privilege which has been extended to their fellow-subjects in other parts of the country and even in their own province, is not quite a serious political blunder. The allaying of the discontent was one of the main objects of the scheme of reforms. I venture humbly to say that the way in which the reform has been worked out here is certainly not calculated to achieve that end. Every consideration for the welfare of the people and of good administration seems to me to demand that as large a number of men of intelligence, education and influence as may be available should be given the right to exercise a constitutional privilege and thus invited to employ their time and energy in the service of their country.

"Gentlemen, I will not detain you by dwelling on the defects of the regulations for the other provinces. Speaking generally, we find that the regulations have bean vitiated by the disproportionate representation which they have secured to the Mohammedan and to the landed classes, and the small room for representation which they have left for the educated classes; also by the fact that they have made an invidious and irritating distinction between the Muslim and the non-Muslim subjects of His Majesty, both in the matter of the protection of the minorities and of the franchise, and lastly in that they have laid down unnecessarily narrow and arbitrary restrictions on the choice of the electors.

"Such are the regulations which have been promulgated under the reform scheme. I would respectfully invite Lord Morley himself to judge how very far they have departed from the liberal spirit of the proposals which he had fashioned with such statesmanlike care and caution. I also invite Lord Minto to consider if the regulations do not practically give effect, as far as they could, to the objectionable features of the scheme which was put forward in Sir Harold Stuart's letter of August 24, 1907, which were so widely condemned, and also to judge how different in spirit they are from the proposals for which the people of India tendered their warmest thanks to His Lordship and to his noble Chief at Whitehall. Is it at all a matter for wonder that the educated classes in India are intensely dissatisfied with the regulations? Have they not every reason to be so? For more than a quarter of a century they have laboured earnestly and prayerfully through the Congress to promote the common interests of all the classes and sects of the people, and to develop a common feeling of nationality among the followers of all the different religions in India, which is not less necessary for the purposes of a civilised government than for the peaceful progress, prosperity and happiness of the people. The regulations for the first; time in the history of the British rule have recognised religion as a basis of representation, and have thus raised a wall of separation between the Mohammedans and the non-Mohammedan subjects of His Majesty which it will take years of earnest effort to demolish. They have also practically undone, for the time being at any rate, the results of the earnest agitation of a quarter of a century to secure an effective voice to the elected representatives of the people in the Government of their country. It is not that the Congress did not want or does not want, that our Mohammedan fellow-subjects should be fairly and fully represented in the reformed councils. It firmly believed, and it fully expected, that if a general electorate would be formed on a reasonable basis, a sufficient number of the representatives of all the classes of the community would naturally find their way into the councils. But it desired that as they would have to deal as members of the councils, with questions which affect equally the interests of all the classes and creeds, they should be returned to the Councils by the common suffrages of their countrymen of all the classes and creeds, and that their title to the confidence of their countrymen should be based on their ability to protect and promote their interests by their education, integrity and independence of character, and not on the accident of their belonging to any particular faith or creed or of their having inherited or acquired a certain number of broad acres. We are naturally grieved to find that when we had caught a glimpse of the promised land by extremely fortunate combination of a liberal statesman as the Secretary of State and a liberal-minded Viceroy, our old friends of the bureaucracy have yet succeeded in blocking the way to it for at least some time to come.

"Gentlemen, the attitude of the educated Indians towards the reforms has been misinterpreted in some quarters. Some of the criticism has been quite friendly and I am sure we all fully appreciate it. But I wish that our friends looked a little more closely into the facts. Their criticism puts me in mind of a very instructive ancient story. Vishvamitra, a mighty *Kshatriya* King, the master of the vast hordes of wealth and of extensive territories, felt that there was a still higher position for him to attain, viz., that of being a *Brahman*, whose title to respect rests not on any earthly possession or power but on learning and piety and devotion to philanthropic work. He accordingly practised severe austerities, and, except one Brahman named Vashistha, every one acclaimed him a *Brahman*. Vishvamitra first tried to persuade Vashishtha to declare him a *Brahman*; then he threatened him; and having yet failed in his object, he killed a hundred children of Vashishtha in order to coerce him into compliance with his desire. Deeply was Vashishtha distressed. If he had but once said that Vishvamitra had qualified himself to be regarded a *Brahman*, he would have saved himself and his hoary-headed wife and the rest of his family all the sorrow and suffering which Vishvamitra inflicted upon them. But Vashishtha had realised the truth of the ancient teaching– सत्यं पुत्रशताद् वरम्

"He valued truth more than a hundered sons. He would not save them by uttering what he did not believe to be true. In his despair, Vishvamitra decided to kill Vashishtha himself. One evening he went armed to Vashishtha's hermitage with that object. But while he was waiting in a corner for an opportunity to carry out his evil intent, he overheard what Vashistha was telling to his wife, the holy Arundhati, in answer to a query as to whose *tapasya* shone as bright as the moonlight in the midst of which they were seated. 'Vishwamitra's was the unhesitating answer! Hearing this Vashishtha's heart changed. He cast aside the arms of a Kshsttriya, and with it the pride of power and anger too. Then he approached Vashishtha in true humility, Vashishtha greeted him as a *Bramharshi*. Vishvamitra was overcome. After he had got over the feelings of gratefulness and reverence which had overpowered him, and had apologised for all the injuries inflicted by him upon Vashistha, he bagged Vashishtha to tell him why he had not acknowledged him a *Brahman* earlier and thus saved himself the sorrow and Vishvamitra from the sin of killing his sons. 'Vishvamitra' answered, 'Every time you came to me, you came with the pride and power of a Kshatriya, and I greeted you as such. You have come today imbued with the spirit of a *Brahman*; I have welcomed you as such. I had spoken the truth then, and I have spoken the truth today as well.' Even so, gentlemen, I venture humbly to claim, have my educated countrymen spoken in the matter of the reforms. The first proposals published in Sir Harold Stuart's letter were open to serious and valid objections, and they were condemned by them. The proposals published by Lord Morley last year were truly liberal and comprehensive in spirit, and they were welcomed with warm gratitude and unstinted praise. The regulations framed to give effect to them have unfortunately departed, and widely too, from the spirit of those proposals, and are illiberal and retrogressive to a degree. The educated Indians have been compelled to condemn them. They have done so more in sorrow than in anger. Let the government modifiy the regulations to bring them into harmony with the spirit of Lord Morley's proposals, and in the name of this Congress, and, I venture to say, on behalf of my educated countrymen generally, I beg to assure the government that they will meet with a cordial and grateful reception. I do not ignore the fact that there is an assurance contained in the Government's Resolution accompanying the regulations that they will be modified in the light of the experience that will be gained in their working. That assurance has been strengthened by what His Excellency the Viceroy was pleased to say in this connection both at Bombay and Madras. But I most respectfully submit that many of the defects pointed out in them are such that they can be remedied without waiting for the light of new experience. And I respectfully invite both Lord Morley and Lord Minto to consider whether in view of the widespread dissatisfaction which the regulations have created, it will be wise to let this feeling live and grow, or whether it is not desirable in the interests of good administration, and to fulfil one of the most important and avowed objects of the reforms, namely the allaying of discontent; and the promotion of good will between the government and the people, to take the earliest opportunity to make an official announcement that the objections urged against the regulations will be taken early into consideration.

Poverty and High Prices

"I have done, gentlemen, with the reform regulations. There are a few other matters, however, to which, I wish, with your permission, to invite attention. There is no doubt that at the present moment the regulations occupy the greatest portion of public attention. But there are other causes of discontent, and some of them far deeper than the objections urged against the regulations. Amongst them all there is none greater than the deep poverty which pervades the land. I do not wish to enter here into the controversy whether the poverty of the people has increased or diminished since the country came under the British rule. What I ask is whether the condition of the people today is such as might reasonably have been expected from their being placed under a highly organised, civilised administration? Is that condition such as to be a ground for congratulation either to the government or to the people? It is true that a fraction of the population has become more prosperous than it was before. But the vast millions of the people are still dragging a miserable existence on the verge of starvation and large numbers of them have been falling easy victims to plague and fever. This is a question of vital importance, and deserves far graver consideration than it has yet received. The sufferings of the people have been greatly increased by the high prices of food stuffs which have ruled for the last few years. The hardships to which the middle and poorer classes have been subjected can be better imagined than described. Gentlemen, I do not know whether our rulers have taken note of the evil effects which have been produced upon the minds of the people by these hardships to which they have been thus exposed for several years now, from one end of the country to the other, from year to year, from month to month, from week to week, and from day to day. I do not know whether they have obtained any official estimate of the numbers of those that have thus been suffering in silence so long. Nearly two years ago the Government of India was pleased to promise an enquiry into the high prices of food stuffs. Has the enquiry been made? If not, why not? It is not unreasonable to ask that when the government finds that a vast proportion of the people entrusted to its care are so poor as they are in India, and that the prices of food stuffs have suddenly gone up as high as they have, it should lose no time in instituting an expert enquiry into the matter and hasten to adopt the remedies which may be suggested by such an enquiry.

Sanitation and Education

"Along with the high prices that have prevailed, there have been other troubles which have added to the woes of our people. A wave of malarial fever has passed over large portions of the country, and has inflicted a vast amount of suffering and loss upon the people. Death rates have been running high. These are the indications not of prosperity but of deep and widespread poverty. The appalling numbers of deaths from plague during the past few years are again a sadly eloquent and yet an unmistakable indication of the weak condition of the people. It is of course now the duty of the government to take every reasonable step it can to promote the health, stamina and national prosperity of the people. And we are grateful for what the government has done in any of these directions. But we urge that the steps taken have been quite inadequate, and that much more should be done to meet the requirements of the situation. Take for instance the question of sanitation. Sanitation is in a most unsatisfactory condition among vast portions of the population and in the greater portion of the country. The grants made hitherto for it have been wholly inadequate. Take again the question of education. The provision made for it also is woefully short of the needs of the country. The people as a whole are still steeped in ignorance, and that ignorance forms an obstacle to every improvement. Every time an attempt is made to reach them by instructions to help to save them from any great evil, as for instance to tell them to seek the benefit of inoculation against plague, or even to use quinine to protect themselves from malaria, the government finds itself face to face with the stupendous difficulty that they are so largely illiterate. Now that illiteracy, that ignorance lies really at the root of every trouble to which the people are exposed. And yet it is sad to find that progress is not being made in the matter of education as it should be. Nearly two years ago the Government of India virtually promised that primary education would be made free all over the country. But that promise has not yet been fulfilled. The Government of India has for fifty years past by their declarations held out the hope that primary education would be made universal in India. We have been waiting and waiting to see this done. Many measures costing money which should not have been introduced have been carried out. Measures which should have been carried out have been kept back. Among this latter category has unfortunately fallen the question of making elementary education free and universal. Elementary education was made free and compulsory in England so far back as 1870. Japan, an Asiatic power, also made it compulsory nearly forty years ago. It has long been compulsory in America, in Germany, in France and in all the civilised countries of the West. Why should India alone be denied the great advantages which accrue from a system of free and compulsory primary education? That is the one foundation upon which the progress of the people can be built. Is agricultural improvement to be promoted and agricultural education to be imparted for that purpose? Are technical instruction and industrial training to be given? Are habits of prudence and self-respect and a spirit of helpfulness to be fostered among the people? A system of free and general elementary education is needed equally as the basis of it all. I earnestly appeal to the Government of India to take up this question of free and universal primary education as one of the most important questions which affect the wellbeing of the people, and to deal with it as early as may be practicable.

Technical and Industrial Education

"Along with this question should be taken the issue of technical education. If vast millions of people in this country are to be rescued from poverty, if new avenues of employment are to be opened and prosperity spread over the land, it is essential that an extensive system of technical and industrial education should be introduced in the country. The examples of the countries having made progress doing the same point out that this is the road to prosperity. Germany was not at one time known as a manufacturing country. It has so greatly improved its position as to become a formidable rival to England. America has enriched herself beyond description by multiplying her manufactures and industries. Japan has in the course of thirty years altered her position from a mainly agricultural into a largely manufacturing country. The industrial progress and prosperity of every one of these countries has been built upon a wide-spread system of scientific, technical and industrial education. The people of India are not lacking in intelligence or industry. They are willing to undergo any amount of labour that may be required of them. But they lack education, the skill of the trained man, and are therefore being beaten day by day by the manufacturers of every foreign countries who have built up a system of technical education, and thereby laid the foundation of its industrial prosperity. The manufactures of these countries are flooding our markets and impoverishing our people. It is high time that the government take up the question in right earnest, and adopt a system of technical education co-extensive with the needs of the country.

Provincial Decentralisation

"Gentlemen, I have no doubt that the council regulations will be improved. I have no doubt the reforms foreshadowed in Lord Morley's despatch will sooner or later be carried out in their entirety. But even when the regulations have been improved and those reforms have been carried out, there will still not be much hope for a real improvement in the condition of the people, unless and until one other essential measure of reform is carried out, and that is a decentralisation of financial power and responsibility from the Government of India to the various provincial governments. It appears from some remarks in one of Lord Morley's speeches that this question of a larger decentralisation than has been dealt with by the Royal Commission, has not escaped His Lordship's keen eye, but that he has allowed it to stand over for consideration in the future. In order to effect a real advance in the condition of the people, it is essential that the Government of India should make very much larger grants to the various provinces, should allow provincial governments to appropriate a much larger share of provincial revenues to be devoted to provincial needs than at present. But I must say that I have not much hope of this being done unless the vital change that I have referred to above is brought about in the existing system of financial administration. Under that system the Government of India holds itself to be the master of all the revenues of the various provinces, and makes allotments to them, by means of what is called provincial settlement for provincial expenditure. Under this system nearly three-fourths of the entire revenues of the country is taken up for Imperial purposes and only about one-fourth is left to provide for all Provincial expenditure. What hope can there be for improvements being effected in the condition of the people of primary education being made free and universal, of technical education being promoted, of agricultural improvement being brought about, of sanitary surroundings being secured to the people, and of their being saved from malaria, plague and famine unless a very much larger proportion of the revenues derived from the people is allowed to be spent by the provincial governments on purposes which directly benefit the people? What is needed is that the Government of India should require a reasonable amount of contribution to be made for Imperial purposes out of the revenues of each province, and should leave the rest of the revenues to be spent for the Provincial purposes. It should require Provincial Governments to make an addition to their contributions when any special cause may arise therefore, but should look to the revenues derived from what are called the Imperial heads to meet the rest of its ordinary expenditure.

Reduction of Expenditure

"One great advantage of such a system will be that the Government of India will have to somewhat curtail or restrict its expenditure. And it is hardly necessary to say that there is a crying need for such a reduction. In the present condition of the people, it is not possible it will not be just, to raise taxation to a higher level than where it stands. But there is a source of revenue derivable from economy itself, and justice and the highest considerations of good government demand that this source should be tapped to a reasonable extent. For years together the Congress has been begging the government to practise economy in the various departments of its administration. In the first place there is the military expenditure. Such a large proportion of the revenues is absorbed by it, that there is not sufficient money left for expenditure on many more useful directions. The congress has been urging for years that the expenditure should be reduced; but it has unfortunately been very much increased. There are several ways of reducing that expenditure. One is to reduce the number of the men in the army. That probably the government will not agree to. The second is that as the army is maintained not merely for the benefit of India but for the imperial purposes as well, the British treasury should contribute a fair proportion of the military expenditure to the British Indian Empire. This is a prayer which has often been urged in the past and it is a prayer which we must urge yet again.

Higher Careers to Indians

"The cost of the civil administration also is extravagantly high, and can well be reduced. The Congress has urged times out of number that the cheaper indigenous agency should be substituted wherever practicable for the costly foreign agency in all the various departments of the administration. It has urged that the higher appointments should be thrown open to the Indians in a much larger measure than they have been heretofore. We have urged this on the ground of economy as well as of justice. We are thankful to Lord Morley that he has appointed two of our Indian fellow-subjects as members of his council. We are deeply thankful both to him and to Lord Minto for their having appointed an Indian to the Executive Council of the Governor-General. What we feel however is that the claims of Indians to a reasonable share in the higher appointments in the service of their country will continue, to have but a poor chance of being satisfied until all examinations relating to India which are at present held in England only, shall be held simultaneously in India and in England, and until all the first appointments which are made in India shall be made by competitive examinations only. You know, gentlemen, how keenly, how earnestly and perseveringly that prince of patriots Mr Dadabhai Naoroji has been advocating this important reform for nearly forty years. But unfortunately for us the change has not yet come. In order to qualify themselves for service in their own land, the educated youth of India are still required to go several thousands of miles away from their homes, to pass an examination in England for admission to the Civil Service of India. This is entirely unjust, it is unjust not only to our educated young men but to our people as a whole. The system is responsible for keeping up the expenditure on the civil administration at a much costlier scale than is justifiable. We must therefore earnestly press that simultaneous examinations should be held in India and England for admission into the Indian civil service.

"Before I leave this subject, I should refer to the appointment of the Right Honourable Mr Ameer Ali as a member of His Majesty's Privy Council. We all know with what satisfaction the news of that appointment has been received throughout the country. I beg in your name to tender our thanks to Lord Morley for this further remarkable instance of his desire to appoint the Indians to higher offices under the Crown.

"Gentlemen, it is very much to be hoped that the Government will earn the gratitude of Indians by throwing open higher careers in the army also to them. It is too late in the day to say that the Indians shall not be appointed to the higher offices in the army in India. Indians who are loyal, who have proved their loyalty by the life-blood which they have shed in the service of His Majesty, the King Emperor and whose valour and fidelity have been repeatedly recognised, ought no longer to be told that they cannot rise to appointments in the army higher than Subedar-Majorships and Bisaldar-Majorships. Reason and justice favour the departure for which I plead. The Proclamation of 1853 has promised that race, colour or creed shall not be a bar to the appointment of Indians to any posts under the Crown, the duties of which they shall be qualified to discharge. We ask the government to give effect to that noble Proclamation, to do justice to the claims of the people of India, by opening the higher branches of the army for qualified Indians to enter. If the government will accede to this reasonable prayer, it will deepen the loyalty of vast numbers of people in India, and, I venture humbly to say, it will never have any cause to regret having taken such a step. On the other hand, the exclusion of Indians from such appointments is a standing ground of dissatisfaction and complaint. It is in every way desirable that it were removed. By throwing higher careers in the army open to the Indians, the government will open another important door for satisfying the natural and reasonable aspirations of important sections of His Majesty's subjects. Their attachment to the Government will thereby be enhanced, and if the opportunity ever arose, the Government would find a large army of Indians trained and prepared to fight under His Majesty's flag to defend the country against foreign invasion and to help the government in maintaining peace on every possible occasion.

Indians in South Africa

"This brings me to the question of the status of Indians in other countries. It is not necessary for me to say how deeply it has grieved us all to hear of the unjust, the cruel, the disgraceful treatment to which our countrymen in the Transvaal have been subjected. The indignities which have been heaped upon them, the hardships and harrassments to which they have been exposed, have excited deep feelings of indignation and grief throughout the country. These feelings are not confined to the educated Indians alone. They are shared by the literates and the illiterates alike. They have penetrated even into the *zenana*, as is evident from the lists of subscriptions collected from ladies which have appeared in the press. Touching appeals have come to us from our sisters in the Transvaal for brotherly help and sympathy in their trials. We admire the unflinching courage, the unbending determination with which our noble brother Mr Gandhi and our other countrymen have been fighting for the honour of the Indian name. Our hearts go forth to them in sympathy, and we are sorely grieved to find that the Government of His Majesty have not yet been able to come to their rescue. Our brethren have repeatedly appealed for protection and support to the Sovereign and Parliament of England, whose sway they live under. And it is a matter of deep grief to them, and to us, that, being the subjects of His Majesty the King-Emperor of India, and being the fellow-subjects of Englishmen they should find themselves so long without protection against cruel and unjust treatment, against humiliating insults, in a colony of the British Empire. It is not right to say that the British Government cannot exercise any influence upon the Boer-British Government. It was but yesterday that the Government of England went to war with the Boers, one of the avowed grounds being that Indians had been badly treated by the Boers. Has the position become weaker since the government has established the might of its power there, that it is afraid to require that the Boer-British Government should follow a course of conduct towards its Indian fellow-subjects different from the one pursued before a course of conduct consistent with the claims of a common humanity and of fellowship as subjects of a common Sovereign? I have no doubt, gentlemen, that the Government of India have made many and earnest representations in this matter to the imperial government. I have no doubt that they will make further representations still. For the honour of the Empire itself, let us hope that the imperial government will yet interfere to bring about an early and honourable settlement of this painful but momentous question. But however that may be, the Government of India is bound in honour and in duty to their Indian fellow-subjects to take steps now to actively resent and to retaliate the treatment which is accorded to them in South Africa. And the least that they ought to do is to withdraw all the facilities for enlisting the indentured labour for South Africa, until the white colonists there agree to recognise the Indians as their equal fellow-subjects. The matter has been under discussion too long. The intensity of feeling which it has created throughout the country demands that it should no longer be allowed to rest where it is. I will not detain you longer on this question, as time will not permit me to do this. I have no doubt that you will pass a strong resolution expressing your sympathy and admiration for our brethren, Hindus, Mohammedans, Parsis and Christians, who are fighting a heroic fight for the honour of the Motherland in South Africa, and urging upon the Government both in India and in England for the justice and necessity of an early and honourable settlement of this great Imperial problem.

Anarchical Crimes

"Gentlemen, there is yet another painful matter for which I must claim attention, and that is the evil of the advent of anarchical ideas of the assassin's creed into our country. It has filled us with grief to find that this new evil has come to add to our sorrows and to increase our misfortunes. Earlier in the year the whole country was shocked to hear that Sir William Curzon Wyllie was shot dead by a misguided young man, and that while attempting to save Sir William Curzon Wyllie, Dr Lalkaka also lost his life at the hand of the assassin. The detestable crime filled all the decent Indians with grief and shame, with grief that a gentleman who had done no one any harm, who had on the contrary befriended many young Indians in England, and who was trying to befriend his assassin even at the moment when he was attacked by him, should have been killed without any cause, without any justification; wish shame, that an Indian should have been guilty of such an atrocious crime. The pain caused by the news was widespread and deep. There was one circumstance however, of melancholy satisfaction in the tragedy; and that was that if one Indian had taken the life of Sir William Curzon Wyllie, another Indian had nobly given up his own in the attempt to save him. Gentlemen, in the name and on behalf of the Congress, I beg here to offer to Lady Curzon-Wyllie and to the family of Dr Lalkaka our deepest sympathy with them in their sad bereavements.

"As though we had not had enough cause for sorrow, we have recently had the misfortune to hear of another equally atrocious crime committed at Nasik. The murder of Mr Jackson has sent another thrill of horror and sorrow throughout the country. Mr Jackson was being entertained at a party by

Indians who honoured and esteemed him because of the good service he had rendered, and because of the sympathy he bore to them. And it was at such a party that a young man, filled with ideas as impotent to produce any good as they are wicked, took away his life. The news has been received with unutterable grief throughout the country, and the deepest sympathy is felt for Mrs Jackson in her cruel bereavement. I bag to offer to her also our sincerest condolence.

"And there was another wicked attempt at a similar crime, though it happily proved unsuccessful. I refer of course, to the bomb which was thrown the other day at Ahmedabad on the carriage of His Excellency the Viceroy. It is a misfortune that Lord Minto has had to introduce several measures of repression. But I believe that there is a general feeling all over the country that His Lordship has throughout meant well, and that he has laboured as a friend to promote what he has conceived to be the interests of the people. The large-hearted liberal-mindedness which Lord Minto has shown in connection with the scheme of reform has entitled him to our lasting gratitude and esteem. And it has been a matter for profound regret throughout the country that an attempt should have been made even upon His Excellency's life. That feeling has happily been relieved however by an equally profound feeling of satisfaction and thankfulness as His Lordship's providential escape.

"I do not know, gentlemen, in what words to express the abhorrence that I am sure we all feel for these detestable, dastardly and useless crimes. It fills me with great grief to think that in this ancient land of ours where *ahimsa,* abstention from causing hurt has been taught from the earliest times to be cue of the greatest virtues which can be cultivated by the civilised man; where the great law-giver Manu has laid down no man should kill even an animal that does not cause any hurt to others; where the taking away of life generally is regarded as a great sin, the minds of any of our young men should have been so far prevented as to lead them to commit such inhuman acts of cold-blooded murder without any provocation. Such crimes were confined until a few years ago to some of the countries of Europe. We had no doubt occasional cases of religious fanatics called *ghazis*, who now and then took away the life of an Englishman on the frontier. But we are grieved to find that these new political *ghazis* have now risen in our midst, and have become a new source of shame and sorrow to the country. I am sure we are all of one mind in our desire to do all that we can to eradicate this new evil from our land. But we do not know what steps should be taken to do so. We have repeatedly denounced these outrages, but those who commit them have obviously gone beyond the reach of our influence. It should be obvious to the meanest understanding that these crimes cannot do any good to our country they have never done any good to any country, but, on the contrary, they have done and are doing us a great deal of injury. They are condemned by our *shastras* and are opposed to the noblest traditions of our race. अयुद्ध्यमानस्य वधो नि:शेषकरणं स्मृतम् the killing of a man who is not standing up to fight is a sin which leads to the extinction of the sinner, says the *Mahabharat*. The whole of the *Mahabharata* illustrates and emphasises the great truth that it is righteousness alone that wins, because its victory is real and lasting, and that unrighteous and wicked deeds though they may secure a temporary seeming advantage, lead eventually to certain degradation and destruction. It proclaims that even in a war, we should not think of winning a victory by wicked means "धर्मेण निधनं श्रेय: न जय: पापकर्मणा" better death by pursuing a righteous course of conduct than victory by means of a wicked deed. It is inexpressibly sad to think that in a country where wise and noble teachings have come down to us through long ages, the assassin's creed should have found acceptance in the minds of any person, young or old. Let us endeavour to instil these noble teachings into the minds of our young men. We owe it to them and to our country, to try so far as it lies in our power, to keep them from being misled into the path of evil and dishonour. Let us do it, and let us hope and pray that such crimes, which we all deplore and detest, will soon become matters of past history.

Deportations and The Partition

"Gentlemen, I have referred in an earlier portion of my address to some of the causes of discontent. I should refer to two other matters which have contributed largely to swell it in the last few years. One of them is the deportation of Indians without any trial. The government cannot be more anxious than we are in the interest of our country's progress, to see good will and confidence grow ever more between the Government and the people. And we are pained to find that by resorting to a lawless law like the Regulation of 1818, to punish men against whom no offence has been openly urged and established, the government by its own action excites a great deal of ill-feeling against itself. We all remember how intensely strong was the feeling excited by the deportation of Lala Lajpat Rai, and how deep and general was the satisfaction when after six month's confinement, he was restored to liberty. Since then, however, nine other gentlemen from Bengal have been similarly deported. The reasons which have led to their deportation have not been made known. Every effort to induce the government to publish those reasons has failed. Public sympathy is consequently all on the side of those who have been deported and all against the government. This cannot be regarded as a gain to good administration. If the government will only have recourse to the ordinary law of the land to bring to justice any person or persons who might be guilty of encouraging violence or lawlessness or of promoting ill-will or hostility to the government, there will be no room left for complaint. The Indian people are an eminently reasonable people. Let them know that a brother has been guilty of a crime; let the government only satisfy the public that there is reasonable ground for depriving any man of his liberty, and they will cease to sympathise with the offender. Where sympathy will not entirely die out, its nature will be greatly changed. There will be no feeling left against the government. But to send away the men who have been leading peaceful and honourable lives to the distant lands, and to confine them under the deportation regulation without giving them any opportunity to hear and answer charges which have been formulated behind their backs, is a course unworthy of the British Government, and it ought to be put an end to as early as possible. Even the Egyptian law of deportation is better in this respect than the Indian law. Under that law an opportunity is given to the person whom it is proposed to deport to hear the charges laid against him, through in camera and to answer them. In that way in justice is largely if not entirely avoided. I hope that if the government is determined to retain the Regulation of 1818 and similar regulations in the Statute book it will at any rate recognise the necessity in the interests of good administration as much as in the interests of justice, of introducing amendments in the said Regulations to make them similar in the particular respect pointed out, to the law of Egypt. I cannot leave this subject without referring to the great service which Mr Mackarness has been rendering to the people of India in this connection. It is only right that we should make a grateful acknowledgment of that service.

"The other matter to which I think it my duty to invite attention is the question of the partition of Bengal. It is unnecessary for me to say what an amount of discontent and bitterness this question has created in Bengal. That discontent and that bitterness has travelled far beyond the limits of Bengal, and has produced a most deplorable influence in the country. It may appear to be a vain hope, but I do hope that the government will yet reconsider this question. I do not propose to take up your time by recapitulating the arguments which have been urged against the partition, and the pleas which have been put forward for a modification of the partition so as to bring together the entire Bengali-speaking community in Bengal under one government. But I will mention one new and important fact in support of my recommendation. And that is this that under the reform scheme the people of Western Bengal are to receive the benefit of a Council Government, Eastern Bengal is not to have it, and finds that the destinies of its 31 millions of people are still left to be guided by one single man. This gives an additional ground of complaint, and dissatisfaction to the people of Eastern Bengal. The partition as it has been made cannot be defended. It ought therefore to be mended. If the government will modify the partition it will restore peace to Bengal, and win the good will and gratitude of millions of men there. It will also enhance thereby its prestige in the eyes of the people throughout the country, as they will feel that the Government can afford to be as just as it is strong.

"The mention of these grievances of Bengal reminds me of some of the grievances of the Punjab. My friend the Chairman of the Reception Committee has already referred to some of them. They will be laid in due course before you, and I trust that you will give them the consideration which they deserve. It is true that some of these questions affect only one province now: but they involve questions of principle, and may affect other provinces in the future. One of these, the imposing of restrictions on the alienation of land, already affects two provinces. The Punjab Land Alienation Act has been followed by a similar act for a portion of the United Provinces, and there is no knowing when the similar acts may not be extended to other areas. These acts have revived a procedure of protecting the interests of the agriculturists which has become obsolete in civilised countries. The right course for the Government to follow is to illumine the minds and strengthen the wills of the *zamindars* and agriculturists by means of education, so that they may he able to protect their interests and increase their incomes. Instead of pursuing that natural and healthy course, the government has had recourse to an obsolete and not very rational method of helping them to protect their properties by depriving them of the power of dealing freely with them, and by compelling the agriculturist to sell his land to a brother agriculturist only. This gives the richer agriculturist the opportunity of buying up his humbler brother, and prevents the latter from obtaining as fair a price as he would get if he were to sell his property in the open market. It also prevents the non-agriculturists from acquiring land, and from investing their capital in enriching it. The subject is a very important one, and I trust you will give it your attention.

The Constitution of The Congress

"Ladies and gentlemen, I have detained you very long. But I must crave your indulgence for a few minutes more. I wish before I conclude to say a few words about the constitution and the present position of the Congress. Ever since the unfortunate split at Surat, the Congress has come in for a great deal of criticism, both friendly and unfriendly. It is said that there has been a division in the Congress camp. It is true, it is sad. We should have been happy if it was not. We hear a great deal of disapproval, of condemnation, of a disunited Congress, and great desire expressed for a united Congress. I ask, gentlemen, how are we a disunited Congress? Are we not here a united Congress, united in our aims and our methods, and in our determination to adhere to them? If we are not a united Congress who is responsible for the disunion? Have we departed in the smallest degree from the lines on which the Congress was started twenty-four years ago? Have we shut out any fellow countryman of ours who wishes to work with us on those lines from coming to the Congress? I emphatically say, no. It is said that we have adopted a creed. Yes, we have done so, because it had become necessary, owing to the influx of some new ideas into the country, to define the objects for which the Congress was organised, to prevent a misinterpretation or misrepresentation of those objects. The creed we have adopted is however no new creed. It has been the creed of the Congress from the beginning. The foundation of the Congress rests on loyalty to the British Government. That has always been the basic principle of the Congress. The Congress has at no time done or sanctioned anything being done which would give the smallest countenance to any idea that it wanted to overthrow the British Government. I believe that the vast bulk of the thoughtful people in India, I mean, of course, those who can and do understand such questions, are as much convinced today as they were when the Congress was started, that the British rule is good for India, and that it is to our advantage that it should continue for a long time to come. That certainly is the feeling of the vast bulk of educated Indians. And, my countrymen, let me personally say this, that if I did not believe that british rule was good for India, I would certainly not say so. If the fear of the law of sedition would deter me then from speaking against it, I would hold my peace, but not soil my lips with a lie, and thereby expose myself to a far more terrible punishment than any that can be inflicted for infringing the law of sedition. I do believe that the British rule is meant for the good of India, meant to help us to raise our country once more to a position of prosperity and power. Our duty to our country itself demands that we should loyally accept that rule, and endeavour steadily to improve our position under it, so that while we suffer some certain inevitable disadvantages of that rule, we should realise all the advantages which we can undoubtedly derive by our being placed under it. That being our position, gentlemen, ever since the Congress was organised, it has made it its duty to bring the grievances of the people to the notice of the government, with a view to their removal by the government, and to secure constitutional changes in the administration which could only he brought about by the government. I may say in passing, that it is the strongest and most unanswerable proof of the loyalty and good will of the Congress towards the government that it has tried during all these years to press those questions on the attention of the government which affected the weal or woe of the people and therefore constituted a real grievance of the people. The raising of the minimum of assessment of the income tax, the reduction of the salt-tax, the prayer for the larger admission of Indians into the public services and the many other reforms urged by the Congress, all illustrate the point. If the Congress was hostile or unfriendly to the government, it would have left the grievances of the people alone, and let discontent grow among them. It is true that there were at one time some narrow-minded officials who regarded the Congress as disloyal. Their race, I hope, is now extinct. I hope that among the officials of government there is not a responsible man now who thinks that the Congress means any harm to the government: I believe that there are a good many among them now who are satisfied that it is the best helpmate that the government could have to help it to conduct the administration of the country on sound and popular lines. I have referred to this not to defend the Congress against any accusation of unfriendliness to the government, but to emphasise the fact that though the Congress did not for a long time adopt a written constitution, it was clear as day-light from the very beginning that it was an organisation whose object it was to bring about reforms in the existing system of administration and redress the grievances of the people by appealing to the constituted authority of the government. Later on, when some of our brethren earnestly urged that the Congress should have a written constitution, such a constitution was agreed upon, at the Lucknow session in 1899, and it laid down in clear words that the object of the Congress was to agitate for reforms on constitutional lines. That is the object of the Congress today. The cardinal principle of the Congress has now been formulated in even more explicit, more unmistakable language. The change has been in the direction of amplifying the objects not of narrowing them. The first Article of the Constitution of the Congress, the Congress creed as it has been called, runs as follows,

> The objects of the Indian National Congress are the attainment, by the people of India, of a system of government similar to that enjoyed by the self-governing members of the British Empire, and a participation by them in the rights and responsibilities of the Empire on equal terms with those members. These objects are to be achieved by constitutional means, by bringing about a steady reform of the existing system of administration, and by promoting national unity, fostering public spirit, and developing and organising the intellectual, moral, economical and industrial resources of the country. I should like to know, gentlemen, if there exists another organisation throughout the length and breadth of this vast Empire which has set nobler objects before itself to achieve. We have made it absolutely clear that we want Self-Government within the British Empire; a system of government, that is to say, similar to that enjoyed by the self-governing members of the British Empire; and that we want to participate on equal terms in the rights and responsibilities of that Empire with those other members.

"Gentlemen, what higher aim could a sensible practical patriot and statesman place before himself? Bear in mind the present status of our country and you at once see how noble, how honourble is the desire to raise it to the position of being a member of a great federation of a great Empire under one Sovereign, holding some objects in common for the benefit of the Empire and pursuing others independently for its own special benefit. Japan is an entirely independent power. And yet Japan considered it an advantage to enter into a friendly alliance with England, and England to do the same with Japan. Some good people tell us that we have gone too far in fixing our aim. Others tell us that we have not gone sufficiently far. But I have not heard one single responsible man put forward any programme of agitation which goes even as far as ours, leaving alone of course one or two irresponsible talkers, whose wild talk is happily not heard now in this country. We have fixed our aim with the utmost deliberation. We consider it high enough to give opportunity for the utmost exercise of patriotic feeling. We feel that with this ideal before us, we can rise to our growth under the British Government by agitating by lawful and constitutional means for obtaining all the privileges which our fellow-subjects in England and other countries enjoy.

"It is sometimes urged against us that our representations are not heard and that in spite of many years of constitutional agitation, we are still labouring under various disabilities and disadvantages. That is unfortunately true; But only partly so. The success achieved by us is by no means ignoble. But even if we had entirely failed that would not establish the inefficiency of constitutional agitation. It would only prove the necessity for more persistent, more strenuous agitation. It is again said that several repressive measures have been introduced during the last two years and that they have made the task of even honest workers difficult. I fully share the regret that these measures have been passed. Let us hope that they will soon cease to be operative, if they may not be repealed. But making allowance for all that, I venture to say that the freedom of speech and action which we yet enjoy under the British Government will enable us to carry on a constitutional agitation to achieve all the great objects which the Congress has set before us. I ask you, my countrymen, not to allow the aspersions which are made against the Congress to go unanswered any longer, and to dispel the wrong notions which have been created in the minds of some of our people about its objects. I ask you to tell all our people that those objects are high and honourable enough to demand the steadfast devotion of the most patriotic minds, and to ask them to co-operate with us in realising them. It is a great change that we want to bring about in the system of administration, a change by which the affairs of the people shall be administered by the voice of the representatives of the people. That change cannot be effected in a day, nor yet in a decade. But I venture to say that if we can educate all our people to stand aloof from and to give no countenance whatever to seditious movements; I do not mean to suggest that they in any way do encourage such movements at present; if we can prevent sedition from throwing obstacles in our path, and teach our people to devote themselves to build up national unity, to promote public spirit among ourselves and to agitate more earnestly and steadfastly that we have yet done to further the constitutional reform, we shall in ten years' time succeed in obtaining a larger measure of reform than was foreshadowed in Lord Morley's dispatch. The objects of the Congress are large and comprehensive enough to afford occupation to the most varied inclinations in the minds of our people. If there are some amongst us who do not wish to take part in agitation for political reforms, let them devote themselves to the promoting of national unity, to the fostering of public spirit, and to the developing of the intellectual, the moral and the economic resources of the country. Here is work enough for every Indian who feels the fervour of a patriotic impulse to take up. Let him choose the work which he finds most after his heart and labour to promote it. But let it not be said that the Congress has narrowly circumscribed the scope of its organisation. Lest it not be said, for it is not true, that the objects of the Congress are not high and honourable enough to satisfy the cravings for activity of the most patriotic minds. The problems which press for consideration at our hands are both vital and numerous. The condition of our people is deplorable. The vast millions of them do not get sufficient food to eat and sufficient clothing to protect themselves from exposure and cold. They are born and live in unsanitary surroundings and die premature and preventable deaths. Humanity and patriotism alike demand that, in addition to what the government is doing, and may do, we should do all that lies in our power to ameliorate their condition. Let every particle of energy be devoted to the loving services of the motherland. There is no land on earth which stands more in need of such service than our own. It is true that we are labouring undue numerous difficulties and disadvantages. Let not those difficulties and disadvantages daunt us. Duty demands that we must solve them; and let us remember that they will not be solved by having small divisions and narrow parties amongst as. In union alone lies the hope of a happy future for our country. Differences often arise among workers wherever there is a large association of men. But differences should be brushed aside, and all earnest patriots, all true lovers of the country, should unite in a common endeavour to promote common objects by methods and ways about which there is a common agreement throughout the country.

The National Ideal

"And here, gentlemen, I wish to say a few words to our brethren of the Muslim League. I deeply grieve to say it, but I think it would be well perhaps that I should say it. I am grieved to think that our brethren have allowed the interest of a sect nay of a party, to predominate in their counsels over the interests of the country that they have allowed sectarian considerations to prevail over patriotic considerations. Gentlemen, no Indian is entitled to the honour of being called a patriot, be he a Hindu, Mohammedan, Christian or Parsi, who desires for a moment that any fellow-countrymen of his, whatever his race or creed may be, should be placed under the domination of the men of his own particular persuasion or community, or that any one section should gain an undue advantage over any other section or all other sections. Patriotism demands that we should desire equally the good of all our countrymen alike. The great teacher Veda Vyasa held forth the true ideal for all religious and patriotic workers to pursue in the noble prayer which he taught centuries ago:

सर्वे च सुखिन: सन्तु, सर्वे सन्तु निरामया: ।
सर्वे भ्रद्राणि पश्यन्तु, मा कश्चिद् दु:खभाग्भवेत् ।।

" 'May all enjoy happiness; may all be the source of happiness to others; may all see auspicious days; may none suffer any injury.' "

"That is the ideal which the Congress has placed before us all from the moment of its birth.

"I am a Hindu by faith, and I mean no disrespect to any other religion when I say that I will not change my faith, for all the possessions of this world or of any other. But I shall be a false Hindu, and I shall deserve less to be called a Brahman, if I desired that Hindus or Brahmans should have any unfair the advantage as such over the Mohammedans, Christians, or any other community in India. Our brethren of the Muslim League have by their sectarian agitation at a critical period of our history, thrown back the national progress which we have been endeavouring for years to achieve. It is painful and humiliating to think that this has been so. But it is no good fretting too much about an irrevocable past. Let us try to forget it. It is a relief to know that there are many amongst them who realise that a mistake has been committed; many who realise that any temporary advantage which a few members of one community may gain over the members of other communities is a trifle which does not count in the consideration of large national interests. What does it matter to the vast masses of the people of India that a few Hindus should gain some slight advantage over a few Mohammedans, or that a few Mohammedans should gain some small advantage over a few Hindus? How ennobling it is even to think of that high ideal of patriotism where the Hindus, Mohammedans, Parsis and Christians, stand shoulder to shoulder as brothers and work for the common good of all. And what a fall is there when we give up that position, and begin to think of furthering the sectarian interests of any particular class or creed at the expense of those of others. I invite my brethren to respond to the higher call, and to feel that our lot having been cast in this now our common country, we cannot buildup a national life such as would be worth having, in separation, but that we must rise or fall together.

"And I have to say a word in this connection to some of my Hindu brethren also. I have been grieved to learn that owing to the unfortunate action of the members of the Muslim League, and let me say here once again that I do not make a single one of these remarks without a feeling of pain: I say what I say not to offend any brother, but in order that a better understanding should grow between the two great communities; I say, gentlemen, that owing to the action of our brethren of the Muslim League, owing to the manner in which the agitation for securing what they had persuaded themselves to believe would be a fair representation for their community, and especially owing to several unfortunate and regrettable things that were said during the course of that agitation, a great estrangement has taken place between the Hindus and Mohammedans generally all over the country, but particularly in the Punjab and the United Provinces. Under the influence of this feeling, some of my Hindu brethren have been led to think and to advocate that the Hindus should abandon the hope of buildingup a common national life, and should devote themselves to promote the interest of their own community as the Mohammedans have tried to promote those of theirs. They have also said that the Congress agitation has done harm to the Hindu community. With all respect to those who have taken this view, I wish to ask what harm the Congress has done to the Hindus? Have not the Hindus benefited equally with other communities by the raising of the minimum of assessment of the income-tax and the reduction of the salt tax, and by the other measures of reform which the Congress has successfully agitated for? But, it is said, some of the officials of the government have shown preference for Mohammedans over the Hindus in the public service because the Hindus have offended them by agitating for reforms, while the Mohammedans have not. Well, I am sorry to think that there seems to be some ground for such a complaint as this in the Punjab and the United Provinces. But, gentlemen, these are mere passing incidents, things of the moment. The favours shown are not to live. Let it be remembered that ex-hypothesis those favours have been shown not out of any love for our Mohammedan brethren, but in order to keep them quiet, to keep them from standing shoulder to shoulder with their Hindu brethren to agitate for reforms. Let the delusion disappear, let Mohammedans begin to take their fair share in agitating for the common good of all their countrymen, and those favours will cease to come. If there was a real partiality for our Mohammedan brethren, one should have expected to see some real concession made to them, for instance, in some privileges which are denied to us all in the matter of the Arms Act or Volunteering, being extended to them. But the thought of extending such a privilege to the Mohammedans has not, you may safely assume, ever entered the minds of even those among the officials, who have been known to be most inclined to favour them. No, gentlemen, this policy of partiality will not live, as it does not deserve to live. And any temporary disadvantages which may have been caused by it to our Hindu brethren in some parts of the country ought not to lead them to swerve from the path of duty, wisdom and honour which the Congress has chalked out for all the patriotic Indians to follow. I do not object to the representations being made to prevent any unjust preferential treatment being shown to the members of any particular community. It seems to me to be not inconsistent with the true spirit of a Congressman to point out and protest against any partiality shown to any member or members of any community on the ground of his or their belonging to that particular community. If a Mohammedan, Hindu or Christian is appointed to a post in the public service, on account of his merit, such an appointment is for the benefit of the public, and no one can have any reason to complain. If a Hindu is preferred to a Mohammedan, not because he has superior qualifications to serve the public, but merely because he is a Hindu, that is a just ground of grievance to the Mohammedans; and not only Mohammedans but all the communities will be entitled without departing from the principles of the Congress, to protest against such an appointment on the broad ground of equal justice for all and because it will excite jealousy and promote ill-will and disunion among people who ought to live in amity and good will. If on the other hand a preference is shown to a Mohammedan over a Hindu who is not surperior but inferior to him in merit and qualifications, a Hindu can protest as much as any other community against such an appointment without departing from the principle of the Congress. But pray let it be done, when it must be done out of a regard for the public interests which demand equality of treatment, and equal justice for all the communities. Let it be done with the desire of avoiding the causes of disunion. Let it not be done out of a feeling of narrow sectarian jealousy. Let us endeavour to win over our brethren who differ from us to the noble ideals which we have hitherto placed before us. Let not their faults lead us to turn away from those ideals. I have faith in the future of my country. I have no doubt that the policy of the preferential treatment of one community over another and all other obstacles which keep the great communities of India from acting together, will slowly but steadily disappear, and that under the guidance of a benign Providence feelings of patriotism and brotherliness will continue to increase among the Hindus, Mohammedans, Christians and Parsis, until they shall flow like a smooth but mighty river welding the people of all the communities into a great and united nation, which shall realise a glorious future for India and secure to it a place of honour among the nations of the world."

[In this congress 243 delegates were registered which was held on December 27-29, 1909 at Lahore]

CONGRESS AND THE POLITICAL REFORMS

The following speech was delivered by Malaviya in proposing a vote of thanks to the President of the Lucknow Congress in December, 1916.

"When we started in 1885, we reposed great trust and

confidence in those to whom the Providence had entrusted the guidance of the affairs of India. For the time we began with appealing, with praying, with begging, with entreating. resolution after resolution has been passed during the last 30 years; it is a written record which nobody can destroy or remove; it is a record showing the patience, the confidence the people of India had in the administrators of India. Their willingness to proceed by gradual steps, almost painfully slow steps, towards evolving a better system of administration. The record of these 30 long years tells us how we have asked not once, not twice, but repeatedly during these so many years. It is now, after an experience of 30 years, that the conviction has sunk into our hearts that those to whom the Providence has entrusted the administration of the affairs of India, the members of the Indian civil service as well as the members of the British parliament have failed and sadly failed to respond to the call of reason and justice. I am sorry to say it. I should have rejoiced if I could say in gratitude they had made a response worthy of the members of the great British nation. There has been some response in some of the small matters and for that we do feel grateful, but the response in all the most important matters has either been wanting or it has been sadly slow. The result of this is, that the conviction has come to us that unless we ourselves have a potent and determining voice in the administration of our country's affairs, there is not much hope for that progress which it is the birthright of every civilised people to achieve.

"We have on our record a repetition of resolutions asking for such simple justice as the separation of judicial and executive functions; we have on our record a cry of children for bread; repeated year after year to be given some education; we have on our record the fact that while we have prayed that primary education should be made compulsory and universal, the provision that has been made for it up to this time is extremely disappointing and unsatisfactory. We have on our record that even with the enlarged councils, when our dear brother Gokhale did make an attempt by introducing a Bill into the council to make provision for the permissive introduction of compulsory education, that effort was baffled by the solid official majority which sits in the council, to do no other work than simply to vote against the resolutions moved by popular representatives. On the other hand, what has happened to bring home the conviction to us we know. In Russia, there was no Self-Government until few years ago, but after being beaten by Japan, Russia learnt wisdom and roused herself into consciousness of what the conditions of modern civilisation required. The first Duma that met, I think in 1903, resolved, being conscious that primary universal education was one of the potent causes of building up a people, upon making education universal and compulsory. It introduced a programme of 19 years, during which period it decided that the elementary education shall become universal, and in the year 1916, nearly three-fourths of that programme has been carried out, and by 1922, the Russians will have provided elementary education to children of school-going age.

"That was the result of power being transferred from a sovereign authority or from a bureaucracy to those who know where the shoe pinches, who feel the need and the effect of unhappy conditions, and who understand how their interest can be best promoted. I have given to you that one illustration among many already given to you as showing the urgent, pressing need of having Self-Government for the people in order that they may administer their own affairs. Let nobody accuse the educated Indians of having put forward a proposal of reform in a light-hearted manner. That reform, so far as the government is concerned, is supported by the entire people, though there may be some small differences, as unfortunately there are with regard to some details. But so far as the government is concerned for the transfering of the power from the Government to the people themselves, this is a united demand on behalf of India and is made in no light-hearted fashion. This conviction is borne after 30 years of self-sacrificing labours in the country's cause, after having held 31 sessions of the Congress in the various parts of the country, which involved no small expenditure of time and money and comfort; this conviction is borne after the question had been weighed in all the possible aspects. The conclusion is forced on our mind that those who have the power are unwilling to part with that power and that those who have the power are unwilling to give the time and the attention to the consideration of your affairs, as the members of the British parliament are and that conviction once arrived at is not likely to be shaken or departed from.

"The reforms which you have put forward do not represent the maximum that you desire. They represent the minimum that is necessary. Let there be no misunderstanding about it. There are some very kindly friends who caution us and wish us to proceed slowly. We have proceeded cautiously and slowly for 30 years. It does not lie in the mouth of any member of the Indian civil service there are some very fine generous-hearted men amongst them—it does not lie in the mouth of any member of the Indian civil service or any member of the British parliament to say that the Indians are asking for an unreasonably large measure of reform today, or that they want to take a long jump. We do not want to take a long jump. There are certain conditions which determine what is necessary and what is not. It is the right of every people to govern itself. No government can be so good as the government of a people by their own people. That being accepted in England, that being accepted for the greater part of the rest of the civilised world, with what reason or justification can it be advanced here that we should be content to let our affairs be administered by a few men who, without any previous training, without any knowlege of our traditions, of our history, come to this country to enjoy a good salary and to spend a good period of their time in the sunny climate of our land? How can we expect they will be able to administer our affairs in the way in which we can? Objections have been urged but they have been refuted one by one. I do not want to detain you by recapitulating them.

"I wish and hope and pray that we shall realise fully the importance of the measures that we have put forward today, and that we shall be prepared to work to bring about their accomplishment. I hope that we will not be content with an expression of our gratitude to our president and expressing satisfaction at the result of this Congress, but that we are determined, as honest, honourable, manly men, to carry out to do our share of the duty of promoting these reforms and carry them into execution. For, remember that there is no greater duty than is cast upon us to see that these reforms are carried out and granted at an early date. Remember it is not a question of personal character with any one of us. We see millions of our countrymen suffering from the evil effects of the administration lacking in one direction or another to come up to the standard of their requirements. We see that those who have the power have failed to do it and what is more regrettable, do not show any willingness to respond to their call. I will draw your attention to one other matter only. There is the question of the employment of the Indians in the higher ranks of the army. You have proved by the blood our people have shed on the battlefield that you are not inferior to any other community or nationality on the face of the earth in bravery, in devotion, yet the ranks of the army have not been opened to our people. So also with regard to the Indian civil service. A Commission was appointed, a report has been made and it was presented to the government. It seems to be so ugly a production that the government have hesitated long to put it before the public. Now when that is the state of affairs, you cannot hope to bring about healthy, necessary reforms unless you get power into your own hands That is the conviction borne in upon us by these 30 years of labour, and I hope you will do all that is necessary to carry this conviction into effect. When you do so, this great gathering of the Congress will be remembered always as the one congress where this decision was arrived at, and you will always associate in your mind with the success of the Congress the arduous, the strenuous, the patient labours of our esteemed president, who has guided our deliberàtions for these four days."

INDIAN DEMANDS

Malaviya delivered the following speech in Hindi at the special provincial congress at Lucknow, on August 10, 1917.

A Retrospect

"Sisters and brethren, In order to understand the present political situation in India it is necessary to make a survey of the past which has led up to it. In doing so we must remember that the two great communities which inhabit India, the Hindu and the Mohammedan, are the inheritors of the two ancient civilisations. The Hindus ruled over this land for the thousands of years and attained a high degree of progress in civilisation which can be compared favourably with the other civilisations of the past or the present. When the Mahomadans came to India they brought with them their own unique civilisation and culture, which left its mark in Europe, and settled down in this country as its permanent inhabitants. Their best representatives achieved a high degree of success in the administration which they established here. Thus until a little over 150 years ago, when the British established a footing in India with a short interval India had been governed mainly by its own people. And even today nearly one-third of India is being governed by the Indians. In the face of these facts it is absurd for anybody to suggest that the Indians are not fit for governing themselves. But like every other great country India passed through a period of national decadence. It was at such a time that the representatives of certain European nations endeavoured to obtain political power in India. Of these the English were successful in doing so. They were distinguished among all the nations of Europe for having a liberal and popular system of administration. They were the first in the modern history to establish the principle of the government of the people by the people on a sound and unshakable basis. Other nations of Europe, America and Japan have taken their lessons in the parliamentary government from England and prospered under it. The Indians reconciled themselves to the English system of administration because it was based on the liberal principles. So long as the administration of what had come to be the British India was in the hands of the East India Company, the Charter which that Company held from the English Parliament was limited to the short period of twenty years. Every time the charter had to be renewed, the parliament made an enquiry into the administration of the country to satisfy itself that their administration of India was carried on in a manner calculated to promote the moral and material well-being of its inhabitants. On one of such occasions, in 1833, an act was passed by the English parliament which laid down that the natives of India shall, without distinction of race or creed, be admitted to the highest offices in the public services of their country for which their education and character qualified them. When, after the mutiny in 1858, the Government of India passed directly under the Crown, the great Queen of England, speaking as the representative of the people of the United Kingdom, gave solemn pledges to the people of India that they would be regarded as the equal fellow-subjects of the British people. When the Government of India Bill of 1858 was under discussion in the Parliament objection was taken to it on the ground that the principle of popular representation had not been recognised in the measure. It was urged that there was no better security for good government than national representation and the free expression of public opinion. But it was said in reply that 'You cannot have national representation at present in India.' But education was to be promoted and the Indians were to be employed in the high offices with the view, among other reasons, to fit them for the anticipated enlargement of their political powers. It was thus made clear that the intention was gradually to let the people of India have their proper share in governing themselves through their representatives.

Congress Demand for the Self-Government

"Under the Indian Councils Act which was passed in 1861 some of the Indians were appointed as members of the legislative council, but their presence counted practically for nothing, and as education advanced Indians began to feel that the affairs of their country were not being properly administered and would not be so administered unless and until they allowed a proper share in the administration. The very first Indian National Congress which met at Bombay in 1885 gave expression to this general conviction in its third resolution. Speaking in support of that resolution our revered countryman Mr Dadabhai Naoroji said that they had learnt from the English people how necessary representation is for good government; without it what good is it to India to be under the Britishers way. It will be simply another Asiatic despotism. We are only British drudges or slaves.

"At its second session, which was presided over by Mr Dadabhai Naoroji, the Congress recorded its fixed conviction that the introduction of the representative institutions would prove one of the most important practical steps towards the amelioration of the condition of the people, and that the reform and expansion of the imperial and provincial legislative councils had become essential alike in the interests of India and England. The Congress put forward a definite, well-considered scheme of such reform. It is important to recall the essential features of that scheme. Not less than one-half of the members of such enlarged councils were to be elected. Remember, this was thirty years ago. Not more than one-fourth were to be the officials having seats ex-officio in the councils, and not more than one-fourth were to be nominated by the government. All the legislative measures and financial questions including all budgets, whether they involved new or enhanced taxation or not, were to be necessarily submitted to and dealt with by these councils. The decisions of the legislative councils were, to be ordinarily binding upon the executive government, but the executive government was to possess the power of overruling the decision arrived at by the majority of the council in every case in which in its opinion the public interests would suffer by the acceptance of such decision. It was provided, however, that whenever this power was exercised a full exposition of the grounds on which this had been considered necessary should be published within one month, and in the case of the local governments they should report the circumstances and explain their action to the Government of India, and in the case of the latter, it was similarly to report and explain to the Secretary of State and in any such case, on a representation made through the Government of India and the Secretary of State by the overruled majority, a standing committee of the House of

Commons was to consider the matter, and, if needful, report thereon to the full House. You will note that in its essential features that scheme was similar to the one that was adopted last year by the Congress and the Muslim League as a definite step towards the Self-Government. In moving the resolution by which it was recommended, our esteemed countryman Mr Surendranath Banerjee said in 1886: 'Self-Government is the ordering of nature, the will of Divine Providence.' Every nation must be the arbiter of its own destiny such is the omnipotent fiat inscribed by nature with her own hands and in her own eternal book. But do we govern ourselves? The answer is, no. Are we then living in an unnatural state? Yes, in the same state in which the patient lives under the ministrations of the physician. Other speakers spoke in the similar strain.

"You know what happened afterwards. At the request of the Congress Mr Bradlaugh introduced a bill in the parliament to bring about a reform of the legislative councils. Thereupon the government introduced a bill which became a law in 1892 by which the councils were somewhat reformed. The reform, however, did not satisfy the needs of the country, and in 1905 our lamented brother Gokhale, speaking as the president of the Congress at Benares urged the further enlargement of the imperial and provincial councils and an expansion of their powers. He said that the goal of the Congress was that India should be governed in the interests of the Indians themselves and that in course of time a form of government should be attained in this country similar to what exists in the self-governing colonies of the British Empire. In the following year, Mr Dadabhai Naoroji, presiding in his 82nd year at the Congress at Calcutta, spoke in clearer and more emphatic language of the pressing need of the introduction of Self-Government in India. The whole of his address deserves to be read and re-read many a time. He claimed for the Indians in India all the control over the administration that the Englishmen had in England. He urged that this was a necessity if the great economic evil which was at the root of Indian poverty was to be remedied and the progress and welfare of the Indian people was to be secured. 'The whole matter', said our Grand Old Man, 'can be comprised in one word—Self-Government or *Swaraj*, like that of the United Kingdom or the Colonies.' In concluding his memorable address, the late revered countryman said: 'Self-government is the only and chief remedy. In Self-Government lies our hope, strength and greatness, I do not know what good fortune may be in store for me during the short period that may be left to me, and if I can leave a world of affection and devotion for my country and countrymen.' I say: 'Be united, persevere and achieve Self-Government so that the millions now perishing by poverty, famine and plague, and the scores of millions who are starving on scanty subsistence may be saved and India may once more occupy her proud position among the greatest and civilised nations of the world.'

"Mr Dadabhai Naoroji did not say that the complete Self-Government should be introduced at once. 'Has the time arrived', asked he, 'to do anything loyally, faithfully and systematically as a beginning at once, so that it may automatically develop into the full realisation of the right of Self-Government?' And he answered: 'Yes. Not only has the time fully arrived, but had arrived long past, to make this beginning. If the British people and statesmen make up their mind to do their duty towards the Indian people they have every ability and statesmanship to devise the means to accord Self-Government within no distant time. If there is the will and the conscience there is the way.'

"It was in response to our agitation that the Morley-Minto Reforms were introduced in 1909. They fell far short of the requirements of the situation, but we accepted them as a liberal instalment of the reforms needed to give the people a substantial share in the management of their affairs. But the experience of four years of the working of the reformed councils, showed the utter helplessness of the representatives of the people in those councils and a desire for a further substantial measure of reform began again to be urged at the Congress and in the press. The desire for a substantial step towards the Self-Government continued to express itself more and more in an emphatic manner in the years that followed.

In the Congress that was held at Bombay in 1915, the President Sir S.P. Sinha urged that the only satisfactory form of the government to which India aspires is government of the people, for the people and by the people.

"You will thus see that the cry for the Self-Government was- not raised merely during the present War and because of it, but is at least as old as the Indian National Congress itself. I have dwelt at such length upon this aspect of the question because efforts have been made in some quarters to create a prejudice against our proposals by the unfounded assertion that the cry for the Self-Government or Home-Rule was for the first time raised by Mrs Annie Besant two years ago and has since been taken up by the Congress. Mrs Annie Besant has done perhaps more than any other person during the last twelve months to carry on an active propaganda in support of the scheme of the Self-Government passed by the Indian National Congress and the All-India Muslim League. But she has not put forward any new or separate scheme of her own. There are not different schemes of the Indian National Congress and of the Muslim League and of the Home Rule League before the country and the Government. There is but one scheme, and that is the scheme jointly adopted by the Congress and the Muslim League. The Home Rule League has declared that it is carrying on a propaganda in support of the Congress and Muslim League scheme. If anybody is to blame for that scheme, it is the Congress and the Muslim League and not the Home Rule League.

Other Demands

"From what has been stated above it is clear that the Indians had been endeavouring for nearly a generation to obtain a real measure of the Self-Government in their country's affairs when the present War broke out in Europe. She had also been complaining for thirty years that the invidious distinction which the government made between the Indians and Europeans in the military administration of the country should be obliterated. She had long and repeatedly asked that the unmerited slur which the Arms Act, as at present administered, cast upon the Indians and the disadvantages to which it exposed them should be removed and that the rules under the act should be suitably modified to achieve these objects. She had asked that the commissioned ranks in the Indian army should be thrown open to all the classes of the Indian subjects to reasonable physical and educational tests, and that a military college or colleges should be established in India where proper military training should be given to the Indians. She had asked that the Indians should be allowed to join or raise the volunteer corps as their European fellow-subjects were allowed to do. These were some of the other long-standing grievances of India when the War broke out.

This Impetus of The War

"At the outbreak of the War His Majesty the King-Emperor was pleased to send a gracious message to the princes and people of India that he had entered upon the War in defense of the treaty rights and obligations and the cause of justice and liberty and the unmolested independent existence of nations, small and great. The princes and people of India loyally responded to His Majesty's appeal to stand up to fight for the right and the Empire. India will ever be grateful to Lord Hardinge for the courage, sympathy and statesmanship which he showed in deciding to send the Indian Expeditionary Force to Europe to fight for the King and Empire at a critical period of the War. India's loyal response and the splendid heroism of her sons in the battlefield won the hearty admiration and just appreciations of the leading members of the two Houses of Parliament, and of the press of England. Such was the situation.

What Did It Demand

"The first thing it demanded was that all invidious distinctions between the Indian and European fellow-subjects of His Majesty should once for all be obliterated. But it was a master for deep regret that except the limited unencouraging opening made under the Indian Defence Force Act, these distinctions remain as they were before the War broke out. Along with many others I have been urging for the last three years that commissions in the Indian army should be thrown open to Indians. I have been repeatedly told that the matter has been under consideration. I cannot but regret that the consideration has been so prolonged. The matter is one of simple justice. Expediency also demands that the exclusion of which Indians have so long complained should no longer continue to hurt and discourage them, particularly in view of the fact that the end of the War is not yet in sight and that there may yet be an unending call upon Indians to fight for the King and the country. For the same reasons the rules under the Arms Act which have produced a deplorably emasculating effect upon a large section of the people should be suitably modified. It is also essential that the recommendations which were made in the shape of amendments to the Indian Defence Force Bill and which were unfortunately rejected should be accepted by the government and provision made for the military training of the Indian youths between the age of 16 and 18 as has been made in the case of Europeans, and for the enrolment of Indians of higher age for Local military service as also had been made in the case of Europeans.

Constitutional Reforms

"As regards the constitutional reforms, the Congress and the Muslim League have recommended that His Majesty the King-Emperor should be pleased to issue a proclamation announcing that it is the aim and intention of the British policy to confer Self-Government on India at an early date. In view of the pronouncements of the responsible statesmen of England and some of the highly-placed officials in this country I cannot understand why the government cannot make such a pronouncement at once as there is evidently no serious difference of opinion about the Self-Government being the goal of British policy in India. As regards the definite steps towards the Self-Government which the Congress and the Muslim League have recommended should be taken after the War, there is no doubt a difference of opinion between some of the officials of the government and the representatives of the public. The difference reduces itself in reality to a question of the pace at which progress should be made towards the Self-Government. One should have thought that such a difference of opinion would not lead to a quarrel. But unfortunately this has not been so. There are some highly-placed officials in the Government of India and in several of the local governments who evidently think that the proposals of the Congress and the Muslim League in this direction are extravagant. His Excellency the Viceroy has told us that he and his councillors were engaged for six months during the last year in framing proposals of reform which in their opinion should be adopted at the end of the War and which they have submitted to the Secretary of State for the consideration of His Majesty's Government. Judging from the utterances of several provincial Governors these proposals seem to be of a minor character and to fall far short of the demands of the Congress. The public do not yet know what those proposals are. Our repeated request that they should be published has not been granted. They know that those proposals have been pressed upon the Secretary of State for his acceptance. It therefore clearly becomes our duty to carry on an educative and demonstrative propaganda in support of the proposals which the Congress and the Muslim League have jointly placed before the government.

"If the scheme of reforms which we have urged is adopted in full at the end of the War, as we desire it should be, it will not alter the form of our government. It will not break up the existing machinery and replace it with something new. The institution and departments which exist will continue. But what will happen will be that except in certain non-domestic matters, the voice of the legislative council, which will contain an elected majority of members, shall ordinarily prevail over the voice of the executive government, that all the financial proposals shall be laid before the legislative council and passed by it; and that in the executive council half the number of the members shall be the Indians. It is true that if these changes are adopted the character of the government will be radically altered. To the extent it will be, it will become a representative government but no untoward results need be apprehended from it. The Viceroy will have the power to veto any decision of the legislative council whenever he will deem it fit in public interest to do so. If this safeguard should not be considered sufficient to allay apprehension and to inspire confidence among our English fellow-subjects, further reasonable safeguards can be provided. But there is nothing in our proposals which can justify an attitude of anger and alarm on the part of any of our European fellow-subjects. I was amused to hear the other day that one of these and a quite sober and respectable gentleman said that he did not object to our desiring home-rule for ourselves but that he objected to his being placed under our rule. Well, nobody will force him into that position. If he is not prepared to live and work with us as an equal fellow-subject, he will be quite free to quit our country. But the steps towards the Self-Government which we desire to be taken after the War, will not yet convert the Government of India into an Indian government. They will convert it into a mixed government of the Indians and Englishmen. We are not working for a separation from England. We desire that even when the full Self-Government has been established in India, the connection between India and England should continue for our mutual advantage. There is nothing in that idea to hurt our national sentiment. The most powerful of the nations have found it necessary or advantageous to maintain friendly alliances with the other nations. But whether our connection with England will continue will depend very much on the attitude of our British fellow-subjects towards us, nor is there any occasion for those of our European fellow-subjects who are engaged in trade and commerce, to be alarmed at our proposals. If they are carried out and, if we get a fair chance of promoting the trade and prosperity of our country, we shall be able to do much greater trade with each other than we do at present. The history of several countries proves this beyond question.

Repression

"But unfortunately some of the advocates of the official proposals seem to have been so convinced of the reasonability of their own proposals, and of the extreme undesirability of the proposals of the Congress that they seem to have thought it their duty to use their official authority to discourage agitation in support of the popular proposals. I have not seen the circular which the Government of India is said to have issued to the provincial governments. But I have no doubt in my mind that such a circular was issued and that the several provincial governments based upon it the policy of repression which they have followed. It is also my conviction that the order of internment passed against Mrs Annie Besant, Mr Arundale and Mr Wadia was passed in pursuance of that policy. I do not say that Mrs Annie Besant never wrote anything which was open to the legal objection nor do I say that she did. What I do say is that if she infringed the law in speaking or writing, and if the infringement was serious enough to deserve action being taken upon it, she should have been proceeded against according to the ordinary law of the land. I consider that in the proceeding as the Madras government did against her and her two colleagues, they had abused the power which they possessed under the Defence of India Act.

"The Defence of India Act was clearly meant to be used against the enemies of the government. I do not believe and the Indians generally do not believe that Mrs Annie Besant is an enemy of the British Government. It is in this view that a feeling of great injustice is ranking in the public mind and it will continue to do so until she and her colleagues are released. It would be evidence of strength and not of weakness on the part of government, if out of deference to the Indian public feeling, it would cancel the order of internment in question, It should similarly cancel the orders of internment under which Messrs Mohammad Ali and Shaukat Ali have so long been deprived of their freedom of movement, without any definite charge being formulated and proved against them.

"We are often told that we ought not to agitate while the War is going on. Everyone will agree that those who are really busy with work connected with the War should not be disturbed. But how many people are really absorbed in work connected with the War? A War cabinet has replaced the ordinary British Cabinet and has set a number of the British Statesmen free to consider and work out many proposals of the reform, even constitutional reform of a far-reaching character. The Electoral Reform Bill has been passed. The Irish problem is nearing solution. Various committees have been busy formulating schemes for the development of the British trade after the War and the schemes of the improved national education. In India also it is but a few who are really so absorbed in the work connected with the War as not to be able to devote time to the other questions. His Excellency the Viceroy and his councillors did find time to formulate the proposals of reform. Owing to the War activities in several departments has been curtailed, and I hope I am not wrong in thinking that at no previous time did the officers of the government here find themselves so little pressed for time as many of them do at present. So far as we Indians are concerned, while we must do our duty in making such contributions to the War in man and money as we can, I shall be glad to know that outside the army there are many Indians in the country who have had the honour of any responsibility connected with the actual conduct of the War being placed upon them. Anyhow, many of us feel that as matters stand, we should be failing in our duty to our country and country-men and to our King-Emperor if we did not do what lies in our power to press the reforms which we consider to be essential for the progress and welfare of our people upon the consideration of the government. And this brings me to the question of what the Situation Demands of Us.

"The first thing is a clear realisation of what we desire to achieve. And the second, a firm determination to do all that is necessary to achieve it. As regards the first, I am sure that we educated men understand what the Self-Government or Home-Rule means. I am equally sure that there is a vast body of our countrymen and countrywomen who have to be taught to understand what the Self-Government means and to feel an earnest desire to obtain it. Let us remember that our English fellow-subjects are not easy to persuade. You must convince them that not only a few but the great bulk of our people desire Self-Government. And in this connection I cannot do better than remind you of the earnest advice given to us by Mr Dadabhai Naoroji in his presidential address in Calcutta in 1906. Said our revered leader: 'While we put the duty of leading us on the Self-Government on the heads of the present British statesmen, we have also the duty upon ourselves to do all we can to support those statesmen by, on the one hand, preparing our Indian people for the right understanding, exercise and enjoyment of the Self-Government, and, on the other hand, of convincing the British people that we justly claim and must have all the British rights. I put before the Congress my suggestions for their consideration. To put the matter in right form, we should send our "Petition of Rights" to His Majesty the King-Emperor, to the House of Commons and to the House of Lords, 'The next thing I suggest', said Mr Dadabhai, 'for your consideration is that the well-to-do Indian should raise a large fund of patriotism. With this fund we should organise a body of the able men and good speakers, to go to all the nooks and corners of India and inform the people in their own languages of our British rights and how to exercise and enjoy them; also to send to England another body of the able speakers, and to provide means to go throughout the country and by large meetings to convince the British people that we justly claim and must have all the British rights of Self-Government. Agitate, agitate over the whole length and breadth of India in every nook and corner peacefully of course if we really mean to get justice from John Bull. Satisfy him that we are in earnest. All India must learn the lesson of sacrifice of money and of earnest personal work. By doing that I am sure that the British conscience will triumph and the British people will support the present statesmen in their work of giving India responsible Self-Government in the shortest possible period. We must have a great agitation in England as well as here.' Agitate; agitate means inform. Inform, inform the Indian people what their rights are and why and how they should obtain them and inform the British people and why they should grant them. The organisation which I suggest, and which I may call a band of the political missionaries in all the provinces will serve many purposes at once to inform the people of their rights as the British citizens, to prepare them to claim those rights by petitions and when the rights are obtained, to exercise and enjoy them.'

"It was a matter of regret and reproach to us that we had not carried out this earnest advice of our revered leader so long. The Morley-Minto reforms of 1909 lulled us into the belief that we had got a liberal instalment of reform. But the experience of the last few years had shown that those reforms have not given any effective voice to the representatives of the people in the administration of the country's affairs; and now that the need for a substantial measure of reform towards the Self-Government is more keenly realised and the time forces are in a special degree favourable to the cause of freedom and Self-Government. I hope that we shall loyally respond to the exhortation of our departed Grand Old Man and earnestly carry on the agitation for the Self-Government on the lines indicated by him. I may here inform you that a petition to the parliament is under preparation, and will soon be ready and begin to be circulated for signatures. I trust you will obtain as large a number of signatures to it as you can. It is essential that between now and the meeting of the next Congress, we should thoroughly organise ourselves in the way suggested by Mr Dadabhai Naoroji and should preach the doctrine of Self-Government or Swaraj in every nook and corner of our provinces. We should establish Self-Government or Swaraj Leagues or Home-Rule Leagues, to propagate the idea and to enlist the intelligent and earnest support of our people for our proposals. I hope you will all endeavour to carry out this idea. I expect that the next Congress which will meet at Calcutta will be attended by a very large number of people. I presume you are aware that the joint session of the All-India Congress Committee and of the Council of the Muslim League has recommended that on the day the Congress will be held in Calcutta a Congress Durbar should be held in every district at which a translation of the presidential address should be read and the resolutions on the Self-Goveroment which were passed by the last Congress and the Muslim League in December last at Lucknow should be adopted. I feel certain that if we shall carry out the advice of Mr Dadabhai Naoroji we shall demonstrate that we deserve Self-Government and we shall win the first substantial step towards it, urged in the scheme of the Congress and the Muslim League within twelve months of the end of the present War. Right aud justice are on our side. The time spirit is with us. English statesmen have acknowledged and that India has freely given her lives and treasure in the cause of the Empire and that things cannot therefore be left as they are. If we do not win Self-Government now the fault will be entirely ours. To ensure success it is necessary that our agitation should be universal and intense. It is equally necessary that it should be strictly constitutional. Our position is clear and strong. We are not asking for separation from England. We are asking for Self-Government within the Empire under the British Crown. The cause of Self-Government does not require to be supported by the arguments showing wherein a foreign system of administration has failed. Self-government is the natural system of government. An alien government even at its best entails many inevitable disadvantages. Macaulay truly observed that no nation can be perfectly well governed till it is competent; to govern itself; and we are familiar with the dictum of Sir Henry Campbell-Bannerman that 'Good government could never be a substitute for government by the people themselves'. As Mr Dadabhai Naoroji put it we claim Self-Government as our right as British subjects, and even if the British system of administration in India were much less open to just criticism than it is, even then we should have been justified in asking for Self-Government. But while we frankly acknowledge the good that the British Government has done us in many directions, we cannot shut our eyes to its many shortcomings. Take for instance the question of education. Think of the state of general education in India when the English came to this country and compare it with what it is at present, and you cannot but feel grateful for what has been accomplished. But consider at the same time what remains to be done in the field of education. Compare the progress in education which the self-governing Japan achieved in thirty years with what has been achieved in double that period in India. In 1872, when Japan introduced its system of national education only 28 per cent of the children of school-going age were at school; by 1903 the percentage had risen to 90; it stands higher now. In India, after nearly 60 years of the great education dispatch of 1854 and the organisations that followed the percentage of the children of school-going age is still below 20! For decades past we have been urging that more and more should be done for the education of the people, but the progress achieved has been woefully slow. You will remember our lamented brother Gokhale introduced his Elementary Education Bill which would have permitted elementary education being made compulsory in certain areas in certain conditions, and you will remember that the bill was defeated by the opposition of the bureaucracy that governs us. It is surprising that we have come to the conviction that we shall never be able to properly promote the education of our people until we have a voice in the administration of our affairs! Similarly there is much to complain of in many other departments. Let us take the question of the employment of the Indians in the higher public services of the country. You know that the examination for admission into the Indian civil service is held in far-off England only. It is a manifest injustice to the Indians. Mr Dadabhai Naoroji began an agitation in 1867 that examinations for admission into the Indian Civil Service should be held simultaneously in India and in England to enable the youths of this country to have a fair chance of competing for the higher services of their own country. But half a century of agitation has not sufficed to secure that small justice to us. The result is, as has been pointed out by my friend Pandit Hirday Nath Kunzru in his recently published and excellent pamphlet on the public services in India, that on the April 1, 1917, out of 1,478 posts ordinarily reserved for the members of the Indian civil service, only 146 or about 10 per cent, were held by statutory natives of India! It hardly needs saying that if India had been governed in the interests of the Indians, we should have found the very reverse of this, viz., that 90 per cent, of the posts in question were held by the Indians and only 10 per cent, by the Europeans. The state of affairs out of the Indian civil service was hardly better. The total number of appointments, carrying a salary of ₹ 500 and upwards, was 5,390 in 1910, and of these only 17 per cent, were held by the Indians and 83 per cent, by the Europeans and Eurasians! This is on the civil side. So far as the army is concerned, it is entirely officered by our British fellow-subjects. Notwithstanding our repeated prayers, the commissioned ranks of the Indian army have never yet been opened to the Indians. Notwithstanding all the fidelity, devotion and heroism with which the Indians have served His Majesty and his predecessors for over a century they cannot yet rise beyond the position of *subedar-major* and *risaldar-major*.

"I will draw attention to only one other matter. We appreciate at its proper value the growth of the Indian trade and commerce. But it is largely in the hands of the Europeans. We have not been helped to obtain our fair share in it. And our industries have not been developed as they could have been developed and as they ought to have been developed. What is it that is responsible for these and many others of our grievances? It is the existing system of administration. Generally speaking, our English-fellow subjects who come to this country at the age of 25 or 21 and who retire from it for good at 55, cannot take that keen and abiding interest in promoting the interests of India and the Indians as we Indians can do; and, in the matters where there is a conflict between the interests of India and the Indians on the one side and of England and the Englishmen on the other, many of them not unnaturally place the interests of their own country and people before our interests. These and many other economic and administrative considerations which vitally affect the moral and material well-being of our people and determine our political status in the scale of nations, have ingrained the conviction in us, so well expressed by Mr Dadabhai Naoroji, that Self-Government is the only and chief remedy, and that in Self-Government lies our hope. Sisters and brethren, let us now put forth a sustained effort commensurate with the depth and earnestness of this conviction for achieving that which we consider to be best for our country and our people. Let us act without fear and without reproach, doing no wrong ourselves but not desisting from our duty even if a wrong should be done to us. It is a matter for thankfulness that unlike some of the other provincial governments the government of these provinces have taken up the correct attitude of not interfering with constitutional agitation for the Self-Government. I have every hope that they will continue in that attitude and that so far as these provinces are concerned there will be no unnecessary obstacles placed in our path. But notwithstanding this, and whether our work lies here or in the other provinces, it is essential that in taking up serious constitutional agitation, we all should have a clear mind and a firm determination as to how we shall discharge our duty. We should take every care to do nothing that is wrong, nothing that will expose us to just reproach. But if in spite of it, trouble should overtake us in the exercise of our constitutional rights, we must suffer it with calm determination and not run away from it. If we shall so bear ourselves, I feel sure that either obstacles will not arise in our path, or if they do, they will not take long to melt. We have really no enemies to be afraid of if we do not harbour an enemy within ourselves, which makes us slaves of fear and of personal selfish considerations. The path of our duty is clear. Let us tread it as men.

"Sisters and brethren, I have detained you very long, but before I resume my seat I should like to say just a few words which I wish would reach the ears of our fellow-subjects of the Indian Civil Service and the non-official European community in India. They both possess great influence and power in this country and they can influence opinion in England also. Many of them have lived long in or been connected with this country. We are entitled to claim sympathy from them in our aspirations and help and co-operation in realising them. It is possible that some of our proposals appear to some of them as impracticable and even extravagant. We are prepared to justify them, and where we cannot, to modify them. We do not claim infallibility for our judgment. I appeal to them to approach a consideration of our proposals in a spirit of friendliness and sympathy, and to help in bringing about a change in the constitution of the Government of our country which will be in consonance with the principles of liberty, justice and the free and unmolested existence and development of every people, for which the British Empire has been making an enormous sacrifice of life and treasure and which alone can ensure the right measure of happiness and prosperity to India and glory to England. I have the privilege of knowing several men among them who, though they do not see eye to eye with us, take a large-minded view of the relations which should exist between India and England in the future, who desire that justice should be done to India's claims. I appeal to them actively to throw the weight of their influence in favour of justice and freedom. And I hope I do not appeal in vain.

"But, however that may be, my countrymen, let us remember that the duty of working out our salvation lies principally upon ourselves. Let us do it faithfully and unflinchingly. Let us organise ourselves without any further loss of time, and arrange to preach the great *mantra*, the humane religion of Self-Government or *Swaraj* or home-rule in every home, in all the parts of our country. Let us teach every brother and sister Hindu and Mussalman, Parsi and Christian etc., young and old, humble as well as high, to understand the meaning of Self-Government, to desire it and to work for it, each to the extent of his or her ability with all the earnestness he or she can. In one word let us put our soul into the business, and God willing success will crown our efforts sooner than many of us at present imagine."

SELF-GOVERNMENT FOR INDIA

Speaking in support of the Self-Government Resolution at the Calcutta Congress of 1917, Pandit Malaviya said:

"We ask that the representatives of the people should have power to determine how the taxes should be raised as otherwise representation would be meaningless. The next demand that we make is that the representation of the people whom the government admitted into the councils should have power to control the executive. When the government introduced representative institutions in this country they must have foreseen, and if they have not they were very unwise, that representative institutions are a misnomer, if they did not carry with them power and responsibility of the people's representatives to control the action of the executive government. With that power follows the power of the purse. Our English fellow-subjects have taught us through their glorious literature that it is the people who pay the taxes, who ought to determine, through their representatives in the councils, how these taxes should be spent. That power of the purse is a national growth and development of the representative institutions. We have dealt with, the realities of the situation and we have to deal with the facts as you find them here today. The Congress-League scheme is a natural and rational advance upon the lines under which the political institutions have been working so far in this country. It is therefore no good telling us that our scheme does not fit in with the schemes formulated in the other countries. The Congress-League scheme is suitable to the conditions in India. Some of our critics tell us that the responsible government means a government which is responsible to the representatives of the people and removable at the pleasure of the representatives. I wish these critics showed a little more consideration, a little more generosity, in dealing with us and credited us with a little more commonsense. Self-Government means that the Executive is responsible to the people. When we spoke of Self-Government we spoke of Self-Government on the colonial lines. In the colonies the executive is responsible to the Legislature. That being so it is entirely wrong to say that in asking for Self-Government we are asking for something less than responsible government. It is said that we might have put into our scheme a little more generosity and a little more enthusiasm but you must remember that when they who put it forward had not only to think of you and me but of the bureaucracy and all those who are represented by Lord Sydenham and the framers were probably wiser in couching it in a language which may not satisfy us, but which has in it all the promise of the realisation of the responsible Government in the near future. The resolution says that Self-Government should be introduced in stages. The Congress did not ask that Self-Government on the colonial lines should be introduced at once. The next stage would be conferring of responsible Government to this country. The Congress programme is not inconsistent with the pronouncement made in the Parliament in August last. But you must remember that there are some who would make these stages occur at longer intervals than we desire. Let us, however, hope that our united voice and judgment will prevail against the voice of those who want to delay the period when the full responsible Government should be established in this country."

DELHI (33rd Session) PRESIDENTIAL ADDRESS

Pandit Madan Mohan Malaviya delivered the following Presidential Address in 1918:

"Mr Chairman, Brother-Delegates, Ladies and Gentlemen. I thank you all from the bottom of my heart for the honour you have done me in inviting me to preside over this great assembly. As has often been said the presidentship of the Congress is the highest honour which the people of this country can bestow upon any one. It is doubly so when it is conferred a second time. This honour is enhanced in the present instance by the fact that you have been pleased to call upon me to guide the deliberations of our great national assembly at a time when the momentous events which affect India as well as the rest of the civilised world are taking place, and when questions of the most far-reaching importance, which have a direct and immediate bearing on our future, are to be considered by the Congress. I am most deeply grateful to you for this signal mark of your confidence in me. I am also grateful to my esteemed friend Mr Vijiaraghavachariar, whom I so much miss in the imperial legislative council where his unyielding independence and incisive logic made him a source of great strength to the people's cause, for having retired in my favour because his selfless anxiety for the country's cause, and his partiality for an old friend, led him to think that my election would serve that cause better at this particular juncture. I sincerely wish I could feel that I deserved all this honour and confidence. I pray to God that with your generous help I may prove not unworthy of it, and that our deliberations may be such as will rebound to our credit and the honour and advancement of our country.

"The importance of this session of the Congress does not need to be emphasised. We meet today in this ancient capital of the Indian Empire, hoary with all its historic traditions and associations. It irresistibly brings to our minds a crowd of thoughts, happy and the reverse, of glories and the vicissitudes which our ancient land has undergone. The impulse to dwell upon them is strong, but 1 will not do so at this place. I will dwell here rather upon the living present. We are meeting at a time when the civilised world is celebrating the happy end of the greatest and bloodiest War known to history. That the end was announced in a memorable utterance by the distinguished Premier of England when, addressing the people of Britain, he said:

> You are entitled to rejoice, people of Britain, that the Allies, the Dominions and India have won a glorious victory. It is the most wonderful victory for liberty in the history of the World.

"You, too, my countrymen, are entitled to rejoice as you have actually been rejoicing, that this great victory has been won. You are also entitled to feel justly proud that our country has played a noble part in this great War, and made a magnificent contribution to its glorious end. As His Excellency the Viceroy very well said the other day:

> She was early in the field helping to stem the rush of Teutonic hordes and she has been in at the end, and her troops largely contributed to the staggering blow in Palestine which first cause our foe to totter to his fall.

"India had many grievances against England when the War broke out. But she had not lost faith in Britain's love of justice and liberty. And the moment the message of His Majesty the King of England and Emperor of India was received, announcing that he had been compelled to draw the word in defence of liberty and of treaty rights and obligations, India loyally put aside her grievances, buried her differences, and her princes and people readily identified themselves with the cause which England had taken up because it was the cause of fairness and liberty. Both our national traditions and our national aspirations predisposed us to that attitude. In days long past, the memory of which is still cherished, our ancestors had waged the greatest war recorded in our history—the *Mahabharata*—and sacrificed the entire manhood of the nation to establish "the triumph of righteousness". And for thirty years we had been carrying on a constitutional agitation to obtain some measure of power to administer our own affairs. Consequently all the classes and communities of our people enthusiastically united in giving an assurance of unswerving loyalty and unflinching support to His Majesty the King-Emperor in the prosecution of the War to a successful end.'[1]

"The ruling princes and the people of India made what His Majesty was pleased lovingly to describe in his gracious message of September 14, 1914, as "prodigal offers of their lives and treasure in the cause of the realm". Let us thank God that our deeds have been as good as our word. We have helped to the full extent of the demand made upon us, and more, in men, money and material. Both our honoured ruling princes and our peasants have contributed their quota of service to the War, and both have made money contributions in the numerous instances beyond their means. From the day His Majesty's message was received, India urged with one voice that her valiant soldiers should be sent to France to be in the forefront of the conflict. Our late Viceroy, Lord Hardinge, who was trusted by the Indians and who was trusted of them, appreciated our proposal and with the foresight and courage that distinguished him, he despatched the Indian troops to France. Both India and the Allies owe him gratitude for this act of statesmanship. Our troops saved the situation in France in 1914 and covered themselves with the glory. The full value of the contributions of the princes and people of India in money and resources remains to be calculated. But we know that it amounts to over two hundred millions, or three hundred crores. As regards our contributions in men, the Secretary of State for India stated the other day in the parliament that 1,161,789 Indians had been recruited since the War began and 1,215,338 men had been sent overseas from India, and that of those 101,439 had become casualties. These are the contributions of which we have every reason to be proud of. More proud are we of the fact that throughout all these four years of trials and tribulations, in the face of the extreme suffering which the War inflicted upon our people, and even when the sky seemed to be much overcast, India remained unshaken equally in her loyalty to the King-Emperor and in her resolve to do her utmost to help the Empire till the end. This is particularly noteworthy in the case of our Musalman brethren. Every one knows how deep are their religious sentiments towards Turkey, and how profound their concern in everything that affects her. When, therefore, unfortunately, Turkey was persuaded by the Central Powers to join them against our King-Emperor and his Allies, the feelings of our Mohammedan brethren were put to the sorest test.[2]

"No thoughtful Mohammedan could be indifferent to the fate which might overtake Turkey. But it must today be a source of the sincerest satisfaction to every Indian Mohammedan who loves his country and community, that the community did not at any time allow its religious sentiments to overpower its sense of duty to the King and to the motherland, and that it remained firm in its support of the cause of the Empire. This is a fact of great moment in the history of our country. It is a matter for sincere thankfulness and congratulations to all our fellow-subjects and ourselves.

"Before we proceed further, let me ask you, men and women of all faiths, whom it is my privilege at this moment to address, and who worship our one common God under different names and in diverse ways, to join in offering Him our humble and profound thanks that the War has come to a happy end, and in praying that it may prove to be the precusor of a lasting, just and universal peace. Let me next, on your behalf and on mine, offer our loyal greetings and dutiful congratulations to His Majesty the King-Emperor on the happy termination of the War.

"It gives us Indians particular satisfaction to think that while the despotic monarchs of the other lands have disappeared, our noble King-Emperor, exercising his beneficent power in consonance with the constitution of the country and the will of his people, sits even more firm in the affections of the people than before. We also offer our cordial congratulations to our fellow-subjects of the Britain, and their sturdy children in the dominions overseas, on the glorious result of their great efforts and sacrifices in the cause of liberty and right. If England had not joined the War and thrown her whole strength and resources into the fight, like Belgium, France would long ago have been compelled to give up the fight, and Germany's ambitions would have been realised. Great have been the sacrifices England has made.

"But greater therefore is the glory she has won. I am sure you also wish to offer your cordial congratulations to the noble people of France, who have won imperishable glory by sustaining the most splendid fight against tremendous odds in defence of their great land of liberty, equality and fraternity. We watched their struggle with the deepest sympathy and with the sincerest admiration; and it is a matter of particular pride and gratification to us to think that our Indian Expeditionary Force was able to reach France in the nick of time to be of help to them and to save the cause both of the Allies and of civilisation in the fearful struggle of 1914-15. Lastly, we must offer our thanks and congratulations to the great people of America whose unselfish entry into the War, involving all the tremendous sacrifice of men and money it did, was the finest tribute to the righteous character of the War which the Allies had been waging, as well as the greatest contribution to the cause of liberty and justice. Humanity owes a deep debt of gratitude to America for the decisive part which she has played under the wise and firm guidance of its noble President in the overthrow of the German militarism. Adopting the words of the president:

We must all thank God with the deepest gratitude that the

> Americans came into the lines of battle just at the critical moment when the whole fate of the world seemed to hang in the balance, and threw their fresh strength into the ranks of freedom in time to turn the whole tide and sweep off the fateful struggle.

"It is our privilege and our pride to send our congratulations to the people of those great nations because our soldiers fought on the same side with them on the battlefields of France and Flanders, and thereby established between them and us a comradeship in a righteous cause which we fervental hope will be the basis of lasting friendship between us."[3]

The Hand of Providence in the War

"Ladies and gentlemen, to my mind the hand of Providence is clearly discernible both in the development of this War and its termination. The world, and particularly the European world, needed a correction and a change. It had been too much given up to materialism and had been too much estranged from spiritual considerations. It had flouted the principle that righteousness exalteth a nation. In spite of the vaunted civilisation of Europe, some of its nations have been living in a state of international anarchy and their relations to one another and to the outer world turned upon force. They have been dominated by an overpowering passion for wealth and power, and in their mad pursuit of it have trampled upon the rights and liberties of the weaker states and peoples. Spain, Austria, and France each sought the mastery of Europe in the past. Germany attempted it this time. England has not, since the fifteenth century, attacked the independence of any European State, but has befriended them when they have been threatened by their more powerful neighbours. But she too has followed a different policy in Asia and Africa. During the last half century only, she has waged wars to annex Egypt, the Sudan, the South Africa Republics, and Burma, besides several other minor Wars. There have been great quarrels among the nations of Europe about markets and colonial possessions. There have been contentions between France and Germany for the control of Morocco, between Russia and Austria for the: control of the Balkans, between Germany and the other powers for the control of Turkey. These great rivalries among them have led them to live in constant fear of war, and ever to keep themselves prepared for it. The earth has been groaning under the burden of big battalions and armaments. There have been treaties and alliances, but they were entered into to keep up the balance of power among them. The determining factor in the international relations has been force. Any nation which wished to attack another could do so with impunity if it made itself superior to that other in brute force. England had, by a long course of events, gained the highest position and power among the nations of Europe. She naturally wanted to maintain it at all costs. Her younger sister Germany became jealous of her and was fired with the ambition to outshine her. For decade past she pursued a systematic policy of national development—military, naval, industrial, economic—with the object of striking a blow for word-power. She converted a whole nation into a wonderfully well-organised disciplined, and equipped army. It is difficult to imagine how any nation can prepare itself better to carry everything before it by force than did Germany. She wanted only to breake the peace of the world when she thought it was most advantageous for her to do so. Her force was strengthened by the forces of her stubborn allies. On the other side were arrayed the forces of the Allies—English, French, Russian, Italian the people of the dominions and of India. It is difficult to imagine a stronger array of forces on either side than there actually was in this War. If diplomacy had not led Russia to fail the Allies, they might probably would have succeeded earlier. But the purpose of the War would not have been served in that way. The War therefore went on in its grim horror. A few months before the termination of hostilities it seemed as if the Germans were going to succeed. The hearts of France and England and the rest of the allied world trembled with fear that in spite of all the combined efforts of the Allies and all the sacrifices which they had undergone for four years, the Germans were going to succeed in their wicked ambilion. But they were not to succeed because they were in the wrong. Providence had decreed that the Allies should succeed because they were in the right. But Providence did not yet bless their efforts, for they still had to learn that the laws of Karma are inexorable and that 'Our acts our angles, are good or ill. Our fatal shadows that walk by us still.'

"Many of the Allies also had too often in the past acted on the evil principle that might is right, and not all of them perhaps were yet prepared to act in their dealings, with all the nations and people on the principle that right is might.

"At the special Service of penitence and humble prayer held on the third anniversary of the War, the high-souled Lord Bishop of Calcutta dwelt upon the fact that time and again the Allies had been held back from victory by the circumstances which were not or could not be expected. And His Lordship said: 'What was God saying all this while to our nation and the Empire? 'you must change, you must change, before I can give you victory.' You must change, is addressed to the nation as a whole and to all the individuals of it. The United States of America joined with us, and their adhesion makes the continuation of the War certain. Thus our nation is granted another chance to change itself. The same divine demand is reiterated, 'you must change before I can give you the victory.'

"It was the evident purpose of the Providence that the powerful nations of the world should undergo a moral rebirth and not only that this War should re-establish the principle that might is right, but that international anarchy should be ended and the warring nations of the world should agree to establish a moral order and a permanent arrangement among them to ensure just and fair dealings with one another and the rest of the human family in the future. For the accomplishment of this purpose it was necessary that the War should not end until America joined it and until the nations agreed to the peace proposals which were to be the basis of this order. It was therefore only when they had so agreed that the Providence enabled America to come in at the critical moment to help the Allies and to turn the scale against Germany.

"This is not a matter of mere inference and argument. President Wilson has distinctly said that America did not come into the War merely to win it. As he put it, 'She came in to be instrumental in establishing peace against the violence of the irresponsible monarchs and the ambitions of the military coteries and make ready for a new order, for new foundations of justice and fair dealing.'

" 'We are about to give order and organisations,' said the great American who has evidently been appointed by God to be the master mason in building the new temple of the international justice, 'We are about to give order and organisation to the peace not only for ourselves but for the other people of the world as well, as far as they will force us to serve them. It is the international justice that we seek and not the domestic safety.'

"He had outlined the basis of peace. The allied government had accepted his proposals at once; the central powers when, they could not help doing it. And he is now at the Conference at Paris to help in the settlement of peace. As he recently said, 'Peace settlements which are now to be agreed upon are of transcendant importance to us and to the rest of the world. The gallant men of our forces on land and sea have consciously fought for the ideals of their country. I have sought to express, these ideals and they have been accepted by statesmen as substance of their own thought and purpose. As the associated governments have accepted them, I owe it to them to see to it so far as in me lies that no false or mistaken interpretation is put upon them, and no possible effort omitted to realise them. It is now my duty to play my full part in making good what they offered their lives and blood to obtain.'

The Ideals of America

"Now what are the ideals that America has fought for? President Wilson stated them in the clearest terms in his memorable address to the Congress on the 9th of January last. It is necessary to recall them to mind. He said:

> The way of conquest and aggrandisement and secret understanding is past. We entered the War in consequence of the violations of right which touched us to the quick and made our life impossible unless they were corrected and we would be secure against their recurrence. We therefore demand that the world should be made safe and fit to live in. All people of the

world are in effect partners in this interest. Therefore, the programme of the worlds peace is our programme.

"He then enumerated his famous fourteen points. Briefly put these were:

1. Open covenants of peace openly arrived at without any secret diplomacy
2. The freedom of the seas subject to certain international conditions
3. Removal of all the economic barriers and equality of trade conditions among all people consenting to the peace and associating for its maintenance
4. National armaments to be reduced to the lowest point consistent with the domestic safety
5. Free, open-minded and absolutely impartial adjustment of all the colonial claims based on the strict observance of the principle that in determining such questions the sovereignty and interest of the populations concerned must have equal weight with the equitable claims of the government whose title is to be determined
6. The evacuation of all the Russian territories and the securing to her of unhampered and unembarrassed opportunity for independent determination of her own political development and national policy
7. The evacuation of Belgium and the complete restoration of her sovereignty
8. The evacuation of all the French occupied territories and the restoration of Alsace-Lorraine
9. The readjustment of the frontiers of Italy along the clearly recognisable lines of nationality
10. Securing to Austria-Hungary the opportunities for autonomous development
11. The settlement of the disputes of the Balkan States by mutual agreement and international guarantees of their political and economic independence and territotrial integrity
12. Securing sovereignty to Turkey over the Turkish

portions of the present Ottoman Empire, but assuring security of life and autonomous development to the other nations now under Turkish rule

13. The creation of an independent Polish State with international guarantees of the political and economic independence and territorial integrity, and
14. The formation of a general association of nations under specific covenants for the purpose of affording mutual guarantees of political independence and territorial integrity for the great and small states alike.

"President Wilson concluded his message to the Congress with the following summary of the ideals of America:

> An evident principle runs through the whole programme I have outlined. It is the principle of justice to all the people and nationalities and their right to live on equal terms of liberty and safety with one another. Unless this principle be made its foundation, no part of the structure of the international justice can stand. The people of the United States could act upon no other principle; and in vindication of this principle they are ready to devote their lives and honour and everything they possess. The moral climax of this culminating War for human liberty has come, and they are ready to put their own strength, their own highest purpose, their own integrity and devotion to the test.

"These noble sentiments are worthy of the great people of America and, I am sure, they have filled all the lovers of right and liberty with gratitude and the hope of a better world. There have been attempts made before this to have international disputes settled by arbitration. There have been organisations made for preventing wars and preserving peace among nations. But never before in the history of the world has there been such a great attempt at establishing new foundations of justice and fair dealings among the nations and at forming a worldwide organisation to carry out the scheme. The Great War was needed to bring this about. The fact that three such liberty-loving nations as Great Britain, France and America are united in purpose to give effect to these proposals, and that Germany, Russia and all the other nations concerned have accepted them, is a matter for most sincere thanks-giving and congratulation. If the proposals are carried out, as we must all hope and pray they will be, they will go far to establish a reign of righteousness among the nations and usher a new era of peace on earth and goodwill among men. If this comes about, the enormous sacrifices of life and treasure which the War has entailed will have been made to good purpose. I am sure, my countrymen, that you who are the inheritors of the great spiritual civilisations, most heartily and reverently welcome these proposals and that you will be willing to undergo any sacrifices to give them your cordial support. I would suggest that as representatives of the one-fifth of the human race and of this great and ancient land, we should send to the gentlemen who are engaged in this holy task at Paris, our respectful good wishes and our fervent prayers for the success of their noble undertaking. I venture to suggest that we may also convey to them a humble expression of our willingness to contribute whatever lies in our power to the success of the scheme. We may assure them that thousands of our young men will gladly and gratefully enroll as Soldiers of God in any international organisation that may be formed to support the proposed League of Nations.

India and the Peace Conference

"You will remember, ladies and gentlemen, that when speaking of our contributions to the War, Mr Lloyd George had promised that India's necessities would not be forgotten when the Peace Conference would be reached. We are thankful to him and to the British Cabinet generally for having recognised the justice of India's claim to be represented at the Conference. We are also thankful that the Government has appointed an Indian—our distinguished countryman Sir S.P. Sinha—to represent her at the Conference. But he has been appointed by the Government of India without any reference to the public. As he has been so appointed, presumably he will represent at the Conference views which are in consonance with the views of that Government. It may be that those views will be in agreement with the views of the Indian public, or it may not be so. We do not know what are the conditions under which

Sir S.P. Sinha has been appointed, or what instructions the Government of India has given him. Unfortunately, the Government of India is not yet responsible to the Indian public; and, as matters stand, there often is a great divergence of views between them and the public of India. This being so, one may be allowed to say, without any reflection against my esteemed friend Sir S.P. Sinha and without forgetting how much he has by his character and talents contributed to the cause of the Indian progress, that it would have been more in consonance with the spirit and aim of the Conference, and also in keeping with the proposals of the constitutional reform which contemplate the appointment of ministers from among the elected members of the councils, if the government had seen their way to ask the Congress and the Muslim League which they knew were going to meet here this week, or the elected members of the imperial and provincial legislative councils, to recommend an Indian or Indians for appointment by the Government as India's representatives at the Conference. In view of the fact that Canada is going to have as many as six representatives, it need not have been apprehended that a request that India should be allowed to have more than one representative would be regarded as unreasonable. There is a widespread opinion in the country that something like this should have been done. This view is not urged because of any delusion that the proposals for the constitutional reform relating to India will be discussed at the Peace conference. I suppose every one understands that they will be discussed in the British Parliament. But it is urged because of the belief that the principles, and even some of the concrete proposals which will be discussed and settled at the Peace Conference, will have a great, direct and indirect, bearing on interests of our country. This cannot be disputed. If it were not so, there would have been little meaning in appointing as an Indian to represent "India's necessities" at the Peace Conference. I am glad that His Highness the Maharaja of Bikaner will be there to represent the views of the Indian States and Ruling Princes, whose steadfast loyalty to and support of the King-Emperor during this War has been of ten times greater value than their liberal contributions in men and money alone. But it will remain a matter for regret that British India will not be represented at this great Conference by a person appointed by the government on the recommendation of the elected representative of the people.

India's Position

"India, ladies and gentlemen, occupies at present an anomalous and unhappy position. The people of India—Hindus, Muslim, Parsis and Christians—are the inheritors of great and ancient civilisations. About a hundred and fifty years ago, the whole of India was under the rule of Indians. At that time she was passing through one of these periods of decay and internal disorder which are not unknown in the history of other nations. By an extraordinary combination of circumstances, which had their origin in the conditions then prevailing, India came to be placed under the rule of the people living six thousand miles beyond the seas and strangers to the Indians in race, religion and civilisation. As has often been said, India was never conquered by the English in the literal sense of the term. The English became the paramount power in India by a series of events carried on by the help of the Indian soldiers and the Indian allies.

"The people supported them and welcomed them because they promoted order and peace and introduced justice and good administration. In the early days of British rule in India, English statesmen regarded it as of a temporary character. They clearly said that it was their duty to so administer India as to help her to take up her own government and to administer it in her own fashion. But as time rolled on, and the vested interests grew up and became strong, a contrary spirit came to dominate British policy in India. The administration came to be conducted less and less in a manner conducive to the development of the people as a nation and more and more so as to perpetuate their subjection. Indians noted it and protested against it. Many large-hearted Englishmen deplord it. Foreign critics also noted the fact. An eminent Frenchman, M. Challey, wrote in his book puplished a few years ago:

> Had England taken as a motto 'India for the Indians', had she continued following the idea of Elphinstone and Malcolm to consider her rule as temporary, she might, without inconsistency, grant to the national party gradual and increasing concessions which in time would give entire autonomy to the Indians, but that is not now her aim.

"For half a century and more, Indians and Liberal-minded Englishmen had been urging England to adopt the policy of giving power and opportunity to the Indians to administer their own affairs. Thirty years before the War, the Indian National Congress came into existence and it had ever since its birth urged that a fair measure of Self-Government should be given to the people. The scheme of reform which the Congress put forward in 1886, was calculated to secure them such power but they have not got it till now. Since 1908 we had specially stated that Self-Government on the colonial lines was our goal.

"I draw attention to these facts so that it may be remembered that we had been pressing for recognition of our right to Self-Government long before the War. It is not the War, its events, and its results that have led us to ask for Self-Government for the first time. Even if the War did not come, our claim to it should have been granted, long ago as a mere matter of right and simple justice. The War, no doubt, came to help us. The contributions which we were able to make brought about a happy change in the angle of vision of English statesmen. In December 1916, our two great national institutions, the Congress, and the Muslim League, that is to say, the representatives of thinking India, jointly, put forward a well-considered moderate scheme of reform which would have given to the people a substantial measure of Self-Government. It is an open secret now that the response which the Government of India suggested to this demand was so poor and inadequate that Mr Austen Chamberlain returned the proposals and suggested the preparation of a more liberal measure which would give some responsibility to the people. In the meantime, agitation in support of the Congress-League scheme was growing. The executive governments in India, imperial and provincial, were generally strongly opposed to the proposals, many of them showed this opposition by trying to suppress the agitation by orders internment under the Defense of India Act and in other ways, and created much unnecessary tension in public feeling. On the other hand, besides the Indians there were Englishmen and Englishwomen who urged that the promise of Self-Government should not be delayed. That high-souled Englishman, the Lord Bishop of Calcutta, said in the course of the service to which reference has been made before: 'We must not look at our paramount position in the light of our new war ideals. The British rule in India must aim at giving India opportunities of self-development according to the natural event of its people. With this in view the first object of its rules must be to train Indians in Self-Government. If we turn away from any such application of our principles to this country, it is but hypocrisy to come before God with the plea that our cause is the cause of liberty.'

"The situation rendered an early announcement of the intentions of the government necessary. It was in this state of affairs that the Secretary of Stale for India made the now famous declaration of the August 20, 1917, in which he definitely stated that the gradual development of self-governing institutions with a view to progressive realisation of the responsible government in India as an integral part of the British Empire was the policy of His Majesty's Government and that they had decided that substantial steps in this direction should be taken as soon as possible.

"It was a momentous utterance. But it was unnecessarily cautious and cold. We did not like all the qualifying conditions with which it was weighted. But we looked at it as a whole. It promised that substantial steps in the direction of the goal of the responsible government in India would be taken as soon as possible, and that His Majesty's Government had decided that, accepting the Viceroy's invitation, the Secretary of State should shortly visit India to consider what those steps should be and to receive suggestions of representative bodies and others regarding them. It also promised that ample opportunity would be afforded for public discussion of the proposals which would be submitted in due course to the parliament. We therefore welcomed the announcement and were grateful for it. Though dissatisfied with its many qualifying conditions, in the circumstances then existing, we accepted it with hope and gratitude. Mr Montagu came to India with a deputation of the distinguished men. Taking the announcement of the 20th August as laying down the terms of their reference, he and Lord Chelmsford elaborated proposals as to the first substantial steps which should be taken to give effect to the policy enunciated in it. The limitations of the announcement naturally had their effect in determining the nature and extent of their proposals. These proposals have now been before the public for several months. They have been criticised by the various bodies. On the first publication of the proposals, while some of our prominent publicmen gave them a cordial welcome, others condemned them as unsatisfactory and disappointing. Some urged their total rejection. The Congress-League scheme which had been put forward with the unanimous support of the public men of the country was calculated to transfer control to the representatives of the people, both in the provincial government and, subject to certain reservations, in the Government of India. The official scheme proposed a limited measure of control in the provincial governments and absolutely none over the imperial government. The official proposals thus fell very short of the Congress-League scheme. They were, therefore, generally regarded as inadequate. It was clear that while acknowledging that the proposals constituted an advance on existing conditions in certain directions, the bulk of the public opinion in India was not satisfied with the scheme as it stood. Almost everybody who was anybody wanted more or less important modifications and improvements in the scheme. But the scheme proposed the introduction of a certain measure of the responsible government in the provincial governments, and was in this respect more in conformity with the announcement of the 20th August than the Congress-League scheme, and many of us urged that the official proposals should be accepted subject to the necessary modifications and improvements. This view found general acceptance in the country.

"When the special Congress met at Bombay, it was apprehended in some quarters that the opinions of those who were in favour of insisting upon the acceptance of the Congress-League Scheme and the rejection of the official proposal, might prevail, at the Congress. But proceedings of the Congress lent no support to these apprehensions. While the Congress made its acknowledgments to Mr Montagu and Lord Chelmsford for the earnest attempt to inaugurate a system of the responsible government in India, it made it clear that it regarded the proposals as they stood as unsatisfactory and disappointing. At the same time it recognised that the official scheme was more in consonance with the announcement of August 20th, and it therefore decided to accept that scheme in its outline and to urge modifications and improvements consistent with the outline which, in its opinion, were absolutely necessary to make it a substantial first step towards responsible government in India, that is, both in the central and provincial the governments. The All-India Muslim League also adopted the same view. Two months after, conference, organised by those of our prominent public men who had more cordially welcomed the proposals of reform than the great bulk of the public, met at Bombay. They too agreed with the Congress and the League in asking for certain essential modifications and improvements in the scheme. It has thus become as clear as noon-day light that enlightened Indian public opinion is unanimous in urging that the principle of the responsible government should be introduced in the Government of India simultaneously with a similar reform, in the provinces, and that there should be a division of functions in the central government into reserved and transferred as a part of the first instalment of reforms. It is unanimous in urging the fiscal freedom for India. It is unanimous in urging that half the number of the members of the council of state should be elected.

"It is unanimous in urging that the Indians should constitute one-half of the executive government of India. It is unanimous in asking that the popular houses should elect their presidents and vice-presidents. It is unanimous in requiring that the elective majority should be four-fifths; and that the reserved list should be as small and the transferred list as large as possible. It is unanimous in asking that the Ministers should be placed on a footing of perfect equality with the members of the executive council. It is unanimous in asking for a complete separation of the judicial from the executive functions. It is unanimous in urging that 50 per cent of the posts in the Indian civil service, and to start with, 25 per cent of the King's Commissions in the army, should be secured to the Indians, and that the adequate provision for training them should be made in the country itself. It is unanimous in urging that the ordinary constitutional rights, such as freedom of the press and public meetings and open judicial trials should be safeguarded, though there is a difference of opinion about the methods suggested to secure the end. I have not attempted an exhaustive enumeration. My object here is to show that there is notwithstanding differences over unimportant matters and notwithstanding all that we hear of divisions and parties, practical unanimity in the country about the most essential changes and improvements which are needed in the proposals of reform. I will not anticipate your decisions. It is for you to decide whether in view of the events which have taken place since the Congress met, you will reconsider any or all of the matters which were considered by the special Congress, or whether you will let its decisions stand as they are. Considering how grave and momentous are the issues involved, I would reconsider them and welcome any suggestions which would improve them. Since the Congress met, events have taken place which would obviously justify such a course. As a mere illustration, I draw attention to one. In the resolution relating to the provincial government, while holding that the people are ripe for the introduction of full provincial autonomy, the Congress said it was yet prepared, with a view of facilitating the passage of the reforms, to leave the departments of law, police and justice (prisons excepted) in the hands of the executive government for a period of six years. Since this resolution was passed, the Functions Committee as well as the Franchise Committee have already visited several provinces, and in two of the major Provinces it has been urged that the full provincial autonomy should be granted there at once, namely, the United Provinces and Bombay, in the former by the Provincial Congress Committee, and in the latter by the non-official members of the Bombay Legislative Council, among whom are such esteemed gentlemen of known moderate views as the Hon'ble Gokuldas Parekh. We may assume that Bengal and Madras also will demand full provincial autonomy. In view of these facts the resolutions of the Congress on the subject may well be reconsidered.[4]

India and The Results of the War

"But, ladies and gentlemen, by far the most important event which has taken place since the Congress met is the happy termination of the War. In concluding their report on the Indian Constitutional Reforms Mr Montagu and Lord Chelmsford said:

> If anything could enhance the sense of responsibility under which our recommendations are made in a matter fraught with consequences so immense, it would be the knowledge that even as we bring our report to an and far greater issues still hang in the balance upon the battlefields of France. It is there and not in Delhi or Whitehall that the ultimate decision of India's future will be taken.

"Happily for India and the rest of the civilised world that decision has now been taken. It was announced in the memorable utterance of the Premier referred to before, in which he said:

> You are entitled to rejoice, people of Britain, that the Allies, Dominions and India have won a glorious victory. It is the most wonderful victory for liberty in the history of the world.

"How does this great event affect our position? How far is India going to share the fruits of the glorious victory to which it has been her privilege to contribute? It is highly encouraging in this connection to remember how generous has been the appreciation expressed by the distinguished Premier and other statesmen of Great Britain of the services of India to the War.

Let me recall a few of their utterances. Speaking in September, 1914, Mr Asquith, the then Prime Minister of England, said:

> We welcome with appreciation and affection India's preferred aid in the Empire which knows no distinction of race or class, where all alike are the subjects of the King-Emperor and are joint and equal custodians of her common interest and fortunes. We hail with profound and heart-felt gratitude their association side by side and shoulder to shoulder with the Home and Dominion troops under a flag which is a symbol to all of the unity that the world in arms cannot dissever or dissolve.

Mr Bonar Law said: 'I do not think we fully realise how much these Indians who have fought and died by the side of our soldiers have helped us through these long months.

"Speaking on the 9th September, Lord Haldane, the then Lord Chancellor of England, said: 'Indian solders are fighting for the liberty of humanity as much as ourselves. India has freely given her lives and treasure in humanity's great cause; hence things cannot be left as they are.' Speaking in February 1917, in the House of Commons, Mr Lloyd George said: 'The contribution of the Dominions and of India has been splendid. The assistance they have given us in the most trying hours of this campaign has been incalculable in its value.'

"In the introduction to Col Merewether's Indian Corps in France, Lord Curzon said: 'Indian Expeditionary Force arrived in the nick of time, that it helped to save the cause both of the Allies and of civilisation after the sanguinary tumult of the opening weeks of the War, has been openly acknowledge by the highest in the land from the Sovereign downwards. I recall that it was emphatically stated to me by Lord French himself. The nature and value of that service can never be forgotten.'

"Speaking again in the House of Commons Mr Llyod George said:

> And then there is India. How bravely, how loyally, she has supported the British Armies. The memory of the powerful aid which she willingly accorded in the hour of our trouble will not be forgotten after the war is over, and when the affairs of India come up for examination and for action.

"Speaking on the 8th of November, Mr Lloyd George said:

> These young nations (the Dominions) fought bravely and contributed greatly and won their place at the Council Table. What is true of them is equally true of the Great Empire of India, which helped us materially to win these brilliant victories which were the beginning of the disintegration of our foes. India's necessities must not be forgotten when the Peace Conference is reached. We have had four years of great brotherhood. Let it not end there.

"I am sure, ladies and gentlemen, we all feel most deeply grateful to our English fellow-subjects for their generous appreciation of our contributions to the War. The question now is to what extent is India going to benefit by the principles for which she gave her lives and treasure, namely, the principles of justice and liberty, of the right of every nation to live an unmolested life of freedom and to grow according to its own God-given nature, to manage its own affairs, and to mould its own destiny. The principles for which Great Britain and the Allies fought have now been embodied in the Peace proposals of President Wilson to which I have referred before. These principles have been adopted with the hearty concurrence and support of Great Britain.

"Indeed, the credit for adopting them is in one sense greater in the case of Britain and France than in the case of America. For Britain and France had borne the brunt of the War for four years and by their unconquerable courage and heroic sacrifices had also been incomparably greater than those of America and their feelings far more deeply injured. It was the more praiseworthy of them, therefore, that they readily agreed to the Peace proposals, which ran counter in some instances to the decisions which they had themselves previously arrived at.

"Now the principle that runs through the Peace proposals is the principle of justice to all people and nationalities and their right to live on equal terms of liberty and safety with one another. Each nation is to be given freedom to determine its own affairs and to mould its own destinies. Russia is to have an unhempered and unembarrassed opportunity for independent determination of her own political development and national policy. Australia-Hungary is to be accorded the opportunity of autonomous development. International guarantees of political and economic independence and territorial integrity are to be secured to the Balkan States, and to the independent Polish States which are to be created. Nationalities other than Turkish now under Turkish rule are to be assured security of life and autonomous development.

"In the adjustment of the colonial claims the principle to be followed is that in determining such questions the sovereignty and interests of the population concerned are to have equal weight with the equitable claims of the government whose title is to be determined. How far are these principles of autonomy and self-determination to be applied to India? That is the question for consideration. We are happy to find that the governments of Britain and France have already decided to give effect to these principles in the case of Syria and Mesopotamia. This has strengthened our hope that they will be extended to India also. Standing in this ancient capital of India, both of the Hindu and Mohammedan periods, it fills me my countrymen and countrywomen, with inexpressible sorrow and shame to think that we, the descendants of Hindus who have ruled for four thousand years in this extensive empire, and the descendants of Musalmans who have ruled here for several hundred years, should have fallen from our ancient state, that we should have to argue our capacity for even a limited measure of autonomy and self-rule.

"But there is so much ignorance among those who have got a determining voice in the affairs of our country at present that, if I but had the time, I would tell them something of the capacity of our peoples—Hindus and Musalmans—till the advent of the British rule in India. I may refer those who care to know it, to the papers published at pp. 581-624 of Mr Dadabhai Naoroji's book—*Poverty and un-British Rule in India*. I will content myself with saying that one-third of India, comprising a population of nearly 60 millions, is still under Indian rule, and that the administration of many of the Indian States compared favourably with that of the British India. Has the fact of our being under British rule for 150 years rendered us less fit for self-rule than our fellow-subjects in our Indian States are?

"Are the people who can produce a scientist like Sir J.C. Bose, a poet like Sir Rabindranath Tagore, lawyers like Sir Bhashyam Iyengar and Sir Rash Behari Ghosh, administrators like Sir T. Madhava Row and Sir Salar Jung, judges of the High Court like Sir Syed Mahmood and Telang, patriots and public men like Dadabhai Naoroji, Mahadev Govind Ranade, Pherozeshah Mehta and Gopal Krishna Gokhale, industrialists like J.N. Tata and his worthy son Sir Dorab Tata and a servant of humanity like Mr Mohandas Karamchand Gandhi and soldiers who have rendered a good account of themselves in all the threatres of War, unfit for a measure of Self-Government in their domestic affairs? I hope that the insult of such an assumption will no longer be added to the injury that is being done to us by our being kept out of our birthright to Self-Government, and that the principle of self-determination will be extended to India.[6]

The Principle of Self-determination

"Ladies and gentlemen, let us make it clear what we mean when we talk of self-determination. There are two aspects of self-determination, and it has been spoken of in the Peace proposals. One is that the people of certain colonies and other places should have the right to say whether they will live under the suzerainty of one power or of another. So far as we Indians are concerned we have no need to say that we do not desire to exercise that election. Since India passed directly under the British Crown, we have owed allegiance to the Sovereign of England. We stand unshaken in that allegiance. We gladly renewed our allegiance to His Majesty the King-Emperor in person when he was pleased to visit India in 1911 after his Coronation in England. We still desire to remain the subjects of the British Crown.

"There is, however, the second and no less important aspect of self-determination, namely, that being under the British Crown, we should be allowed complete responsible government on the lines of the Dominions, in the administration of all our domestic affairs. We are not yet asking for this either. We are asking for a measure of Self-Government which we have indicated by our Congress-League Scheme of 1916. We urge that the measure of Self-Government, i.e., of responsible government, to be given to us should be judged and determined in the light of the principle of self-determination which has emerged triumphant out of this devastating War. In order that this should be done it is not necessary that the proposals of reform which have been elaborated by Mr Montagu and Lord Chelmsford should be laid aside and a brand-new scheme be prepared. The Special Congress and the Muslim League have expressed their willingness to accept those proposals with the modifications and improvements which they have advocated. This great Congress representing the people of all classes and creeds—Hindus, Mussalmans, Parsis and Christians—representing all interests, landholders and tenants, merchants and businessmen, educationists, publicists and representatives of the other sections of the people is assembled here today to express the mind of the people on this question. One special and particularly happy feature of this Congress is the presence of merely nine hundred delegates of the tenant class who have come from far and near, to join their voice with the rest of their countrymen in asking for a substantial measure of Self-Government. The representative Congress of the people of India will determine and declare what in its opinion should be the measure of reform which should be introduced into the country. Let the British Government give effect to the principle of self-determination in India by accepting the proposals so put forward by the representatives of the people of India. Let the preamble to the statute which is under preparation incorporate the principle of self-determination and provide that the representatives of the people of India shall have an effective voice in determining the future steps of progress towards complete responsible government. This will produce contentment and gratitude among the people of India and strengthen their attachment to the British Empire.

Our Caluminators

"Ladies and gentlemen, I think I have said enough to show how strong is our case on the ground of justice for a substantial measure of the responsible government. While we have noted with thankfulness the attitude of the British statesmen towards the cause of the Indian reform, while we have noted with satisfaction that in their election manifestoes, Mr Lloyd George, Mr Bonar Law, Mr Asquith, in short, leaders of all parties in the United Kingdom, have pledged themselves to the introduction of the responsible government in India, we regret to find that a Limited Liability Company of businessmen known as the Indo-British Association have organised themselves in London with the distinct object of opposing the cause of the Indian reform. This Indo-British Association and other narrow-minded European and Anglo-Indian bodies in India and in England, who are opposed to any power being transferred to Indians have been misusing the Rowlett Committee Report to create a wrong impression in the minds of the British public that the people of India are disaffected towards the British Crown. This is a wicked attempt. One should have thought that with the overwhelming evidence of the loyalty of the people of India to the British Crown, fresh in the minds of the English people and of the Allied world, not even the worst detractors of Indians would venture to make such a dastardly attempt at this juncture. The Rowlett Committee itself has brought the fact of that loyalty into great prominence. The committee have summed up their conclusions as follows:

> We have now investigated all the conspiracies connected with the revolutionary movement. In Bombay they have been purely Brahmin and mostly Chitpavan. (I am quoting from the Report and not expressing my own opinion). In Bengal the conspirators have been young men belonging to the educated classes. Their propaganda has been elaborate, persistent and ingenious. In their own province it has produced a long series of murders and robberies. In Bihar and Orissa, the United Provinces, the Central Provinces and Madras it took no root but occasionally led to crime or disorder. In the Punjab the return of emigrants from

> America bent on revolution and bloodshed produced numerous outrages and the Ghadr Conspiracy of 1915. In Burma too the Ghadr Movement was active but was arrested. Finally came a Mohammedan, conspiracy confined to a small clique of fanatics and designed to overthrow the British Rule with foreign aid. All these plots were directed towards one and the same objective—the overthrow of the British Rule in India by force. Sometimes they have been isolated, sometimes they have been interconnected, and sometimes they have been encouraged and supported by the German influence.

"Now, ladies and gentlemen, assuming that the whole of this statement is correct, let us see what the committee says further about these plots. They say, 'All have been successfully encountered with the support of Indian loyalty.' This should be enough to silence the calumniators of India. Mr Montagu and Lord Chelmsford observed in their report on the Indian Constitutional Reforms: 'Whatever qualifications may be needed in the case of the particular classes, the people of India as a whole are in genuine sympathy with the cause which the Allies represent. However much they may find fault with the government, they are true in their loyalty to the British Crown.' In another place they truly observed: 'The loyalty of the country generally was emphasised by the attempts made by a very small section of the population to create trouble.' I most sincerely deplore as I am sure every thoughtful Indian does, that any of our youths should have been misled into what the Rowlett Committee has described as a movement of perverted religion and equally perverted patriotism. I deplore that even a few of our young men should have been misled into criminal organisation or conspiracy against the government. I equally deplore that they should have committed acts of violence against any of their follow-men. But let not the misdeeds of a small number of the unfortunately misguided youths be pitted against the unswerving loyalty of 320 millions of people of India. It is not fair.

"But unfair though it is, our opponents are making a strenuous endeavour to defeat the cause of reform or to whittle down the reform proposals by misrepresenting us and it is necessary for us to correct their misrepresentations and to show

how strong is the case for reform. We have to emphasise that apart from any considerations of the government here being a good or bad government, we are entitled to have Self-Government as every other nation is entitled to have it. Sir Henry Campbell-Bannerman said years ago that 'Good government is no substitute for Self-Government.' Speaking in the House of Commons at a much earlier period, in the thirties of the last century, Macaulay truly observed that 'No nation can be perfectly well governed unless it governs itself.' No arguments are therefore needed to justify our request that we should also be allowed to govern ourselves. The justice of our case is overwhelmingly strong. With all the advantages that it has, and which we gladly and gratefully acknowledge, the system of government which has been introduced into India, has numerous defects in it. We have acknowledged its good points repeatedly; we have also pointed out its weak points repeatedly. By way of illustration I will invite attention to some of these here. Every nation is entitled to administer its own affairs. It follows that the people belonging to the Indian nation should manage their own affairs. As I said before, when the British Government was established in this country, their idea was that their rule should be temporary, only to enable the Indians to regain, to readjust their lost balance and be able to take charge again of their own affairs. A number of the British statesmen have said that they were only the guardians of the welfare of the people of India.

Europearising The Service

"But the system of administration which has been established is opposed to this idea. Under it, the European Agency has been introduced into the administration in such an enormous way that all the services are dominated in the higher branches by the Europeans. The result has been that the opportunities have not been given to the Indians to exercise the power of administration, which alone could enable them to exercise power successfully and satisfactorily, and the Europeans have been imported in large numbers from England, not only for the military services but also for the civil services. At present the position is, and has been from 1833, when the statute was passed, that the statute declared that no Indian subject of His Majesty would be debarred from obtaining, or holding any appointment, for which he is qualified. This is a rule for which we have often expressed our gratitude. But, ladies and gentlemen, in justice the rule should have been different and more liberal so far as the Indians are concerned. It should have been that the Indians should be employed in the various public offices of their country and that only where the circumstances made it necessary, should the Europeans, who possessed expert or special knowledge, be employed in any department. Thus, the correct rule which should have been followed has not been followed. In spite of the Statute of 1833, very few Indians were appointed. Then came the Mutiny and the Indian Civil Service Act was passed. It was decided that the examination for the civil services would be held in London only. For examining even the Indians as to their qualifications for serving in India, the examination was to be held in England; the Indians prayed that the examination should be held at least at the same time in India also. A committee appointed by the Secretary of State reported in favour of the simultaneous examinations in both the countries. But that recommendation has been disregarded. Mr Dadabhai Naoroji spent sixty years of his life in agitating for this simple measure of justice. It is painful to remember that he died without seeing it accepted. The result has been that though an agitation for the admission of the Indians into all the higher departments of the public services of the country has been carried on for over sixty years, we have not yet got a fair footing in those services. At the time when the Public Services Commission reported in 1914, less than 10 per cent of the posts were filled by the Indians and over 90 per cent were filled by the Europeans. That was in the Indian civil services. In the other services also the Europeans have had a practical monopoly of all the higher posts.

Taking the Military Services

"For a long time past the Indians have been urging that a fair number of commissions in the army should be thrown open to them. The demand has not been met. The Duke of Connaught recommended many decades ago that a military college should be established in India for training the Indians as officers. Since the Congress met in 1885, it has repeatedly urged that such a college should be established and commissions in the army should be thrown open to the Indians. This was not done. I know it for a fact that when the Coronation Durbar was to take place in India in 1911, Lord Hardinge had recommended that the Kings' Commission should be thrown open to the Indians. That was not done. Years rolled along, but the bar justice which the Indians had been praying for was not done. Then came the War. We offered, unanimously and from all sides, our loyal support to the government. We urged that our soldiers should be sent to France and Flanders to fight in defense of the Empire and in vindication of the principles of liberty and justice. We also prayed with an unanimous voice that commissions in the army should be regularly thrown open to the Indians. The War went on for three years without our last prayer being heeded. When the Indian soldiers serving in the ranks had won Victoria Crosses, when they had again established their valour and fidelity in many fields, then came the announcement that ten commissions in the army would be open to the Indians and only five persons, I understand, have so far been nominated to these commissions; for, four men were given only temporary commissions. We naturally feel that justice has not been done to us inspite of all that we have done during this War.

"Ladies and gentlemen, there are so many other matters in which our reasonable demands have not been conceded, in which justice has not been done to us. The administration has been unnecessarily expensive. In the military services and in the civil services, high salaries are paid, mostly to the Europeans, and the country thus loses every year an enormous amount of money which should be distributed among its own children. If three-fourths of the expenditure on the European services were to be spent upon the Indians, India would be in a far more prosperous condition than she is or can be in so long as the existing state of things continues. But our repeated requests for a reduction of high salaries is met by a further increase in those salaries and the substitution of Indians for the Europeans is still a matter for further consideration.

General Failure of the Bureaucracy

"Take again the question of education. We have been praying that education should be made universal and better. We have not been able to persuade the government to do so. Gokhale introduced a bill to make it permissive for the municipalities to make primary education compulsory. That bill was not allowed to pass. We acknowledge with gratitude all that the Government has done since then in the matter of education—primary, secondary, university. But we feel that what has been done is very small compared with what remains to be done.

"Then there is the question of the poverty of the people and of public health. Poverty has been very deep and widespread. We have urged measures to remove it. There have been numerous famines during the last century, and we have lost millions of people from death and famines. Public health has been low. The mortality from plague has been very great. During the last 20 years we have lost many times more lives from plague than what have been lost during the whole of this devastating War in Europe. The vitality of our people is poor; the average duration of life is shortened. The whole situation is painful. As a partial but important remedy, we have urged and urged, the Famine Commission also urged, that indigenous industries should be promoted and encouraged. They did so in 1880. Since then the Congress has repeated the prayer, but that prayer has not been listened to. It was only when the War broke out that the Industrial Commission was appointed and you have only to read its report to realise how great, how sad, has been the loss which the country has suffered by reason of industries not having been encouraged. There are many other departments in which the existing system of government has failed the people. Take for instance the question of currency. The needs of the great bulk of the people of India, who owned their little savings in silver, were not sufficiently considered when the mints were closed to silver in 1893. In other respects also the needs of the people of India have not been met in the matter of currency and banking. I do not want to prolong the list. My object in drawing attention to these is to emphasise the fact that the bureaucratic system which exists at present has failed. While we gratefully acknowledge that it has achieved a good deal, while we acknowledge all the good that it has done, we say that it has failed very largely to promote the welfare of the people as it should have promoted. I cannot express this idea better than in the words of Lord Mayo who said many years ago:

> We have not done our duty to the people of this land. Millions have been spent on the conquering of the race which might have been spent in enriching and in elevating the children of the soil. We have not done much and we can do a great deal more. We must first take into account the inhabitants of the country. The welfare of the people of India is our primary object. If we are not here for their good. We ought not to be here at all.

"This was said by Lord Mayo nearly fifty years ago. Of course, things have improved in some directions; but a great deal more yet remains to be done. This is a very brief and imperfect summary of our complaint against the system which exists, and it is our settled conviction that Self-Government is the only remedy. It is therefore that we press for it with all the earnestness we can command.

"And now, ladies and gentlemen, I wish to put in a word of appeal here to the Indian Civil Services. I was surprised and pained as I am sure, you all must have been, to read a circular issued by the Secretary to the Indian Civil Service Association or somebody like that in Bihar, asking them for an organised expression of opinion on behalf of the civil services with regard to the reform proposals. Of course everybody is free and every civilian as much as any one else, to hold, and if he so chooses, to express his individual opinion about any matter in which he feels interested. But that members of the Indian civil services should as a service organise a united expression of their opinion against the Reforms, is a thing which has shocked Indian sentiments. The circular points out that an impression has gained that the Service is favourable to the proposals and that this effort has been made to remove that impreression or correct it. The circular further says that such an effort is being made in every province. I appeal to the members of the Indian civil service to think whether this is a right course for them to pursue in the matter of constitutional reforms in India. They have covenanted to serve India. Many of them have served her well and we feel grateful to them for it. Many Indian civil servants have laid India under a deep obligation. We cherish the honoured name of Allan Octavian Hume who was the founder of the Indian National Congress. We revere the memory of the godly Sir William Wedderburn who devoted all his time up to the last moment of his life to the promotion of the good of India. We have the respected name of Sir Henry Cotten whose lifelong service to this country will not easily be forgotten. Even now there are many members of the Indian civil service retired, and even in the service itself, who are really and truly the friends of the people of India. I expect every fair-minded man among them will agree that any attempt made by the service as a body to prejudice the cause of reform or to oppose it, will be a matter for most serious complaint to the people of India. We look forward to their co-operation in any measure of reform that may be introduced. We hope that the advice which Lord Hardinge gave them would be remembered by them, and that they would all put their intellect and strength of character in supporting the liberal reforms and making them successful rather than in opposing them or getting them whittled down. I have already referred to the misuse which is being made by some of our opponents of the Rowlatt Committee's recommendations. There is also unfortunately the opposition organised in England by the British Indian Association and the opposition of the Europeans in this country. If the Indian civil services will at this critical juncture throw in their united weight against the proposals for reform, it would be a matter of which India will have serious reason to complain. This is a juncture when it is necessary that the cause of India should be correctly and faithfully represented, and we expect that members of the Indian civil service will stand up for the interest of India and of the Indians, for justice to the people of the country in the service of which they have enrolled themselves and spent the best of their years.

"Ladies and gentlemen, I have shown that we have many complaints against the existing bureaucratic system. I have also said that Self-Government is the only remedy. It is our conviction that if we Indians had an effective share in the administration of our affairs, we should have managed things very differently. How we should have managed them is not a mere matter of conjecture, but is clearly shown by the resolutions that we have passed during the last 32 years in regard to many questions of public interest Those resolutions show that if we had an effective voice, an effective control in the administration of our country's affairs, we would probably have achieved at least half as much progress as the Japanese have achieved, that our people would have been more prosperous, more contented, and in every way more happy then they are at present. We ask for this opportunity of the national self-development, and trust that our British fellow-subject, including those in the Indian civil service, will support and help us in this demand. It is particularly necessary that they should help us against those who are misrepresenting us and making a misuse against us of the recommendations of the Rowlatt Committee. I have expressed before this my whole-hearted condemnation of the ways pursued by some of our misguided youths. I deplore that they were misled. But what is now of importance is to remember the circumstances under which the evil tendencies grew up among them. I would ask every Englishman who considers this question to make a mental survey of what passed in India from the period of 1897 to 1915. I would ask him to remember that it was the Plague Administration in Poona that gave rise to alarm and resentment among the people and led to the unfortunate murder of the two Englishmen and to the deportation of the Natu brothers. I would ask him to remember the partition of Bengal. I would ask him to remember the repressive measures which were adopted to put down the agitation against the partition; also the various other repressive measures passed between 1817 to 1915. I will then ask him to consider what has been done by the government in the same period in the matter of reforms and in redressing the grievances of Indians. He will have to recognise that while on the one side there were causes created for discontent, the reasonable demands which the Indians had been making were not granted. Our industries were not encouraged. The difficulty in finding careers for our young men was growing. Education was not sufficiently spread; poverty was increasing, racial inequality was kept up between the Europeans and Indians: there were invidious distinctions made between the Indians and Europeans in the services and in the matter bearing arms. All these causes contributed to a state of feeling which might well lead, deplorably but pardonably, some Indian youths into the paths of sedition. If our English friends will bear these facts in mind, I think they will arrive at a more just judgment that they are likely to do otherwise. All that I would say to them is that remedy for the state of things which the Rowlatt Committee deplore, assuming their conclusions to be correct, lies not in forging any repressive legislation but in granting large and liberal measures of reform, which will remove the root-causes of discontent and promote contentment and satisfaction among the Indian people.

The president then referred to the urgent need of sending a deputation to England to plead for India's cause and concluded as follows:

Self Determination

"Ladies and gentlemen, I have already tried your patience hard and I would not detain you longer. But before I conclude let me say one final word to you. The situation is this. Our cause is just; the opportunity for pressing it is favourable. But our opponents are strong and well-organised. There is great need of sending a strong deputation to England so that our cause may not suffer for want of good and proper advocacy. I hope therefore that you will decide to send such a deputation at an early date. But the strength which your deputation will possess, the influence which it will exercise, will be derived from you. So it is the organisation which you will create in India, the solid sentiment upon which your political organisation will be built up here, which will determine the strength and influence which your deputations will have in England. To that end I ask your attention to the one principle which seems to be very much in favour with you just now. And that is the principle of self-determination. You have asked that the British Government should extend the principle of self-determination to India in her political reconstruction. I ask you, my brothers and sisters, to apply that principle to your affairs so far as it lies in your power. I ask you to determine that henceforward you shall be equal fellow-subjects of your British fellow-subjects and equals of all the rest of your fellow-men in the world. I ask you to determine that hereafter you will resent, and resent most strongly, any effort to treat you as an inferior people. I ask you to determine that henceforward you will claim, and claim with all the strength that you command that in your own country you shall have opportunities to grow as freely as Englishmen grow in the United Kingdom. If you will exercise this much of self-determination, and go about inculcating these principles of equality, of liberty and of fraternity among our people, if you will make every brother, however humble or lowly placed he may be, to feel that the ray Divine is as much in him as in any other man, however highly placed he may be; if you will make every brother realise that he is entitled to be treated as an equal fellow-subject, you will have determined your future for yourself, and then those who are in power will not long be able to resist any of your reasonable demands. I ask you, my brethren, to give this matter your most earnest consideration. You have got the opportunity now. The scheme of reforms which has been proposed gives you the opportunity. Whatever may be the powers which may be entrusted to the provincial and the central governments, electorates must be formed and the councils must be expanded. The formation of electorates gives you the best chance to instruct every one of your fellow-men in the political principles which you wish he should understand and follow, and upon which our future construction should rest. I appeal to you to begin your efforts, to organise and instruct our future electorates, that is to say our fellow-men who will exercise the power that we seek should be given to them. I appeal to you to establish Congress committee in every *Taluka* and every *Tehsil* and see that the people understand these principles. If you will do this, if you will work in that spirit with that determination, if you will show that much of self-determination and work unitedly with one purpose, I am sure, God will grant us self-determination earlier than we many of us imagine we are going to get it."[8]

Resolutions Adopted by the Congress

1. India's Loyalty

Resolved that this Congress most respectfully begs to convey to His Majesty the King-Emperor its deep loyalty and profound devotion to the Throne and its congratulation on the successful termination of the War which was waged for the liberty and freedom of all the peoples of the world.

2. Allied Forces

(a) Resolved that this Congress desires to place on record its profound appreciation of the brilliant gallantry of the Allied Forces and particularly of the heroic achievement of the Indian Troops in the cause of Freedom, Justice and self-determination.

(b) That the foregoing Resolution be communicated to the Government of the Allied Nations and the United States of America through His Majesty's Secretary of State for India and to His Excellency the Commander-in-Chief of India.

3. Re-Affirmation of the Resolutions

Resolved that this Congress re-affirms resolutions 2, 3, 4, and 11 passed at the Special Session of the Indian National: Congress held in Bombay.

4. Self-Government

(a) Resolved that this Congress also re-affirms Resolution No. 5 relating to the Self-Government passed at the Special Session of the Congress held in Bombay, subject to this, that in view of the expression of the opinion in the country since the sitting of the said Special Session, this Congress is of opinion that so far as the provinces are concerned, full Responsible Government should be granted at once and that no part of the British India should be excluded from the benefit of the proposed constitutional reforms.

(b) That non-official Europeans should not be allowed to form the separate electorates on the ground that they represent the mining or the tea industries, and if they are allowed such representation they should be limited to their proportion compared to the population of the Provinces concerned.

5. Indian Civil Service

Resolved that this Congress re-affirms No. 6 of the Special Congress demanding that 50 per cent of the Indian civil services should be recruited in India.

6. Reform in the Punjab

Resolved that this Congress views with grave apprehension the attempt made in certain quarters to assign an inferior position to the Punjab in the reform-scheme, and urges that having regard to its political, military and historical importance, its wealth, education, social advancement and its magnificent services during the last war, the Punjab should be placed on a basis of equality with Bengal, Madras, Bombay, and the United Provinces.

7. Reform in Delhi

Resolved that this Congress strongly recommends that Delhi should be constituted into a Regulated Province, that it should have legislative council to assist the Chief Commissioner, and that it should have at least two representatives in the legislative assembly.

8. Reform in Ajmer-Merwara

Resolved that having regard to the special importance of the Ajmer-Merwara and British Rajputana as a model for the

Native States, this Congress supports the claim of that Province that its status should be that of a Regulated Province, and that a Council consisting of a majority of the elected representatives of the people, should be provided in the reform Scheme, and that the two elected representatives of the Province should be allowed on the proposed Legislative Assembly.

9. Women's Franchise

Resolved that this Congress urges that women, possessing the same qualifications as are laid down for men in any part of the scheme, shall not be qualified on account of their sex.

10. Rowlett Committee

Resolved that this Congress views with alarm the recommendations of the Rowlatt Committee which, if given effect to, will interfere with the fundamental rights of the Indian people, impede the healthy growth of the public opinion and would also prejudicially effect the successful working of the constitutional reforms.

This Congress urges on the Government to remove from the Statute Book immediately The Defense of India Act, Bengal Resolution HI of 1818, Bombay and Madras Resolution of 1819 and 1827 respectively, the Press Act, the Seditious Meetings Act, the Criminal Law Amendment Act, and the other similar repressive measures curtailing the liberty of the subject.

This Congress further urges upon the Government that all the detenues, interned or externed, under the Defence of India Act, or the aforementioned regulations, and all the political prisoners should at once be set at liberty as an act of amnesty in view of the victorious termination of the War, as also to ensure the success of the new regime under the new scheme.

11. Self-Determination

Resolved that in view of the pronouncement of President Wilson, Mr Lloyd George, and other British statesmen, that to ensure that future peace of the world, the principle of self-determination should be applied to all the progressive nations.

Be it resolved—

1. That this Congress claims the recognition of India by the British Parliament and by the Peace Conference as one of the Progressive Nations to whom the Principle of Self-Determination should be applied.
2. That in the practical application of the principle in India the first step should be:
   (a) The removal of all the hindrances to free discussion, and therefore the immediate repeal of all the laws, regulations and ordinances restricting the free discussion of the political questions whether in the press, private or public meeting, or otherwise, so that the legitimate aspirations and opinions of all the residents in India may be fearlessly expressed; further, the abolition of the laws, regulations, and ordinances, which confer on the Executive, the power to arrest, detain intern, extern, or imprison any British subject in India, outside the processes of ordinary Civil or Criminal Law, and the assimilation of the law of sedition to that of England.
   (b) The passing of an Act of Parliament which will establish at an early date complete responsible Government in India.
   (c) When complete responsible government shall be thus established, the final authority in all the internal affairs shall be the supreme Legislative Assembly as voicing the will of the Indian Nation.

Resolved further—

(d) That in the reconstruction of the Imperial policy, whether in matters affecting the inner relations of the nations constituting it, in questions of foreign policy or in the League of Nations, India shall be accorded the same position; as the Self-Governing Dominions.

12. The British Indians

Resolved that this Congress re-affirms the resolutions, passed at the previous Sessions of the Congress, on the subject of the status of the British Indians in the Self-Governing Dominions and the Crown Colonies of the Empire, and once again places on record its sense of resentment and ever-growing dissatisfaction at the continued ill-treatment of the Indian settlers in the Dominions and the Colonies, earnestly hoping that in view of the readjustment of the relations between the component parts of the Empire the statesmen and people of Great Britain will endeavour to redress the grievances of the Indian Settlers.

13. Representation at the Peace Conference

Resolved that this Congress urges that injustice to India, it should be represented by an elected representative or the representatives, to the same extent as the Self-Governing Dominions at any Conferences that may be held to deliberate on or settle the terms of peace or reconstruction.

In view of the shortness of time, and in anticipation of the request made in the preceding part of the resolution being acceded to by His Majesty's Government, this Congress elects as its representatives Bal Gangadhar Tilak, M.K. Gandhi and Syed Hasan Imam.

14. The Industrial Commission

Resolved that while generally welcoming the recommendations of the Industrial Commission and the policy that in future the government must play an active part in promoting the industrial development of the country, the Congress hopes that in the practical application of this principle, the object kept in view will be the encouragement of the Indian capital and enterprise and the protection of this country against the foreign exploitation, with the sole aim of making India industrially and economically self-contained and self-dependent.

This Congress places on record its regret at the exclusion of the tariff-question from the scope of the Commission's inquiries and reiterates its opinion that the industrial development of the country is impossible without the fiscal autonomy being granted to her.

This Congress agrees with the Commission that industry

should have separate representation in the Executive Council of the Government of India but it is of the opinion that an Imperial Industrial Executive Board is not necessary.

This Congress welcomes the recommendation of the Commission that the Provincial Department of the industries should be constituted at an early date and urges the same on the Government of India.

This Congress urges that Imperial and Provincial Advisory Boards should be constituted for the purposes of promoting industrial development and that they should the consist of the Indians elected by the Indian industrial and trades associations and by the Chambers of Commerce.

This Congress is of the opinion that the proposed Imperial Industrial and Chemical Services should be constituted on a scale of salary and with the object of having them manned fully by Indians but that the Europeans who are experts in any line should be engaged on short-term agreements till they can be replaced by the duly-qualified Indians.

This Congress is of the opinion that the government should invite the universities to establish commercial colleges and should help them to; do so by the substantial grants.

This Congress regrets the absence in the report of the recommendations for the adequate organisations for financing industries and urges upon the government the urgent necessity of starting the Industrial Banks on a scale commensurate with the vast and costly machinery recommended in the Report.

This Congress conveys to the Hon'ble Pandit Madan Mohan Malaviya the profound gratitude of the country for his able, closely-reasoned and comprehensive minute, attached to the Report which puts the case for the Indian industrial development in an unanswerable form.

15. War Expenditure

Resolved that having regard to the unprecedented economic strain to which India has been subjected during the period of the War, and considering the injury likely to be caused to the infant or the nascent industries of the country by the addition of any further burden of heavy taxation, as well as by the facilities enjoyed by the competing foreign industries, and in view of the cessation of hostilities, the Congress urges that the Government will, as indicated by Sir William Meyer in his introductory speech, reconsider the matter and relieve India of the burden of the contribution of £45 millions for the War purposes.

16. Release of Ali Brothers

Resolved that this Congress again most earnestly requests the government to release Shaukat Ali and Mohammad Ali who are now at the beginning of their fifth year of internment.

17. Responsible Government

Resolved that this Congress approves of the submission to H.M. the King-Emperor of an address of congratulation on the successful termination of the War and a petition to a High Court of the parliament in England enunciating our demand for the responsible government as an integral part of the British Empire and embodying the resolutions of the Congress regarding such demands, and appoints,

N.C. Kelkar, K.M. Munshi, B.G. Horniman and V.J. Patel to draft them and desires the All-India Congress Committee to arrange for their preparation and presentation.

18. Deputation to England

Resolved that a Committee consisting of the President, Syed Hasan Imam, Hakim Ajmal Khan, Pandit Gokaran Nath Misra, C. Vijiaraghava Chariar, G.S. Khaparde, N.C. Kelkar, C.R. Das, V.J. Patel, Barkat Ali, Lala Harkishan Lal and Fazl-ul-Haq be appointed (a) to select the members of the Deputation to proceed to England to advocate and press the demands of the Congress contained in the resolutions of this Congress, and (b) to cooperate with the Provincial Congress Committees in collecting the necessary funds, with Kelkar as the Convener.

19. Indigenous System of Medicine

Resolved that recognising the comparatively wider prevalence of the Ayurvedic and Unani systems of medicine in India and their undeniable claims of usefulness, this Congress strongly recommends to the Government of India the eminent desirability of taking the definite steps to secure to them the advantages vouchsafed to the western system under the present administrative policy of the Government.

That the consideration of the opinions of the local governments, with respect to placing the indigenous system of medicine on a satisfactory basis as revealed in the summary laid before the Imperial Legislative Council at Simla this year, should be postponed pending a thorough inquiry by a mixed committee of the representative Vaidyas, Hakims, their sympathisers and the experts and such other medical practitioners as may be nominated by the Government.

20. Amendments in the Constitution

Resolved:

(a) That in the opinion of this Congress, the Congress Constitution should be so amended as to bring the work of the British Congress Committee into coordination with that of the other component parts of the Congress organisation.

(b) That in the opinion of this Congress it is necessary to make the newspaper *India* more attractive and to associate an Indian or Indians in its editorial management.

(c) That in the opinion of this Congress half the delegation fee which is now ear-marked for the British Congress Committee be set apart to be utilised generally for propagandist work in England.

(d) That in the opinion of this Congress the deputation which will proceed to England in connection with the Constitutional Reforms be authorised to enter into negotiations with the authorities of the British Congress Committee to make the necessary arrangements on the lines suggested above.

21. Congress Constitution

Resolved that the Congress desires the All-India Congress Committee to consider and report what changes may be introduced in the working of the Congress constitution and rules in the matter of the electorates, elections, etc., and in the procedure of the Congress Session and the Subject Committee.

22. *Remission of Delegates Fees*

Resolved that the payment by the delegates of the delegation fees under Art. 21 may be remitted for this year and for 1919 only in the case of the tenant delegates and other members of the poorer classes as the recommendations of the respective Provincial Congress Committees.

23. *Thanks to the Secretaries*

Resolved that this Congress records the valuable services rendered by the Secretaries of the Congress for the last year, namely the Hon'ble Bhurgri and C.P. Ramaswamy Iyer and P. Xesava Pillai.

24. *Office Bearers*

That this Congress appoints V.J. Patel, G.N. Misra and Fazl-ul-Haq as the Joint General Secretaries for the year 1919.

[In this Congress 4865 delegates registered which was held on Dec. 26-31, 1918 at Delhi]

CALCUTTA (47th Session) PRESIDENTIAL ADDRESS

The following are the exerpts from Pandit Madan Mohan Malaviya's Calcutta presidential address, which he was not able to deliver, owing to his detention in Asansol:

"I offer my profound thanks for the honour of being called upon to preside over the deliberations of the Indian National Congress. That the honour has been conferred on me at a time when the country is placed in very abnormal circumstances, when our revered countryman, Mahatma Gandhi and a large number of India's patriotic sons and daughters are still undergoing imprisonment, makes my gratefulness for this signal mark of confidence in me all the more greater. I also fully realise the responsibility which has thus been placed upon me. I pray that I may prove equal to it.

"When I was entering Delhi to preside over the Congress the last year, I was arrested and detained in jail until some time after the Congress had met and passed its resolution in spite of the efforts of the police to prevent it from doing so. This fact and the attitude of the Government towards the Congress as disclosed in the recent official announcements, had prepared people to apprehend that I would not be allowed to attend the Congress this year also. This is no longer a matter of conjecture. While writing this note this morning I received the following letter from the Collector of Benares:

> Dear Pandit ... The Bengal government have advised. the local Government that the Public Safety Act is in force in Bengal and that if you and the other leaders proceed to Calcutta, for the Congress sessions, you will not be allowed to attend it. I am directed to communicate the above to you and I request that you will be so good as to pass on the warning to the other leaders who may be in Benares at the present time.

"I appreciate the action of the Bengal government in sending me this warning in this courteous manner. I have informed them however that I see no justification for their decision that we shall not be allowed to attend the Congress, and have told them by which train I intend to leave for Calcutta.

"Last year the government arrested a large number of people on their way to attend the Congress at Delhi. This year also I hear that the police are very active in preventing people from going to attend the Congress. The Police Commissioner of Calcutta has issued a press notification warning the public that whosoever harbours, receives or assembles in any houses or premises in his occupation or charge or under his control a person whom he knows to have been deputed to Calcutta as a delegate to the Indian National Congress, 1933, will render himself liable to prosecution under the Penal Code. He has also warned all the landlords, that the reception committee of the said Congress has been declared an unlawful association and that any place which in the opinion of the Bengal government is used for the purpose of the said unlawful association is liable to be notified and taken possession of by the police who may direct any person therein and take possession of the movable property found therein.

"The Government has thus obviously done all they could severely to discourage and prevent the holding of the Congress at Calcutta.

"Its present attitude is morally indefensible and politically unwise. It cannot be too strongly condemned. The Congress may well be described as the unofficial Parliament of India. It is the greatest and most active political organisation of the country. It has been in existence now for forty-seven years. It has a great record behind it. The most important constitutional and administrative reforms which have taken place in India during the last half century have all been due to the work or pressure of the Congress. It has been the constant and fearless champion of the people's right for freedom and Self-Government. The forty-six volumes of its reports, the numerous reports of its provincial and District Conferences and the proceedings of the Imperial and Provincial Legislative Councils all eloquently attest how the Congress has been fighting for this measure with only one object in view namely, the amelioration of the condition of the people and their national advancement in all the important directions.

"It has always pleaded for the equal political rights and equal justice to all the classes and sections of the people. During the last thirteen years, the most respected of the Congressmen have repeatedly suffered imprisonment for the sake of the country's cause.

"For all these reasons the people regard the Congress as their best friend and guide and are ever willing to listen to its advice, even when it involves a sacrifice of the personal interests.

"Ever since the Montford proposals were published, the Congress has been pressing for the introduction of responsibility in the Central Government of India. Finding that the government gave no sign of willingness to respond to the request the Congress declared in 1929 that if the government would not announce its willingness to grant British Dominion Status to India up to the end of the next year, the Congress would advise the country to declare itself for complete independence. The Viceroy did make a declaration on the first November 1929, but that did not meet the requirements of the Congress and consequently on the first day of the January, 1930 the Congress declared the complete independence to be its goal.

"On March 12, succeeding, Mahatma Gandhi started the Civil Disobedience Movement to bring pressure to bear upon the government to concede to minimum national demand which he clearly defined, the government adopted strong measures to suppress the movement. But it failed to do so. Then after nearly a year's resolute administration Lord Irwin's government considered it wise and just to make a truce with the Congress through Mahatma Gandhi which is known as the Gandhi-Irwin Pact. The Pact was made with the approval of the British Government.

"The Congress was then invited by the prime minister of England to send its representatives to the Round Table Conference because it was felt by the government that without Congress the Conference could not be regarded as fully representative. The Congress made Gandhiji its sole representative and he attended the Conference as such. He returned to India anxious to cooperate with the government in the further work of the Conference. But while the Conference was going on in London, the General election in England brought a large Conservative majority into the Parliament and a strong Conservative became the Secretary of State for India.

" 'As the result of the election' in the words of Mr Benthall, who represented the Conference, the policy had undoubtedly changed. The right wing of the new government made up its mind to break up the conference and to fight the Congress. The Muslims who did not want the central responsibility were delighted. Government undoubtedly changed her policy and tried to get away with the provincial autonomy with a promise of central reform.'

" 'We had made up our minds', continues Mr Benthall, 'before this that a fight with Congress was inevitable and we felt and said that the sooner it came the better. But we had also made up our minds that for a crushing success we should have all the possible friends on our side. The important thing to us seemed to be to carry the Hindus in the street represented by such people as Sapru, Jayakar, Patro and the others. If we could not get them to fight the Congress, we could at least ensure that they would not back the Congress. We pressed upon the government that the one essential earnest of the good faith which would satisfy these people was to undertake to bring in the provincial and the central constitution in the one act. So we joined with the strange companions. The government saw the argument; and the conference instead of breaking up in disorder with the 100 per cent of the Hindu political India against us ended in promises of cooperation by 99 per cent of the Conference, including even such people as Pandit Madan Mohan Malaviya, while Gandhi himself was disposed to join the standing committee.'

"This needs no comment. The subsequent pronouncements and actions of the government culminating in the statement of January 4, 1932, have made it clear that even before the return home of Mahatma Gandhi, the government had decided upon launching a strong, carefully planned, comprehensive attack on the Congress and had coolly concerted their plans for it. In the light of these facts it becomes easy to understand why the Viceroy refused to grant an interview to Mahatma Gandhi when he so earnestly sought it with a view to remove the differences which had arisen between the government and the Congress in some provinces and to avert resort to the Civil Disobedience. The government did not give him that opportunity and had kept him interned since that time. The attack on the Congress was hurled like an avalanche. The most drastic ordinances were promulgated and extended to all the parts of India.

"It is estimated that nearly 120,000 persons including several thousand women and quite a number of children have been arrested and imprisoned during the last fifteen months.

"It has been repeatedly said on behalf of the government that its quarrel with the Congress is due to the adoption of the Civil Disobedience, by the Congress. I have shown above by quoting the letter of Mr Benthall that the Conservative Party and the European community of Calcutta decided to fight the Congress, not because it had taken up the Civil Disobedience Movement, but because it insisted upon a real transfer of power from the British to the Indian hands, in other words, upon having the substance of independence in the management of the country's affairs. It must be remembered that as Sir Samuel Hoare boartfully stated, the initiative this time has been with the government. The Congress offered Civil Disobedience in defence of the rights of the people which were attacked by the government by means of the ordinances passed under the existing laws. It has throughout the campaign been in the power of the government to stop Civil Disobedience or by abandoning the policy of repression.[2]

"Under the English constitution, the British parliament exercises soverign power as a legislature, and in theory it has a right to make or unmake any laws whatever for the Britishers. But as a great English writer, Dicey has pointed out, the actual exercise of authority by any sovereign whatever, and notably by the parliament is limited on every side by the possibility of the popular resistance.

"Further on he says, 'The external limit to the real power of a sovereign consists in the possibility or certainly that his subjects, or the large numbers of them will disobey or resist his laws', and still further, 'a soverign may wish to do many things which he either cannot do at all or can do only at great risk of serious resistance, and it is on many accounts worth observation that the exact point at which the external limitation begins to operate, that is, the point at which the subjects will offer serious or insuperable resistance to the commands of a ruler whom they generally obey is never fixed with precision.' Another great writer cited by Dicey has said, 'If a legislature decided that all the blue-eyed babies should be murdered, the preservation of the blue-eyed babies would be illegal. But legislators must go mad before they could pass such a law and subjects be idiotic before they could submit to it.' This limitation exists even under the most despotic monarchies.

"It is indisputable therefore that if a legislature or a despot should promulgate a law which is obviously unjust or oppressive and attacks our elementary liberties, the people have the right to disobey such a law and to offer to it 'serious and insuperable resistance'. The right of disobedience or resistance is a most valuable constitutional weapon in the hands of a people, by the fear of which they can force the legislators or despots to exercise their powers within the limits of reason and justice, and by which they can re-establish their natural rights and liberties when they have been attacked or invaded.

"The greatest of our liberties is the liberty of opinion. It was said by Erskine that 'Other liberties are held under government, but the liberty of opinion keeps governments themselves in due subjection to their duties. This has produced the martyrdom of truth in every age, and the world has been only purged from ignorance with the innocent blood of those who have enlightened it.'

"Not withstanding all the assurance of equality of treatment in the days of the War, after the War was over England has changed her attitude towards India. It has never yet agreed that India should exercise the right of self-determination to establish which she contributed her lives and treasure. On the contrary, she has treated Indians during the last thirteen years as a race whose pace of progress towards the Self-Government must be determined by the Parliament of England.

"England has gone on preparing a constitution for the future of the Government of India with the help of some Indians of its own selection and liking. It has framed the constitution under the claim that it is the right and moral obligation of the British Parliament to determine to what extent and with what limitations and safeguards it will allow India to administer its own affairs. The White Paper is an ugly revelation of the attitude of the British statesmen who dominate the English Parliament today towards India and her problems. It constitutes a deliberate affront to the patriotism and intelligence of India. Indeed it proposes to make the position of the Indians worse than it is today.

"It was idle to expect that a constitution born under the

influence of the attitude which the British statesmen entertain towards India could be the one which could be acceptable to the Indian people. It is not surprising that the White Paper is being condemned all over the country. I hope that no self-respecting Indian who has a correct sense of his duty towards the motherland will take part in any further confabulations regarding the White Paper unless and until the British Government should change its present policy and should make up its mind to treat the Indians as the equal fellowmen who are as much entitled to complete independence in the management of their own affairs as England herself is in regard to her own affairs.

"I appeal to my countrymen to wake up to the reality of the situation. I take it that every Indian wants that we should have complete freedom for the management of our own affairs. The attainment of this freedom will become easier if we will unite and work with one mind and purpose to achieve it. I implore all the Hindus and Mussalmans, Sikhs, Christians and Parsis and all the other countrymen to sink all the communal differences and to establish political unity among all the sections of the people.

"The unity Conference which was laid at Allahabad has nearly brought about the communal agreement. I earnestly hope that the Conference will soon resume its work and complete it to the satisfaction of all the communities. Our national political aims are common to all the parties and with the disillusionment which the White Paper has brought about I have every reason why we should not be able to establish political unity in the country. If we succeed in doing so, the pressure of the United India is bound to induce the British Government to revise its attitude towards India and the Indians and to invite them to exercise their right of self-determinations and to prepare a constitution which shall give India real independence to manage her own affairs.

"In the midst of much darkness, I see a clear vision that the clouds which have long been hanging over our heads are lifting. Let every son and daughter do his or her duty to expedite the advent of the dawn of the day of the freedom and happiness. Truth is on our side. Justice is with us. God will help us. We are sure to win. *Vande Mataram.*

Resolutions Adopted by the INC

The following resolutions were passed by the forty-seventh session of the Indian National Congress held in Calcutta on April 1, 1933.

Goal of Independence

This Congress reaffirms the resolution passed at its 44th session at Lahore in 1929 declaring complete Independence as its goal.

Civil Disobedience, A Legitimate Weapon

This Congress holds the Civil Disobedience to be a perfectly legitimate means for the protection of the right of the people for the vindication of the national self-respect and for the attainment of the national goal.

Adherence to the Civil Disobedience Programme

This Congress reaffirms the decision of the Working Committee arrived at on the January 1, 1932. On a careful survey of all that has happened during the past fifteen months, the Congress is firmly of the opinion that in the situation in which the country is placed, the Civil Disobedience movement should be strengthened and extended, and the Congress therefore calls upon the people to pursue the Movement with greater vigour on the lines laid down by the Working Committee in the aforesaid resolution.

Boycott

This Congress calls upon all the classes and sections of the people in this country to completely eschew foreign cloth, to give preference to *Khaddar* and to boycott all the British goods.

White Paper

This Congress holds that no constitution framed by the British Government while it is engaged in conducting a campaign of ruthless repression, involving the imprisonment and internment of the most trusted leaders of the Nation and thousands of their followers, suppression of the Fundamental Rights of free speech and association, stringent restraint on the liberty of the press and replacement of the normal civil law by the virtual martial law, deliberately initiated by it on the eve of Mahatma Gandhi's return from England with a view to crush the national spirit, can be worthy of consideration by or acceptable to the people of India.

The Congress is confident that the public will not be mislead by the scheme outlined in the recently-published White Paper which is inimical to the vital interests of India and is devised to the perpetuate foreign domination in this country.

Gandhiji's Fast

This Congress offers its congratulations to the country on the successful termination of Mahatma Gandhi's fast of September 1932 and hopes that untouchabilty will before long become a thing of the past.

Fundamental Rights

This Congress is of the opinion that to enable the masses to appreciate what Swaraj, as conceived by the Congress, will mean to them, it is desirable to state the position of the Congress in a manner easily understood by them. With this object in view it reiterates Resolution No. 15 of the Karachi Session of the Congress of 1931. (See Appendix No. 6).

[47th Congress to be held in Calcutta in March 1933 was banned as was 46th (Delhi) Congress to be held on 24 April 1932]

APPENDIX NO. 1

What Happened at Calcutta

The following statement was issued by Pandit Madan Mohan Malaviya with regard to the events that took place in Calcutta during the Congress Session held on April 1, 1933.

"My regret at not having been allowed to attend the 47th session of the Indian National Congress at Calcutta to preside over it was buried under the satisfaction I felt along with millions of my countrymen at the Congress having been held at Calcutta in spite of all the measures taken by the authorities to discourage and prevent the delegates from attending it. That in spite of those measures over 2500 delegates started for Calcutta and were arrested either on route or at Calcutta is the best proof of the strength of the Congress movement. Of these delegates nearly a thousand were arrested and detained before they could reach Calcutta. The rest of them, i.e., over 1500 reached Calcutta and notwithstanding the notice issued by the Police Commissioner were given accommodation at various places in the city. It is interesting to note that among these delegates there were 48 members of the All India Congress Committee, 83 Muslims, 117 ladies, 23 Sikhs, 7 Parsis and 2 Christians. The delegates came from all the parts of the country as is shown below:

United Provinces 673	Maharashtra 25	Sind 5
Bengal 300	Bombay 22	Ajmer 3
Bihar 285	Gujarat 31	Delhi 17
Orissa 43	C.P. Hindi 50	Assam 29
Andhra 23 Tamilnadu 27	C.P. Marathi 22 Berar 15	Punjab 31 N.W.F.P. 6
Kerala 7	Karnatak 3	

"When the news was received at Calcutta that I had been arrested on my way, it was announced on behalf of the Congress that Mrs Nellie Sen Gupta would preside over the Congress. The time and place for holding the Congress were also announced nearly twenty-four hours in advance. And it is worthy of note that notwithstanding all the stringent and laborious measures taken by the Police over 250 delegates representing all the parts of the country met at the appointed place punctually as the clock struck 3. Mrs Nellie Sen Gupta was there at her post and started reading her address. All the seven resolutions adopted by the Subjects Committee on the previous evening were read out and passed. Eventually the police made a lathi charge, dispersed the huge crowd which had gathered and arrested the delegates. They bore the assault calmly. Delegate after delegate as he stood up to move resolutions was violently attacked by the sergeants wielding lathis with all their might. Care was taken by the sergeants not to aim at their heads, but serious injuries were sustained by the delegates at other parts of their bodies. One delegate, a *Vakil* from Arrah who kept persistently reading a resolution in spite of a shower of blows had his spectacles broken and one of his eyes severely injured he was even kicked. Women delegates were not beaten, though some of them who tenaciously struck to the National Flag were roughly handled in an attempt to snatch the flag from them. All honour to these delegates who conducted themselves as worthy soldiers of the peaceful army of the Congress and stood the most severe test of their adherence to non-violence. I have referred to the manner in which they were beaten and assaulted not in order to complain of the violence and provocation of the police but to give an idea to the public of the ordeal through which the Congress had to pass.

"But there is one event which took place in Calcutta before the session of the Congress to which I wish to draw attention. It relates to the behaviour of the police on the evening of the 30th March. Eighty-nine delegates from U.P. after having been taken into custody in the course of a police raid, were assaulted by the European or Anglo-Indian Police Sergeants in the Lai Bazar Thana. The assault was wanton, brutal and evidently premeditated. Many of the delegates suffered severe contusions on their faces and heads for which some are still under medical treatment. Some of these delegates occupy high positions in society and are well known in their districts. The facts of the shameful incident as represented by Mr Jwaran Paliwal of Farrukhabad, the leader of the group, and several other victims, are briefly as follows:

"At 5 p.m. on the 30th March the Police raided a building in Nawab Badruddin Street and arrested 89 delegates all of whom were from U.P. including 3 from Meerut. The prisoners were taken to the Kolutala Thana and kept there for about half an hour. The behaviovr of these delegates, as all other delegates arrested at different times and in different places, was entirely peaceful. No resistance was offered by anybody either at the time of arrest or while they were being hustled into the prison vans. From Kolutala Thana they were removed to the Lai Bazar Thana at about 7-30 p.m. When the prisoners arrived sergeants came rushing from the different directions and lined themselves up in two rows facing each other between the exit of the vans and the gate of the lock-up in which the prisoners were to be kept. They were about 30 in all. Some of them were seen wrapping their hands with cloth as though preparing for a boxing contest. Shouts of "ready", "ready" were raised among the sergeants which the prisoners clearly heard. The prisoners were thereupon ordered to alight one by one. Each one of them on alighting was set upon by the sergeants and belaboured with sticks and fists. Only a few of the sergeants had sticks, the main body of them used their fists. Blows were freely directed at the stomach, chest, face, eyes and head. Delegates who tottered under a blow which fell on the right side received another immediately on their left. When a prisoner who had been cuffed in the stomach placed his hands there a shower of fists fell on his unprotected head and face. Anyone who lowered his head got a violent punch on his chin. Those who fell down under the assault were kicked with heavy boots. One delegate from Etawah who tried to protect his head with his hands was seized by several sergeants who dashed his head against a wall and kept him pressed to it by the throat. His head was badly injured and bled profusely. Several delegates were unconscious or semi-unconscious for a long time after the assault was over. Over a dozen delegates bled either from a torn lip, an injured eye, broken teeth or a broken head. The sergeants kept punctuating their brute-like beating with foul abuse. Every one of the delegates had perforce to pass through the double row of sergeants and none of them escaped the assault. Some who happened to come out of their vans in groups got off lightly as compared to those who came out in singles. At length when the sergeants' appetite was appeased the medical attendant of the Thana administered first aid, while sergeants kept jeering and joking at the plight of their victims. Tincture Iodine was applied to the wounds. Some who were senseless or were suffering due to severe pain particularly from blows received on the stomach and ribs were attended to by their fellow delegates who fanned them with handkerchiefs and gave them water to drink. Moulvi Abdul Latif of Lucknow who had fainted due to injuries in the ribs and was in a serious condition had to be treated with fomentation and was eventually sent to the police hospital at night. Pandit Shiva Datta Pande of Lucknow whose condition caused grave anxiety, was also sent to the Police Hospital for the treatment of injuries in the stomach. Others with similar injuries spent the night in the Thana in agony. Next day; i.e., on the 31st March, they were all removed to the Presidency Jail where the injured had to be specially attended to. Some had to be immediately admitted to the Jail Hospital. The blood on the face of several of them was washed and their blood-stained clothes changed in jail. Pandit Kapil Dev Pande of Gorakhpore, Pandit Jay Dev Shastri of Farrukhabad and Pandit Shiva Prasad Shukla of Behraich still carry prominent marks of injuries on their eyes and nose. Pandit Om Prakash Tiwari of Agra and Pandit Satya Narayan Datt of Etawah display torn lower lips. Thakur Kamal Singh of Agra and Sjt. Devi Dass of Jhansi bear marks of severe injuries on the nose while a number of delegates still continue to suffer acute pain in the stomach and ribs. Three delegates Maulvi Abdul Latif and Pandit Shiva Datt of Lucknow and Pandit Shiv Prasad Shukla of Bahraich were kept in the Jail Hospital throughout their detention, and the former two were unable to sit up or move by themselves even when they were released on the 6th April. Sjt. Virendra Kumar Sadh of Farrukhabad who had been badly injured in the ribs had to be detained in Calcutta for treatment.

"Since writing the above, other incidents of a similar nature that took place at Kalighat and in the Bhowanipore Thana have come to my notice. The prisoners who were assaulted in this Thana and on their way to it were released only on the 7th i.e., the day I left Calcutta. Some of them have since seen me in Benares and related details of assaults on delegates who had been arrested at Kalighat on the 30th March and 1st April. The facts are briefly as follows:

"On the 30th March about 180 delegates were arrested at Kalighat. They were marched to the Bhowanipore Police Station on foot under police escort. A sergeant whose name is known to the delegates distinguished himself by want only assaulting several delegates while putting them under arrest, as also after arrest. He set upon Mr Fakir Chand of Kanpur for shouting slogans and beat him with a stick in several parts of the body. Mr Fakir Chand bears marks of violent blows on the head, left arm and other parts of the body. His condition having become grave, he was sent at midnight in a riskshaw to the Police hospital. Similarly, Sjts. Ram Saroop and Maujilal of Unao were beaten by the same man raising slogans. Both these delegates had to be sent to the police hospital at night. Sjt. Naroang Singh of Gonda was given a blow with the stick on his face so that two of his teeth were broken and the upper lip badly injured. Sjt. Sukhdev Prasad of Gorakhpore was struck several blows causing profuse bleeding. He too was treated later on in the Police hospital. Sjt. Ram Palak Singh and Sjt. Sampuran Tiwari of Basti got violent blows on their heads causing bleeding wounds. Sjt. Mata Prasad of Gonda was hit on his private parts. He is still suffering from the injuries and finds urination extremely painful. Nearly 40 persons in the batch of about 180 received injuries caused mainly by one sergeant.

"The other incident relates to the arrest of 21 delegates of U.P. who occupy leading positions in the Congress. The batch was arrested on the 1st of April at Kalighat at about 11 a.m. They were taken to the Bhowanipore in a bus. At the Thana they were given chairs and benches to sit on. While the names and other particulars were being taken down the same stout sergeant mentioned above appearing on the scene suddenly pulled Thakur Munshi Singh of Hardoij by the ear and shouting 'you cried, down with the British Government eh?' punched him several times heavily on the temples. The sergeant was interrupted in his brutal attack on Thakur Munshi Singh by a telephone call. But he returned from the telephone and began to belabour his Victim again. When Mr Rustom Satin a delegate from Jhansi tried to remonstrate on behalf of his companion the sergeant struck a heavy blow with his stick on his head causing a big swelling. The sergeant then kept growling and brandishing his encased revolver at the delegates. He retired eventually on the arrival of a Magistrate who had been summoned in view of the important arrests of these men. Later Mr L.G. Kher a leading Congressman and *Vakil* of Jhansi who was one of the delegates refused to supply any more particulars as regards the name; and addresses of his group unless the incident of the wanton attack on Thakur Munshi Singh and Mr Rustom was duly noted by the Police. Eventually their demand was complied with the fact of the assault recorded in the police diary.

"The beating during the actual Congress Session might have been expected. But one could hardly believe that the prisoners in custody would be treated in the atrocious manner described above. I make a present of these facts to those who are in power. To those who suffered I offer my respectful sympathy and my congratulations on the cool courage with which they bore the cowardly assaults. Their silent suffering will soon kill the system which permits human beings to be so brutally treated and humiliated for no other crime than that they desire the same freedom for their country that their oppressors enjoy in their own."

Benares — Madan Mohan Malaviya

April 9, 1933.

APPENDIX NO. 2

Mahatma Gandhi's Statesment dated April 30, 1933:

"A tempest has been raging within me for-some days. I have been struggling against it. On the eve of the '*Harijan* Day', the voice became insistent, and said: 'Why don't you do it?' I resisted it. But resistance was in vain and the resolution was made to go on an unconditional and irrevocable fast for the twenty-one days commencing from Monday noon the 8th May and ending on Monday noon the 29th May.

"As I look back upon the immediate past, many are the causes too sacred to mention, that must have precipated the fast. But they are all connected with the great *Harijan* cause.

The fast is against nobody in particular, and against everybody who wants to participate. But it is particularly against me. It is a heart-felt prayer for the purification of self and associates for greater vigilance and watchfulness. But nobody who appreciates the step about to be taken is to join me. Any such fast will be a torture of them and of me. Let this fast, however, be a preparation for many such facts to be taken to be purer and more deserving persons than myself.

"During all these months since September last, I have been studying the correspondence and literature and holding prolonged discussions with men and women, learned and ignorant, *Harijans* and non-*Harijans*. The evil is greater than even I had thought it to be. It will not be eradicated by money, external organisation and even political power to the *Harijans,* though all these three are necessary. But to be effective, they must follow or at least accompany inward organisation, and inward power, in other words, self-purification. This can only come by fasting and prayer. We may not approach the God of truth in arrogance of strength, but in the meekness of the weak and the helpless.

"But the mere fast of the body is nothing without the will behind. It must be a genuine confession of an inner fast, an irrepressible longing to express truth and nothing but the truth.

"Therefore, those only are privileged to fast for the cause of truth, who have worked for it and who have love in them even for the opponents, who are free from animal passion, and who have abjured earthly possessions and ambition. No one, therefore, may undertake without previous preparation and discipline, the fast I have foreshadowed.

"Let there be no misunderstanding about the impending fast. I want to live for the cause, though I hope I am equally prepared to die for it. But, I need for me and my fellow-workers greater purity, greater application and dedication. I want more workers of unassailable purity. Shocking cases of impurity have come under my notice. I would like my fast to be an urgent appeal to such people to leave the cause alone.

"I know that many of only *Sanatanist* friends and others think that the movement is a deep political game. How I wish this fast would convince them that it is purely religious.

"If God has more service to take from this body. He will hold it together despite deprivation of earthly food. He will send me spiritual food. But he works through earthly agents and everyone who believes in the imperative necessity of removing untouchability will send me the food I need by working to the best of his or her ability, for the due and complete fulfilment of the pledge given to the *Harijans* in the name of the Caste Hindus."

4

Dissent Note in the Indian Industrial Commission

NOTE ON REPORT OF INDIAN INDUSTRIAL COMMISSION

Pandit Madan Mohan Malaviya was a member of the Indian Industrial Commission representing. Indian Legislative Council along with others he submitted the following note in response to his dissenting views of the main Report submitted by the commission.

Introductory

On March 21, 1916 the Hon'ble Sir Ibrahim Kahimtoola moved a resolution in the imperial legislative council urging the appointment of a committee to consider and report what measures should be adopted for the growth and development of the industries in India. Among the matters which he suggested might suitably be referred for the consideration of the committee, he put this question in the forefront:

> Whether representation should be made to the authorities through the Secretary of State for India for securing to the Government of India full fiscal autonomy, specially in reference to import, export and excise duties.

In the course of his speech in supporting the resolution, the Hon'ble member laid great stress on this point. He said:

> I readily recognise that efforts are being made by the government in many directions to meet the needs of the situation. It appears

> to me, however, that, unless the hands of the Imperial Government are free in fiscal matters, the results will not be adequate. If the Government of India were free to adopt measures solely in the interests of the people of this country, without any restrictions or limitations in fiscal matters, our industrial development would be in a fair way of successful accomplishment. India wants fiscal autonomy as the first step towards her industrial regeneration, and if Indian publics opinion is to have any weight in the determination of this question, we ought to get it at once.

"The Hon'ble Sir William Clark, the then Member for Commerce and Industry, accepted the Resolution on behalf of the government. He announced that the government had anticipated the recommendation of the Resolution, and had already taken steps to constitute not a committee, but a more important body, a commission, whose duty it will be to consider and report upon the possibility of the further industrial development in this country. He said at the same time for the reasons which he put before the Council, the scope of the enquiries entrusted to the Commission would not include a consideration of the question of the fiscal policy of the government. Sir William Clark noted that in the opinion of the mover of the Resolution a Government of India, uncontrolled by the Secretary of State, untrammelled by the conceptions of the fiscal policy which may be held by the British Government of the day, would be a far more potent instrument for the development of the industries in India and administration of this country under its present constitution. He also recognised that there was a weighty body of opinion tending in that direction. But he said that 'His Majesty's Government feel that the fiscal relationships of all the parts of the Empire as between one another and the rest of the world, must be reconsidered after the War, and they wish to avoid the raising of all such questions until that fortunate time shall have arrived. It was therefore stated in the Resolution appointing this Commission that any consideration of the present fiscal policy of the government; has been excluded from its enquiries, and that the same considerations apply with even greater force to any proposals involving the imposition of the duties for the specific purpose of protecting the Indian industries, a policy which would very directly affect the fiscal relations of India with the outside world. This will explain why, as Sir Frederick Nicholson puts it in his statement submitted to us 'The part of Hamlet must be totally omitted.'

"The Commission has been instructed to examine and report upon the possibilities of further industrial development in India and to submit its recommendations with special reference to the following questions:

(a) Whether new openings for the profitable employment of the Indian capital in commerce and industry can be indicated;

(b) Whether and, if so, in what manner, government can usefully give direct encouragement to the industrial development;

  (i) By rendering technical advice more freely available;

  (ii) By the demonstration of the practical possibility on a commercial scale of the particular industries;

  (iii) By affording directly or indirectly the financial assistance to the industrial enterprises; or

  (iv) By any other means which are not incompatible with the existing fiscal policy of the Government of India.

"In the course of the speech to which the reference has been made, Sir William Clark made it clear that 'The building up of the industries where the capital, control and management should be in the hands of the Indians was the special object; which we all have in view.' He emphasised that it was of immense importance alike to India herself and to the Empire as a whole, that the Indians should take a larger share in the industrial development of their country. He deprecated the taking of any steps. if it might merely mean that the manufacturer who now competes with you from a distance would transfer his activities to India and compete with you within your boundaries. It was the same object of finding out how to help the Indians to develop industrial and commercial enterprise, that led the Government of India to depute Professor C.J. Hamilton, the Mintc Professor of Economics in Calcutta, to visit Japan to obtain more detailed particulars for the use of the Industrial Commission, so that we may know exactly what her Government has done to aid her people in the notable advance which they have made, having developed a structure of modern industrial and commercial enterprise from a past which knew nothing of the western economic conditions. We have to keep this object clearly before our mind in dealing with the questions which we have to examine and report upon.

India Past and Present

In the revised note which Professor C.J. Hamilton submitted to the commission, after dwelling on the rapidity with which Japan has transformed herself from a country where agriculture absorbed the energies of the bulk of the population to one of the important manufacturing countries of the modern times, he says:

> The second fact, even more arresting from an Indian point of view, is that this remarkable transformation has been achieved by an Asiatic community. The Asiatics have long been regarded as intensely conservative, unprogressive, needing the help and guidance of the western nations for the maintenance of law and order and, even with their assistance, being with difficulty persuaded to adopt the modern aims and methods associated with the economic progress.

"Mr C.J. Hamilton does not stand alone in this view. In the course of my work connected with this Commission, I have repeatedly been reminded of the erroneous notion which many a European hold that India is, and must remain, a mainly agricultural country, that the people of India are by nature and tradition deficient in industrial capacity and commercial enterprise, and that these qualities are inherent in the nations of the West. It is necessary to combat this notion, for it vitiates judgment regarding the capacity of the Indians. It is also necessary for a proper appreciation of the present industrial condition of India and of the possibilities of its future development, that the facts and circumstances of the past should be correctly known and appreciated.

"I agree with my colleagues that at a time when the West of Europe, the birthplace of the modern industrial system, was inhabited by the uncivilised tribes, India was famous for the wealth of her rulers and for the high artistic skill of her craftsmen, and that even at a much later period when the traders from the West made their first appearance in India, the industrial development of this country was at any rate not inferior to that of the more advanced European nations. But I do not agree with them as to the causes which they assign for the subsequent growth of the industries in England, and, by implication, for the want of the growth of such industries in India. They say:

> But the widely different social and political conditions of the West had helped the middle class to establish itself on a foundation of the commercial prosperity, and the struggles for the political freedom and religious liberty in which it had taken its share and endowed it with a spirit of enquiry and enterprise that was gradually and increasingly directed to the attainment of the industrial efficiency, and that it was to this middle class that the so-called industrial revolution of the eighteenth century was mostly due.

(Paragraph 1 of the Report.)

"Similarly it is stated in the paragraph 134 of the Report that:

> The history of the evolution in the West of the new industrial methods which culminated in the rapid and striking changes of the latter half of the eighteenth century shows that a large part was played therein by the educated as well as by the capitalist classes. The encouragement of the scientific research and its practical application by the Royal Society, and at a later stage by the Society of Arts, was closely paralleled by the fresh industrial ventures constantly being set on foot by the merchants and other persons with capital at command. When the results began to reach India in the shape of machine-made imports, the movement had passed beyond the stage where the gradual evolution which in England had taken place could be readily imitated in India.

"In my opinion this does not give a correct view of the matter, and is calculated to support the erroneous ideas about the natural capacity of the Indians and Europeans for the industrial enterprise, and to stand in the way of the right conclusions being reached as to the possibility of the industrial development in India with the co-operation of the government and the people. I must therefore refer a little more fully to the economic history of India and of the 'industrial revolution' of England which has greatly affected the history of India A manufacturing as well as an agricultural country 'The skill of the Indians,' says Professor Weber, 'In the production of delicate woven fabrics, in the mixing of colours, the working of metals and precious stones, the preparation of essences and in all manner of the technical arts, has from early times enjoyed a world-wide celebrity.' There is evidence that Babylon traded with India in 3000 B.C. Mummies in Egyptian tombs, dating from 2000 B.C., have been found wrapped in Indian muslin of the finest quality. 'There was a very large consumption of Indian manufactures in Rome. This is confirmed by the elder Pliny, who complained that the vast sums of money were annually absorbed by commerce with India.' 'The muslins of Dacca were known to the Greeks under the name of Gangitaka... Thus it may be safely concluded that in India the arts of cotton spinning and cotton weaving were in a high state of proficiency two thousand years ago where as...cotton weaving was only introduced into England in the seventeenth century.' (Imperial Gazetteer of India, Volume III, page 195.)

"As regards iron manufactures, Professor Wilson says; 'Casting iron is an art that has come ento practise in England only a few years back. The Hindus have known since time immemorial the art of smelting iron, of welding it, and of making steel.' Mr Ranade wrote in 1892: 'The iron industry not only supplied all the local wants, but it also enabled India to export its finished products to the foreign countries. The quality of the material turned out had also a world-wide fame. The famous Iron Pillar near Delhi, which is at least fifteen hundred years old, indicates great amount of skill involved in the manufacture of wrought iron, which has been the marvel of all who have endeavoured to account for it. Mr Bill (The Geological Survey of India) admits that it is not many years since the production of such a pillar would have been an impossibility in the largest factories in the world, and, even now, there are comparatively very few factories where such a mass of metal could be turned out. Cannons were manufactured in Assam of the quality, Indian woods or steel furnished the materials out of which Damascus blades of a world-wide reputation were made; and it paid Persian merchants in those old times to travel all the way to India to obtain these materials and export them to Asia. The Indian steel found once considerable demand for cutlery even in England. This manufacture of steel and wrought iron had reached a high perfection at least two thousand years ago.' ('Ranade's Essays on Indian Economics', pp. 159-160).

"There is abundant testimony to prove that at the date of the invasion of Alexander, as for the centuries before it, the people of India enjoyed a high degree of prosperity, which continued to the breaking up of the Mughal Empire in the eighteenth century.

" 'All the descriptions of the parts of India visited by the Greeks,' Mr Elphinstone tells us, 'give the idea of a country teeming with population, and enjoying the highest degree of prosperity...The numerous commercial cities and ports for foreign trade, which are mentioned at a later period (in the *Periplus*) attest the progress of the Indians in a department which more than any other shows the advanced state of a nation (p. 363)... Arrian mentions with admiration that every Indian is free.... The army was in constant pay during war and peace...The police are spoken of as excellent. Megasthenes relates that in the camp of Sandrocottus, consisting of 400,000 men, the sums stolen daily did not amount to more than about 3 pound...The fields were all measured, and the water carefully distributed for irrigation; taxes were imposed upon trade, and an income-tax levied from the merchants and traders. Royal roads are spoken of by Strabo and mile-scones...Gold and gems, silks and ornaments were in all the families; the professions mentioned show all that is necessary to the civilised life...The number of kinds of grains, spices, etc., which were grown afford proofs that the country was in a high state of cultivation...Their internal institutions were less rude; their conduct to their enemies more humane; their general learning much more considerable; and, in the knowledge of the being and nature of God, they were already in possession of a light which was but faintly perceived, even by the loftiest intellects in the best days of Athena.' (*History of India*, p. 53).

"The author of the *Periplus of the Erythrian Sea* fully describes Indian commodities for which there was a great demand in the West, especially in at Rome, about the first century of Christ. Many a travellers from the West have similarly described the trade of India. In the fourth and sixth centuries two Chinese travellers visited India, and have fully recorded their views on its material condition, which included flourishing arts and industries.

"Then came the period of the Crusades and the beginning of the Levantine trade which culminated in Venice becoming the greatest trader with India; and later on, Genoa. Marco Polo came to India in the 13th century and has left a record of his impressions.

"The waves of conquest which commenced from the eleventh century no doubt greatly hampered the Indian industrialists and industries for some time. But the establishment of the Mughal Empire and the safety and securities of the reign of Akbar seem to have fully revived the Indian industries and handicrafts. Bernier, who visited India in the reign of Shahjahan, gives a glowing description of his capital. He speaks of his immense treasures, gold and silver and jewellery, 'A prodigious quantity of pearls and precious stones of all sorts'... and marvels over the incredible quantity of the manufactured goods, 'Embroideries, streaked silks, tufts of the gold turbans, silver and gold cloth, brocades, net-work of gold,' Tavernier also gives etc. lengthy description of the manufactured goods, and dwells with wonder on the marvellous peacock-throne wishing the natural colours of the peacock's tail could be worked out in jewels, the carpets of silk and gold, satins with streaks of gold and silver, the lists of the exquisite works of minute carving and other choicest objects of art are endless.

The East India Company

"It was this trade and prosperity that lured the traders of Europe to India. As the historian Murray puts it: 'Its fabrics, the most beautiful that human art has anywhere produced, were sought by merchants at the expense of the greatest toils and dangers.' (*History of India*, p 27.) After the decline of Venice and Genoa, the Portuguese and the Dutch captured the Indian trade. The merchants of England viewed their trade with envious eyes, and formed the East India Company which obtained its charter from Queen Elizabeth on 31st December 1600, to trade with the East India, not to exchange as far as possible the manufactured goods of England for the produces of India (Report, para 2) for there were few English manufactures then to be exported but to carry the manufactures and commodities of India to Europe.

" 'At the end of the seventeenth century,' says Lecky, 'great quantities of cheap and graceful Indian calicoes, muslins, acid chintzes were imported into England, and they found such favour that the woollen and silk manufacturers were seriously alarmed. Acts of Parliament were accordingly passed in 1700 and 1721 absolutely prohibiting, with a very few specified exceptions, the employment of printed or dyed calicoes in England, either in dress or in furniture, and the use of any printed or dyed goods, of which cotton formed any part.' (*Lecky's History of England in the Eighteenth Century*).

"When Clive entered Murshidabad, the old capital of Bengal, in 1757, he wrote of it: 'This city is as extensive, populous, and rich as the city of London, with the difference that there were individuals in the first possessing infinitely greater property than in the last city.' (H.J.S. Cotton, in *New India*, published before 1890.)

" 'Less than a hundred years ago,' wrote Sir Henry Cotton in 1890, 'the whole commerce of Dacca was estimated at one crore of rupees, and its population at 200,000 souls. In 1787 the exports of Dacca muslin to England amounted to 30 lakhs of rupees; in 1817 they had ceased altogether. The arts of spinning and weaving, which for ages offered employment to a numerous and industrial population, have now become extinct.

Families which were formerly in a state of affluence have been driven to desert the town and betake themselves to the villages for a livelihood. The present population of the town of Dacca is only 79,000. This decadence has occurred not in Dacca only, but in all the districts. Not a year passes in which the Commissioners and District Officers do not bring to the notice of the government that the manufacturing classes in the parts of the country are becoming impoverished.'

" 'In the first four years of the nineteenth century,' says Mr Romesh Chandra Dutt, 'in spite of all the prohibitions and restrictive duties, six to fifteen thousand bales of cotton piece goods were annually shipped from Calcutta to the United Kingdom. The figure rapidly fell down in 1813. The opening of trade to the private merchants in that year caused a sudden rise in 1815; but the increase was temporary. After 1820 the manufacture and export of the cotton piece-goods declined steadily; never to rise again.' (*Economic History of British India*, p. 296)

How India Came to be an Agricultural Country

" 'At an early period of the Company's administration, British weavers had begun to be jealous of the Bengal weavers, whose silk fabrics were imported into England and so not only were the Indian manufacturers shut out from England, but a deliberate endeavour was now made to use the political power obtained by the East India Company,' says Romesh Chandra Dutt, 'to discourage the manufactures of India. In their letter to Bengal, dated March 17, 1769 the Company desired that the manufacture of raw silk should be encouraged in Bengal, and that of manufactured silk fabrics should be discouraged. And they also recommended that the silk winders should be forced to work in the Company's factories and prohibited from working in their own homes.'

"In a letter to of the Court of Directors, quoted in Appendix 37 to the Ninth Report of the House of Commons Select Committee on the Administration of Justice in India, 1783, (quoted by Mr Romesh Chandra Dutt on p 45 of his book) it was stated:

'This regulation seems to have been productive of very

good effects, particularly in bringing over the winders, who were formerly so employed, to work in the factories. Should this practice (the winders working in their own homes) through inattention have been suffered to take place again, it will be proper to put a stop to it, which may now be more effectually done, by an absolute prohibition under severe penalties, by the authority of the Government.'

'This letter, as the Select Committee justly remarked, 'contains a perfect plan of policy, both of compulsion and encouragement which must in a very considerable degree operate destructively to the manufactures of Bengal. Its effects must be (so far as it could operate without being eluded) to change the whole face of the industrial country, in order to render it a field for the produce of crude materials subservient to the manufactures of the Great Britain.' (Ibid)

"Furthermore, according to Mr Digby, in 1813, Indian cotton manufactures were liable to the following charges in England:

	£	$	*d.*
Calicoes or dimities for every £100 cf value ...	81	2	11
Cotton, raw (per 100 Ibs.)	0	16	11
* Cotton, manufactured	81	2	11
Hair or goal's wool, manufactures of, per cent.	84	6	3
Flowered or stitched muslins of white calicoes (for every £ 100 in value)... ...	32	9	2
Other manufactures of cotton not otherwise charged	32	9	2

" 'These burdensome charges were subsequently removed, but only after the export trade in them had, temporarily or permanently, been destroyed.' (*Prosperous British India*, p. 90) On the other hand, ever since the English power was established in India, English goods entered India either with no import, or with a merely nominal import duty. At the time Indian cotton goods were liable to the heavy duty of £81 per cent, in England, English cotton goods imported into India were subject to a duty of only 2½ per cent. In addition to this, the steam engine and the power-loom had in the meantime been perfected in England, and English manufactures had begun to come in increasing quantities to India. The result was well described by Mr Henry St. George Tucker, who had, on retirement from India, become a Director of the East India Company. Writing in 1823, he said: 'The silk manufactures, (of India) and its piece-goods made of silk and cotton intermixed, have long since been excluded altogether from our markets; and, of late partly in consequence of the operation of a duty of 67 per cent, but chiefly from the effect, of superior machinery, the cotton fabrics which heretofore constituted the staple of India, have not only been displaced in this country, but we actually export our cotton manufactures to supply a part of the consumption of our Asiatic possessions. India is thus reduced from the state of a manufacturing to that of an agricultural country.' Memorials of the Indian Government, being a selection from the papers of Henry St. George Tucker (London 1853, p. 494, quoted by Mr Romesh Chandra Dutt at p. 262 of his *Economic History of British India*.

"H.H. Wilson, the historian of India, also wrote as follows:

> It was stated in evidence (in 1813) that the cotton and silk goods of India up to the period could be sold for a profit in the British market at a price from 50 to 60 per cent, lower than those fabricated in England. It consequently became necessary to protect the latter by duties of 70 and 80 per cent, on their value, or by positive prohibition. Had this not been the case, had not such prohibitory duties and decrees existed, the mills of Paisley and Manchester would have stopped in their outset, and could scarcely have been again set in motion, even by the power of steam. They were created by the sacrifice of the Indian manufacture. Had India been independent, she would have retaliated, would have imposed prohibitive duties upon British goods, and would thus have preserved her own productive industry from annihilation. This act of self-defense was not permitted to her; she was at the mercy of the strangers. British goods were forced upon her without paying any duty, and the foreign manufacturer employed the arm of political injustice to keep down and ultimately strangle a competitor with whom he

> could not have contended on equal terms. (Quoted by Romesh Chandra Dutta, Ibid, pp. 262-3).

"Another important Indian industry which succumbed to the jealousy of the English manufacturers, was ship-building. That ship-building was an ancient industry in India, and that the Indians carried on navigation to far distant east, and west, has been fully established by Dr Radhakumud Mukerjee in his valuable *History of Indian Shipping*. Both Darius and Alexander had hundreds of vessels constructed in India. Indian river craft navigated Africa and went as far as Mexico. Again around the Coromandel Coast Indians navigated as far as Java, Sumatra, Borneo and distant Canton.

" 'A hundred years ago,' says Mr Digby, 'ship-building was in so excellent a condition in India that ships could be (and were) built which sailed to the Thames in company with British-built ships and under the convoy of British frigates.'

"The Governor-General (Lord Wellesley) reporting in 1800 to his masters in Leadenhall Street, London, said:

> The port of Calcutta contains about 10,000 tons of shipping, built in India, of a description calculated for the conveyance of cargoes to England...From the quantity of private tonnage now at command in the port of Calcutta from the state of perfection which the art of ship-building has already attained in Bengal (promising a still more rapid progress and supported by abundant and increasing supplies of timber), it is certain that this port will always be able to furnish tonnage to whatever extent may be required for conveying to the port of London the trade of the private British merchants of Bengal. (Quoted by Mr Digby in *Prosperous British India*, p. 86).

"But, says Mr Taylor:

> The arrival in the port of London of Indian produce in the Indian-built ships created a sensation among the monopolists which could not have been exceeded if a hostile fleet had appeared in the Thames. The ship-builders of the port of London took the lead in raising the cry of alarm; they declared that their business was on the point of ruin, and that the families of all the shipwrights in England were certain to be reduced to starvation, (*History of India*, p. 216).

"The cry prevailed. The Court of Directors opposed the employment of the Indian ships in the trade between England and India. 'In doing so,' says Mr Digby, 'they employed an argument which, in some of its terms, sounds very curious at the present time, when so many lascars are employed by all the great lines of steamers running to the East. After reciting other reasons against ship-building and ship manning in India, the Court said in their dispatch, dated January 27, 1801: 'XVII. Besides these objections which apply to the measure generally, there is one that lies particularly against ships whose voyages commence from India, that they will usually be manned in great part with lascars or the Indian sailors. Men of that race are not by their physical frame and constitution fitted for the navigation of cold and boisterous latitudes; their nature and habits are formed to a warm climate, and short and easy voyages performed within the sphere of the periodical winds; they have not strength enough of mind or body to encounter the hardships or perils to which ships are liable in the long and various navigation between India and Europe, especially in the winter storms of our northern seas, nor have they the courage which can be relied on for the steady defense against an enemy... But this is not all. The native sailors of India are...on their arrival here, led into scenes which soon divest them of the respect and awe they had entertained in India for the European character. The contemptuous reports which they disseminate on their return cannot fail to have a very unfavourable influence upon the minds of our Asiatic subjects, whose reverence for our character, which has hitherto contributed to maintain our supremacy in the East, will be gradually changed...and the effects of it may prove extremely detrimental...Considered, therefore, in a physical, moral, commercial and political view, the apparent consequences of admitting these Indian sailors largely into our navigation, form a strong additional objection to the concession of the proposed privilege to any ship manned by them.' (Appendix No. 47 Supplement to the Fourth Report, East India Company, PP 23-4, quoted by Mr Digby in the *Prosperous British India*, at pp. 101-3.)

"The lascars of today are only the successors of those who

emerged from the ports of Kathiawar and navigated from thence to Aden and Mocha to the East African coast and to the Malay Peninsula. It is possible an Indian lascar in the early nineteenth century, finding himself in London, may have indulged himself just as Jack today does, when he lands in any important Indian port. But it cannot but be regretted that such small considerations were allowed to weigh at all against the Indian navigation to England. And it is difficult to express in words the economic and political losses which this attitude has meant for England as well as India. How much better would have been the position of India, how infinitely stronger that of England, if Indian shipping had been allowed to grow, and had grown as shipping in other countries has grown during the last forty years, and been available to India and the Empire in this hour of need.

"Mr Romesh Chandra Dutt has shown in his *Economic History of British India* that this continued to be the settled policy of England towards India for fifty years and more; that it was openly avowed before the House of Commons and vigorously pursued till 1833 and later; and that it effectually stamped out many of the national industries of India for the benefit of the English manufactures. Mr Arnold Toynbee has expressed the same view:

> The English industries would not have advanced so rapidly without protection, but the system, once established led to the perpetual wrangling on the part of the rival industries, and sacrificed India and the Colonies to our great manufactures (*The Industrial Revolution of the Eighteenth Century in England, by Arnold Toynbee,* p. 58).

"Let us now turn to England to see what happened there during the same period. The industrial revolution, which has powerfully affected Indian industries, is said to have begun in England in 1770: 'In 1770,' says Mr Cunningham, 'there was no Black Country, blighted by the conjunction of coal and iron trades; there were no canals or railways, and no factory towns with their masses of population. All the familiar features of our modern life, and all its most pressing problems, have come to the front within the last century and a quarter.' (*The Growth of the English Industry and Commerce* by W. Cunningham. Part II, p. 613)

"Up to the middle of the eighteenth century English industry was in a very backward condition, The state of that industry is thus described by John Richard Green: 'Though England already stood in the first rank of commercial states at the accession of George III, her industrial life at home was mainly agricultural. The wool trade had gradually established itself in Norfolk, the West Riding of Yorkshire and the countries of the south-west; while the manufacture of cotton was still almost limited to Manchester and Bolton, and remained so unimportant that in the middle of the eighteenth century the export of cotton goods hardly reached the value of fifty thousand a year. There was the same slow and steady progress in the linen trade of Belfast and Dundee and the silks of Spitalfields. The processes of manufacture were too rude to allow any large increase of production... But had the processes of manufacture been more efficient, they would have been rendered useless by the want of a cheap and easy means of transport. The older main roads had broken down. The new lines of trade lay often along mere country lanes which had never been more than horse-tracks...A new era began when the engineering genius of Brindley joined Manchester with its port of Liverpool in 1767 by a canal; the success of the experiment soon led to the universal introduction of water-carriage, and Great Britain was traversed in every direction by three thousand miles of navigable canals. At the same time new importance was given to coal which lay beneath the soil of England. The stores of iron which had laid side by side with it in the northern countries had laid there unworked through the scarcity of wood which was looked upon as the only fuel by which it could be smelted. In the middle of the eighteenth century a process for smelting iron with coal turned out to be effective; and the whole aspect of the iron trade was at once revolutionised. Iron was to become the working material of the modern world and it is its production of iron which more than anything else has placed England at the head of the industrial Europe. The value of coal as a means of producing mechanical force was revealed in the discovery in which Watt in 1766 transformed the steam engine from a mere toy into the most wonderful instrument which the human industry had never had at its command. Three successive inventions in the twelve years, that of the spinning jenny in 1764 by weaver Hargrieves, of the spinning machine in 1768 by Barber Arkwright, of the 'mule' by 'Weaver Crompton in 1776, were followed by the discovery of the power loom. But these would have been comparatively useless had it not been for the revelation of a new inexhaustible labour-force in the steam engine. It was the combination of such a force with such means of applying it that enabled Britain during the terrible years of her struggle with France and Napoleon to all but monopolise the woollen and cotton trades, and raised her into the greatest manufacturing country that the world had seen.' (Green's *Short History of the English People,* pp. 791-92)

"But as Mr Cunningham has pointed out: 'Inventions and discoveries often seem to be merely fortuitous; men are apt to regard the new machinery as the outcome of a special and unaccountable burst of inventive genius in the eighteenth century. But to point out that Arkwright and Watt were fortunate in the facts that the times were ripe for them is not to detract from their merits. There had been many ingenious men from the time of William Lee and Dodo Dudley; but the conditions of their day were unfavourable to their success. The introduction of expensive implement, or process, involves a large outlay; it is not worthwhile for any man, however energetic, to make the attempt, unless he has a considerable command of capital and has access to large markets. In the eighteenth century these conditions were being more and more realised. The institution of the Bank of England, and of other banks, had given a great impulse to the formation of capital; and it was much more possible than it had ever been before for a capable man to obtain the means of introducing costly improvements in the management of this business.' (*Growth of English Industry and Commerce, Part II,* p. 610)

"The Bank of England had been formed in 1694 as an instrument; for procuring loans from the people at large by the formal pledge of the State to repay the money advanced on the demand of the lender, 'but for more than sixty years after the foundation of the Bank, its smallest note had been for pound 20, a note too large to circulate freely, and which rarely travelled far from Lombard Street. Writing in 1790, Burke said that when he came to England in 1750, there were not twelve bankers shops in the provinces, though then (in 1790) he said, they were in every market town. Thus the arrival of the Bengal silver not only increased the mass of money, but stimulated its movement; for at once, in 1759, the bank issued pound 10 and pound 15 notes, and in the country private firms poured forth a flood of paper,' (Brooks Adams, *The Law of Civilization and Decay*, pp. 263-264 quoted by Mr Digby at p 33 of his book).

'In 1756, when Clive went to India, the nation owed pound 74,575,000, on which it paid an interest of 2,753,000. In 1815 this debt had swelled to pound 861,000,000, with an annual interest charge of 32, 645,000.' (Ibid, p. 33)... 'The influx of the Indian treasure, by adding considerably to the nation's cash capital, not only increased its stock of energy but added much to its flexibility and the rapidity of its movement.' (Ibid, p. 31)... 'Very soon after Plassey, the Bengal plunder began to arrive in London, and the effect appears to have been instantaneous, for all the authorities agree that the 'industrial revolution', the event which has divided the nineteenth century from all the antecedent time, began with the year 1760. Prior to 1760, according to Baines, the machinery used for spinning cotton in Lancashire was almost as simple as in India; while about 1750 the English iron industry was in full decline because of the destruction of the forests for fuel. At that time four-fifths of the iron used in the kingdom came from Sweden.' "

" 'Plassey was fought in 1757, and probably nothing has ever equalled the rapidity of the change which followed. In 1760 the flying shuttle appeared, and coal began to replace wood in smelting. In 1861 Hargreaves invented the spinning jenny, in 1779 Crompton contrived the mule, in 1785 Cartwright patented the power loom, and chief of all, in 1768 Watt matured the steam engine, the most perfect of all events of centralising energy. But, though those machines served as outlets for the accelerating movement of the time, they did not cause the acceleration. In themselves inventions are passive, many of the most important having laid dormant for centuries, waiting for a sufficient store of force to have accumulated to set them working. That store must always take the shape of money and money not hoarded, but in motion.' (Brooks Adams, *The Law of Civilisation and Decay*, pp. 259-260)

"Money came from India.' Mr Digby says in Prosperous British India.

" 'England's industrial supremacy owes its origin to the vast hoards of Bengal and the Karnatik being made available for her use....Before Plassey was fought and won, and before the steam of treasure began to flow to England, the industries of our country were at a very low ebb. Lancashire spinning and weaving were on a par with the corresponding industry in India so far as machinery was concerned; but the skill which had made Indian cottons a marvel of manufacture was wholly Wanting in any of the Western nations. As with cotton so with iron; industry in Britain was at a very low ebb, alike in mining and in manufacture.' (Ibid, pp. 30-31)

"Though the power loom was constructed in 1784, power weaving did not become a practical success until the dressing-frame was invented in 1803. Up to 1801s, the cotton goods sent out from England to India amounted in value pound 21,000; by 1813 they had risen to pound 108,824. When the Charter of the East India Company was renewed in that year, its monopoly of trade with India was abolished, and British traders obtained a fresh outlet into this extensive Empire. The enormous increase of the imports of English manufactured cottons into India in the subsequent years hardly needs description. By the end of the century, India had become the largest single market for them, its demands for British cotton goods having been just under pound 20,000,000. In the year before the war they had risen to pound 44,581,000.

Effects of the Exports of Raw Produce

"Another factor which has powerfully contributed to India becoming more and more agricultural is the policy pursued by the British Government in India of encouraging the exports of its raw produce. Paragraph 5 of our Report has discussed the effects of these exports and that of the advent of the railway and the steamship. But it seems to me that, for an adequate appreciation of the results, the matter requires to be treated at greater length.

"In the eighteenth century the Colonies of England were looked upon as 'plantations' where raw produce was grown to be sent to the mother country, to be manufactured and sent back to the colonies and to the rest of the world. After the American War of Independence the new colonies were allowed to work out their own destinies, and they began to develop their manufacturing power by protection even against British manufactures. Since then, in the expressive language of Mr Ranade: 'The great Indian dependency of England has come to supply the place of the old Colonies. This dependency has come to be regarded as a plantation, growing raw produce to be shipped by the British agents in the British ships, to be worked into Fabrics by British skin and capital, and to be re-exported to the dependency by the British merchants to their corresponding British Firms in India and elsewhere.' (Essays, p. 99)

"This is best illustrated by the case of cotton. The Court of Directors of the East India Company began so early as 1788 to take an interest in the question of the cultivation of cotton in India, and expended considerable sums in various attempts to stimulate its growth. Since 1858, the Government of India have, at the instance of British manufacturing interests, taken steps from time to time, to improve the quality and quantity of cotton produced in India. The latest evidence of this is the appointment of the Indian Cotton Committee of the last year. I do not complain that this has been done. On the contrary, I think enough has not been done in this direction. I think India can grow, and ought to be helped to grow, much more and better cotton, and should be able to help both England and herself with it. But my point is that the policy which the Government has hitherto pursued has been of encouraging the exports of the raw produce. Its policy has not been to encourage the conversion of our raw cotton into manufactures.

The doctrines of free trade and of laissez faire, and an undue regard for the English interests and the fear of interference with English trade, have prescribed the policy which it has had to pursue.

Railways and Commerce

"The construction of railways in India was mooted first by Lord Hardinge. He left a minute in 1848, and his successor, Lord Dalhousie took up the subject. It was in 1853 that Lord Dalhousie wrote his great Railway minute and gave the first stimulus to railway construction. India is indebted to him for the railway, as also for the telegraph. Says his eminent biographer, Sir Willam Hunter: 'This was Lord Dalhousie's masterly idea not only would he consolidate the newly–annexed territories of India by his railways, and immensely increase the striking power of his military forces at every point of the Empire, but he would also use a railway construction as a bait to bring the British capital and enterprise to India on a scale which had never entered the imagination of any previous Governor-General.

" 'In all these arrangements,' continues Sir William Hunter, 'Lord Dalhousie had from the outset a vigilant eye to the mercantile aspects of his railway routes. The commercial and social advantages,' he wrote in his masterly minute on Railways, 'which India would derive from their establishment are, I truly believe, beyond all the present calculation. Great tracts are teeming with produce they cannot dispose of. Others are scantily bearing what they would carry in abundance, if only it could be conveyed whither it is needed. England is calling aloud for the cotton which India already produced in some degree, and would produce sufficient in quality, and plentiful in quantity, if only there were provided the fitting means of conveyance for it from distant plains to the several parts adopted for its shipment. Every increase of facilities for trade has been attended, as we have seen, with an increased demand for articles of the European produce in the most distant markets of India; and we have yet to learn the extent and value of the interchange which may be established with people beyond our present frontier, and which is yearly and rapidly increasing. Ships from every part of the world crowd our ports in search of produce which we have, or could obtain in the interior, but which at present we cannot profitably fetch thence; and new markets are opening to us on this side of the globe under circumstances which defy the foresight of the wisest to estimate their probable value or calculate their future extent.'

" 'Lord Dalhousie provided free play for the mercantile possibilities of the railways by removing the previous checks and hindrances on the Indian trade. Sir Edwin Arnold sums up these measures in a pithy marginal note' 'All ports in India made free.'

" 'The unprecedented impulse which Lord Dalhousie thus gave to the Indian trade may be realised by the following figures. During his eight years of rule the export of raw cotton more than doubled itself from 1½ millions sterling to close on 3½ millions. The export of grain multiplied by more than threefold from 890,000 pound in 1848 to 3,900,000 in 1856. The total exports of merchandise rose from 13½ millions sterling in 1818 to over 23 millions in 1856.

" 'The vast increase of productive industry, represented by these figures, enabled the Indian population to purchase the manufactures of England on an unprecedented scale. The imports of cotton goods and twist into India rose from three millions sterling in 1848 to 6-$^{1}/_{3}$ millions in 1856. The total imports of merchandise and treasure increased during the eight years from 10½ to 25½ millions.' (*Dalhousie, Rulers of India Series* by Sir W. W. Hunter, pp. 191, 193-6)

"I am fully alive to the advantages which railways have conferred on India. I have quoted from Sir W.W. Hunter to show how their introduction affected the Indian industries. As Lord Dalhousie's minute shows, one of the objects which they were intended to serve was the promotion of English trade and commerce with India. That was then the policy of the government. I do regret that it was not then also the policy of the government to promote Indian industries, for then India would have prospered as well as England. It is particularly to be regretted that when they decided to develope a vast system of railways in India, they did not also decide to develop the iron and steel industry. For if they had done so, there would have been a much greater and more rapid extension of railways, because they would have cost India much less according to official testimony, the price of iron was increased fifty per cent, by reason of freight and landing charges and would have spelled much greater benefits to the country than they have. The adoption of such a policy had been urged long ago both by the Indians and by Englishmen. In a paper which be read before the Industrial Conference at Poona in 1893, Mr Ranade said: 'Many years ago Captain Townsend of the Ordnance Department observed in his work on the Mineral Wealth of India that nothing strikes the stranger who studies Indian economy so much as the contrast between the bounty of Nature and the poverty of Man in the matter of this iron industry. Endowed more richly in iron ore than almost any other country in the world, India has in a commercial sense, no iron industry at all.' Essays, pp. 158-9).

" 'Mr Ball, Deputy Superintendent of the Geological Survey, in his work on Economic Geology observes that if the government had started the manufacture of iron on an extended scale at the time of the first opening of the railways, great benefits would have accrued to the State. If the state was justified in undertaking the construction of its own railways, there was nothing inconsistent with principle in its undertaking the manufacture of its own iron any more than in its manufacture of salt or opium. The effect of its establishing factories for iron manufacture throughout India would have, in Mr Ball's opinion, enabled the state to keep vast sums of money in circulation, and would have given employment to large numbers of people who now resort to agriculture as their only resource. The golden opportunity was allowed to pass, and we find ourselves in the anomalous situation that after one hundred and fifty years of British rule, the iron resources of India remain undeveloped, and the country pays about ten crores of rupees yearly for its iron supply, while the old race of iron smelters find their occupation gone.' (Essays, pp 164-5).

"That this could have been done is proved by the success of the great Tata Iron and Steel Works. The Government have earned the gratitude of the Indians by the support they gave to the scheme, and it is a matter of great satisfaction that the firm has rendered signal services to the Government and the Empire during this War by a ready supply of rails and shell steel for use in Mesopotamia and Egypt. But if the Government had taken up the question of the manufacture of iron and steel when the schemes of railways were projected, or even later, the industry would have been established in the country much earlier and the entire industrial prospect of the country would have been altered and improved. It was not done because unfortunately for India it was not the policy of the government then to promote Indian industries.

"I have dealt some length upon these facts to remind my English fellow-subjects how largely England is indebted for her industrial efficiency and prosperity.

"The value of these imports had risen by 1913-11 to 25 crores to her connection with India, and how grave an economic wrong has been done to India by the policy pursued in the past, with the object that this should induce them the more to advocate and insist upon a truly liberal policy towards India in the future. I have also done this to dispel the idea that Indians are to blame for the decline of their indigenous industries, or that they suffer from any inherent want of capacity for the industrial development on modern lines, and that the Europeans are by nature more fitted than Asiatics for success in manufacturing pursuits. I have shown that up to the middle of the eighteenth century England herself was an agricultural country; that for thousands of years and up to the beginning of the last century India excelled in manufactures as well as in agriculture, and that if during the century she came to be predominantly agricultural, this was due to the special treatment to which she had been subjected and not to any way of industrial capacity and enterprise among her people.

The Result of the Frequent Famines

"The decline of Indian industries, the growing imports of British manufactures and the exports of raw produce from

India, led inevitably to the impoverishment of the manufacturing classes in all the parts of the country and drove a growing proportion of the population to depend more and more upon the land. Out of a total record export of 58¾ millions in 1878-79, only 6½ per cent, represented the value of what could properly be called manufactured goods, 93½ per cent, being mere raw produce. In 1880 the imports of manufactured goods were valued at round 51,397,561. By the combined operation of these two causes the country was reduced to an economic condition which exposed it to the aggravated evils of the frequent famines. Sir Horace Plunkett whose inability to join us I most sincerely regret, pointed out in his valuable Report of the Recess Committee of 1896, that similar causes had led at an earlier period to the similar results in Ireland. Speaking of the effect of the legislation which had struck at all the Irish industries, not excepting agriculture, he said:

> It forced the population into entire dependence on the land and reduced the country to an economic condition involving periodical famines.

"In India there were five famines between 1800 to 1825: two between 1825 to 1850; six between 1851 to 1875; eighteen between 1876 to 1900. According to Mr Digby, the total mortality according to the official records, between 1854 to 1901 was 28,825,000. Writing in 1901, Mr Digby said:

> Stated roughly, famines and scarcities have been four times as numerous during the last thirty years of the nineteenth century as they were one hundred years earlier, and four times more widespread.

"I agree with my colleagues that, apart from the other advantages which the railways have conferred upon India, they have had an important effect in lessening the disastrous results of famines. Grain can be carried to tracts affected by famine with much greater ease now than could be done before, and deaths from actual unavailability of food can be prevented. Since 1900, when the second Famine Commission, over which Sir Antony MacDonnell (now Lord) presided, made its report, the problem of famine relief and famine administration has also been placed on a satisfactory basis, and an admirable Famine Code has been drawn up, 'In regard to palliatives much has been done; but in respect of prevention, the hand has been slack. And this I regret to say, notwithstanding the fact that many of the remedies which we recommend today were recommended nearly forty years ago.'

"After the disastrous famine of 1877-78, the government was pleased to appoint an Indian Famine Commission to enquire how far is it possible for the government; by its action, to diminish the severity of famines, or to place the people in a better condition for enduring them. In their Report the Commission said: 'A main cause of the disastrous consequences of the Indian famines, and one of the greatest difficulties in the way of providing relief in an effectual shape, is to be found in the fact that the great mass of the people directly depend on agriculture, and that there is no other industry from which any considerable part of the population derives its support. The failure of the usual rains thus deprives the labouring class, as a whole, not only of the ordinary supplies of food obtainable at prices within their reach, but also of the sole employment by which they can earn the means of procuring it. The complete remedy for the condition of things will be found only in the development of industries other than agriculture and independent of the fluctuations of the seasons.

"The principal recommendations which that Commission made for the encouragement of a diversity of occupations among the people are so valuable, and so much in line with many of our own recommendations, that I reproduce them below. They said: 'We have elsewhere expressed our opinion that at the root of much of the poverty of the people of India, and of the risks to which they are exposed in seasons of scarcity, lies the unfortunate circumstance that agriculture forms almost the sole occupation of the mass of the population, and that no remedy for present evils can be complete which does not include the introduction of a diversity of occupations, through which the surplus population may be drawn from the agricultural pursuits and led to find the means of subsistence in manufactures or some such employments.'

"And, after referring to the obstacles that then stood in the way of the investment of English capital in India, and after urging the reasons why direct State aid could not then be given, they proceeded to say: 'There are however, directions in which we have no doubt the Government might usefully aid in fostering the inception of new industries. The introduction of tea cultivation and manufacture is an instance of the successful action of the government which should encourage further measures of a like character. In this case, the government started plantations, imported Chinese workmen, distributed seed, and brought the industry into a condition in which its commercial success was no longer doubtful. It then retired from any share in it, sold its plantations, and left the field to private capitalists. The cultivation of cinchona is a measure of a somewhat similar description though it has not yet passed entirely into the hands of private persons.

"In treating of the improvement of agriculture, we have indicated how we think the more scientific methods of Europe may be brought into practical operation in India by the help of specially–trained experts, and the same general system may, we believe be applied with success both to the actual operations of the agriculture and to the preparation for the market of the raw agricultural staples of the country. Nor does there appear any reason why action of this sort should stop at agricultural produce, and should not be extended to the manufactures which India now produce on a small scale or in a rude form, and which with some improvement might be expected to find enlarged sales, or could take the place of similar articles now imported from foreign countries.

"Among the articles and processes to which these remarks would apply may be named the manufacture and refining of sugar; the tanning of hides; the manufacture of fabrics, cotton, wool and silk; the preparation of fibers of other sorts, and of tobacco; the manufactures of paper, pottery, glass, soap, oils and candles.

"Some of these arts are already practiced with success at government establishments, such as the tannery at Cawnpore, which largely supplies harness for the army, and the carpet and other manufactures carried on in some of the larger jails; and these institutions form a nucleus, around which we may hope to see a gradual spread of the similar industry. They afford practical evidence of the success of the arts practiced, and are schools for training the people of the country in improved methods; and so long as any such institutions fairly supply a government want, which cannot be properly met otherwise, or carry on an art in an improved form, and therefore guide and educate private trade, their influence can hardly fail to be beneficial. The same may be said of the workshops of the government and the railway companies which are essential for the special purposes for which they are kept up, and gradually train and disseminate a more skilled class of artisans.

"The government might further often afford valuable and legitimate assistance to the private persons desiring to embark in a new local industry, or to develop and improve one already existing, by obtaining needful information from other countries or the skilled workmen or supervision, and at the outset supplying such aid at the public cost. So far as the products of any industries established in India can be economically used by the government, they might properly be preferred to the articles imported from Europe, and generally the local markets should be resorted to for all the requisite supplies that they can afford. We are aware that steps have been taken within the last few years to enforce these principles, but more can certainly be done, and greater attention may properly be paid to the subject.

"Otherwise than as above indicated, we do not think it desirable that the government should directly embark in any manufacture or industry in an experimental way. Such experiments to be really successful or valuable must be carried out on a commercial basis. The conditions of any Government undertaking are rarely such as to give it this character, and the fear of incurring an undue expenditure on what is regarded as only an experiment will often lead to failure, which will be nonetheless mischievous because it was thus caused.

"There is no reason to doubt that the action of the government may be of great value in forwarding technical, artistic, and scientific education, in holding out rewards for efforts in these directions, and in forming at convenient centers museums or collections by which the public taste is formed and information is diffused. The great industrial development of Europe in the recent years has doubtless received no small stimulus from such agencies; and the duty of the government in encouraging technical education is one to which the people of England are yearly becoming more alive, and which it is certain will be more adequately performed in the future. All the causes which render such action on the part of the government desirable in Europe apply with greater force to India. Experience, however, is still wanting, even in England, as to how such instruction should be given, and for India it will be hardly possible at present to go beyond the training of ordinary workmen in the practice of mechanical or engineering manipulation.

"To whatever extent it is possible, however, the government should give assistance to the development of industry in a legitimate manner, and without interfering with the free action of the general trading community, it being recognised that every new opening thus created attracts labour which would otherwise be employed to comparatively little purpose on the land, and thus sets up a new bulwark against the total prostration of the labour market, which in the present condition of the population follows on every severe drought.

The Cry of The Indians for the Promotion of Technical Education and Indigenous Industries

"This valuable Report was published in 1880, but it seems that little heed was paid to its most important recommendations. Little was done to encourage indigenous industries; less to promote technical education. In the meantime the Indian National Congress, which was organised to focus Indian public opinion and to represent the wants and wishes of the Indian public to the government, came into existence in 1885. At its third Session in 1887 it passed the following resolution:

> That having regard to the poverty of the people, it is desirable that the government be moved to elaborate a system of technical education, suitable to the condition of the country, to encourage

> indigenous manufactures by a more strict observance of the orders, already existing, in regard to utilising such manufactures for State purposes, and to employ more extensively than at present, the skill and talents of the people of the country.

"At its next session, in 1888, the Congress urged the appointment of a mixed Commission to enquire into the industrial condition of the country as a preliminary to the introduction of a general system of technical education. It reiterated this request in 1891, 1892 and 1893. In 1894 it affirmed in the most emphatic manner the importance of increasing public expenditure on all the branches of education, and the expediency of establishing technical schools and colleges. It repeated the same request in 1895. In 1896 when a famine had broken out in a more or less acute form throughout India, it again urged that 'the true remedy against the recurrence of famine lies in the adoption of a policy which would enforce economy, husband the resources of the State, foster the development of indigenous and local arts and industries which have practically been extinguished, and help forward the introduction of modern arts and industries. In 1898 it again prayed, that having regard to the poverty of the people, and the decline of the indigenous industries, the government will introduce a more elaborate and efficient scheme of technical instruction, and set apart more funds for a better and more successful working of the same. In 1904 the Congress urged the establishment of at least one central fully–equipped polytechnic institute in the country, with minor technical schools and colleges in different provinces and repeated that prayer in 1905. In 1906 it urged that primary education should be made free, and gradually compulsory, all over the country, and that adequate provision should be made for technical education in the different provinces, having regard to local requirements. It reiterated the same prayer in 1908, 1909, 1910, 1911 and 1913. After the outbreak of the War in 1914, the Congress urged the government to adopt immediate measures to organise and develop Indian industries. As the years rolled on, the need for industrial development was more and more keenly felt by the Indians. Since 1905, an Indian Industrial

Conference has met year after year, as an adjunct of the National Congress, and it repeatedly pressed upon the government the need for providing technical, industrial and commercial education throughout the country. It has also urged various other measures for the encouragement of indigenous industries. But neither the recommendations of the Indian Famine Commission nor the representations of the Indian National Congress, nor those of the Indian Industrial Conference, produced much effect. Speaking at the Industrial Conference convened by Government in 1907, Sir John Hewett, the then Lieutenant-Governor of the United Provinces, said:

> The question of technical and industrial education has been before the government and public for over twenty years. There is probably no subject on which more has been written or said, while less has been accomplished.

"The earlier portion of the Chapter X of our Report, dealing with the industrial education, shows how little has been done up to this time to provide such education for the people. A few years ago the Government of India instituted scholarships of the annual value of 150 pound, not exceeding ten in number, to enable the Indians to proceed to Europe and America for special training, but it was not necessarily to be technical. Under this system 100 students have hitherto gone abroad for such training. Finding the provision to promote the scientific and industrial education of the Indians in the country wholly insufficient, a few Indians and European gentlemen started an Association in Calcutta in 1904, one of the objects of which was to enable the distinguished graduates of Indian Universities to prosecute further studies in science in Europe, America, Japan or other foreign countries. Since 1910, the Bengal Government helped the Association with an annual grant of ₹ 5,000, which has been reduced to ₹ 2,500 since the War. Rai Jogendra Ghose Bahadur, Secretary of the Association, told us that over 300 students had been sent abroad with the assistance of this Association for such education, and that 140 of them had returned, of whom 130 were employed. He also told us that his students had started twenty new factories and were in charge of several factories employing a capital of over forty lakhs of rupees. This shows how keen is the desire of the Indians to obtain technical education and to devote themselves to the industrial regeneration of their country. The Government of India has recently increased the number of technical scholarships to thirty and have revised the rules regulating the grant of such scholarships, which are in some respects an improvement on those they have superseded. But these scholarships are too few to meet the requirements of the situation. Adequate provision for imparting useful industrial and technical education both at home and abroad, remains yet to be made for the youth of India.

"In the book—*Progress of the other Nations in Manufactures, and its Effect on India*, reference has been made in Chapters II, VI and VII of our Report to the growth of certain industries in India during recent years with the Indian capital and Indian control, the most important among them being the cotton mill industry, the Tata Iron and Steel Works and the Tata Hydro-Electric Works. So far as this goes, this is a matter of sincere satisfaction. But the progress is altogether small. In the meantime, since 1870, other nations have made enormous progress in manufacturing industries. I would particularly mention Germany, Austria, the United States and Japan, as their progress has specially affected India. They have each done so by devising and carrying out a system of general and technical education for their people, accompanied by a system of State aid and encouragement of industries. And these nations and several others besides most of which have built up their industries by some form of State aid or protection have taken full advantage of the policy of free trade to which India has been subjected, to purchase raw produce from India and to flood her markets with their manufactured goods. India has thus been exposed to ever-extending commercial subjugation by these nations, without being armed and equipped to offer a resistance and without being protected by any fiscal walls or ramparts. This incessant and long-continued attack has affected her agricultural as well as manufacturing industries. Her indigo industry has nearly been killed by Germany. Before 1897, when Dr Bayer produced artificial indigo, Germany had been importing vegetable indigo of the value of over one million sterling, A few years afterwards she was exporting artificial indigo of three times that value. Germany's bounty fed beet sugar gave the first serious shock to the ancient sugar industry of India, and it has suffered and is continually suffering from the competition of foreign sugar. In 1913-14 Germany and Austria purchased from India, raw materials amounting to 24,220,400 pound in value, or just a little less than one-sixth of the total output. While the imports to India from these two countries amounted to 11,304,141 pound. The exports to the United Kingdom in the same year amounted to 38,236,780 pound, and the imports from the United Kingdom to 78,383,149 pound. Forty or fifty years ago, Japan was far behind India both in agriculture and industries. But her government and people, working in conjunction, have brought about a wonderful development of her industries built upon a system of technical education which included everything required to enable her to occupy her proper place among the manufacturing nations of the world. Japan takes in a large proportion of the exports of our cotton, and she sends us an increasing quantity of her cotton goods and other manufactures. The average of her total imports of the five pre-War years 1909-10 to 1913-14 was 2.5 per cent, of our total imports. The share of her imports in the year ending March 1917, was 8.9 per cent, of the total. The total imports of India (excluding 28,959,766 pound of treasure, but including government stores) amounted, in the year ending March 31st 1914, to 127,538,638 pound. In the imports of the five pre-War years 1909-10 to 1913-14, the average share of the United Kingdom was 62.8 per cent; of the other parts of the British Empire, 7 per cent of the allies (excluding Japan), 4.6 per cent of Japan, 2.5 per cent of the United States, 3.1 per cent of Java, 6.4 per cent and of the other foreign countries (principally Germany and Austria-Hungary), 13.6 per cent. The share of the principal countries in the imports of the year ending March 31, 1917 was the United Kingdom, 587 per cent; other parts of the British Empire, 7 per cent: allies (excluding Japan), 3.3 per cent; Japan 8.9 per cent; the United States, 7.3 per cent; Java,

8.9 per cent; and the other foreign countries 5.9 per cent. The extent to which India has thus come to be dependent; upon the other countries for the raw materials and the manufactured articles necessary in the daily life of a modern civilised community is deplorable. The following classified table of the imports which came into India in the year ending March 1914, will give an idea of the extent of this dependence:

	£
I. Food, drink, and tobacco ...	16,441,330
Fish (excluding canned fish) ...	208,330
Fruits and vegetables	753,583
Grain, pulses and flour	185,560
Liquors	1,251,642
Provisions and oilman's stores ...	1,649,087
Spices	1,154,875
Sugar	9,971,251
Tea	152,409
Other food and drinks, i.e., coffee (other than roasted or ground) hops, etc. ...	511,623
Tobacco	501,923
II. Raw materials and produce, and articles mainly unmanufactured ...	7,088,380
Coal, coke, and patent fuel ...	710,920
Gums, resins, and ice	175,764
Hides and skins, raw	101,066
Metallic ores and scrap iron or steel for manufacture	41,977
Oils	2,934,611
Seeds, including oil seeds ...	53,431
Tallow, steering, wax	150,638
Textile materials	1,204,510
Wood and timber	515,590
Miscellaneous (including shells, chink, cowries, fish manure, pulp of wood and rags for paper)	1,149,873
III. Articles wholly or mainly manufactured	96,769,443
Apparel	1,669,389
Arms, ammunitions and military stores.	236,713
Carriages and cars, including cycles and motor cars	1,422,667
Chemicals, drugs and medicines ...	1,605,699
Cutlery, hardware, implements (except machine tools) and instruments ...	4,291,140

	£
Dyes and colours	1,510,933
Furniture, cabinet-ware, and manufactures of wood	224,323
Glassware and earthenware ...	1,728,667
Hides and skins, tanned or dressed, and leather	266,683
Machinery of all kinds (including belting for machinery)	5,508,397
Metals, iron and steel and manufactures thereof	10,633,249
Metals, other than iron and steel and manufactures thereof ...	41,010,801
Paper, paste board, and stationery ...	1,524,982
Railway plant and rolling stock ...	6,689,794
Yarn and textile fabrics ...	50,360,043
Miscellaneous (including prints, engravings, pictures, rubber manufactures, smoker's requisites, soaps, spirits perfumed, sticks and whips, stones and marble, toilet requisites, toys, and requisites for games and sports, umbrellas and umbrella fitting-) ...	5,055,963
IV. Miscellaneous and unclassified, including living animals, fodder, bran pollards and articles imported by post ...	1,916,135
V. Government stores	5,373,350
Total value of all imports, excluding treasure	£127,538,638

"Chapter IV of our Report gives a more analysed and critical summary of the industrial deficiencies of India. It similarly points out that the list of industries which, though the materials and articles we import are essential alike in peace and war, are lacking in this country is lengthy and ominous; and that until they are brought into existence on an adequate scale, Indian capitalists, will, in times of peace, be deprived of a number of profitable enterprises, whilst, as experience has shown in the event of a war which renders sea transport impossible, India's all-important existing industries will be exposed to the risk of stoppage, her consumers to great hardship, and her armed forces to the gravest possible danger. With the abundance of our raw materials, agricultural and mineral, with the great natural facilities for power and transport, with a vast borne market to absorb all that we may manufacture, it should not be difficult to effectively cut down this list, if the government will equip the people for the task by providing the necessary educational and banking facilities and extending to them the patronage and support of the State. How the government may best do this is the question we have to answer.

Government Industrial Policy in Recent Years

"I have little to add to the history of the Government industrial policy in the recent years which is given in Chapter VIII of the Report. The account given there of the efforts made by the government for the improvement of the Indian industries shows how little has been achieved. But I do not agree with my colleagues when they say (paragraph 111) that this has been owing to the lack of a definite and accepted policy, and to the absence of an appropriate organisation of the specialised experts. I share with them the regret that Lord Morley did not approve that part of the proposal of the Madras Government made in 1910, which urged that the government agency should be employed to demonstrate that certain industrial improvements could be adopted with commercial advantage; and I am thankful that in modification of that order, Lord Crewe, by his telegram, dated February 1, 1916, authorised the Government of India, pending final orders on this Commission's Report, to instruct local governments that in cases in which they desire to help the particular industries they may do so subject to your approval and to the financial exigencies, without being unduly restricted by my predecessor's rulings.' But I cannot endorse that part of the Report which speaks of 'the deadening effect produced by Lord Morley's dictum of 1910 on the initial attempts made by the government for the improvement of the industries.

"(Introductory, page xix.) I think my colleagues have taken an exaggerated view of the effect of Lord Morley's refusal to sanction the particular part of the Madras Government's proposal to which reference has been made above. In justice to Lord Morley, and in order that the orders which he passed on the subject of technical education may be properly appreciated,

I will quote below the following two paragraphs from the dispatch in question, dated July 29 1910. Said his Lordship: 'I have examined the account which the Madras Government has given of the attempts to create new industries in the province. The results represent considerable labour and ingenuity, but they are not of a character to remove my doubts as to the utility of State effort in this direction, unless it is strictly limited to industrial instruction and avoids the semblance of a commercial venture. So limited interference with private enterprise is avoided, while there still remains an ample and well-defined sphere of activity. The limit disregarded, there is the danger that the new state industry will either remain a petty and ineffective plaything, or will become a costly and hazardous speculation. I sympathise with the Conference and the Madras Government in their anxiety for the industrial development of the province, but I think that it is more likely to be retarded than promoted by the diversion to the State-managed commercial enterprises of funds which are urgently required for the extension of the industrial and technical instruction.

" 'The policy which I am prepared to sanction is that State funds may be expended upon familiarising the people with such improvements in the methods of production as modern science and the practice of the European countries can suggest; further than this the State should not go, and it must be left to the private enterprise to demonstrate that these improvements can be adopted with commercial advantage. Within the limits here indicated it appears to me that the objects which the Industrial Conference had in view can all be accomplished by the means of technical and industrial schools; it is in such schools that a knowledge of new industries and new processes can be imparted, that the use of new implements can best be taught and the technical skill of the artisans most readily improved. In a leather school the method of chrome tanning can be demonstrated and taught; in a weaving school the indigenous handloom can be improved and the advantage of the improvement demonstrated. If the schools are properly managed they will supply the private capitalist with instructed workmen and with all the information he requires for a commercial venture. To convert the leather or weaving school into a government factory in order to demonstrate that articles can be manufactured and sold to the public at a profit, goes, in my view, beyond what is desirable and beyond what is found necessary in the other provinces. My objections do not extend to the establishment of a bureau of industrial information, or to the dissemination from such a centre of intelligence and advice regarding new industries, processes or appliances, provided that nothing is done calculated to interfere with private enterprise.

"As Lord Crewe pointed out in his dispatch No. 24, Revenue, dated March 125, 1912: 'The Government of Madras seemed to have placed too limited a construction upon the orders given in my predecessor's dispatch of July 29, 1910. The policy which he then sanctioned was that the state funds might be expended upon familiarising the people with such methods of production as modern science and the practice of the European countries could suggest. This need not he interpreted as confining instruction solely to the industrial schools. I am prepared to recognise that in certain cases instruction in the industrial schools may be insufficient and may require to be supplemented by the practical training in workshops, where the application of new the processes may be demonstrated; and there is no objection to the purchase and maintenance of the experimental plant for puprose of demonstrating the advantage of improved machinery or new processes and for ascertaining the data of production.

"Indian public opinion no doubt desired that the government should go farther than Lord Morley had sanctioned. But even so, they would have been grateful if action had been taken within the ample and well-defined sphere of activity which he had sanctioned; if the funds which it was proposed to divert to the state-managed commercial enterprises; had been devoted to the extension of the industrial and technical instruction for which his Lordship said, 'They were "urgently required" if the state funds had been 'expended upon familiarising the people with such improvements in the methods of production as modern science and the practice of the European countries could suggest.' Their complaint was that that was not done. It is said in paragraph 199 of the Report that the Government of India had neither the organisation nor the equipment to give effect even to the comparatively limited policy sanctioned by Lord Morley. The obvious answer is that the necessary organisation and equipment should have been created.

A Welcome Change

"The outbreak of the War drew forcible attention to the extent of India's dependence upon the countries outside the British Empire, particularly upon Germany and Austria, for the supply of many of the necessities of life for her people, and some time after the commencement of the War, the Government of India resolved to examine the question of the industrial policy which the government should pursue in the altered state of things in India. In their dispatch to the Secretary of State dated November 26, 1915, Lord Hardinge's government put the case for a change of policy in very clear and forceful language. They said: 'It is becoming increasingly clear that a definite and self-conscious policy of improving the industrial capabilities of India will have to be pursued after the War, unless she is to become more and more a dumping ground for the manufacture of foreign nations who will be competing more keenly for the markets, the more it becomes apparent that the political future of the larger nations depends on their economic position. The attitude of the Indian public towards this important question is unanimous and cannot be left out of account. Manufactures, politicians and the literate public have for long been pressing their demands for a definite and accepted policy of State aid to the Indian industries and the demand is one which evokes the sympathy of all classes of Indians whose position or intelligence leads them to take any degree of interest in such matters. The dispatch emphasised the need for an industrial policy which will enable technical education in India to produce its best results, and which will lighten the pressure on purely literary courses and reduce the excessive demand for employment in the services and callings to which these courses lead up. Finally the Government said: 'After the War India will consider herself entitled to demand the utmost help which her government can afford to enable her to to take her place, so, far as circumstances permit, as a manufacturing country.'

"The acceptance of this policy by the Secretary of State for India and the appointment of this commission to consider and report in what ways this help may be given was welcomed by the Indians with feelings of gratitude and hope, like the dawn of day after a dark and dreary night. But the hope is occasionally clouded by a recollection of the fact that the Labour Party joining with the Irish Nationalists and the Lancashire vote mobilised its force against the government in England against the raising of the import duty on cotton goods in India even while the Indian cotton excise duty which India has regarded as a great and crying grievance all these twenty-one years, was still allowed to continue and that so highly honoured a statesman as Mr Asquith gave his support to the government policy only on the understanding that this in common with all other fiscal issues would be reconsidered at the end of the War. Indians remember, however, with gratitude the firm attitude which Mr Austen Chamberlain, the then Secretary of State of India, adopted in the matter, and the reply which he gave to the Lancashire deputation that waited on him with reference to that simple fiscal measure, without which, as he told the deputation, it would have been impossible for India to make the contribution of 100 millions to the costs of the War.

"The brief narrative which I have given here of the industrial relations of India, with England, and of the policy which England has pursued towards India, will, I hope, lead some of those of my English fellow-subjects who are unwilling to let the Government of India protect and promote Indian industries under a wrong apprehension that would injure English interests, to recall to mind how much India has contributed to the prosperity of England mainly during a century and a half, and how much she has suffered by reason of the illiberal policy which has hitherto been pursued towards her. It will lead them, I hope, to reflect that the result of this policy is that, after a hundred and fifty years of the British Rule, India, with all her vast natural resources and requirements, is the poorest country in the world, and that comparing her pitiable condition with the prosperous states of the self-governing dominions which have enjoyed freedom to develop their industries, they will recognise the necessity and the justice of allowing India's liberty to regain national health and prosperity. Such a policy will not benefit India alone. It will benefit England also. For if India will grow rich, if the standard of living in India will rise, her vast population will naturally absorb a great deal more of imports than it does at present. This view was repeatedly urged by Mr Dadabhai Naoroji and it is fully supported by the history of other countries which have become prosperous during the recent times. The United States offers an illustration. The following figures show how their imports have grown with their prosperity:

Year	**Imports in millions of dollars**
1860	353
1870	435
1880	667
1890	789
1900	849

"The same truth is illustrated by the history of the commerce of Japan. As Japan has been developing her own manufactures and growing in affluence, she has been furnishing a rapidly- growing market to the merchants of the world. The following table makes this clear:

Annual Average Imports of Japan in Recent Decades.
Values in Millions of Yen

From	*U.K.*	*Germany*	*USA*	*Other Countries*	*Total*
1881-1890 ...	19.6	3.4	4.2	19.3	46.5
1891-1900 ...	46.6	14.8	22.8	87.0	171.2
1900-1909 ...	84.3	36.1	65.8	199.8	386.0

"Commenting on the growth and variety of the imported manufactures in the United States noted above, Mr Olive Day says in *History of Commerce* (p. 568): 'It is probable that the United States will always continue to import manufactured wares like those named above, in great variety and amounting in the total to considerable value. We cannot afford to refuse the contributions of peoples who have specialised in various lines, and by reason of inherited taste and skill, or with the aid of exceptional natural resources, can offer us what we cannot readily produce ourselves.'

"This is exactly what I would say with regard to our future, assuming that we are allowed to develop our home industries to the fullest extent we can. But I need not labour this point further. I am glad to find that the Committee on Commercial and Industrial Policy after the War of which Lord Balfour of Burleigh was the Chairman, has expressed the same view. In paragraphs 232 and 233 of their Final Report they say: 'Whilst Europe as a whole may be said to be divided into settled fields of international competition where local circumstances, convenience of transport, and suitability of production for local needs, have become the controlling factors, there remain vast markets still practically untouched for the future development of the exporting nations of the world. China, with its 400 millions of population, an old and industrious civilisation, must in the near future develop its already great and growing demands for products of our trades. There are great potentialities in India and there is also the demand of Siberia and the smaller Far Eastern countries, which are likely in future to afford profitable markets. It is true that in this sphere the competition of Japan will have to be increasingly reckoned with, but we have no doubt that with a rise in the standard of living of Eastern peoples, there will come a corresponding increase of the quantity and improvement of the goods demanded. This development cannot fail to be of advantage to the British industry, and for this reason, if for no other, we desire to emphasise the importance of all the measures, including particularly the rapid extension of Railways, likely to promote the economic well-being of India. The hope of

Indians for the industrial development of their country has been further strengthened by the knowledge that, like their noble predecessors in office, the present Viceroy and the Secretary of State are also convinced of the necessity of a liberal policy being adopted in respect of Indian industrial development. They have read the following passage in the Report on Constitutional Reforms with great satisfaction: 'On all grounds, a forward policy in industrial development is urgently called for, not merely to give India economic stability; but in order to satisfy the aspirations of her people who desire to see her stand before the world as a well-poised, up-to-date country; in order to provide an outlet for the energies of her young men who are otherwise drawn exclusively to government service or a few overstocked professions; in order that money now lying unproductive may be applied to the benefit of the whole community; and in order that the too speculative and literary tendencies of Indian thought may be bent to more practical ends, and the people may be better qualified to shoulder the new responsibilities which the new constitution will lay upon them. These considerations led Lord Hardinge's Government to recommend the appointment of the Industrial Commission which is at present sitting. These are political considerations peculiar to India itself. But both on economic and military ground the imperial interests also demand that the natural resources of India should henceforth be better utilised. We cannot measure the access of strength which an industrialised India will bring to the power of the Empire; but we are sure that it will be welcomed after the War. How far the hope so raised will be reaped, will depend largely upon the decision of the vital question whether the power as well as the responsibility of promoting the industrial development of India, shall be placed in the Government of India, acting under the control of the elected representatives of the people in the legislative council. This factor governs all our recommendations. Industries and Agriculture.'

"In Chapter V of the Report dealing with industries and agriculture my colleagues say: 'We take this opportunity of stating in the most emphatic manner our opinion of the paramount importance of agriculture to this country, and of the necessity of doing everything possible to improve its methods and increase its output. Such improvement will, we anticipate, be mainly effected by the organisations which are in process of development under the charge of the imperial and provincial departments of agriculture, and though the results attained are not yet of much economic importance, they are steadily growing and will eventually demand large manufacturing establishments to produce the machinery, plants and tools which the *ryots* will find advantageous as labour-saving devices.'

"They point out the possibilities of improved agricultural methods and suggest that there is much scope for the use of power-driven machinery in agriculture for lifting water from wells, channels, tanks and rivers, for irrigation and for other purposes, and for improving the land by draining low-lying ground and by deep ploughing, etc. They also recommend the provision of hand machinery of improved types, especially for the reaping, threshing and winnowing of crops. They go on to say:

'India is not at all accustomed to the free use of mechanical appliances, and it should be an important function of the Departments of Industries and Agriculture to encourage their introduction in every possible way. For a long time to come the employment of machinery in agriculture in India will largely depend upon the completeness and efficiency of the official organisation which is created to encourage its use and to assist those who use it.'

"In this connection I would draw attention to the opinion of Mr James MacKenna, the Agricultural Adviser to the Government of India. At page 29 of his valuable pamphlet on 'Agriculture in India', published in 1913, he says: 'We have seen that the introduction of European machinery has always figured prominently in the efforts of the amateur agricultural reformer. Much success has undoubtedly been obtained in the introduction of grain-winnowers, cane-crushing machinery, etc. But in recommending the introduction of reaping machines or heavy English ploughs, caution is necessary. Reaping machines may be useful on large estates where labour is scarce, but the whole rural economy of a tract where population is dense may be upset by their use. A large amount of cheap labour which ordinarily does the reaping is thrown out of employment; the gleaners lose their recognised perquisites. In the case of heavy ploughs, the advisability of deep ploughing has first to be proved. In both cases the capacity of the available cattle and the difficulty of replacing broken spare parts and of carrying out repairs are serious obstacles to the introduction of foreign machinery. As in the case of plants, the improvement of the local material which the cultivator can himself make and repair and which his cattle can draw, seems the more hopeful line of improvement.' I entirely endorse this opinion. The difficulties pointed out by Mr MacKenna apply with equal if not greater, force in the case of power-driven machinery for the purposes indicated above. As my colleagues have observed in India agricultural conditions are widely different from those in Europe and Germany, and as yet very little of mechanically–operated plant has come into use here, chiefly because holdings are small and scattered, and the *ryots* possess little or no capital. The results achieved in this direction in the south of India are also not very important perhaps if measured by their immediate economic effect. While, therefore, I appreciate the value of the use of power-driven machinery in the development of agriculture, when economic conditions should favour its introduction, I do not agree with the recommendation that it should be an important function of the Departments of Industries and Agriculture to encourage their introduction in every possible way. I apprehend that with such a recommendation from the commission, the zeal for promoting mechanical engineering interests and establishments may push the use of the power-driven machinery without due appreciation of the economic interests of the agriculturists in the present circumstances of the country. For these reasons, and because in any case the introduction of the power-driven machinery will take a long time, I think it my duty to draw attention to the other means of improvement, particularly to the agricultural education.

"The history of agriculture in India during the British rule has recently been told by Mr MacKenna in his pamphlet referred to above. Agriculture is by far the greatest of the industries of India, and nearly 200 millions of its immense population are dependent for their livelihood on agriculture or on industries subsidiary to it. The Famine Commission of 1860 made very strong recommendations as to the necessity of the establishing departments under a Director in each province to promote agricultural enquiry, agricultural improvement and famine relief. The departments were constituted, but by a Resolution published in 1831 the Government of India decided to postpone agricultural improvement until the scheme of agricultural enquiry had been completed. Nothing was done till 1889, at the end of which year the Secretary of State sent out Dr Voelcker of the Royal Agricultural Society to enquire into and advise upon the improvement of Indian agriculture. After touring all over India and holding many conferences, Dr Voelcker recommended a systematic prosecution of the agricultural enquiry and the spread of general and agricultural education, and laid down in considerable detail the lines on which the agricultural improvement was possible. An agricultural chemist and an assistant chemist were appointed in 1892 to carry on the research and to dispose of the chemical questions connected with forest and agriculture. In 1901 an Inspector-General of Agriculture was appointed. Two other scientists were added to the staff in 1903. Mr MacKenna says: 'The object aimed at was to increase the revenues of India by the improvement of agriculture; but nothing was done for that improvement, and the expansion of the Land Records staff and the compilation of statistics almost entirely occupied the attention of the provincial departments. An Agricultural Research Institute was established in Pusa in 1905 with the help of a generous donation of 30,000 pound made to the Viceroy by Mr Henry Phipps of Chicago. In 1905-06 the Government of India announced that a sum of 20 lakhs (subsequently raised to 24 lakhs) would annually be available for the improvement of agriculture. Agricultural colleges were accordingly reorganised or started at Poona, Cawnpore, Sabour, Nagpur, Lyallpur and Coimbatore. These colleges have been doing good work, but very little progress has been made with the agricultural education of the people. I wish to acknowledge here the improvement which has been brought about in agriculture by means of our large irrigation works, which the government has constructed, the improvement of wheat and cotton and in other ways. That improvement has been great and the government is entitled to full credit for it. But I wish to draw attention to the urgent need and great possibilities of the further improvement. Irrigation requires to be much more extended. A more systematic and extended programme of the improvement requires to be adopted, the most important item in which should be the agricultural education.

Agricultural Education

"Writing in 1915 on this subject Mr MacKenna said:

'There is probably no subject connected with agriculture on which so much has been written as agricultural education none, perhaps in which less has been effected, it is a constant anxiety to the agricultural workers who mainly strive after an ideal which seems untenable. It has been debated at the numerous conferences and has been the text of many writers, but there are practically no results to show. The Famine Commissioners, so long ago as 1880, expressed the view that no general advance in the agricultural system can be expected until the rural population had been so educated as to enable them to take a practical interest in agricultural progress and reform. These views were confirmed by the Agricultural Conference of 1888... The most important, and probably, the soundest proposition laid down by the conference was that it was most desirable to extend primary education amongst the agricultural classes. But with the enunciation of this basic principle other resolutions were passed which, while containing much that was excellent, probably led to the extraordinary confusion of the subsequent years. For some time the dominating idea was that it was necessary to teach agriculture somehow or the other in the rural schools.

Fortunately this idea has now been abandoned. It is now agreed that agriculture, as such, cannot be taught in schools; that rural education must be general and agricultural education technical....The view now taken is that, instead of endeavouring to teach agriculture as such an attempt should be made to impart to the general scheme of education a markedly agricultural colour and to encourage powers of observation and the study of nature with special reference to the surroundings of each school. With this object the text books are being re-written so as to include lessons on familiar objects; nature study is being taught and school gardens have been started. There are, however, serious difficulties in obtaining suitable teachers. But, as I have already said, more will depend on the natural awakening of the intelligence of pupils by the spread of general education than on the specialised training. And in primary schools the essential thing is to establish general education on a firm basis so that the pupils may develop power of observation and of reasoning. If this be done interest in their surroundings will naturally follow.

"Mr MacKenna says in the end: 'Any attempt to teach agriculture in India, before investigation has provided the material, it is a fundamental mistake which has seriously retarded development, and this mistake has affected not only elementary, but to a much greater extent collegiate education. This is where we stood after thirty-five years of inquiry, discussion and trial! Other civilised countries took a much shorter period to decide upon a definite course of agricultural education and have prospered on their decision. In Sir Horace Plunkett's *A Report of the Recess Committee of 1896* an account is given of the systems of state aid to agricultre and industry which were prevalent before that year in the various countries of Europe. Though these countries, as also America and Japan, have made much greater progress since then both in agricultural education and improvement, that report is still of great value to us and will amply repay perusal. I will extract only one passage from it here. Said Sir Horace Plunkett and his colleagues:

'The most positive action of the state in assisting agriculture is taken in connection with education. Everywhere it is accepted as an axiom that technical knowledge and general enlightenment of the agricultural class are the most valuable of all the levels of progress. The great sums spent by the various countries in promoting technical education as applied to agriculture, as well as to the other industries, prove this.' M. Marey-Oyens, the head of the Dutch Board of Commerce and Industry, and president of the agricultural council, says: 'Every guilder spent in the promotion of agricultural teaching brings back profit hundredfold.' 'Every franc spent in agricultural teaching brings a brilliant return,' says the Belgian minister of agriculture in his message to the parliament last year. M. Tisserand attributes the great progress made by French agriculture since 1870, in a large measure to our schools, our professors, our experiment stations, and the illustrious men of science, whom the administration has induced to devote themselves to the study of agricultural questions. Mr M.H. Jenkins, in his report to the Royal Commission on Technical Instruction says, 'The results of agricultural education in Denmark have been something extraordinary. Danish butter is now the best in the world; in 1830 it was described by the British Vice-Consul at Copenhagen as execrably bad; the progress since is directly traceable to agricultural education.' (Report, pp. 54-55).

"It is hardly necessary to refer at any length to the great progress of agricultural education and improvement in America or to the enormous wealth and prosperity which has resulted therefrom. But I might refer here to the case of Japan. We know that Japan has made remarkable progress in agriculture. She developed an excellent system of agricultural education many years ago. 'In the valuable *Note on Agriculture in Japan* which Sir Frederick Nicholson submitted to the commission along with his written evidence, he describes the system of agricultural education which he found at work in Japan in 1907.' It is not necessary for me to describe the system here. My object simply is to draw attention to the necessity, in the interests of the improvement of agriculture and agriculturists, of early steps being taken to devise a system of both general and agricultural education for the masses of our agricultural population.

"I would also recommend that the attention of the agricultural department be invited to the desirability of carrying out those other recommendations of Dr. Voelcker which have not yet been carried out, particularly those relating to the establishment wherever possible of Fuel and Fodder Reserved. Our attention was particularly drawn to the facts that the high prices of fuel and fodder are inflicting serious hardship and loss upon the people in general and of the agriculturists in particular. I may note that we were informed that last year about 40,000 acres of irrigated plantation were established by the forest department in the Punjab, in order to meet provincial requirements.

"The high prices of the foodstuffs and the consequent suffering to which the bulk of the people are exposed have made the question of increasing the yield of our food crops also one of great and pressing importance. In his pamphlet on the Agricultural Problems of India, which Rai Gangaram Bahadur submitted to the Commission, he argues that, 'We are producing in a normal year, just enough to meet our requirements (of food consumption) with no surplus to meet the contingency of a failure of the rains in the ensuing year. We are also confronted with the fact that in India the yield per acre of crops is very much lower than what it is in other countries. The figures given by Rai Gangaram Bahadur at page 12 and in Table VIII of his book are instructive. The average yield per acre of wheat in Bombay and the United Provinces was 1,250 Ibs.; in the United Kingdom, it was 1,973 Ibs.; in Belgium, 2,174 Ibs,; in Denmark, 2,526 Ibs.; in Switzerland, 1,858 Ibs. The average yield per acre of barley in the United Provinces was 1,300 Ibs.; in the United Kingdom, 2,105 Ibs.; in Belgium, 2,953 Ibs.; in Denmark, 2,456 Ibs. in Switzerland, 1,940 Ibs. The average yield per acre of maize in the North-West Frontier was 1,356 Ibs.; in Canada, 3,487 Ibs.; in New Zealand, 3,191 Ibs. in Switzerland, 2,198 Ibs. The average yield per acre of rice in India is only half of what it is in Japan. The possibilities of development that lie before us are therefore vast, and the call for measures for improvement is urgent and insistent. It is the call both of India and of the Empire, and I strongly recommend that the matter should receive prompt and adequate attention from the agricultural departments both imperial and provincial.

"In this connection I desire also to draw attention to the necessity of providing greater financial facilities for agricultural improvement. So long ago as 1882, that revered friend of India, Sir William Wedderburn, advocated the establishment of agricultural banks for this purpose. The Indian National Congress pressed the suggestion upon the attention of government. But it has not yet been carried out. I would draw attention to the very valuable paper on 'The Reorganization of Rural Credit in India', which was read by Mr Ranade before the first Industrial Conference at Poona in 1891. (Ranade's Essays, pp. 41-64). It is a powerful plea for the establishment of agricultural banks. I might add that, besides other countries mentioned by Mr Ranade, Japan has provided such facilities as are here recommended for the improvement of its agriculture. *The Japan Year Book for 1917* says: 'There are two kinds of agricultural credit. They are long credit and short credit, the former for the purchase of farm land and for the development of farm land and other permanent improvements for which a loan for a term of 50 years or less is allowed. The short-term credit is one that is to be used mostly for the purchase of fertilisers, farm implements, or food for cattle. Our banks usually give credit for a term of five years or less. There are also credit associations for supplementing these agricultural banks.'

Technical Education

"The modern system of technical education may be said to date from the famous Universal Exhibition held in London in the year 1851. Speaking generally, Englishmen did not believe in the value of technical education, and much effort has been necessary in England itself to make them do so. One of the earliest of these efforts was made by Mr J. Scott Russell, who published a valuable book in 1869, named *Systematic Technical*

Education for the English People. In this book, after showing that education should be both general and special, he said: 'The highest value in the world's markets will be obtained by that nation which has been at most pains to cultivate the intelligence of its people generally, and afterwards to give each the highest education and training in this special calling. In other words, the value of the nation's work will vary with the excellence of the national system of technical education. All I have said above seems axiomatic. To me it is so, but I trust the reader will not be offended if I am obliged to treat it quite otherwise. The English people do not believe in the value of technical education. Still less do they believe in the value of a national system of education, and still less in the duty of the Government, the legislature, and the educated part of a community, to undertake the education of a whole people. I am therefore compelled to prove as mere matters of facts that which the accomplished scholar, the observant traveller takes as an axiom on which argument is vested. It is the object of this chapter to prove that technical education has brought good of a national and commercial kind to those who possess it; that the want of it is attended with pecuniary loss, and that there is social danger to the community in our continued neglect of it.

"Of late years a series of great public events have been taking place, which have been of great national value in serving to awaken the British people—For half a century they had been enjoying the fruits of the inventions of a few men of genius who had created the whole system of modern manufacturing, and the Providence had also endowed them with the accumulated wealth of countless centuries stored up in the bowels of the earth in the shape of coal and iron, ready to be used or wasted and worked out in this manufacturing century. The genius of a few men having set coal and iron to do the manufacturing work of mind and man, the citizens of England had begun to think that it was they who were superior in intelligence and civilisation to the un-coaled, un-ironed, un-engineered nations around them. For half a century nothing occurred to awaken them from this dream, and for that half century the works of English engineers and English iron and coal bore the highest reputation, and earned the highest prices in the world. Eighteen years ago there began a series of competitive trials of intelligence and skill between the citizens of the different civilised nations of the world. The scene of the first trial was in London in 1851. It was the famous Universal Exhibition of the Industries and Products of all nations. In that great school the civilised nations of Europe had their first lesson in technical education. They were able to see in how many things England retained her hereditary excellence and England was able to see in how many branches of taste and skill other nations possessed qualities in which she was wanting. (*Systematic Technical Education for the English People*, by J. Scott Russell. London, Bradbury, Evans & Co., 11 Bouveverie Street, 1869, pp. 79-81.)

"Mr Russell went on to say that up to 1851 and for many years after, England held supremacy in the great objects of manufacturing and constructive skill. But she lagged behind other nations in some other arts. For instance: 'The Exhibition of 1851 had disgusted the whole nation with its blue earthenware plates, cups and saucers, borrowed from the 2,000 years' tradition of China, and with its huge lumps of glass, called decanters and glasses, out or moulded into hideous distortions of form... Entire England was struck by the amazing superiority of some continental nations in the beauty and grace of design, which sufficed to convert the rude and nearly worthless material of clay and flint into valuable and invaluable works of art, in earthenware and glass. She occupied the four years' interval between the Exhibitions of 1851 and 1855 in collecting and diffusing through the manufacturing countries the best models of the best masters, in establishing for the potteries and glass works schools of design, and in training teachers for art workmen. These young institutions already bore fruit in 1855, and when the second Exhibition took place in Paris in 1855 England was no longer outstripped in pottery and glass. On the other hand, the Exhibition of 1851 made the French and German nations fully realise their inferiority to England in the manufactures of iron and steel, the great instruments of skill, industry, mechanical power, and transport. When the Exhibition of 1855 took place, it was found that they had already recorded much advance in the manufacture of iron, steel and other metal. They had already established schools in every metropolis, large town, or centre of industry for educating professional men and masters, for training foremen and skilled workmen, and for educating apprentices.'

"The fourth Exhibition took place in Paris in 1867. It gave the nations, and especially England, a final lesson. 'By that Exhibition,' says Mr Scott Russell, 'we were rudely awakened and thoroughly alarmed. We then learnt, not that we were equalled, but that we were beaten not on some points, but by some nation or other on nearly all those points on which we had prided ourselves... England was convinced that she had been asleep, and that a whole generation of wakeful, skilled workmen had been trained in other countries during the interval between 1851 and 1867.' (Ibid, p 86).

"The jurors who had been appointed at the Paris Exhibition and the government reporters made their report. On this report the government sent abroad a Commissioner to ascertain whether the alleged defects of the English system of education, and the inferiority of the English to some other people in some sort of technical skill, were real or imaginary. Mr Samuelson, MP, travelled in France, Belgium and Germany, examining as he went the most famous establishments on the continent which stood in direct rivalry to England. 'He found', said Mr Bussell, 'everywhere in these establishments men of all ranks better educated than our own; working men lees illiterate foremen and managers well-educated, and masters accomplished, well-informed, technical men.' He summed up the result of his examination as follows: 'I do not think it possible to estimate precisely what has been the influence of continental education on continental manufactures... That the rapid progress of many trades abroad has been greatly facilitated by the superior technical knowledge of the directors of works everywhere, and by the comparatively advanced elementary instruction of the workers in some departments of industry, can admit of but little doubt...Mean while we know that our manufacturing artisans are imperfectly taught, our agricultural labourers illiterate; neither one nor the other can put forth with effect the splendid qualities with which Providence has endowed our people. Our foremen, chosen from the lower industrial ranks, have no sufficient opportunities of correcting the deficiencies of their early education; our managers are too apt, in every case of novelty, to proceed by trial and error, without scientific principles to guide them; and the sons of our great manufacturers too often either despise the pursuits of their fathers, as mere handicrafts unworthy of man of wealth and education, or else, overlooking the beautiful examples which they afford of the application of natural laws to the wants of men, follow them solely as a means of heaping up more wealth, or at the best for want of other occupation: to the evils of such a condition not only our statesmen, but also our people, are rapidly awakening and the disease being once acknowledged, I believe the remedy will soon be applied.'

"The following statement of one of the jurors consulted by the commissioner expressed the general sense of those who had been examined. Said Mr Mundella: 'I am of the opinion that English workman is gradually losing the race, through the superior intelligence which foreign governments are carefully developing in their artisans...The education of Germany is the result of a national organisation, which compels every peasant to send his children to school, and afterwards affords the opportunity of acquiring such technical knowledge as may be useful in the department of industry to which they were destined...If we are to maintain our position in industrial competition, we must oppose to this national organisation one equally effective and complete; if we continue the fight with our present voluntary system, we shall be defeated generations, hence we shall be struggling with ignorance, squalor, pauperism and crime: but with a system of national education made compulsory, and supplemented with art and industrial education. I believe within twenty years England would possess the most intelligent and inventive artisans in the world.'

"The people and parliament of England recognised the soundness of this opinion. The Elementary Education Act was passed in 1870, an expenditure of many millions a year was agreed upon, and elementary education made compulsory. The provision for supplementing this education with industrial and technical education was slower to come, but come it did. England has made a great deal of provision since then for imparting technical and scientific education in her schools, colleges and universities. The number of these latter has been raised from 1860 from nine to eighteen. It is this which has enabled England to maintain her high position and to keep up her industrial eminence. It is this which has enabled her to fight the splendid fight she has fought in this War. For, though every lover of liberty must rejoice at the invaluable help which the United States of America are now giving to the cause of freedom, it is but bare justice to say that, unprepared though England was before the War, it is British brains and British technical skill united no doubt with French brains and French technical skill, and supported by British and French hearts of steel, that have enabled Britain and France to baffle Germany, and made it possible for the Allies to achieve a final victory. And yet as the reports of the various departmental committees of the Committee on Commercial and Industrial Policy after the War show, the wisdom and experience of England is loudly calling for widespread and far-reaching changes in respect of primary and secondary education and apprenticeship, and for better technical and art education, for her people in order that her industrial position after the War may be quite secure.

"I have referred at length to the history of the progress of education, both general and technical, in England, as it has a great lesson and an inspiration for the US. Our education today is in many respects nearly in as bad a condition as was England's in 1869; and, in my opinion, the course which was then suggested by Mr Mundella and Mr Samuelson in the passages I have quoted above, is the exact course which should be adopted here. It was the misfortune of India that when our English-fellow-subjects, who have taken upon themselves the responsibility for the welfare of the people of India, were convinced of the need of universal elementary education in England, they did not introduce it at the same time in India also. If this had been done, India would not have stood so far behind other nations as she does today. However, the neglect of the past should be made up as much as possible, by the adoption of prompt and effective measures now. The need for such measures has become greater by the great changes which have taken place during the interval. The commercial war which has long been going on will become much keener after the War. India will be much more exposed to the competition of nations which have built up their industries upon a widespread and comprehensive system of technical education. In this category come not only the nations of Europe and America, but also Japan. As the Government of India deputed a special officer to Japan to obtain information for us, so that we may know exactly what her government has done to aid her people in the notable advance which they have made, I invite particular attention to the progress of education in that country.

"It is clearly established that the development of the Japanese industries has been built upon 'a system of technical education which included everything required to enable her to occupy her proper place among the manufacturing nations of the world. If the industries of India are to develop, and Indians to have a fair chance in the competition to which they are exposed, it is essential that a system of education at least as good as that of Japan should be introduced in India. I am one with my colleagues in urging the fundamental necessity of providing primary education for the artisan and labouring population. No system of industrial and technical education can be reared except upon that basis. But the artisan and labouring population do not stand apart from the rest of the community; and therefore if this *sine qua non* of industrial efficiency and economic progress is to be established, it is necessary that primary education should be made universal. I agree also in urging that drawing and manual training should be introduced into primary schools as soon as possible. In my opinion until primary education is made universal, if not compulsory, and until drawing made a compulsory subject in the primary schools, the foundation of a satisfactory system of industrial and technical education will be wanting. Of course this will require time. But I think than that is exactly why an earnest endeavour should be made in this direction without any further avoidable delay.

"Sir Frederick Nicholson says in his Note on Japan: 'The leap at education which the whole nation has made under the compulsory system is shown by the fact that while the primary school system was only formulated in 1872, by 1873 the number at these schools had already reached 28 percent, by 1833, 51, by 1893, 59, and in 1904, 93 per cent, of children of a school–going age.'

"This furnishes us with an estimate of the time that will be needed and also an exhortation to move forward. It is upon this basis that industrial and technical education now rests in Japan, but the two kinds of instructions have grown together there, and so I think they should largely grow together here also. Towards this end, I should connect; the measures of industrial and technical education which my colleagues have proposed, a little further with the system which already exists in the country. I would utilise the existing schools as far as possible not only for imparting a progressive course of drawing, but also for offering an optional course in elementary physics and chemistry, and carpentry and smithy. I would suggest that the Directors of Public Instruction of each province may be asked, in consultation with the Directors of Industries, to recommend changes in the curriculum of the schools, primary, secondary and high, with, a view to make them practical, so that they may form a part of the system of technical education.

"I cannot close this portion of my note better than by adopting, with necessary modifications, the concluding remarks of Mr Samuelson on the subject of technical education: 'In conclusion I have to state my deep conviction that the people of India expect and demand of their government the design, organisation, and execution of the systematic technical education, and there is urgent need for it to bestir itself, for other nations have already sixty years' start of us, and have produced several generations of educated workmen. Even if we begin, tomorrow the technical education of all the youths of twelve years of age who have received sound elementary education, it will take seven years before these young men can commence the practical business of life, and then they will form but an insignificant minority in an uneducated mass. It will take fifteen years before those children who have not yet begun to receive an elementary education shall have passed from the age of 7 to 21 and represent a completely–trained generation; and even then they will find less than half of their comrades educated. In the race of nations, therefore, we shall find it hard to overtake the sixty years we have lost. Tomorrow, then, let us undertake with all energy our neglected task; the urgency is twofold—a small proportion of our youth has received elementary, but no technical education; for that portion let us at once organise technical schools in every small town, technical colleges in every large town, and a technical university in the metropolis, the rest of the rising generation has received no education at all, and for them let us at once organise elementary education, even if compulsory.'

The Training of Mechanical Engineers

"I fully agree with my colleagues as to the necessity of a full measure of the practical workshop training for the artisans, foremen and mechanical engineers. But I have doubts whether the system they propose would give sufficient general liberal education to even would-be mechanical engineers. I also apprehend that the schools attached to the railway workshops will not admit of a sufficient number of the Indians obtaining training in them. My colleagues also say that as the development of the country proceeds the number of students will increase. I join with them, therefore, in recommending that the existing engineering colleges should make provision for the higher technical instruction of mechanical and electrical engineers. I would only add that substantial grants should be given to these colleges for this development and the standard of education demanded of the mechanical engineers whom they are to educate should not be, inferior to that of a BSc in Engineering of the University of London. This would be best secured by attaching these colleges to universities, where this is not already the case.

"There are at present only two teaching universities in India. I hope that the Calcutta University will soon develop further teaching functions. In my opinion every teaching university should be encouraged to provide instruction and training in mechanical and electrical engineering under its own arrangements. The needed measure of workshop practice can be provided by the arrangements with railway and other workshops existing in or near the cities or towns where they exist; and where this may not be feasible, they should be encouraged to establish sufficiently large workshops to be run on commercial lines as a part of their engineering departments. Under such an arrangement the students will be able to spend their mornings in the workshops and their afternoons at the classes at the university, they will live in an atmosphere of culture, and will cultivate higher aims and ideals than they are likely to, in schools attached to the railway workshops. As our mechanical engineers are to play a great part in the future development of the country, its seems to me highly desirable that they should combine culture and character with expert knowledge and technical skill. And nothing is better calculated to ensure this than that they should be brought up under the elevating influences of a university and should bear its hall-mark.

"I would also recommend that provision for the training of the electrical engineers should be made simultaneously with that for the mechanical engineers, and should not be postponed to an indefinite future date. I think it will not be long before electrical manufactures will be started in India. The need for these is fully pointed out in the chapter on the industrial deficiencies of India. The use of the electrical machinery is steadily growing, and will grow at a more rapid rate in the future; and, if even for present requirements, we leave it to the managers of the electrical undertakings to train their own men, we shall be driving an increasing number of Indian youths to go abroad to be trained as the electrical engineers.

Higher Technological Training

"I agree with my colleagues that it is urgently necessary to prepare for a higher technological training which will provide the means whereby the science students of the colleges affiliated to the universities may learn to apply their knowledge to the industrial uses, and that the simplest way of meeting this demand will be to expand the engineering colleges by the creation of the new departments for the higher technical instruction of the mechanical and electrical engineers. But I doubt whether it would be best to add the departments of general technological chemistry to these engineering colleges where they are not parts of a teaching university. Where they are not, I think that they should be developed into full colleges of engineering, by provision being made for teaching other branches of engineering in them, such as railway engineering, and sanitary engineering, for which no satisfactory provision exists here at present.

"As regards the teaching of general technological chemistry, I would recommend that this should be developed at the teaching universities and at the first-rate colleges affiliated to universities. Every one of the these has a more or less well– equipped laboratory, and by the special grants, such as are given by the Board of Education to the Universities and University Colleges in the United Kingdom, they should be helped to strengthen their staffs and to improve their laboratories for this purpose. We should thus give a practical value to the teaching of chemistry which is going on at present in our colleges, In view of the industrial expansion which we expect, the demand for the students trained in the general technological chemistry is likely to be very great. If provision is made for teaching it at the Universities or University Colleges, a much larger number of students is likely to be attracted to it than if it is made at the engineering colleges. A sufficient number of scholarships and fellowships should be provided at every one of these institutions to attract and encourage bright students to devote themselves to the subject.'

Imperial Engineering Colleges or an Imperial Polytechnic Institute

"My colleagues think that it will be necessary ultimately, if not in the immediate future, to provide India with educational institutions of a more advanced character. They think that, for some time to come, the demand for this higher training can best be met by the provision of scholarships to enable students to proceed abroad; but that as soon as our foregoing recommendations have had time to develop their full effect, it would be advisable to proceed further and establish at least two imperial colleges of the very highest grade, one of which should cover every branch of engineering, while the other should be devoted mainly to metallurgy and mineral technology, the developments of which are certain to be on a very extensive scale. They say that this ideal should always be kept in sight as the goal.

"I agree with my colleagues that in the immediate future the demand for the higher training here contemplated can only be met by the provision of scholarships to enable students to proceed abroad. I go further. I think that even when we have established our proposed higher colleges, we shall have to send our best scholars abroad to improve and perfect their knowledge. With all the provision for the higher education which Japan has made in her own country, she has continued to send a large number of her students abroad. The Japanese Year Book for 1917 shows that there were 2,213 Ryugakusei or foreign-going students, staying abroad in 1915 the bulk of them in the United States of America. The number of students of both the sexes which Japan has sent to Europe and America since the opening of the country to the foreign intercourse must reach enormous figures, says the same Year Book, especially when the students who have gone abroad at their own expense are included. The demand for the expert knowledge and technical skill will be so great in India, if we are to achieve in any measure the progress we desire, that it is desirable that the provision for scholarships should be greatly increased, and the students should be largely selected as is done in Japan, from among those who have done teaching work for some years after completing their academic course.

"But after all that may be done in this direction, the large needs of the education of the youth of a country which is equal to the whole of Europe minus Russia cannot be met in this manner. Those needs, and the vast possibilities of the development which lie before us demand that at least one first class Imperial Technological or Polytechnic Institute should be established in India without any further delay. Indian public opinion has long and earnestly pleaded for the establishment of such an institute in the country, as witness of the resolutions of the Indian National Congress and the Indian Industrial Conference, and of the various Provincial Congresses and Conferences. Here again Japan furnishes us an example. Japan recognised the need and value of a similar institution when she started on her present career. 'When Iwakura's embassy was in London in 1872, the attention of Mr (now Marquis) Ito was drawn to the advisability of starting an engineering college in Tokyo to train men for the railways, telegraphs and industries which were to be started in Japan, and be procured, through a Glasgow Professor, the services of Mr Henry Dyer to organise this college, eventually merged in the University of Tokyo,' (*The Educational System of Japan* by W.H. Sharp. 1906, p 206.) 'Since then Marqais Ito has repeatedly spoken of the establishment of this college as one of the most important factors in the development of Japan, since from it have come the majority of engineers who are now working the resources and industries of that country.' (*Japan by the Japanese*, p. 65). Mr Dyer was assisted by a number of foreigners to whom Japanese were added as soon as possible. The course then extended over six years, the last two years being spent wholly on practice. The college being under the Public Works Department, the students had the run of all the engineering establishments and works under its control; and graduates who were sent abroad for further work invariably distinguished themselves.

"I earnestly hope that with the distressful record, to which our Report bears witness, of all the loss and suffering which India has undergone owing to the want of sufficient; and satisfactory provision for technical and technological instruction in this country, the government; will be pleased not to delay any further the institution of an Imperial Polytechnic Institute in India. This is absolutely demanded in the interests of the country and the large recommendations which we make for industrial development.

"My colleagues have recommended that there should be at least two imperial colleges established, one to cover every branch of engineering, and the other to be devoted mainly to metallurgy and mineral technology. I think both these departments should be combined in one polytechnic institute, and that all the important branches of chemistry should be provided for in the third department. My colleagues have not recommended an imperial college of chemistry, evidently because they have recommended the institution of a separate service for chemistry. Even assuming that a separate service is to be constituted for chemistry, it cannot be accommodated better for its headquarters than as department of the Central Imperial polytechnic Institute of India.

"Under the heading of the Miscellaneous Educational Proposals my colleagues refer to the question of providing for training in navigation and marine engineering. I hope this will be done at an early date. I do not share the doubts of my colleagues that the industry of shipbuilding is not likely to be materialised for some time in India. I hope that, considering the huge volume of import and export trade of India and considering also the indigenous resources for ship-building, with those that exist in the country at present and those that are likely to be developed in the near future, ship-building should be specially encouraged by the government, even if it should be necessary for some time to import plates and sections from abroad. And for this reason I think that a school should be started in India at an early date to train people in navigation and marine engineering.

Commercial Education

"Among other proposals my colleagues have drawn attention to the importance of commercial education. While appreciating the good work of the Sydenham College of Commerce, they say: 'There is a strongly–expressed desire for similar colleges in the other parts of India, and we think that the other Indian Universities might well consider the possibility of satisfying this demand. Industry and commerce are bound to go on expanding with rapidity, and they will be glad to pay a higher price for more efficient employees.'

"I entirely agree with this opinion. But I think that in view of the great and growing importance of the commercial education, the government should invite the universities to establish commercial colleges and should help them to do so by the substantial grants. I would reproduce here what I wrote in 1911 on this subject: 'The importance of commercial education, that is, a special training for the young men who intend to devote themselves to commercial pursuits as a factor in national and international progress is now fully recognised in the advanced countries of the West. Those nations of the West which are foremost in the commerce of the world have devoted the greatest attention to commercial education. Germany was the first to recognise the necessity and usefulness of this kind of education. America followed suit; so did Japan; and during the last fifteen years England has fully made up its deficiency in institutions for commercial education. The Universities of Birmingham and Manchester have special faculties of commerce with the Diploma of Bachelor of Commerce. So has the University of Leeds. Professor Lees-Smith, who came to India two years ago at the invitation of the government of Bombay, in addressing the Indian Industrial Conference at Madras said: 'The leaders of commerce and business' need to be scientifically trained just as a doctor or a barrister or professional man is...Modern experience shows us that business requires administrative capacity of the very highest type. It needs not merely technical knowledge, but it also needs the power of dealing with new situations, of going forward at the right moment and of controlling labour. These are just the qualities which the universities have always claimed as being their special business to foster; and we therefore say that if you are going to fulfil any of the hopes which were held out yesterday by your president, if you are going to take into your own hands the control of the commerce of this nation, then you must produce wide-minded, enterprising men of initiative, men who are likely to be produced by the University Faculties of Commerce. The university faculty of commerce is intended, of course, to train the judgment and to mould the minds of men. It is claimed that although it must give primarily a liberal education, it is possible to give that education which has a direct practical bearing on business...That kind of man (a man so trained) has immense possibilities in the world of commerce; he is the kind of man on whom you must depend to lead you in the industrial march in the future.'

"When it is remembered that the export and the import trade of India totals up more than 300 millions every year, it can easily be imagined what an amount of employment can be found for our young men in the various branches of commerce, in and out of the country, if satisfactory arrangements can be made to impart to them the necessary business education and training. Here also the experience and practice of Japan afford us guidance and advice. Higher commercial education has made great progress in Japan during the last twenty years. Before the end of the last century the candidates who sought advanced commercial education at the Tokyo Higher Commercial School exceeded a thousand a year, though the school could accommodate a much smaller number then. Since 1901 Higher Commercial Schools have been established at Osaka, Kobe, Nagasake and Yamaguchi and at the Waseda University. In banks and other firms, graduates of commercial schools have been employed to an increasing extent every year. Formerly it was held that no advanced education was needed for a merchant. But today stern reality shows that the managements of any large-scale enterprise must be undertaken only by the highly educated. Experience in Japan has shown that though in the earliar years, the talented youth of the country sought places in official circles, as commerce and industry began to grow even those who had made a special study of the politics and law not infrequently chose to enter the commercial world; and I believe that in view of the industrial development which our recommendations foreshadow, if a College of Commerce is established in every major province of India, a number of our young lawyers, who find the bar overcrowded, will be glad to take advantage of such education and become efficient means of promoting the growth of industry and commerce in the country.

Land Acquisition in Relation to Industries

"Section 39 of the Land Acquisition Act lays down that the provisions of sections 6 to 37 (both inclusive) shall not be put in force in order to acquire land for any company, unless with the previous consent of the local government, and section 40 of the Act says that 'such consent shall not be given unless the local government be satisfied by an inquiry held as hereinafter provided, (a) that such acquisition is needed for the construction of some work, and (b) that such work is likely to prove useful to the public. There is no appeal against an order of the local government giving its consent to the acquisition of any land on the ground that it is likely to prove useful to the public, and complaint has been made that the power given by the act to the local government has been misused. I know of one instance where this power was used two or three years ago to acquire land to enable the Young Men's Christian Association to establish a club and recreation ground. The protest of the unfortunate house-owners who were dispossessed were unheeded. It cannot be disputed therefore that the section as it stands has been differently interpreted. A remedy may be provided against its being further misinterpreted by having the expression 'is likely to be useful to the public' qualified by an amending Act. But however that may be, I do not share the doubt whether that Act can be fairly used by a local government on behalf of an industrial company. I think it cannot be.

"Nor can I join my colleagues in making the recommendation that the local government may acquire land compulsorily from private owners on behalf of an industrial concern, even in the circumstances and under the conditions specified by them. The Indian Act is framed on the analogy of the English Acts on the subject of the compulsory acquisition of land for public purposes. If the expression 'likely to be useful to the public' is interpreted in the manner in which it would be interpreted under the English Acts, there will be little room left for doubt as to its meaning, describing the scope of the Lands Clauses Acts, *The Encyclopaedia of the Laws of England* (Vol. 8, pp. 3-6), says: 'The provisions as to the incorporation of the Lands Clauses Acts apply to all the acts authorising the purchase of lands whether general or local. Such acts fall into three classes:

1. Acquisition of lands for purposes of national defense or general government.
2. Acquisition of lands for public purposes of a local or municipal character.
3. Acquisition of lands by corporations or individuals for commercial purposes of public utility.

Dealing with 3, i.e., commercial purposes of public utility, it says:

'Under this head fall the bulk of the special, local, and personal acts which incorporate the Lands Clauses Acts. They fall into the following main classes:

1. Cemeteries.
2. Electric lighting, effected by provisional orders confirmed by statute.
3. Gasworks.
4. Harbours.
5. Markets and Fairs.
6. Waterworks.
7. Railways and light Railways.
8. Tramways.

'In all the cases, except that of the ordinary railways, these undertakings can, under general Acts, be entrusted to municipal bodies.'

"A glance at the list given above is sufficient to show that every one of the commercial objects for which land may be required is an object of public utility i.e., one to the benefit of which every member of the public has an equal right with every other member, by complying with the rules which may be prescribed therefore. The test of it is clearly indicated in the last sentence which says that 'In all cases, except that of ordinary railways these undertakings can, under general Acts, be entrusted to the municipal bodies.' The justification for depriving a man of his property against his will may be found in the fact that it is being done for the benefit of any individual or group of individuals, but for the benefit of the public of which he also is a member, and that he will be entitled to share the benefit of the undertaking as much as any other person. Where an undertaking is not "likely to be useful to the public," in the sense indicated above, the provisions of the Act, or the power of the government, cannot in my opinion be rightly used to compulsorily acquire land for it. In my opinion when an industrial concern, the members of which have the right to shut out every one outside their body from participation in the benefit of their business, desires to acquire land, it must do so by exchange, negotiation or moral suasion.

Industrial Finance

"We were asked to report in what manner the government could usefully give encouragement to the industrial development by direct or indirect financial assistance to the industrial enterprises. We are all agreed upon that the lack of financial facilities is at present one of the most serious difficulties in the way of the extension of such industries, and that it is necessary that much greater banking facilities should be provided than existing at present. We have come to the unanimous conclusion that along with the other measures of assistance which we have to recommend, the establishment of the industrial banks, working on approved lines, would be a potent means of removing these difficulties and of affording help to industrialists, and that such difficulties are of sufficient national importance to justify government assistance. The recent establishment of the Tata Industrial Bank is a matter of sincere satisfaction. But there is need for more institutions of the same class. And it is because we had not sufficient material before us to enable us to formulate a definite scheme for the industrial banks, that we have recommended that an expert committee should be appointed at the earliest possible date to consider what additional banking facilities are necessary for the initial and for the current finance of the industries; what form of government assistance and control will be required to ensure their extension on sound lines as widely as possible throughout the country; and whether they should be of provincial or of imperial scope, or whether both these forms might not be combined in a group of institutions working together.

"As the adequate extension of the industrial banks will be a matter of time we have recommended a scheme to meet the need experienced by the middle-class industrialists for current finance. I do not quite like the scheme, as it involves too much of spoon-feeding. But as it is professedly a temporary arrangement, I raise no objection to it. I only hope that its acceptance will not in any way delay the adoption of a scheme of the regular industrial banks, and that it will be unnecessary to continue this temporary scheme very long.

"If the industrial development is to take place on any thing like the large scale which our Report contemplates, nothing is more important than that regular banking facilities should be multiplied manifold, and that as early as may be practicable. To clear the ground for this it is necessary to remove some misconceptions. Since the failures of certain Indian banks in 1913 and 1914, an opinion has grown up in certain circles that the Indians lack the capacity to manage joint-stock banks. When those failures occurred certain foreign papers held these Swadeshi banks up to ridicule. That there were mistakes both of policy and of management in the case of some of these banks is indisputable. But these mistakes should not be exaggerated, and they should not be made the basis of an indiscrimination or condemnation of the Indian capacity for the joint-stock banking and for extolling the capacity of the Europeans for each business. A certain number of failures has been a common feature in the history of joint-stock banking in England and America as well. Englishmen regard the Bank of England, and with pardonable pride, as the greatest financial institution in the world and yet even that institution that safest bank in the whole of the United Kingdom has had its share of vicissitudes, 'From 1819 to 1890, the Bank of England came to the verge of bankruptcy every ten years' (*History of the Bank of England* by Dr Andreades, p. 404), while the list of the banks that failed in England is of enormous length. To mention only a few, during the years 1791 to 1818 about a thousand banks suspended operations in England. In the financial depression of 1839, 29 banks went out of existence, out of which 17 had never paid any dividend. In the year 1862 the Limited Liability Law was passed, and within the space of three years 300 companies were formed with a nominal capital of 04 million pounds, of which 270 failed shortly afterwards. This was followed by financial crisis in which a large number of banks failed, and the greatest of them, Operand Gurney, with the liabilities of 18,727,917 pound closed its doors on the morning of what is known in the history of banking in England, as the Black Friday. Other banks failed also. The estimated liability of the various failures amounted to 50 millions and the losses were also very great. In 1890 the great firm of Baring Brothers, which had helped the Bank of England out of its difficulties in 1839, failed. Have these numerous failures led to any general condemnation of Englishmen as being unfit to manage joint-stock banks? Why then should the failures of a few banks started by the Indians lead to any such general inference being drawn against them?

"Let us now turn to the history of banking in India. The first joint-stock bank was started in 1770 by Messrs. Alexander and Co. It was called the Hindustan Bank. It issued notes. These notes, though not recognised by the Government, obtained a local circulation which occasionally reached 40 or 50 lakhs. They were received for many years at all the public offices in Calcutta scarcely excepting treasury itself. This bank failed in 1832. In 1806 was established the Bank of Bengal, but it received its charter of incorporation in 1809. The East India Company contributed one-fifth of the capital and appointed three of the Directors. Since 1809, and more particularly from 1813 when the Act was passed which removed certain restrictions from the Europeans settling in India, banking received a stimulus and several banks were established. Between 1829 and 1833 most of these agency houses failed. In 1838 a joint-stock bank named the Union Bank was started. It was intended to afford ID the money market that facility which the Bank of Bengal owing to its charter could not afford. The bank failed in January 1818, although long before that it was known to be in a hopelessly insolvent state. The dividends it declared and of which it made so great a parade were taken not from the capital, for that had gone long before, but from the deposits that people were still confiding enough to make. The bank had indiscriminately invested in indigo and the Directors freely helped themselves to the bank money. On one English firm were debtors to the bank of 24 lakhs of rupees, one-fourth of the whole capital of the bank, and another firm had taken cash credits to the amount of 16 lakhs of rupees. There were scandals connected with the failure of the first Benares Bank in 1849. The Bank of Bengal itself violated its charter in the crisis of 1829-32. The first Bank of Bombay was established in 1840, the Bank of Madras in 1843. These banks were established under conditions similar to those of the Bank of Bengal, with the East India Company as a share-holder of one-fifth of the capital. In 1868 the Bank of Bombay failed. A Commission was appointed to enquire into the causes of the failure. The Report of the Commission which was published in 1869, ascribed the failure to the following causes:

(a) The Charter Act which removed many restrictions contained in the former Act and permitted the bank to transact business of an unsafe character;
(b) The abuse of the powers given by the Act by weak and unprincipled secretaries;
(c) The negligence and incapacity of the directors;
(d) The very exceptional nature of the times.

"Sir C. Jackson (president of the Commission) summed up his views on this point, in the dictum that the great lesson the failure taught was that banks should not lend money on promissory notes in a single name or on the joint promissory notes, when all the parties were borrowers and not, any of them sureties for others. (*An Account of the Presidency Banks*, p. 31)

"I draw attention to this with special reference to the statement contained in the paragraph 281 of our Report that we have received evidence in favour of a relaxation of the restrictions of the Presidency Banks Act which prevent loans from being for longer than six months, and require the security of two names.

"Another bank of the same name with the similar rights, but this time without the contribution of the government was started in the same year in Bombay. It worked well till 1874, in which year appeared a famine in Bengal. The government balance at the bank was one crore, and it was intended that 30 lakhs might be drawn to purchase rice from Burma for the purposes of relief in Bengal. The bank was unable to pay the money. It did not close its doors only because the money was due to the government. This incident gave rise to the Reserve Treasury system, which dates from 1876. In this year was also passed the Presidency Banks Act which imposed important limitations on the Banks.

"Of the seven European banks that existed in India in 1863, all but one has failed. That one is the Allahabad Bank. About 1875 five new banks were established. Of these only one, viz., the Alliance Bank of Simla Limited, the Punjab Banking Co. having been amalgamated with it, survived. Amongst those that failed was the Himalaya Bank Limited, which stopped payment in 1891. Besides these joint-stock banks, the big banking firm of Sir George Arbuthnot failed in 1907. The Bank of Burma was established in 1904. It failed in 1911. When it failed it had a working capital of a crore and 19 lakhs. It was found that one-third of the working capital had been advanced to a firm in which the Directors were interested. Last of all came the failure of the Bank of Upper India. Indians were not responsible for the management of any of these banks. They were all managed by the Europeans. The history of the Indian banks for which the Indiana were responsible is neither so long nor so eventful. It goes back only to the year 1881 in which year the Oudh Commercial Bank was founded. It was followed by some other small banks. The Punjab National Bank was established in 1894. Both these banks have carried on their business without interruption. The People's Bank of India was founded in 1901. When it closed its doors in 1913, it had nearly a hundred branches in various places, mostly in Upper India. The other ill-fated institution, the Amritsar Bank, was started in 1904. It failed in 1913. With the year 1905 the year of the partition of Bengal began an era of new Swadeshi indigenous activities in India and from 1906 there began to be established banks large and small all over the country. These totalled 476 in 1910. The most important of these were the Bank of India and the Indian Specie Bank, started in 1906, the Bengal National Bank and the Indian Bank of Madras in 1907, the Bombay Merchant Bank and the Credit Bank of India in 1909, the Kathiawar and Ahmedabad Banking Corporation in 1910, and the Central Bank of India in 1911, Of the eleven important banks started since 1901, six collapsed during 1913-14. But taking large banks and small, in all about two dozen Indian banks failed. Though the failure of even one bank is a matter for regret, two dozens out of 476 cannot be said to be a very large number.

"There is no doubt that in some of the banks that failed there was a fraudulent manipulation of accounts, and that in the others large sums of money were advanced to the enterprises in which some of the directors were interested. There were also mistakes of policy, as for instance, in the financing of the long-term business with short-term deposits, and the sinking of the far too great a proportion of these funds in a single industry. But that the failures were due more to these causes than to dishonesty and fraud is attested by the fact that the number of the criminal prosecution in connections with these failures has been conspicuously small.

"Regarding the failures in the Punjab, Pandit Balak Ram Pandya, Auditor of Accounts, Lahore, said in his written evidence submitted to us: 'Indeed, when we compare the recent bank and the industrial failures in the Punjab with similar incidents in the other countries, we are astonished at the comparatively small proportion of the cases in which the failures in our case were due to dishonesty or selfishness. The price we have paid for our inexperience is undoubtedly heavy, but it is by no means heavier than what other countries have paid before us. If we have only learnt the lesson which the disasters of the last four years so impressively teach, there is surely no room for despondency.'

"In pursuance of a recommendation contained in the preliminary note on the scope of enquiry by the Indian Industrial Commission, a committee was appointed by the Punjab Provincial Industries Committee to examine and report upon the causes of the recent failures in the financial and industrial enterprises in the Punjab. Their report throws much valuable light upon the subject. The Committee said: 'All the evidences produced before us insisted on the want of business knowledge and experience in company promoters, managers, and staff as a primary cause of failure. There were few competent managers, whether of banks or of industrial concerns. Consequently egregious blunders were made, and some of the so-called dishonesty seems to us very like ignorance; much of it was due to anxiety to cloak losses.'

"After describing the defects and mistakes of the banks, the Committee said: 'Lest, however, it should be imagined that the state of Swadeshi banking and industry was altogether rotten, we must hasten to point out two relieving features: (a) in the first place the survival of the Punjab National Bank showed that a purely Indian directorate and staff were capable of steering a bank through circumstances as trying as ever any financial institution had to face; (b) and again the fact that several banks, as the following statement shows, have paid in full, and others are likely to pay, is evidence that by no means all of the banks were inherently unsound.'

"(I omit the statement because I understand that much more has been paid up since June 1917, when the Committee made their report). The Committee summed up the result of their investigation as follows: 'Thus, speaking generally, our feeling is that the collapse can be referred to the two fundamental causes:

(i) The inexperience, and the defects of the machinery, inevitable to the starting of every new venture;

(ii) The lack of palliation or remedial section such as the government itself, or the quasi government agencies, i.e a State-supported Provincial Bank, might supply. 'Indians need Government Support and Education in Banking'.

"This brief review would, I hope, make it clear that there is little ground for any general disparagement of the Indians in the matter of joint-stock banking. It shows that if the Indians receive (a) the same sympathy and support from the government which the Europeans have received through the Presidency Banks and (b) if they also receive the necessary measure of education in modern banking the Indians will give as good an account of themselves in this branch of important national activity as any other people have given. As regards the first, I would strongly recommend that the question of a Central State Bank, having branches in every province, should be taken up at an early date. The presidency banks have rendered inestimable service to the Europeans in carrying on trade and commerce with India. They cannot under their existing charter help industries. There has also been a complaint that even in the matters of such loans as they can advance, and do advance to the Europeans, these banks do not easily accommodate the Indians. This complaint found strong expression at Lahore. The official Committee of Lahore to which reference has been made before, said in their report. During the crisis there was no co-operation between the Indian Banks themselves, or between them and the English banks, or between them and the old-fashioned Indian banks. We attach peculiar significance to the statements made by the witnesses as to the position of the Bank of Bengal. While the fact that the Punjab National Bank has been received on the clearing list only, however, alter surviving the crisis shows that at present good relations do exist and that there is future possibility of better, yet the absence of a provincial bank probably meant the downfall of the sound banks which might have been saved. The Bank of Bengal is too big, not local in us its sympathy, ignorant of the provincial conditions, and not susceptible to the influence of the provincial government. The Lahore Branch was willing to help and made recommendations to Calcutta, but these were rejected with curtness, and not even on the deposit of the government paper would the Bank of Bengal consent to advance money to the Punjab National Bank. When the government withdrew the right of issuing notes from the presidency banks in 1860, they agreed to help them by allowing the use of the public balances. In a Finance Department memorandum of December 20, 1860 to the Bank of Bengal (quoted by, Mr Brunyate at p 81 of his *Account of the Presidency Banks*) the extent to which the government admitted the obligation to compensate the Banks for the withdrawal of the right of issue was indicated as below: 'The Bank (of Bengal) cannot be admitted to have any claim as of right to compensation, but they are certainly in a position deserving of much consideration and one in which they may equitably look for all the reasonable support on the part of the government.'

"The government agreed to compensate them by giving them their cash balances without interest, to the extent of 70 lakhs to the Bank of Bengal and 50 lakhs to the Banks of Bombay and Madras. In practice the Banks have been allowed to enjoy the use of much larger balances during the decades that have since passed. But as Mr Brunyate points out in his book at p. 99: 'Long before 1876 the Secretary of State had come to the conclusion that the Banks had been sufficiently compensated for the loss of their note issue. It is high time therefore that the government should cease to place public balances with the Presidency and that these balances should be kept in a State Bank, the benefits of which would be available to a larger public. The proposal for a single Bank of India to take the place filled by the three Presidency Banks was before the government between 1860 and 1876. But no decision was arrived at on the subject. The question was taken up by the Royal Commission on Indian Finance and Currency. They expressed no final opinion upon it, but recommended that it should be taken up at an early date. They said in paragraph

222 of their Report: 'We regard the question, whatever decision may ultimately he arrived at upon it, as one of the great importance to India, which deserves the careful and early consideration of the Secretary of State and the Government of India. We think, therefore, that they would do well to hold an inquiry into it without delay, and to appoint for this purpose a small expert body, representative both of the official and non-official experience, with directions to study the whole question in India in consultation with the persons and bodies primarily interested, such as the Presidency Banks, and either to pronounce definitely against the desirability of the establishment of a State or Central Bank in India at the present time or to submit to the authorities a concrete scheme for the establishment of such a bank, fully worked out in all its details and capable of immediate application.'

"This recommendation was made in 1914. The consideration of it was postponed because of the War. I can only express the earnest hope that it will be taken up as early as may be practicable. The interest of the country demands the early creation of an institution which will at once be the central reservoir to which all public balances should belong and the central fountain which will feed all fruitful national activities throughout the country.

"Not the least important advantage of the establishment of a State Bank will be that adequate facilities will be provided for training Indians in banking work. The need for such training is obvious. In paragraph 282 of the Report my colleagues say: 'But there is in India at present a lack of trained bank employees, owing to the absence in the past of the facilities for commercial education and of any regular system of training Indians in banking work, while the countryfolk do not yet realise the advantages to themselves of the organised banking. For these reasons, the extension of banking in the mofussil has been slow. Whereas in the case of the Punjab, no rapid progress was made, it was attended with grave risks and followed by disaster. There was mismanage-ment at the headquarters of the banks, and many of the branches did little but receive deposits.

"The opinion of the Lahore Committee, which I have quoted above, also emphasised the need of promoting a knowledge of banking business. Here again I would draw attention to the marvelous development of banking in Japan. At the time of the Restoration in 1868 ignorance concerning the methods of foreign finance, or of banking, or of joint-stock companies was universal, although Japan was not entirely without some financial machinery. National finance and economy were both in a perilous condition. The Japanese had not been accustomed either to the combination of capital or the formation of corporation. They had undertaken every enterprise individually, and the financial businesses which then existed were not in a prosperous condition. As early as 1870, Mr Hirobumi Ito (afterwards Prince ITO), of the Finance Department, memorialised the government that the proper management of finance and economy was the foundation upon which the state affairs must be conducted, and that unless sound institutions were established for this purpose no good administrative result should be attained. At his suggestion he was sent in the same year to America to study financial institutions and their working. And as the result of his observations he submitted to the government the following three propositions: First, the standard of currency should be gold; secondly, bonds should be issued for the conversion of the notes; thirdly companies should be established for the purpose of issuing paper money.

"After much discussions of these and certain alternative proposals, regulations were drafted in 1871 and promulgated with the sanction of the sovereign for organising national banks. The first national bank was established at Tokyo in 1873, and began business in less than ten months. It is not necessary for me to trace the history of banking in Japan further than to say that there are now five kinds of banks in Japan, viewed in relation to the line of business respectively followed, viz., (a) home trade, (b) foreign commerce, (c) industry, (d) agriculture and (e) colonisation; and that in 1913 the total number of these banks was 2,152, of which 2,100 represented ordinary and savings banks at the end of first half-year, and 52 in number of special banks at the end of the years. The paid-up capital of these banks amounted in 1913 to 436,188,271 yen, the reserve fund to 139,109,917 yen, the total deposits to 10,811,884,300.

"In *Fifty Years of New Japan* (by Count Okuma, Volume I, p. 532) Baron Shibusawa, the president of the first national bank, concludes his chapter on the development of banking in Japan as follows: 'Before concluding this essay the writer cannot refrain from expressing his profound satisfaction at the fact that the small spring of banking business, which had been so insignificant at the time of the restoration, has, by a gradual process of accretion, become a broad, navigable river, as it is now, and his conviction that this is the result of having followed the example of European and American nations, to which the Japanese are much indebted. Again the Japanese are very grateful for the valuable services of Mr Alexander Allan Shand, now a Director of the Paris Bank, London, who came to Japan at the invitation of the Issue Department in 1872, acted as adviser in banking to that department, wrote valuable books on banking, instructed young Japanese in that line and thus paved the way for the development of banking business in the country.'

"India was far ahead of Japan in 1872. She stands far behind Japan today. No doubt banking in India today is far in advance of what it was in Japan in 1872. But if it is to develop as it should, I would recommend that the Government of India should do even now what the Government of Japan did long ago, viz., take definite steps to impart the best instructions to the young Indians in banking through the best teachers it can appoint. Even if a state bank should be slow in coming, the presidency banks and other banks which receive help from the government, should be asked to take in a few Indians perferably graduates of a college of commerce as apprentices for the higher training in banking.

Provincial Departments of Industries

"I agree with my colleagues in recommending the creation or development of the provincial departments of the Industries, subject to the reservations noted below:

1. Report, paragraph 306 (c): 'I think that the control of technical and industrial education should not be placed under this department but either under the Department of Education or under a committee jointly appointed by the Departments of Education and Industries. In my opinion this arrangement will secure that both the theoretical and practical sides of technical and industrial education will receive sufficient attention.

   "The other proposed multifarious duties of the Director of Industries will leave him little time to direct the work of education. It is contemplated (paragraph 331 of the Report) that the Deputy Director should inspect the institutions for technical education. It will not make for efficiency if the Director is made responsible for the duties which he will evidently not be able to perform.
2. Report, paragraph 307: 'I think that the agricultural engineering should be under the control of the Director of Agriculture. Agricultural engineering will not be confined to putting in power plant for agricultural work. It will include questions relating to drainage and irrigation also. These questions are of far greater importance than the mechanical putting in of power plant, which can be carried out by the engineering staff with no less efficiency if the staff be under the control of the Director of Agriculture than if it be under that of the Director of Industries.'
3. Report, paragraph 312: 'I do not think that the Director of Industries should be the Secretary to Government for commercial and industrial subjects. If he is, the object of referring his proposals to the scrutiny of the member in charge of the department will, I fear, be largely defeated in practice. Considering that the Director will deal with large interests, it is desirable that the scrutiny should be real.'
4. Report, paragraph 313: 'The salaries which have been proposed for the Director and the Deputy Director

have evidently been proposed from the point of view that these officers will be Europeans. In my opinion the salaries should be fixed from the point of view that they will be Indians, and it should be provided that, if a European is imported from abroad, an extra allowance of 25 per cent, above the salary shall be given to him. I would suggest that the salary of the Director should be ₹ 1,000 rising to ₹ 2,000.'

5. Report, paragraph 314: 'The salary of the Deputy Director should range from ₹ 500 to ₹ 1000.'
6. Report, paragraph 317: 'The salary of Circle Officers should range between ₹ 200 and ₹ 500.'
7. 'The strength of the staff should be determined after the Director and Board of Industries have been appointed and have submitted a definite programme of work.'

Imperial Department of Industries

Report, paragraph 321: "I agree with my colleagues in recommending that; 'Industry should have separate representation in the executive council of the government of India.'

(Paragraph 322.) "But I venture to doubt the necessity or desirability of the proposed Indian Industries Board. My colleagues have described the duties for the performance of which the board is, in their opinion, needed. They say:

1. 'The imperial department of the Industries would control the administration of the various acts with which it is concerned. The member for industry, with his Secretariat, will certainly not require a board to help him to do this.'
2. 'And (it) would be responsible for the general direction of the accepted industrial policy of the country, including technical and industrial education. Even without any reference to the expected devolution of power to the provincial governments, the member for Industry will not require the assistance of a member of the board to perform this duty either. The member

for education performs a similar duty in regard to education.' In paragraph 352 of the Report my colleagues state what they expect to be done under this head. They say: 'Under heads 9 and 10 (Encouragement of industries, advice to local governments, and industrial and technical education), the only expenditure incurred by the imperial department would be in respect of the staff of visiting experts, who would work directly under the appropriate member of the industries board. The allotment of work among these should be effected by one of them, who might be styled senior visitor. The inspectors would be mainly concerned with the industrial schools; the inspection on behalf of the imperial department of the higher institutions would be largely performed by the members of the industries 'Board and the other high technical officers.'

"I think the proposal to appoint these imperial visiting experts, entirely lacks justification. They will be like the fifth wheel of a coach. But however that may be, all the members of the industries board are expected to do in this direction is to inspect the higher institutions. These institutions will be under provincial governments. They are not likely to suffer for want of such superior inspection, and the member for industry may be expected occasionally to honour them by a visit when he is out on tour.

3. 'The remaining duties of the department would consist of the initiation and running of any imperial pioneer and research factories that may be needed.'

"In paragraph 356 my colleagues say: 'As instances of the experimental factories which could be more appropriately started by imperial agency may be cited (a) glass works, an account of the range of experts needed, (b) wood distillation, which would yield results of very general application and should be applied to a number of different species of trees. It would be for the industries board to decide on the best site for the factory in each case, and to determine the exact object of the experiment which should be placed in charge of a suitable specialist.'

"I do not see any reason why both these suggested factories should not be started as provincial undertakings in any province where conditions may be considered to be suitable for them. But assuming that they may be started as imperial factories, surely the member for industry, acting on expert opinion and advice, may be trusted to sanction such an experiment without the assistance of the proposed board.

4. 'Presumably each full-scale government factory will have its manager or superintendent. When many such have been started, the need for appointing a general superintendent of such factories may be considered. But a highly-paid officer like a member of the proposed board should not be required in connection with the work.
5. "The framing of schemes for assisting private enterprise of a class for which an imperial agency would be required.–'The Member for Industry should be trusted to do this, when it becomes necessary to do it. It should be left generally to the provincial governments to assist private enterprise whenever it may be held to be desirable. The policy should, in my opinion, be to avoid creating a class of enterprise for which an imperial agency would be required.'
6. The supply of stores– 'For this a very large perhaps unduly large staff consisting of a Controller General, four Deputy Controllers, seven Assistant Controllers, six Inspectors, 20 Assistant Inspectors, and a Supervisor of Stores Contracts is proposed. It does not seem that any room is left for work for any member of the Industries Board here.'
7. The collection and dissemination of commercial and industrial information,– 'For this also there is a separate highly-paid Director, and it is proposed to give him two highly-paid Deputies for Calcutta and

Bombay.'

8. 'And the direction of such scientific and technical services and departments as come under its control,' every imperial service and department which may be constituted will have its appropriate head. With such head it should require little direction from outside. Such direction and general control as may be desirable can be exercised by the member for industry.'

"For all these reasons I think the creation of an imperial executive board of industries is not necessary. In my opinion an advisory board should be constituted here also, as it will be in the provinces. It may consist of the members largely elected by the legislative council and partly nominated by the Government. This will mean saving of over two lakhs a year in salaries alone. But not the least important advantage of dropping the proposed board would be that the member for industry would not be left without the charge of any specific branch of work as he would be under the proposal of my colleagues (paragraph 323). The difficulty that my colleagues have felt in recommending where to locate the board of Industries (paragraph 328) strengthens the doubt of its necessity. They say: 'We feel compelled to recommend that the headquarters of the board should be with the Government of India.' They fully realise from the unsatisfactory experience of the past, the imperative necessity of keeping the activities of the board in close touch with the industrial life of the country. But they think that this need will be largely met by the fact that the officers controlling the various departments under it would be working in large industrial centers, while the members themselves would also have had considerable industrial experience and would tour regularly. They have also found it difficult to select an industrial centre as the headquarters of the board, without introducing a bias that might react unfavourably on the other centers. My colleagues therefore reconciled themselves to the idea that the Indian Industries Board should be moving up to Shimla and down to Delhi every year with the Government of India. But this does not seem to me to be a business like arrangement.

Direction of Chemical Research

"I am doubtful as to whether the general direction of the chemical research should be left to the Imperial Department of Industries, (Report, paragraph 324.) In my opinion it should be vested in the faculty of chemistry, of the chemistry department of the imperial polytechnic institute, which I have recommended. It seems to me anomalous and unscientific to entrust the direction of the scientific research to an executive government machinery like the proposed Imperial Department of Industries, I fear that the distinguished chemist who may be attached to the department, will develop in him more and more of an executive head and lose more and more of the scholar. At present a chemist who has completed an investigation is himself responsible for it and free to publish it. In the scheme proposed this freedom will be taken away from him. The judgment of the chief chemist will decide whether the result of any particular research work may or may not be published.

"This is the age of specialisation. In order to achieve the highest distinction as a scientist, a man must specialise in some particular branch of science. It will be difficult if not impossible, to find a chemist, who will be equally strong in more branches of chemistry. Generally speaking, the chief chemist will not therefore be competent to pass the final judgment upon the research relating to any branch other than his own. Dr Bose must be the judge of Dr Bose. It would be impossible for a man like him to work, when an official however eminent a scientist he may be in his own particular subject, will have the power to reject or accept his work.

"In the note submitted to us by Mr Puran Singh of the Dehradun Forest Research Institute, he has put forward a strong argument against research under the control of an administrative officer. The considerations urged by him merit attention. He says:

1. 'Scientific and industrial research when carried on by the government departments, does not become as popular as it would be if it were associated with the universities.

2. 'The work of the university professor, unlike that of the government official, is open to public criticism and valuation not only at the hands of laymen but before the other universities of the world as well. This accounts for the high standard of university work, a standard which is the pride of the professor to maintain, not only for the sake of his own good name, but for the reputation of the university to which he belongs. A government official, on the other hand, has to keep a limited circle satisfied with his work, and his reputation when once made in that circle, runs little risk of being marred, as he is safe under the protection of his official seat.
3. 'Up to this time in no country which encourages scientific research has it been possible for any one to aspire to the dignity of a professor of a university without having first risen through the ranks of student and assistant. On the other band, in this country we see young men fresh from the universities appointed at direct responsible positions of research and educational work, and the stimulus for ever-increasing effort is in most cases lacking.
4. 'Research work by the agency of a government department as such does not carry sufficient weight with the scientific bodies of the world.
5. 'The research officer should be in the nature of a democratic public man rather than a government official, who is bound to become by the very nature of his environment somewhat of an autocrat.
6. 'Many public research institutes that have recently sprung up in this country indicate a desire on the part of the people to be rid of official control in order to carry on research as independently as at present done in the universities of other countries. Though the desire is thus indicated, yet all work in this direction is waste of energy if there exists no clearly defined and harmonious co-operation between the government and these private institutes. Such institutes are bound

to starve finally through the lack of the university atmosphere, and the authority and resources, as distinct from control of the government at their back. The Universities of Tokyo and Kyoto have both the government and, through the government, the people at their back.

7. 'Education when given in colleges run by a government department such as those of the agriculture and forests, as distinguished from the colleges affiliated to the universities, does not tend to efficiency. The teacher therein is neither properly responsible to the students and the public nor to the government. This is because the government has no means of judging the ability of the professor as such. The fact that no government, selection till now has proved a failure in research or in imparting scientific education is due to the government having unwittingly lent to them an authority and position which causes men of average attainments to appear as geniuses.
8. 'And lastly, it is a fact that no country in the world has followed the procedure adopted in this country for organising scientific and industrial research. This point is well-illustrated in a recent number of 'Nature' by Mr Hugh Robert Mill in reviewing a note on an enquiry by the Government of India into the relations between forests and atmosphere and soil moisture. He says, 'To our mind the method adopted could produce no better result than it appears to have done. In a scientific problem such as was set forth, the only function of the state seems to us to be to decide that such an enquiry shall be carried out at the public expense and that every facility for obtaining data shall be given by all the departments and all the government concerns, local and central. It should then be handed over to a competent man of science, set free from all the other duties and supplied with necessary assistants. His report, when complete, will be authoritative and epoch-making, if

> not final, and incidentally his own reputation would be made or marred by his handling of the facts. The total expense would probably be no greater and the labour of many public servants would not be diverted from the work for which they were trained.'

"This comment emphasises exactly the point I am attempting to bring to your notice, viz., that scientific research must be independent and in the hands of the best possible men.

"I would therefore recommend that the control of research should be left not to the Imperial Department of Industries but to the Imperial Polytechnic Institute, if it is established, or to a science council elected by scientists working in the various universities, colleges and other scientific institutions in the country. The Departments cf Industries, both provincial and imperial, should communicate their suggestions for research to the institution or council, and encourage the application of the results, of researches made to industries so far as they can.

The Organisation of Scientific and Technical Services. The Indian Chemical Service. The Imperial Industrial Service.

"In proceeding to discuss the important proposals of my colleagues in relation to the subjects noted above, I think it necessary to recall that the commission was appointed, to examine and report upon the possibilities of further industrial development in India and to submit its recommendations with special reference to the following questions:

(a) Whether new openings for the profitable employment of Indian capital in commerce and industry can be indicated;

(b) Whether, and, if so, in what manner, the government can usefully give direct encouragement to the industrial development

  (i) By rendering technical advice more freely available;

  (ii) By the demonstration of the practical possibility on a commercial scale of the particular industries;

  (iii) By affording, directly or indirectly, financial assistance to the industrial enterprises; or

(iv) By any other means which are not incompatible with the existing fiscal policy of the Government of India.

"In concluding the resolution appointing us, the Government of India expressed the hope that the commission would find it possible to place their report in the hands of the Government of India within 12 months from the date of its assembling in India. This as well as the terms of our reference would show that we are expected to make recommendations as to the openings for the profitable employment of Indian capital in commerce and industry, which could be carried out on an early date.

"Chapter III of our Report which gives a summary of the industrial deficiencies of India, shows how various and how great are the openings in which the Indian capital can be employed, We say there: 'The list of the industries which, though their products are essential alike in peace and war, are lacking in this country, is lengthy and ominous. Until they are brought into existence on an adequate scale, Indian capitalists will, in times of peace, be deprived of a number of profitable enterprises; whilst in the event of a war which renders sea transport impossible, India's all-important industries will be exposed to the risk of stoppage, her consumers to the great hardship, and her armed forces to the greatest possible danger.'

" 'But as my colleagues say at p 4 of our Report' Although much information of the technical and industrial value will be found in the evidence of some of the expert witnesses... We have concentrated our attention on the machinery which we propose should be set up to effect the industrial development generally rather than on the particular industries to be improved. This machinery will, we believe, do what is needed for all the industries and it would be useless for us to attempt to frame the detailed recommendation for which the technical enquiries by experts are required.'

"With due deference to my colleagues, I think that we have concentrated too much attention on the machinery which has been proposed and yet, I fear that, excepting the provincial and imperial Departments of the Industries, the machinery proposed will not promote the industrial development as rapidly as the circumstances of the situation require. The scientific and technical services which they recommended will, on their own showing, take some time to organise, the industrial researches which they wish to promote, will take some time to bear fruit. In my opinion the immediate requirements of the country in the matter of the industrial development require the adoption of measures which will bear fruit more speedily.

"There are two classes of the industrial enterprises which can be taken up in this country. The first class, and this is by far the larger class, consists of those which can be started by the importation of machinery and experts as the first managers. In this class of work we have to imitate and not to initiate. As soon as the Provincial Departments of Industries, with their advisory boards, have been constituted in the provinces, they should decide, with such expert advice as may be necessary, what industries of this class can be started within the province, and should invite and encourage the Indian capitalists by the information and technical assistance to oganise them. It was the adoption of such a course that enabled Germany and Japan to achieve rapid industrial development. Sir Frederick Nicholson urged the adoption of this course on us in the following passage in his note: 'On the whole, then, I consider that the best way both for starting the selected industries in India and for training the future managers is after the fashion of Germany and Japan and the other countries, for the promoters, whether government or private, to draw liberally on Great Britain, etc., for real experts as first managers of any projected industries; then is to select young men, preferably men already trained in technological institutions, and to put them through close, disciplined, industrial and business training under these experts till they are fitted either to start on their own account or as reliable business managers to the capitalists.' (*Minutes of Evidence*, Vol. Ill, pp. 396-7).

"Mr Charles Tower also says, 'In the manufacture of steelware and of machinery, Germany is usually credited, not without justice, with being rather an imitator than an initiator. Her great success in this line has been achieved by the rapidity with which Germany had adopted the improvements invented elsewhere.' (*Germany of today*, Home University Library, p. 137)

"This is also the course which was adopted by America. Up to 1860 America had made little progress in developing the manufacture of steel. In 1862 Park Brothers and Company imported the biggest crucible steel plant of all up to that time, and imported also several hundred English workmen to ensure success. Since then the progress of the steel industry there has been phenomenal. In 1860 the output of pig iron in the States was only 0.8 million tons, and of steel nil; by 1900 America was producing 13.7 millions of tons of pig iron and 10.1 of steel, and in 1913 while the production of pig iron amounted to 10.3 million tons in the United Kingdom, it amounted to 31 million tons in the United States. Last but not the least, we have an eloquent illustration in India itself of the soundness of this policy in the success of the Tata Iron and Steel Works. The works were organised with the advice, and have been carried on under the supervision of the best experts imported from abroad, and they have been a conspicuous success. This, therefore, is the right policy which should be followed in regard to the many other industries, the need for which has been pointed out in our chapter on the industrial deficiencies of India. Raw materials and labour abound, capital exists and only wants organising, the home market is extensive, the machinery and the expert can be imported, the profits to the government and the people will be considerable; all that is needed is that the government, should wholeheartedly lend and assist the Indian capital in organising the industries.

"But to carry out the industrial developments in this manner it is essential, as Mr H.P. Gibbs, the General Manager of the Tata Hydro-Eleotric Supply Company, so well puts in his wrtiten evidence before us, that: 'No man should be imported into India unless he is a recognised expert in his particular line. He too should be engaged on short-time contract and made to understand he is being engaged and paid to teach our local men just as much as to introduce and carry on his work. The young man from abroad who is educated but inexperienced should not be brought to India and allowed to get his practice here.'

"The industries which will be so started will be the best practical schools for training our science graduates as recruits for the proposed imperial services.

Provision for Scientific Research

"The second class of the industries consists of those for which some research work is needed. I fully agree with my colleagues about the need and value of such research. I recognise that, to borrow the language of the Committee of the Privy Council, effective research, particularly in its industrial applications, calls increasingly for the support and impetus that come from the systematised delving of a crops of sappers working intelligently, but under orders. I am therefore not opposed to the idea of creating an Indian Chemical Service and an Imperial Industrial Service at the right time and under the right conditions. But I regret I do not agree with my colleagues as to the time when, and the conditions under which, these services should be organised. In my opinion our first duty is to create the material for these services in this country. One important means of doing this is the strating of industries, as I have urged above, under imported experts and placing our select young men, already trained in the technological institutions, under them.

"The other measures which in my opinion are needed are:

(i) That steps should be immediately taken for developing the teaching of science and technology in our existing universities and other collegiate institutions, (a) by strengthening their staff and equipment, and (b) by awarding a sufficiently large number of scholarships to encourage the study of science and technology at our schools, our colleges and our universities;

(ii) That an imperial polytechnic institute, manned by the most distinguished scientists and engineers, whose co-operation we can secure, should be established in the country, for imparting the highest instruction and training in science and technology; and

(iii) That the provision of scholarships for study in foreign countries should be largely increased to enable the most distinguished of our graduates to finish their education in the best of foreign institutions.

"The view which I humbly urge here is strongly supported by the recommendation made in the Interim Report of the Consultative Committee on Scholarships for Higher Education, of which the Right Hon'ble Mr A.H. Dyke Acland was the Chairman. The Committee was appointed before the War in March 1913. The report from which I am going to quote was adopted by it in May 1916. In a prefatory note to the Report, Sir Selby Bigge, writing on behalf of the Board of Education, said: 'The Board have no need to use the complimentary phrases to convey their estimation of the great value of their work, but on this occasion they may perhaps permit themselves to express their appreciation of the broad spirit in which the report is conceived, of its forcible exposition of the principles, and of the lucid and vigorous style in which it is written.'

"The recommendations are of such great weight and have such a direct bearing on the question I am dealing with, that I make no apology for reproducing them here: 'On the side of science and technology in relation to the industries and commerce of the nation, the greatest needs of the nation are ranged by us in order of practical priority as follows, though their satisfaction should proceed as far as possible contemporaneously and concurrently:

'(129) The first need is the wider recognition, especially by the employers, of the benefit that can be obtained by the employment in industry, agriculture, and commerce, of men trained in science in all grades, but specially for directive and advisory posts. A great improvement is already seen; but public opinion needs further enlightenment.

'(130) Secondly, the most useful thing that can be done without any increase in the means at present at our disposal is to encourage research in existing institutions after graduation. There were probably before the War more men and women fitted to be trained in research than were secured for this public service. The prolongation of the scholarships in suitable cases, which we recommend, is the one means that is available. The other means fall within the province of the Committee of the Privy Council:

(131) 'Given a limited amount of money available annually the next need would be to assist existing institutions for training in science and technology, to enable them to improve their equipment, increase their staff, attract more highly qualified teachers, and introduce new subjects of study; and to establish new places of higher technical and scientific instruction where needed. To bring existing institutions fully up to the national needs a great capital sum and income would be required. But any sum well expended, would be useful. However, in view of the needs of the nation and the empire, it seems probable that the larger sum will be forthcoming, at whatever sacrifices in the immediate future.

'(132) Improved and extended higher secondary education is needed. Side by side with this, with the strengthening of the universities and technical schools, and with an increasing demand for the scientific workers, an increase in the supply of the scholarships from secondary schools and universities will be required. This should move forward *pari passu* with the other improvements.' (pp. 69-70)

"This view also receives support from the conclusions at which the Committee of the Privy Council for Scientific and Industrial Research arrived. In their Report for the year 1915-16 (pp. 40-41), they summarised those conclusions as follows: 'If we were asked to state these conditions (that appear to us necessary for the success of our work) in the shortest possible terms we should reply: First, a largely increased supply of the competent researchers; secondly, a hearty spirit of co-operation among all the concerned-men of science, business, working men, professional and scientific societies. Universities and technical colleges, local authorities and government departments. And neither condition will be effective without the other. Before the War the output of the universities was altogether insufficient to meet even a moderate expansion in the demand for research. The annual number of the students graduating with first and second class Honours in science and technology (including mathematics) in the universities of England and Wales before the War was only about 530, and of these but a small proportion will have received any serious training in research. We have frequently found on inquiry that the number of workers of any scientific standing on a given subject of the industrial importance is very limited. The responsibility for dealing with the grave situation which we anticipate, rests with the education departments of United Kingdom. We shall be able to do some thing to encourage a longer period of training by the offer of research studentships and the like; but that will not suffice. It is useless to offer scholarships if the competent candidates are not forthcoming, and they cannot be forthcoming in sufficient numbers until a larger number of well selected and educated students enter the universities. That is the problem which the education departments have to solve, and on the solution of which the success of the present movement in our opinion largely depends.'

Recruitment of the Scientific Services

"For the recruitment of the scientific services, the Indian Chemical Service, and others my colleagues recommend that 'To the utmost extent possible the junior appointments should be made from the science graduates of the Indian universities, and that the senior and experienced men who will be required to initiate and direct research work should be obtained on special terms from England, when such are not available here' The qualifying clause which I have emphaised must be appreciated at its practical value. My colleagues recognise that a 'relatively small field of selection at present exists in India.' They say: 'As development of science teaching at the universities, and opportunities for the technical training in India increase, we believe that the necessity for importing the specialists will greatly diminish, and that ultimately the services will be mainly filled with officers trained in this country.'

"But they say further on that 'It will be some years before

it will be possible to obtain the full necessary staff in India.'

"They therefore rely for such recruitment mainly on England. But they recognise that 'there will be similar post-war demands made at home and in the dominions for scientific, especially chemical, experts, which will render it difficult to obtain suitable recruits from England. It is probable, consequently, that the salaries higher than the pre-War rates will be demanded by the suitably qualified experts.

"But I think that the qualified English experts will not be available, at any rate in any number for some years even for higher salaries than those of the pre-War period, The committee of the privy council said in their Report for 1915-16: 'It is in our view certain that the number of the trained research workers who will be available as the end of the War will not suffice for the demand that we hope will then exist. We are too apt to forget in this country that with industry as with War, a brilliant group of field officers, and even a well-organised general staff, need armies of well-trained men in order to produce satisfactory results.'

"In view of these facts, it will be wise of us not to rely upon our being able to depend on England for the senior and experienced men who will be required to initiate and direct research work in India. Besides though they advocated that the senior and experienced men should be obtained from England, what my colleagues have actually proposed is very different from it. They have proposed that recruits for these services especially chemical services should be obtained at as early an age as possible, preferably not exceeding 25 years. They leave no room for doubt as to what they mean. They say: "We should thus secure the university graduate, who had done one or perhaps two years post-graduate work, whether scientific or practical, but would not be confirmed in specialisation. We assume that the requisite degree of specialisation will be secured by adopting a system whereby study leave will be granted at some suitable time after three years' service, when a scientific officer should have developed a distinct bent. In their recommendations regarding the recruitment the imperial industrial service also, they say that of 'the age of recruitment should not usually exceed 25 years,' and that they think it desirable, 'If the young engineers whom we propose to recruit are to develop into valuable men, they should be encouraged after about three years' service to take study leave.' It is obvious then that under the scheme proposed by my colleagues the men to be recruited from England will not be "senior and experienced men", but raw graduates from the universities who will be expected to specialise after joining the service in India. Specialisation almost always involves delay. If therefore we must take in only raw graduates and remunerate them during the years they are qualifying themselves for effective research work, I think it is very desirable that we should take in Indian graduates whose training will be less costly, and who will serve the country throughout life, whereas in the case of an English graduate, there will always be the apprehension that he may leave us for higher emoluments elsewhere, and the certainty that he will leave the country after the period necessary to qualify for a pension, taking away with him the knowlegde and experience which he had gained in its service. Having regard to all the considerations which have been urged above, I think the idea of recruiting this service from England should be abandoned, and that it should be decided that it shall be recruited entirely from among graduates of the Indian universities and of the Imperial Polytechnic Institute, which I have recommended. My recommendation has the further merit of being entirely in consonance with the recommendations made by the Royal Commission on the public services in India regarding the recruitment of the scientific and technical services. Indians have a very sore feeling about the imperial Indian services. The importation of experts from England for these services has not only unnecessarily increased the cost of these services to India but has had the very great disadvantage of preventing Indians from being trained for higher work in these services. We can never forget that so distinguished an Indian as Dr P.C. Roy did not find admission into the Indian Educational Service. We know that though the Geological Survey of India, has been in existence for 64 years, up to 1913 only three Indians had been appointed to the superior service in it. In this connection I put the following question to Dr H.H. Hayden, Director of the Geological Survey of India: "Has the department kept it as an object before it that it should train the Indians to qualify themselves for employment in the higher grades of the department?"

"And his answer was:

'We have been for many years training men in the subordinate ranks of the department, but they do not necessarily qualify for appointments in the higher grade. It is always open to them to apply for an appointment in that grade...'

"My Hon'ble colleague Mr Low then asked Dr Hayden: 'You have these research scholars. Is it not one of the objects of research scholarships, that the scholars, if possible, should qualify themselves for recruitment to the department?'

"And the answer was: 'That is one of the objects of the efforts.we have made in educating them in Geology in the Presidency College and the Calcutta University. I think geological education was initiated in Calcutta by the Geological Survey. We have had more Indians in the subordinate branch of the service.'

"The Indian witnesses before the Royal Commission quoted the opinion of Dr Oldham, the first head of the Geological Department, concerning the fitness of the Indians for this department, which showed that he had the most unshakable confidence that with even fair opportunities of acquiring such knowledge (that of the physical sciences) many Indians would be found quite competent to take their place side by side with the European assistants either on this survey or in many other ways, and yet the evidence before the Royal Commission showed that competent Indians had found the door of admission barred against them and that up to 1913, only three Indians had been appointed to the superior service.

"My colleagues say that the ultimate object should be to man the services they propose with the officers trained in this country. Similar language was used in the past in relation to the other imperial departments. For instance, it appears that in the agricultural department the intention of the Government of India from the very commencement was that it should be staffed largely by the Indians.

" 'We adhere firmly,' wrote the Government of India to the Secretary of State in 1910, 'To our frequently declared policy that the service (the agricultural service) should be manned ultimately by the Indians and that the object to be kept steadily in view is to reduce to a minimum the number of experts appointed from England and to train up the indigenous talent so as to enable the country to depend on its own resources for the recruitment of its agricultural staff in the higher branches.'

"But inspite of this clear declaration, the imperial service has become the monopoly of the Europeans, while the Indians have been confirmed to the provincial service. The evidence of Dr Harold Mann and of the representative members of the provincial service before the Royal Commission showed that many highly–qualified Indians, several of whom possessed the European degrees or experience, had been unable to find admission into the imperial service, which had been manned by the recruits imported from Europe, 'Who', said Dr Mann, 'laboured under the serious disadvantage that their experience related to a system of agriculture, which in its organisation is quite foreign to the most parts of India and will be for a long time to come.'

"So also with regard to the imperial forest service. The Inspector-General of the Forests stated in his evidence before the Royal Commission that when the forest department was instituted, and for a long time afterwards, both the Government of India and the Secretary of State expressed the opinion that it was a special department in which the service of the Indians should be utilised as largely as possible.

"Yet from 1891 to 1906 no steps were taken to provide for the direct recruitment to the provincial service, and it was laid down in 1912 that candidates for the imperial forest service must have obtained a degree with honours in some branch of natural science in a university of England, Wales or Ireland, or the BSc degree in pure science in one of the universities of Scotland. At the time the Royal Commission took evidence, the total number of the officers in the superior service in the agricultural, civil, veterinary, forest, geological survey, locomotive and carriage and wagon departments was 407. Of these only six officers were statutory natives of India.

"The Royal Commission recognised the injustice that had been done to the Indians in their practical exclusion from the scientific and technical services. They expressed the opinion that there were no political grounds whatsoever for recruiting the superior staff of such services in Europe. They stated that if the requisite technical training were available in India, the necessity for indenting on Europe for the qualified men would cease to exist, and they therefore recommended that a determined and immediate effort should be made to bring about the conditions which would soon make it possible to meet the normal requirements of the services without requisitioning the services of men from abroad. That effort remains yet to be made; and while my colleagues have proposed the creation of two more imperial services they have recommended that the establishment of the Central Chemical Research Institute and of the Imperial Engineering College may wait for an indefinite future. These facts, coupled with the experience of the past, make me apprehend that, if these two services are created on the lines suggested by my colleagues, the senior appointments in them also will for a long time remain practically the monopoly of the Europeans, and that the Indians will not only be kept out of their emoluments, but also of the opportunities for acquiring high efficiency in the subjects with which the services will be concerned. The Royal Commission recommended that with a view to bring about the conditions which would soon make it possible to meet the normal requirements of the services without requisitioning the services of men from outside, existing institutions should be developed or new ones created and brought up to the level of the best European institutions of a similar character. They recognised that this would require an initial expenditure of a considerable sum of money, but they urged that the outlay would be more than repaid, not only by the additional facilities which such institutions would give to the young men to qualify themselves for the direct appointment, to the higher branches of the public services, but by the contribution they would make to the industrial progress of the country. These recommendations lend strong support to my proposal that a first-class Polytechnic Institute should be established in India as one of the first measures needed for the industrial development of the country. At such an institute provision should be made for imparting the highest instruction and training in all the important branches of science and technology and also in commerce and administration. This will be the best means of creating the army of the trained workers which is needed for promoting the industrial development in this extensive empire. The institution of the proposed services should wait until this has been done. And in the meantime only such appointments should be made in the Departments of Industries as it is absolutely necessary to fill.'

The Estimate of Cost

"The proposals which we have made in the report show that the number of the technically trained man who will be needed to carry on the industrial development and to promote the trade and commerce of the country, will be a very large one, and that it will grow steadily for some time. It is also certain that the public expenditure will rise in the several directions after the War. These considerations demand that expenditure should not be raised in any department beyond what is actually necessary. The salaries which my colleagues have proposed for the imperial, industrial and the Indian chemical services are largely based upon a consideration of what is likely to attract the Englishmen to the senior appointments in the services. If, in view of all that I have urged above, the decision should be arrived at that these services should be manned by Indians, including in that term those Europeans who are statutory natives of India, the proposed expenditure would be largely reduced. This is no mean consideration and should not be ignored. Situated as India is, one cannot too often recall the wise remarks of Sir William Hunter, made many years ago, that 'If we are to give a really efficient administration to India, many services must be paid for at lower rates even then at present. For those rates are regulated in the higher branches of the administration by the cost of the officers brought from England. You cannot work with the imported labour as cheaply as you can with the native labour and I regard the more extended employment of the natives, not only as an act of justice but as a financial necessity. If we are to govern the Indian people efficiently and cheaply, we must govern them by the means of themselves, and pay for the administration at the market rates for native labour.'

"Should this view be accepted, the salaries proposed would be reduced by about 30 to 40 per cent. I do not attempt to make any detailed alternative proposals regarding the cost of the scheme. If any of my suggestions commend themselves to the government, the details will easily be worked out.

"Speaking generally, 1 would say that a substantial part of the expenditure that is proposed for salaries should be saved, partly by reducing the number of the appointments proposed and partly by fixing the salaries at the standard which will be suitable for the Indian graduates and scholars. The expenditure proposed on buildings will also, in my opinion, admit of a very substantial reduction. Here again the example of Japan affords us guidance. They spend very much less on their educational buildings than is spent in India. A scheme for the award of scholarships to encourage the study of science and technology can be best prepared by the Education Department.

"As regards grants to the universities, I would recommend that on an average an annual grant of a lakh and a half should be made to the each university for the purpose of providing instruction and teaching in science and technology, particularly in mechanical and electrical engineering, applied chemistry, commerce and agriculture. A capital grant of about 15 lakhs each should be made for the necessary educational buildings and residential quarters and for equipment. And lastly, I would recommend that, to start with a capital expenditure of 30 lakhs, and the an annual grant of six lakhs a year should be sanctioned for an imperial polytechnic institute.'

Conclusion

"I cannot conclude this note better than by endorsing the following generous and wise words of Sir Frederick Nicholson:

> 'I beg to record my opinion that in the matter of the Indian industries we are bound to consider the Indian interest firstly, secondly and thirdly. I mean by 'firstly' that the local raw products should be utilised, by 'secondly' that industries should be introduced, and by 'thirdly' that the profits of such industry should remain in the country. If measures for the industrial development of India are taken in this spirit, India will become prosperous and strong, and England more prosperous and stronger.' "

5

The Morley-Minto Reforms and the Montagu-Chelmsford Reforms

THE MORLEY-MINTO REFORMS

At the request of the Editor of the *Indian Review* Pandit Madan Mohan Malaviya contributed the following sentiments to the Symposium on the Reform Proposals published in the December Number of 1908.

"The people and the government have both to be congratulated at the proposals of reform which have been put forward by the Government of India and the Secretary of State. The reforms have been conceived in a truly liberal and praiseworthy spirit. They will, when carried out, mark the beginning of a new era, full of hope and promise for the future. His Excellency the Viceroy and Lord Morley are entitled to our lasting gratitude for the statesmanlike wisdom and courage which they have shown in formulating these proposals. They are also entitled to our gratitude for having published the proposals to give the public a full opportunity of expressing their opinions regarding them and making further suggestions.

"I have hopes that the reforms will be made still more liberal and beneficial before they take their final shape. The government is to be particularly congratulated upon deciding to create a non-official majority in the provincial councils. I venture to say that they should have adopted the same course in regard to the supreme council. It would be quite safe and wise to do so, if, however, that must be postponed for the future, then the proposals of His Excellency the Viceroy to have an equal number of the official and non-official members in his council should at least be accepted. The proposed reforms mark the second great triumph of the Congress movement the first having been the passing of the Indian Councils Act of 1892.

Pandit Madan Mohan Malaviya seconded the following resolution at the twenty-third Indian National Congress held at Madras in December 1908:

"This Congress desires to give expression to the deep and general satisfaction with which the Reform proposals formulated in Lord Morley's dispatch have been received throughout the country; it places on record its sense of the high statesmanship which has dictated the action of the government in the matter and it tenders to Lord Morley and Lord Minto its most sincere and grateful thanks for their proposals.

"This Congress is of opinion that the proposed expansion of the legislative councils and the enlargement of their powers and functions, in the appointment of the Indian members to the executive councils with the creation of such councils where they do not exist, and the further development of the local self-government, constitute a large and liberal installment of the reforms needed to give the people of this country a substantial share in the management of their affairs and to bring the administration into closer touch with their wants and feelings. This Congress expresses its confident hope that the details of the proposed Scheme will be worked out in the same liberal spirit in which its main provisions as outlined in the Secretary of State's dispatch have been conceived.

In doing so he said:

"Mr Chairman, and the brother-delegates, while the eloquent voice of my esteemed friend is still ringing in your ears, it seems presumptuous on my part to try to address you on the same subject; but duty has to be done; it can neither be delayed nor abandoned. I crave your indulgence for a few minutes in which I will try to explain the position of the Congress. I am sure we are all of one mind in expressing our sincere appreciation of the liberal and praiseworthy spirit which has dictated the action of the Government of India and which has inspired the proposals of reform which they have formulated. I am sure we feel warmly grateful and we feel that they have done us a real service in formulating these proposals. Therefore, gentlemen, it is that there is such unanimity among all the Congressmen in expressing our gratitude to Lord Morley and Lord Minto for the services they have done to India, for the statesmanlike wisdom, courage, and coolness they have shown in formulating these proposals and in persevering with them. Gentlemen, it is a day upon which not only we have to congratulate ourselves, but it is one on which the great English nation has to be largely congratulated. Twenty three years ago, when the Congress met for the first time in this great city, our late lamented countryman, Raja Sir T. Mohave Rio, speaking as the Chairman of the Reception Committee, said that the Congress was the soundest triumph of the British education and a crown of glory to the British nation. Gentlemen, indeed the Congress has been such a triumph of British administration and crown of glory to the British nation.

"You may remember that nearly fifty years ago when Her Majesty the Queen of England assumed direct control of the Government of India, in that year there was a great deal of discussion in the Parliament as to the system of government to be introduced in this country. During the debate member after member got up and expressed the desire that India should be governed on the most liberal principles. I will not weary you by reproducing many extracts from those speeches, but I will remind you of what Mr Gladstone said, 'There never was a more practical writer than Mr Kaye, and in his history he says: 'The admission of the natives of India to the highest office of state is simply a question of time.' And there is another name entitled to great weight in this house. Mr Hafliday says: 'I believe that our misson in India is to qualify the natives for governing themselves.'

'Other speakers spoke in the same strain and the Proclamation that was issued subsequently by Her Majesty promised definitely that all the privileges that her English subjects enjoyed would be extended to her Indian subjects as they received education and gained more experience, qualified themselves for the discharge of duties which they will be called upon to discharge. Gentlemen, it took many years before these excellent ideas were put into action. But a beginning was made very shortly after the Proclamation. You know how the Councils Act of 1861 had provided that the Indian members should be appointed to tbe Viceroy's Council. Under that provision the Indian members were appointed, but that measure of reform was not sufficient. When the Congress met in 1885 it formulated a definite Scheme of representation of the people of India in the Councils of H.E. the Viceroy and in the local councils. The Congress expressed its earnest belief that the representation of the people of India in the councils was essential for the good administration of the country. Gentlemen, at that time the Congress laid down a scheme and that scheme is the one which we have yet to see being realised in its full measure. In 1886 the Congress expressed the opinion that half the members of the Supreme Legislative Council should be elected, one-fourth should be officials and one-fourth should be nominated. It expressed the same opinion with regard to the provincial councils. It also asked for powers of interpellation, for discussing the budget, for moving resolutions, in fact a complete scheme was formulated in 1886. That same scheme was repeated in greater fullness in 1889 when the late Charles Bradlaugh addressed the Congress meeting at Bombay. Gentlemen, in those early years the gentlemen who spoke to this resolution were the men who had occupied the most eminent positions in this country. The late Mr Justice Telang, Mr Dadabhai Naoroji, Sir S. Subramania Aiyar, Mr Bardley Norton, Mr George Yule, Pandit Ajodhya Nath, men like these had most earnestly supported the proposals which the Congress had put forward, that half the members of the supreme council should be elected, one-fourth should be officials and one-fourth nominated. So also in the case of provincial councils. That was the view which the Congress put forward again and again; that is the view which the vast majority of our educated countrymen hold at this moment to be a sound view.

"We believe that the time has come when, not only in the

provincial councils, but also in the supreme council, half the members at least should be elected the representatives of the people. That being on view, if we come forward to offer our unstinted and grateful support to the proposals of Lord Morley and Lord Minto, it is not that we feel that the country is not prepared to have that measure of reform carried out in respect of the supreme council, it is not that we feel that the need for reform is less urgent or is less pressing than it was 25 years ago, during which we have gained experience by being members of the council and by working other institutions it is not that the need for it is less pressing now; but, we feel that we should continue to act in the wise and sober spirit which the Congress has from the very beginning displayed in receiving the proposals of the government. We asked that half the members of the legislative councils should be elected; that was in 1885-86; yet when the time came for the introduction of the Indian Councils Act, we were contend to receive a very much smaller installment of reform. We feel today as we felt in 1886 and 1889 that half the number of the members of the Viceroy's Council at least should be elected by the people; yet we are prepared to receive the installment of reform which the government is pleased to put forward for our acceptance.

"Now, gentlemen, I only wish to point out that I refer to it because there is an idea in some circles, not only in England, but here, that we are receiving more than ever we asked for. There is an idea abroad, and agitation has been set on foot probably under the impression that Lord Morley and Lord Minto are under the influence of generous and liberal instincts giving to us more than what we asked for, or what is needed in the interests of the country. Nothing of the kind. I have told you and I will give you the reasons very briefly in order to show the value of the support which the Congress is rendering to the government in accepting the proposals. I want to tell you how urgent is the need for reforming the supreme council in the way the Congress has advocated and how beneficial will be the results not only for the people but also to the government. I will refer to only one or two instances. Gentlemen, you know above all things the government of India like all the other governments require the goodwill and moral support of the people over whom the Providence has placed them to govern. That goodwill is a more valuable asset than all the armies which any Government has English statesmen have always recognised that it is so. Mr Gladstone said so; Lord Morley said so; and every liberal and far-sighted statesman has acknowledged that to be the true view even in the case of India. In order to retain the goodwill of the people there is nothing more important than that the Government of India should be able to conduct the administration of the country with a sole eye to the good of the people. They said in 1858, 'We want to govern India for India and not to please the party here, and must adopt the principles which will be thoroughly acceptable and intelligible to the people of India. You know that the Government of India as they are constituted, are to a great extent under the thumb of the Secretary of State, and that the Secretary of State, is under the thumb of the War Office. If you have a good Secretary of State, even he cannot always protect your interests. I will refer to the question of the Military burden imposed on India. Government of India fought against the injustice of imposing the Military charge upon the Government of India. We owe them our deepest thanks for the attitude they have adopted in this matter; yet they found it difficult to get justice done to India. In the matter of cotton excise duty who does not know that the Government of India will not have imposed that unjust taxation if they had been left to themselves? If the Government of India cannot, by reason of position that they occupy in the economy of the British Empire, always command or exercise that independence which is needed to protect the interest of this country, what can be more reasonable in the interest of the Government of India itself than that it should have a larger measure of support from the representatives of the people in the council? If there were half the body of the council composed of the elected representatives of the people, if they recorded their opinions in the clear and certain tones, the Government of England would probably have hesitated a great deal more before they imposed either the military burden or such an impost as the cotton exercise duty upon the people of India. Yet, what is the result? There is any amount of ill-feeling caused in the country by the imposition of such unjust burden. Therefore in the interests of the sound administration itself, it will be an advantage to have half the number of members to be the elected representatives of the people.

"Look at the question from the point of view of the people. There is the question of irrigation vs. railways. Times out of number, not only representatives of the people but some of the highest officials of the government, no less an authority than Lord MacDonnell, presiding over the Famine Commission, expressed the strong opinion that irrigation should receive more attention than railways. Yet what do we find? The Government of India is devoting more money to build railways than to promote irrigation. So also is the matter of primary education; if you had elected representatives in the council their support would enable the Government of India to carry on the administration better and to the greater satisfaction of the people and to the stronger security of the British rule; in that it will win the hearts and affections of the people.

"I have referred to this to show that the need for the reform of the supreme council is very pressing and we feel that it is that we can abandon it; yet as I told you, we are prepared to receive the instalment of reform which the government have put forward, in a truly grateful spirit. That is a remarkable proof, I hope, of the way in which the action of the government will be received by the educated people of India in the all matters where the government take them into their confidence. That shows that if they had admitted us to the supreme council, we should not run away with the mad ideas, pester them with mad ideas, but be reasonable and considerate in pressing for reforms in matters which promote the well-being of the people and would not hamper them in any of their actions.

"I hope, having said that much, I need not take up much more time in dwelling upon the reforms. My esteemed friend has done so, and the resolution very well summarises the main features of the reform. There has not been time enough to discuss all the proposals, but there are one or two points which are matters of importance, which I crave your indulgence to say something about. The most important is about the question of the appointment of the executive members in the councils. We are thankful to the Government of India and to Lord Morley that they have decided to appoint Indians as the members of the executive councils. That again is a prayer which the Congress had been repeating year after year for a long time. Certainly it must be a matter of great satisfaction to the Congressmen that so many of their recommendations have been accepted by the Government. But, gentlemen, with regard to this matter, there is a suggestion which it is important to make. Lord Morley has said that he proposed to take powers under the Act which is to be introduced into the parliament to appoint an Indian member to the executive council of the Viceroy and of the provincial government. I beg to suggest and hope that the Congress is of one mind in this matter that the powers should not be merely taken to appoint a member when the Secretary of State may like, but that it should be provided for in the Statute. There is any amount of reason in support of this suggestion. I will refer you only to the incidents to show that the need for it is urgent. You remember, gentlemen, as a rule, it is our experience that when the matters are not provided for in the Statute, when they are left to the will and pleasure, to the particular idiosyncracies or to the generous instinct of a particular representative of His Majesty who may for the time control the destinies of India, the reforms are not always carried out as the interests of the country demand that they should be. When the Councils Act of 1861 was under discussion in parliament a question was asked by Mr Bright, and in answer to that question the then Secretary of State said that a member of council would be able to propose a resolution to any question of revenue precisely as they could in the House of Commons. That was said in 1861, yet not once was this privilege exercised. It was not put in the statute, it was therefore not recognised as a thing which ought to be brought into practice and it was not brought into practice. I will give you another instance. In the matter of appointment of the Indian members of Council no man could have used more strong, more emphatic, clear and binding language than was the language used by Sir Charles Wood in discussing that measure. Suggestions had been made by the several members that the Act should provide that a certain proportion of the members of council should be Indians. The suggestion received the support of a good number of members, but then in answer it was pointed out by Sir Charles Wood that, while he agreed to the desire that is should be so, he thought that it was not necessary to make a provision in the statute. And mark the language he used. The first ground was that he wanted to regard the Indian members as being equal to the other members in the Councils of the Empire. 'It had been said', said Sir Charles Wood in the course of that discussion 'that their great object ought to be to obliterate the distinctions between the conquerors and the conquered in India.' Now, that was precisely the policy which he wished to carry into effect, Those Bills distinctly provided that the natives should be employed in the legislative councils as well as in the highest judicial Courts, and in the most important executive offices. The same spirit ran through the whole of them, the spirit which animated that policy which Lord Canning had been most successfully carrying out, and which, he believed, with his honourable friend would afford the best security for the permanence of our rule, for it would make the highest class of the natives, as well as those of the lowest degree feel that their own good was bound up in the continuance of our sway. He believed it to be the best mode of consolidating and perpetuating our dominion in that country. He might observe, however, that he had not thought it at all desirable to name the natives expressly in the measure. He held the law of perfect equality before Her Majesty's subjects without distinction of race, birth, or religion, and he would not do anything which could lead to the supposition that he doubted for a moment the existence of that principle. He had never admitted that there was any distinction between any of the subjects of the Queen, whatever might be their differences of birth, of race, or religion. That was the spirit on the occasion of her assuming the direct Government of India; and that was the principle which would continue to actuate him in all his administrative measures.

"Nobler language was never used in the explanations of intentions of Her Majesty's Proclamation. There never could be a clearer determination shown to employ the Indians to the highest executive offices. This was uttered in 1861; we are now in the year of Grace 1908 and not a single member has been appointed either to the Executive Council of the Viceroy or to any of the Local Governments. It may be, I have no doubt you will agree, that Sir Charles Wood was prompted by the same generous instinct which prompts Lord Morley. I believe in Lord Morley's firmness and determination to introduce reforms. I believe, so was Sir Charles Wood. It may be that a member may be appointed today. There is no guarantee that a member will be appointed time after time to the executive councils unless the provision is made for it in the statute. I therefore beg to suggest, I hope the Congress is of one mind in this matter, that there should be statutory provision for the appointment of not only one Indian but at least two in the Viceroy's Executive Council, and the Executive Councils of Governors. There is only one other matter which involves a question of principle. I am sorry I have exceeded the time; it is an old sin of mine; but the matter is of importance. I hope I shall satisfy you that I am not taking up your time uselessly. There is one other important question, that of class representation which we cannot afford to overlook on such an occasion. Now, gentlemen, I believe myself and a vast majority of the educated, that there are no conflicts of interests among the Indians as Indians. In 999 out of every 1,000 matters, the interests of the Hindus, Mohammedans, landholders and the merchants are all the same. We are governed by the same taxation; whatever misfortunes befall the country, we have to share them, together. Therefore I cannot see the need, I beg respectfully to say of having such class representation as has been given a prominent place in the Reform Scheme. There are questions; it is perfectly right, but these questions do not come before the legislative council either of the Viceroy or of the local governments.

In matters of religion the faith and worship different sects may work apart, though not with hostile feelings; but in secular matters their interests do not conflict. Their interests are not the interests of one class against the other. However, if they do, let us consider what the proposals are. Now, gentlemen, I was going to say in the matter of class representation, Lord Morley's proposals, so far as they go, are excellent. There has been expressed a desire in the some quarters that there should be provision made to enable the members of the separate communities to vote apart from the other members, that there ought to be a fixed number of the members in each community, who could sit; in the councils. That will work manifestly injuriously to one community at least in the Upper India. In my own province, the United Provinces, there are 1,246 elected Councillors of whom 436 are *Mussalmans*. According to the proportion of population only 225 will be entitled to sit if the rule suggested were adopted, At present, therefore, I think, gentlemen, we should leave Lord Morley's proposals as they stand in this matter and not ask that any different principle of the representation should be introduced. I will not take up any more of your time. Let nobody be under the delusion that the reforms are final. We must receive them with grace, with warm gratitude. We must hope for more and more. Not enjoyment and not sorrow Is out destined end or way. But to act that each tomorrow finds us farther than today.

"Only by the kind dispensation of an all-kind Providence and by the help of the government which the Providence has placed over us, we are to achieve that measure of Self-Government for which the expression has been given by the best Indians during the last 25 years.

THE MONTAGU-CHELMSFORD REFORMS

Soon after the publication of the Indian Constitutional Reforms by Hon'ble Mr E.S. Montagu and H.E. Lord Chelmsford in June 1918, Pandit Madan Mohan Malaviya wrote the following criticism of the proposals:

"The proposals of the Secretary of State and the Viceroy relating to the constitutional reform are, it is scarcely necessary to say, the result of many months of the earnest discussion and careful deliberation held under the circumstances which are too well-known to require recital. In the words of their authors the proposals are of great intricacy and importance, and it is only right that they should have been published for full and public discussion before being considered by His Majesty's Government in England. Both because of their inherent importance and of the high official position of their authors, the proposals deserve most careful consideration at the hands of the all serious-minded persons who are interested in the future of this country.

"There is much in the proposals that is liberal, and that will mean a real and beneficial change in the right direction, which we must welcome and be grateful for; but there are also grave deficiencies which must be made up before the reforms can become adequate to the requirements of the country. In the first category are the proposals, taking them in the order in which they have been placed in the summary, to place the salary of the Secretary of State on the estimates of the United Kingdom, and to appoint a Select Committee of the House of Commons for the Indian affairs; to increase the Indian element in the Governor-General's Executive Council by the appointment of a second Indian Member; to replace the present Legislative Council of the Governor-General by a Legislative Assembly, which will consist of about one hundred members of whom two-thirds will be elected; to associate Standing Committees, two-thirds of which should be elected by the non-official members with as many Departments of the Government as possible and to allow the supplementary questions to be put by any member of the Legislative Assembly. In the same category come many provisions relating to the provincial governments, for instance, the proposal that in every province (and this will include the United Provinces, the Punjab, Bihar and Orissa, the Central Provinces and Assam) the Executive Government should consist of a Governor and an Executive Council, which should consist of the two members, one of whom will be an Indian, and a minister or ministers nominated by the governor from the elected members of the legislative council; that; these Ministers should be in charge of portfolios dealing with certain subjects; that on these subjects the decisions of the ministers should be final subject only to the Governor's advice and control; that though the power of control is reserved to the Governor, it is expected that he would refuse assent to the proposals of his ministers only when the consequences of the acquiescence would be serious; that it is not intended that he should be in a position to refuse assent at discretion to his minister's proposals; that in the each province an enlarged legislative council with a substantial elected majority should be established; that the members should be elected on as broad a franchise as possible that every member of the council should be entitled to ask the supplementary questions; that the Standing Committees, consisting mainly of the members elected by the legislative council, should be attached to each department; that there should be a complete separation made between the Indian and provincial heads of revenue; that the provinces should make contributions of the fixed amounts to the Government of India, which should be the first charge on the provincial revenues; that the provincial governments should have certain powers of taxation and borrowing and the last, but not the least important, that the budget should be laid before the legislative council and subject to one reservation, should be altered so as to give effect to the resolutions of that council. That the reservation is that if the legislative council should refuse to accept the budget proposals for certain subjects, which are described as reserved subjects, the Governor-in-Council should have power to restore the whole or any part of the original allotment, on the Governor certifying that, for reasons to be stated, such restoration is in his opinion essential either to the peace or tranquillity of the Province or any part thereof, or to the discharge of his responsibility for the reserved subjects. The reservation is no doubt very wide, and it will require to be abandoned or modified. I shall deal with it later. Of the same favourable character are the proposals that complete popular control should, as far as possible, be established in the local bodies; that the racial bars that still exist in regulations for the appointment to the public services should be abolished; that in addition to the recruitment in England where such exists, a system of appointment to all the public services should be established in India; and that percentages of the recruitment in India with a definite rate of increase, should be fixed for all the services, though the percentage suggested for the Indian Civil Service is inadequate and will require to be increased from 33 to 50 per cent, at once. The proposals relating to the Native States also seem to be satisfactory. Taking these proposals as a whole, so far as they go, they obviously constitute a liberal advance upon the existing state of affairs for which Mr Montagu and Lord Chelmsford are entitled to our grateful acknowledgments. But in my opinion they do not go far enough to meet the requirements of the country. The effect of the proposals is summarised by their authors in paragraph 353 of their report in the following words: 'We begin with a great extension of the local self- government so as to train the electorates in the matters which they will best understand. Simultaneously we provide a substantial measure of the Self-Government in the provinces and for the better representation and more criticism in the government of India and for the fuller knowledge in the Parliament, And we suggest the machinery by the means of which at regular stages the element of responsibility can be continuously enlarged and that of the official control continuously diminished, in a way that will guarantee the ordered progress and afford an answer to the immediate representations and agitation.' This certainly means progress, but it means unduly slow progress; whereas if India is to be equipped industrially and politically, to discharge her obligations to her own children and to the Empire in the immediate future that confronts her, it is imperatively necessary that an adequately rapid rate of progress should be ensured by the introduction of a larger measure of self-government in the Provinces and a substantial measure of it in the Government of India itself.

The Congress-League Scheme

"The Congress-League scheme was framed to secure what, in the present circumstances of India, the united wisdom of educated India believes to be the right measure of power to the people, acting through their representatives in the councils, both in the provincial and the Imperial administrations. It reserved absolute power to the central executive government in all matters relating to the defence of the country, war and peace and foreign and political relations. It also reserved sufficient power to every executive government to prevent any legislation or policy being adopted which it considered injurious. It will be obvious from the list of proposals summarised above that Mr Montagu and Lord Chelmsford have adopted many recommendations of the Congress-League scheme; but they have discarded its vital feature, viz., the sharing by the government of power with the representatives of the people, except in so far as they have proposed to give power to the provincial legislative councils in respect of such subjects as may be "transferred" to them. I think: that, they have done so for insufficient reasons. If they could make up their minds to recommend that power should be shared by them with the representatives of the people to the extent urged by the Congress and the Muslim League, the objections which they have urged, could be met by alterations and amendments in the scheme. For instance, all the arguments which they have put forward against the proposal that the Indian members of the executive council should be elected by the elected members of the Legislative Council, could be met by laying it down that the Governor should nominate the Indian Members out of a panel to be recommended by the elected members. The object of the Congress-League proposal clearly is that the Indian members of the Executive Council should be men who enjoy the confidence of the public as represented by the legislative council.. So long as this object was secured, no one would quarrel about the method which might be adopted to attain it. But it is essential that the object should be secured. In summing up their criticism of the Congress-League scheme as a whole, after describing its vital features, the distinguished authors say: 'Our first observation is that in our view such a plan postulates the existence of a competent electorate, and an assembly which will be truly representative of the people.' They believe that both a sound electoral system and truly representative assemblies will be evolved in time, but they say they cannot assent to the proposals which could only be justified on the assumption that such institutions would be immediately forthcoming. Here I respectfully join issue with the authors. I firmly believe that such institutions can be, and that therefore they ought to be, brought into existence now. I will show later on that this can be done.

"In dealing with the proposals of the Congress-League scheme relating to the representation of the minorities, the distinguished authors seem to complain that the separate electorates are proposed in all the provinces even where Mohammedans are in a majority, and that wherever they are numerically weak the proportion suggested is in excess of their numerical strength. But this rule was initiated and established by the government in spite of the protests of the non-Muslims. But having been so established, Hindus could not expect to effect a compromise with the Mohammedans on any other basis at any rate at present. They agreed to an even larger proportion than their present representation for the same reason. The figures of the seats to be reserved for the special Muslim electorates in the various provinces were of course arrived at no other basis than that of negotiation. But the Hindus agreed to them deliberately in order to secure the union and co-operation of Hindus and Mussalmans for the common good of the people as a whole. It is quite true that a privileged position of this kind is open to the objection that if any other community hereafter makes good a claim to separate representation, it can be satisfied only by deduction from the non-Muslim seats, or else by a rateable deduction from both the Muslim and non-Muslim seats. But when the Hindus and Muslims did come to an agreement like the one in question, one need not despair that, in case of a real necessity, their leaders would be able to arrive at some solution. They have learnt; to recognise the truth that compromises have sometimes to be made by the individuals and even by the communities for furthering the common good. The authors themselves also have after weighing the whole situation, rightly, though with justifiable reluctance, assented to the maintenance of the separate representation for the Mohammedans for the present, although they have reserved their approval of the particular proposals set before them, until they have ascertained what their effect upon the other interests will be, and have made provision for them.

"I will not attempt to deal just now with all the criticism which the distinguished authors have bestowed upon the Congress-League scheme. I expect that a statement will be prepared in the due course on behalf of the Congress and the Muslim League in which these objections will be considered at length. Though some of these objections may not be without weight, I believe they can be fairly and fully met; and I still think that with some modifications, which I have no doubt the Congress and the Muslim League will agree to, that the scheme will be best meet the present requirements of the country, and constitute a satisfactory first stage of responsible government in India, responsible not in the strict technical sense in which the word has been interpreted by the authors of the proposals and is generally understood in England, but in a more restricted sense, viz., that every member of the executive government would, before taking office, be informed under the authority of the Parliament; that though he does not hold the office at the will of the legislative council, he must; hereafter consider himself morally responsible to the people to administer their affairs in conformity with their wishes as expressed through their representatives in the councils. But I recognise that the proposals which have been put forward by Mr Montagu and Lord Chelmsford after months of discussion and deliberation, have reduced the chances of the Congresa-League scheme being accepted; and I think that, in the circumstances of the case, the most practical course for us to adopt will be to press for such modifications and expansion of the proposals in question as will make them adequate and complete. If this is done, it will necessarily assimilate them in principle to the Congress-League scheme.

The Conditions of the Problem

Educational Backwardness

"In considering the imitations of the proposals put forward by Mr Montagu and Lord Chelmsford, we have no doubt to bear in mind that they regarded the announcement of the 20th August last as laying down the terms of their reference. But it seems to me that they have put too narrow an interpretation on those terms, particularly on the question of the rate of progress towards the responsible government, and in dwelling to the extent they have done on the responsibility of the British electorate and Parliament for the welfare of the people of India; also in insisting too much and too often that the British electorate could not part with that responsibility until an Indian electorate was in sight; to take the burden on its shoulders. This evidently much influenced their judgment and prevented them from forming an impartial and correct estimate of the conditions of the problem which they had to solve. A perusal of the chapter headed "Conditions of the Problem" is the report leaves a disagreeable impression on the mind that the circumstances which go against the introduction of the responsible government have been given an exaggerated value, and that those that are in favor of it have been under-estimated or ignored. Attention is prominently drawn to two dominating conditions. One is that the immense masses of the people are poor, ignorant and helpless far beyond the standards of Europe and the other is that there runs through the Indian Society a series of cleavages of religion, race, and caste which constantly threaten its solidarity and of which any wise political scheme must take serious heed. The first of the statements is unfortunately quite correct; but it means a strong impeachment of the present bureaucratic system, and supplies an urgent reason for introducing a real measure of popular self-government in India. The bureaucratic system which has had complete sway in India for a century and more has not lifted the immense masses of the people from poverty, ignorance and helplessness. The educated classes of India, who are of the people and live and move with them have made repeated appeals to those in power to allow the representatives of the people a share in the administration, so that they might co-operate with them to reduce this colossal poverty and illiteracy but the bureaucracy and Parliament have steadily refused to part with power and they must be held responsible for the result.

"Great stress is laid upon the very limited extent to which education has spread among the people also upon the fact that the total number of persons enjoying a substantial income is very small. It is noted that in one province the total number of persona the who enjoyed an income of 66, a year, derived from other sources than land, was 30,000; in another province, 20,000...

"According to one estimate, the number of landlords whose income derived from their proprietary holdings exceeds 20 a year; in the United Provinces it is about 126,000 out of a population of 48 millions. It is evident that enormous masses of the population have little to spare for more than the necessaries of life. True, also too true ! But this again furnishes a very strong reason for at least partly transferring power and responsibility from those who have had a monopoly of it for the last hundred years without having it in proper measure to promote a larger production and distribution of wealth.

"It is then urged that the proportion of the people who take an interest in the political questions is very small. After urging that the town-dwellers who take an interest in the political questions, are a fraction of the people. The report says, 'On the other hand it is an enormous country population, for the most part poor, ignorant non-politically minded and unused to any system of election immersed indeed in the struggle for existence. The rural classes have the greatest stake in the country because they contribute most to its revenues but they are poorly equipped for politics and do not at present wish to take part in them. Among them are a few great landlords and a larger number of yeomen farmers. They are not ill-fitted to play a part in affairs, but with few exceptions they have not yet done so. Yes, but were not the bulk of the people in every country and, even in England non-politically minded until they were given an opportunity to exercise the political power until the franchise was extended to them? And is there a better means of getting the people to take an interest in politics than by giving them such power?

"As regards education as a basis for franchise the Indians would certainly desire that in any scheme of election that may be introduced, the possession of a recognised degree of education should entitle a person to a vote without any other qualification. But I cannot help feeling that the argument based on the lack of education among the people, has been unduly pressed against the cause of the Indian constitutional reform. We know that in Austria, Germany and France which have adopted the principle of manhood, or the universal suffrage, a common qualification is that the elector should be able to read and write. So also in Italy, the United States, etc. But except in the case of the eight universities, the franchise has never been based in the United Kingdom on any educational qualification. It is the possession of the freehold or leasehold property of a certain value or the occupation of premises of a certain annual value that gives a vote there, and it is said that this is the most universal qualification in all the countries where a system of popular election has been introduced. Mr Disraeli made an attempt; in his abortive Reform Bill of 1867 to introduce an educational franchise in England. Hansard records that it was met by ridicule, because it proposed a very low educational franchise, so much backward was the education in England at the time. Mr Gladstone's Reform Bill of 1868, based the franchise, like its predecessor of 1832, on property qualifications. It was after the franchise had been so extended to the workmen, that the Englishmen began to say that we must educate our masters, and thus the Elementary Education Act was passed in 1870 making the elementary education universal and compulsory.

"The Duke of Newcastle's Commission of 1861 stated in their report that the estimated number of day scholars in England and Wales in 1833 was one in ll. Speaking in 1868, Mr Bruce stated that they had then arrived at the rate of one in seven or eight. In introducing the Elementary Education Bill

(1870) Mr Forster described the situation as showing much imperfect education and much absolute ignorance, ignorance which we are all aware is pregnant with crime and misery, with misfortune to individuals and danger to the community. So we are not much worse off than England was in 1867-70. Nor are we worse off than was Canada, when on Lord Durham's recommendation, the parliament established responsible government there. It is impossible,' said Lord Durham in his memorable report which led to the change, and to the exaggeration of the want of education among the inhabitants. No means of instruction have ever been provided for them, and they are almost and universally destitute of the qualifications even of reading and writing. Let us have a reform bill based on the principles of that the of 1863, or a substantial measure of responsible government, and one of the first things, if the first thing we should do is to pass an Education Act which will remove the stigma of illiteracy from our land and steadily raise the percentage of the scholars at our schools, until in a decade or so, it will equal the standard which has been reached in the other civilised countries.

"Having dealt with at such length with the argument based on the want of education among the people, I think it my duty to add that though the government have not yet secured them the benefit of education, nature has been much less unkind to them. They have been endowed with a fair measure of common sense, and not only in their caste *panchayats* and conferences but generally in all the matters which concern them, the bulk of the people well understand their interests and come to fairly correct conclusions regarding them, The number of such conferences is steadily growing, Only in February last, the tenants of the United Provinces held a Conference of their own during the *Magh Mela* at Allahabad, when they discussed and adopted a representation to Mr Montagu and the Viceroy, urging what they wanted to be done to protect and promote their interests. They did me the honour of inviting me to address a few words to them; and it gave me genuine pleasure to see how well they understood and appreciated every point that affected their interests, I claim that, allowing for the difference due to the possession or the want of education, our small proprietors, yeomen farmers, and the bulk of our tenants will compare not unfavorably with corresponding classes in the other countries in the possession of natural intelligence. And finally, having regard to the response which they have made, and are still making to the appeal to subscribe to the War loan and to risk their lives in the defense of the Empire, it is wrong and unkind to suggest that they are hopelessly deficient in the capacity to judge whom they should elect as their *panch mukhtar* or representative in the legislative councils. Twelve months of the whole-hearted effort by the officials and non-officials, to educate and organise them, similar to that which has been made for raising the war loan and recruits from the people, will go far to prepare them for the proper exercise of any franchise which may be conferred upon them.

"In discussing the question of electorates it should also be remembered that though it is in every way desirable to make the franchise as broad as possible, it cannot in reason be regarded as a very serious objection that, comparatively speaking, our electorates may not, in the first instance, be as large as in the countries where the elective system has been in vogue for a long time. A reference to the gradual extension of the franchise in England may not be amiss here. We know that up to the year 1832 the majority of the House of Commons were elected by less than fifteen thousand persons. In Scotland, where the population at that time was about 2,360,000, there were only about 3,000 electors. As Mr Gladstone stated in 1881, the Reform Bill of 1832 which was described as the Magna Carta of British Liberties, added about; 500,000 to the entire constituency of the three countries. After 1832 the next reform came in 1886. At that time the total constituency of the United Kingdom reached 1,364,000, and by the bills which were passed in 1867-65 the number was raised to 2,448,000. By 1884, the constituency had reached in round numbers 3,000,000. The Act of 1885 added about 2,000,000 to the number, i.e., nearly twice as much as was added since 1867 and more than four times as much as was added in 1832.

"This brief history contains both guidance and

encouragement for us. With a fairly liberal franchise, we are in a position to start with the electorates the dimensions of which will be regarded by every reasonable man as satisfactory, when all the circumstances of the case are borne in mind.

Religious Differences

"As regards the second dominating condition, it is true that the Indian Society is composed of the vast numbers of people who belong to the different religions, races and castes. But it seems to me an exaggeration to say that this circumstance constantly threatens its solidarity. The people of India are more law-abiding than perhaps those of any other country in the world.

"Differences of religion, race and caste do not stand in the way of their generally living and working together as good neighbors and friends, or of their combining for promoting the common purposes. The occasional outbursts of the religious feeling which no one can deplore more than we Indians do are due to ignorance which the bureaucracy has failed to remove, and to the defects of a foreign system of administration which can only be mitigated by the power being substantially shared with the representatives of the people. Mr Montagu and Lord Chelmsford say that the difficulty that outweighs all the others is the existence of the religious differences. With due deference to them, I venture to say that they have taken much too exaggerated a view of this difficulty. They refer appreciating to the agreement reached at Lucknow in December 1916, between the Muslims and Hindus; but they ask, 'What sure guarantee it affords that religious dissensions between the great communities are over? It should be obvious that this guarantee cannot spring from the agreement in the question itself but from the accomplishment of the object it was intended to achieve, viz., the attainment of the self-Government. If this was done, power and responsibility would be transferred in the fair measure to the educated Hindus and Mohammedans, so that they would be in a position to promote patriotism and public spirit, education and industrial and commercial enterprise among their countrymen which will usher an era of greater co-operation, prosperity and goodwill, and thus make religious riots a matter of past history. Mr Montagu and Lord Chelmsford cannot regard the concordat (of Lucknow) as conclusive. They say: 'To our minds so long as the two communities entertain anything like their present views as to the separateness of their interests, we are bound to regard religious hostilities as still a very serious possibility. How quickly and violently the ignorant portion, which is as far the largest portion of the either great community, responds to the cry of "religion in danger" has been proved again and again in India's history. The record of the last year bears recent witness to it.' As I have said before, no one can deplore and condemn religious riots more than we Indians do. But the distinguished authors are mistaken in thinking that there is any connection between the occasional outbursts of religious hostilities and what they describe as the present views of the two communities as to the separateness of their interests. The proneness of the ignorant portion of the either community to respond to the cry of religion in danger is due not to the religious differences, which are present year in and year out, but to ignorance; and if this ignorance were removed, religions differences would cease to divide and to lead to riots. The distinguished authors are well aware that such regrettable distempers of ignorance have not been unknown even in England. I cannot do better than quote here from a speech of Macaulay delivered in the House of Commons on the 19th of April, 1847. Speaking in support of the Government Plan of Education, and referring to the No Popery riots of 1780, Macaulay said: 'The education of the poor' he (Adam Smith) says, 'is a matter which deeply concerns the commonwealth. Just as the magistrate ought to interfere for the purpose of preventing the leprosy from spreading among the people, he ought to interfere for the purpose of stopping the progress of the moral distempers which are inseparable from ignorance. Nor can this duty be neglected without danger to the public peace. If you leave the multitude uninstructed, there is serious risk that religious animosities may produce the most dreadful disorder.' The most dreadful disorders! Those are Adam Smith's own words; and prophetic words they were. Scarcely had he given this warning to our rulers when his prediction was fulfilled in a manner never to be forgotten. I speak of the 1780. I do not know that I could find in all the No Property Piots history a stronger proof of the proposition that the ignorance of the common people makes the property, the limbs, and the lives of all the classes insecure. Without the shadow of a grievance, at the summons of a madman, a hundred thousand people rise in insurrection. During a whole week there is anarchy in the greatest and the wealthiest of the European cities. The parliament is besieged. Your predecessor sitting trembling in his chair, and expects every moment to see the door beaten in by the ruffians whose roar he hears all round the house. The peers are pulled out of their coaches. The bishops in their lawn are forced to fly over the tiles. The chapels of the foreign ambassadors, buildings made sacred by the law of nations, are destroyed. The house of the chief justice is demolished. The little children of the prime minister are taken out of their bed? And lay in their night clothes on the table of the horse guards, the only safe asylum from the fury of the rabble. The prisons are opened. Highwaymen, house-breakers, murderers, come forth to swell the mob by which they have been set free. Thirty-six fires are blazing at once in London. Then comes the retribution. Count up all the wretches who shot, who were hanged, who were crushed, who drank themselves to death at the rivers of gin which ran down Holborn Hill; and you will find that the battles have been lost and won with a smaller sacrifice of life. And what was the cause of this calamity, a calamity, which, in the history of London ranks with the great plague and the great fire. The cause was the ignorance of a population which had been suffered, in the neighbourhood of palaces, theatres, temples to grow up as rude and stupid as any tribe of the tattooed cannibals in New Zealand, I might say as any drove of beasts in Smithfield market.

"The instance is striking, but it is not solitary. To the same cause are to be ascribed the riots of Nottingham, the sack of

Bristol, all the outrages of Ludd, and Swing, and Rebecca, beautiful and costly machinery broken to pieces in Yorkshire, barns and hay stalks blazing in Kent, fences and buildings pulled down in Wales. Could such things have been done in a country in which the mind of the labourer had been opened by education, in which he had been taught to find pleasure in the exercise of his intellect, taught to revere his Maker, taught to respect legitimate authority, and taught at the same time to seek the redress of the real wrongs by the peaceful and constitutional means?

"It seems to me that not only did the learned authors fail to trace the riots to their true cause, but that they did not also take it into account that there are unfortunately some among the European officials in India who feel a satisfaction in seeing religious differences at work, not only between the Hindus and Mohammedans, but even between the two sects of Mohammedans, men who evidently think with Sir John Strachey that the existence side by side of these hostile creeds is one of the strong points in our political position in India. The painful story of the Camilla and Jamalpur riots need not be repeated here, but the mind irresistibly goes to it in a discussion like this. It is important to move in this connection that Hindu-Mohammedan riots seldom take place in the Indian States. Not only this, but even in British India, districts which have been placed in charge of the Hindu or Mussalman Magistrates or Superintendents of Police, have passed peacefully through periods of stress and anxiety, while there were disturbances in several of those which were in charge of the European officers.

"Here again it ought not to be forgotten that India is not the only country which has known the trouble of the religious differences among her sons. England herself has not been a stranger to this. Her history contains a sad record of the evils which she experienced owing to the bitter differences between the Protestants and Catholics. The long-lasting persecution to which the latter were subjected by the former, particularly in Ireland, is a matter of not very remote history, when the House of Lords, the House of Commons, the Magistracy, all corporate offices in towns, all the ranks in the army, the bench, the bar, the whole administration of the government or justice, were closed against the Catholics; when the very right of voting for their representatives in the Parliament was denied them; when in all social and political matters, the Catholics, in the other words the immense majority of the people of Ireland, were simply hewers of wood and drawers of water to their Protestant masters. The Catholic Emancipation Bill which admitted [Roman Catholics to Parliament, and to all but a few of the highest posts, civil or military, in the service of the Crown, was passed only in 1829]; the Bill for the disestablishment of the church in Ireland, only in 1869!

"But it speaks volumes for the growth of the religious toleration among the Protestants of England of the period that the Catholic Emancipation Bill was passed by a Parliament which did not contain a single Catholic as a member. This is a happy illustration of the liberalising effect which the representative institutions produce upon the people of the country where they are established. But this is a digression. I thank God that except in the limited periods and areas, the relations between the Hindus and Mussalmans in India, have generally been far happier than those that subsisted so long between the Protestants and Catholics in Great Britain and Ireland. For centuries they have lived together, all over this wide country as good neighbours, trusting each other, co-operating with each other, and having close and intimate social and business relations with the each other. The regrettable outbursts of the religious animosities have been occasional and fleeting and remediable, and have been confined to a few places in the country. Last year in some of these places, the blame for the origin and spread of the trouble that arose, was openly ascribed by the people to the officials. In Delhi, the Capital of the Empire, the Hindus refused to celebrate the Bamatila not owing to any misunderstanding between themselves and the Mohammedans, but with the local authorities. It was owing to the official obstinacy and callousness that the whole of the Hindu Delhi kept its large business suspended for eleven days and suffered serious loss and hardship over it. But notwithstanding this, the relations between the Hindus and Mohammedans remained undisturbed. In the country as a whole, the attitude of the officials and the people left no room for complaint!. In not a few places, notably Lahore, Hindus and Mohammedans cooperated with each other, with cordial good will, to see their two celebrations pass off in peace and harmony.

"Before I leave this subject I should like to say further, that the difficulty arising out of our religious differences, such as they are, is much less serious than that which arose out of the enmity which prevailed between the French and the English in the two provinces of Canada in 1837, when Sir James Craigh wrote that 'The line of distinction between us is completely drawn; friendship, cordiality are not to be found; even common intercourse scarcely exists,' and when Lord Durham said, in his memorable report in which he recommended the establishment of the responsible government in Canada. 'I found the two nations warring in the bosom of a single state. I found a struggle not of principles but of races. It is encouraging to note that the existence of this deep-seated and widespread animosity between the two large sections of the people was not held to be a bar to the introduction of the responsible government there, but rather a strong reason for and an effective remedy against it. The subsequent events have fully vindicated the wisdom of that decision. The fact lends strong support to the view that the introduction of a system of the self-government in which power and responsibility must be vested in an increasing measure in the leaders of the communities, will prove the most effective means of preventing the religious differences from leading to the undesirable results.

The Interests of the Masses. The Bureaucracy and the Educated India

"A strong claim is made in the report that the official has been hitherto the best friend of the *ryots*, and that he must therefore retain power to protect him until it is clear that his interests can safely be left in his own hands or that the legislative councils represent and consider his interests. So with the depressed classes no one would quarrel with the desire of the official to take every reasonable precaution to protect the interests of the *ryots* and of the depressed classes. But the claim that the bureaucracy has hitherto been the best friend of these classes can only be conceded in a limited sense and requires to be examined. This has become all the more necessary in view of the fact that it is stated in the report that the prospects of advance very greatly depend upon how far the educated Indian is in sympathy without capable of fairly representing the illiterate masses. We have also been reminded that it is urged that the politically-minded clashes stand somewhat apart from and in advance of the ordinary life of the country. The distinguished authors of the proposals have addressed a very kindly appeal to the educated class that if they resent the suggestion that has bean made that they have hitherto safeguarded their own position and shown insufficient interest in the peasant and labouring population, now is the opportunity for them to acquit themselves of such an imputation and to come forward as leaders of the people as a whole. Several of the proposals for reserving power to the bureaucracy and not extending it to the educated Indian, until the peasant and the labourer has learnt the lesson of self-protection, seem to be based on the idea that the former is their better friend. It has become necessary therefore to go briefly into this question.

"In the early days of the British rule the official did a great deal for the people to establishing peace and order, in promoting protection of life and property, in providing the country with a set of codes of great value, in organising the administration of justice, civil and criminal, and the police and the revenue departments, in promoting irrigation, in improving the existing means of the communications and creating new ones—roads, railways, posts and telegraphs in establishing schools and hospitals to the extent he did, and so on.

"He secured to a large body of the occupiers of the soil the right to retain their holdings, bringing the law in this respect; in consonance with the ancient custom of the country, so long as they paid the rent, and protected them against the eviction and enhancement of the rent except in accordance with the law. For this and more all honour and gratitude to him. But I ask every good man and true man in the bureaucracy and their number is not small to say whether in his opinion the system which he represents has done enough to advance the welfare of the *ryot*, the labourer and the general mass of the people? The report before me bears witness that it has not. The report of the Commission which was appointed after the great famine of 1877-78 drew attention to the fact that the mass of the people were miserably poor, and that no remedy against the evils to which they were exposed in the times of famine, would be complete until a diversity of the occupations was provided them by the encouragement of the industrial pursuits. And yet little worth speaking of has been done in this direction up to this day. The mass of the people are still steeped in poverty. They are also steeped in ignorance. The Education Commission of 1884 recommended the extension of the universal elementary education. But we know to our grief, how, after the lapse of the thirty-three years, we stand in regard to it. So far as the depressed classes are concerned it is particularly a question of education. If the blessings of the education had been secured to them, their position would have immensely improved. But this has not been done. Public health stands low, as is evidenced by the high rate of mortality. The needs of the population in respect of sanitation and medical relief have been poorly met. Technical education has not been promoted, industries not encouraged. Indians have not been admitted in the fair numbers into the higher ranks of the public services civil and military: public expenditure has not been reduced but has on the contrary been raised to an enormous extent. During all this time power has remained absolutely in the hands of the bureaucracy. It has found money for everything thought it fits to provide for, but it has again and again pleaded the want of funds for promoting the services bearing directly on the people's welfare.

"Let us now see what the educated Indians have been doing during this identical period. From 1885 they have been meeting regularly every year in the Congress at great personal sacrifice and earnestly pressing upon the bureaucracy measure after measure calculated to improve the lot of the rural population and the general mass of the people. A glance at the resolutions passed by the Congress during the thirty-three years affords unquestionable evidence of the attitude of the educated Indian towards the mass of his countrymen. In 1886, the Congress stated that it regards with the deepest sympathy, and views with grave apprehension, the increasing poverty of the vast numbers of the population of India, and urged the introduction of the representative institutions as one of the most important practical steps towards the amelioration of the condition of the people. In 1887, it urged that having regard to the poverty of the people, it is desirable that the government be moved to elaborate a system of the technical education, suitable to the condition of the country and to encourage the indigenous manufactures. In 1888, it urged that it was the first duty of the British Government in India to foster and encourage education, general as well as technical, in all its branches, again emphasised the importance, in view of the poverty of the people, of encouraging indigenous manufactures, and advocated the appointment of a Commission to enquire into the industrial condition of the country.

"In 1891, in reply to a telegram from General Both, he said that the sad condition of fifty to sixty millions of the half-starving paupers, constituted the primary raison d'etre of its existence. It again and again pressed the view upon the government that India can never be well or justly governed, nor her people prosperous or contented, until they are allowed, through their elected representatives, a potential voice in the legislatures of their country, and urged a series of measures of retrenchment and improvement with the view of improving the unhappy condition of affairs. For years it urged the reduction of the salt tax and the raising of the taxable minimum for the income-tax from ₹ 500 to ₹ 1,000 before these measures were adopted by the government. It has ceaselessly advocated the adoption of an improved excise policy and the introduction of a simple system of the local option in the case of all the villages, to keep temptation away from the door of the poor. Its advocacy of an improvement in the administration of the Forest laws and for the abolition of the evil system of the forced labour and supplies (*beggar and rasad*), also its strong agitation against the system of the indentured labour and for the proper treatment of the Indians in the colonies, have all been in the interests of the same classes. In the interests of the agricultural development, it has urged that the government should impose a limit upon its land revenue demand and that it should secure fixity of tenure, wherever it does not exist, to the tenant in the land he tills. It advocated the starting of the Agricultural Banks and the adoption of the measures for the improvement and development of agriculture as it has been developed in the other countries and the establishment of a larger number of experimental and demonstration farms all over the country. It has again and again reiterated that fully fifty millions of the population, a number yearly increasing, are dragging out a miserable existence on the verge of starvation, and that in every decade several millions actually perish by starvation, and has humbly urged that immediate steps should be taken to remedy this calamitous state of affairs. When the famine of 1896 occurred, the Congress again drew pointed attention to the great poverty of the people and again insisted that the true remedy against the evils of the recurrence of famine lay in the adoption of a policy, which would enforce economy, husband the resources of the state, foster the development of the indigenous and local arts and the industries which have practically been extinguished, and help forward the introduction of the modern arts and industries.

"It is unnecessary to prolong this list, and to refer to the other resolutions of the Congress of a similar character. I hope this is enough to show how earnestly and pathetically the educated Indian has been pleading for the lifetime of a generation for the adoption of the measures having the one aim of ameliorating the lot of his poorer countrymen. The proceedings of the provincial and even communal conferences and of the imperial and provincial legislative council bear similar testimony, but it is unnecessary to refer to them in detail. I think the educated Indian can safely claim that he has proved that he is at least as much in sympathy with and capable of representing the illiterate masses as our friend the official.

A Contrast Progress in Japan

"It is regrettable to have to note that the British electorate and its responsible agent, the bureaucracy, which has held absolute power during the period in question has responded sub-title to the representations of the educated Indian. In the same period the Japanese, who were in not half so good a position as India so far as material resources and administrative organisation were concerned, have achieved enormous progress; they have made education universal in their country, given technical and scientific education to their youth to fit them to play their part successfully in every branch—civil military or naval of the activity of a civilised country, developed their industries, built up their manufactures, promoted national banking and credit, enhanced the prosperity and strength of their people, and raised their country to the position of a first class world-power whose manufactures are pouring into Europe and India, whose steamers are carrying on its own export and import trade, and whose friendship has been of the incalculable value to the British Government: in the present crisis. The educated Indians feel that if the British electorate and Parliament had agreed to admit them to a share of power as they asked for in 1886, they too would have been able to achieve a considerable degree of the similar progress in their country, and they are naturally anxious that that power should not be withheld any longer from them. The failure of the bureaucracy to do much of what it should have done to build up the national strength and prosperity of the Indian people during the last thirty-three years, in spite of the repeated representations of the educated Indians, has created a widespread conviction among them that the healthy progress of the country will not be ensured unless the power is given to them to promote it. This was a factor in the problem even in 1914. The events of the last four years have intensified its importance and added a new element to the situation,

The Effects of the War

"Before the War the Indians based their claim to a share in the government of their country on the natural right and justice, which was supported by the pledges of the British Sovereign and Parliament. That claim has received additional strength by the part which India has played in the War. India will ever be grateful to Lord Hardinge for having sent her Expeditionary Force to help England and France in the great fight for liberty, right and justice, and she is naturally proud of all the help which her princes and people have given to the British Empire in the hour of her great need. It has been acknowledged that but for the timely and powerful help of the Indian contingent the fortunes of the War would have been very adversely affected in France towards the end of 1914. It is also indisputable that but for India's splendid rally, British prestige would have suffered irretrievably in the East. In view of this achievement of which any nation may be proud, the Indians ask what reason is there for England not permitting them even partly to manage their domestic affairs now as Canada and Australia and the other self-governing British Colonies do. Mr Montagu and Lord Chelmsford have taken full note of the effects of the War on India. They have observed: 'The War has given to India a new sense of self-esteem.' She has in the words of Sir Satyendra Prasad Sinha, 'A feeling of profound pride that she has not fallen behind other portions of the British Empire but has stood shoulder to shoulder with them in the hour of their sorest trial.' She feels that she has been tried and not found wanting, that thereby her status has bean raised, and that it is only her due that her higher status should be recognised by the Great Britain and the world at large. They have further noted that 'the War has come to be regarded more and more clearly as a struggle between liberty and despotism, a struggle for the right of small nations and for the right of all the people to rule their own destinies, that attention is repeatedly called to the fact that in Europe Britain is fighting on the side of liberty, and it is urged that Britain cannot deny to the people of India that for which she is herself fighting in Europe and in the fight for which she has been helped by

India's blood and treasure....The speeches of English and American statesmen, proclaiming the necessity for destroying German-militarism, and for conceding the right of self determination to the nations have had much effect upon the political opinion in India and have contributed to give new force and vitality to the demand for the self-government which was making itself more and more widely heard among the progressive section of the people. This clear and correct statement, for which Mr Montagu and Lord Chelmsford are entitled to our thanks, should have led one to expect that they would recommend the introduction of a substantial measure of the responsible government in India, which would mark a clear recognition of her higher status as also of the principle of self- determination. But their proposals fall far short of that. It is surprising that after taking a full survey of the situation, they could come to the conclusion that at this period of the day the Indians would be satisfied with the proposals of reform which will not give them a real and potential voice in the administration of their country's affairs, in the central as well as in the provincial governments.

The Interests of the Foreign Missionaries, Merchants and Public Servants

"Mr Montagu and Lord Chelmsford have persuaded themselves that the Indians are not yet fit for such a measure. But they cannot persuade the Indians to agree with them. I have already dealt with the principal grounds upon which they have based their conclusions. I have given the sufficient reasons for the belief that the interests of the *ryots* will not suffer at the hands of the educated Indians, I have shown that neither the educational backwardness nor the differences of religion, race and caste stand in the way of reform. I am bound to add that the Indians will resent the further suggestion that if the power were transferred to them, the interests of the missionaries, foreign merchants, and of foreigners in the service of India would suffer. The educated Indians have not shown any hostility towards the missionaries. On the contrary they have pulled very well with many of them. But the anxiety of Mr

Montagu and Lord Chelmsford to place the interests of the persons who professedly come to this country to convert its people from the faith of their ancestors, in the scale against the demands of the country for advance in the direction of the self-government, so vital to the national life and growth, will supply to the unprejudiced minds a new argument in favour of the home rule. It is equally unjust to the people of this country to suggest that if they got power they might use it to the injury of the foreign merchants and public servants. Have not the relations of the foreign merchants with the Indians at all important centers of the industry, been uniformly of good will and fair dealing? What reason is there then to be found in fact to justify the apprehension that if the Indians got power they would indulge in any prejudiced attack on, or allow any privileged competition against, any existing industry? That they will be as foolish as to jeopardise their country's enormous trade import and export by giving any just cause for complaint to the foreign merchant, whom they cannot replace for a long time? That they will not have the sense to recognise that the maintenance and improvement of that trade demands nothing more urgently than that no foreigner should have a suspicion of any but fair and honourable treatment at their hands? As regards the public servant, what reason again is there to doubt that he may not be supported in the legitimate exercise of his functions or that the rights and privileges guaranteed or implied in the conditions of his employment may be tampered with by the government if the Indians got a share in it? Is there any reasonable ground for apprehending that the Indians, representing the best elements of the Indian society, will ever think for attempting to break the covenants which have been solemnly made on their behalf? Will that be the way in which they would expect to attract the foreign expert; and technically trained man whom it will be necessary in their own interests to invite to help them for many a year to come? Clearly these apprehensions are not justified.

Some Important Conditions Insufficiently Appreciated

"I fear that in dealing with the questions noted above as well as with many others, one all-important condition of the problem has not received sufficient consideration. It is this that even if the full measure of the self-government which we Indians have asked for is conceded, the existing system of the administration will not be torn up by the roots. The executive government will continue to be predominantly European. It will still have the decisive voice in all the matters of administration. The entire edifice of the administration which has been built up in a hundred years will remain unshaken. The administration of justice will continue to remain under the High Courts. The existing body of the laws will remain in force. Even if a new legislature should want to alter or repeal an act, it will not be in its power to do so until the head of the government should give his consent to the measure by which it may be sought to do it. The services will continue to be manned by the present incumbents, and, even, if fifty per cent, of the higher appointments should be filled up in India in the future, it will be long, very long, before the services will be half-Indianised. These facts contain in themselves a guarantee, which cannot fail, that the new order of things which may be ushered will not lead to any catastrophe to the any existing interests. And they ought to inspire courage and confidence in the Englishmen dealing with the question of the introduction of a real measure of the self-government in India.

Need For Making India Self-supporting

"There is another vital condition, newly come into existence which demands serious consideration. The War has forcibly drawn attention to the dangers to which India is exposed, in its present condition, both industrially and politically. It is a matter of supreme thankfulness that we have got on so far as we have done. Let us hope and pray that we shall get to the end of the chapter with equal good luck. Let us also hope that this devastating War will soon end, and that the peace which will follow will endure for a long time. But it will not be the part of wisdom and statesmanship to build entirely upon such a hope. It will be safer to think that it may be falsified and that there may be another war within the ten years or so, and to be prepared for it. But how to be prepared for it? That is the question. The learned authors say that the War has thrown strong light on the military importance of the economic development. We know that the possibility of the sea communications being temporarily interrupted forces us to rely on India as an ordnance base for the protective operations in the Eastern theatres of War.

"This is true, but the experience of the War has shown more than this. It has shown that not only should India become self-supporting in the matter of forging weapons of defence and offence, but that India's sons should be trained to use those weapons in larger numbers and in better ways than herebefore. Mr Montagu and Lord Chelmsford have noted the importance of this question, but they have naturally left it for consideration hereafter with the note that "it must be faced and settled." It is devoutly to be hoped that it will be settled soon and rightly, that both in the interest of India and of England. English statesmen will realise that India's safety in the future will depend, to a much greater extent than in the past, upon her own sons being as well trained and equipped to fight as are the sons of the countries that surround her of Afghanistan, of Persia, of Turkey and of Japan. This demands that England should make up her mind to treat India now not as a trusty dependent but as a trusted partner, and to admit her sons on a footing of perfect equality with Englishmen to all the branches and grades of the military service, on land, on the sea and in the air. Both justice and expediency demand that the Indians should be treated by the Englishmen as comrades in arms in the full sense of the expression, and that they should be trained as Englishmen are trained for the all branches of the service, superior as well as inferior. But the very grudging manner in which, after nearly half a century of agitation and after four years of this dreadful War, the question of throwing the King's Commissions open to the Indians has been dealt which makes one despair of the claims of the Indians to be fitted for the defence of their country, being justly dealt with until a substantial measure of the political power is enjoyed by the Indians. Political status depends upon political power.

Mr Montagu and Lord Chelmsford said in their report that the importance of the question of British Commissions outweighs in the eyes of India all others. They recommended that a considerable number of the Commissions should now be thrown open to the Indians. There were 2,689 officers of the British Army serving in India in 1914-15, and 2,771 of the Indian Army, or 5,560 in all. It is estimated that for the new army of half a million about fifteen thousand officers will be required. But the Government of India has decided, with the approval of the Hon'ble Secretary of State for India to nominate only ten Indian gentlemen annually during the War for Cadetships at the Royal Military College at Sandhurst, and to offer a certain number of temporary King's Commissions in the Indian army to the selected candidates nominated partly from the civil life and partly from the army. No number has been fixed for the Commissions which are to be granted under any of the headings (l), (2) or (3). The Indians had hoped that this question of Commissions will be dealt with in a broader spirit. They naturally think that the adequate justice has not been done to their claims, and they feel keenly disappointed. But this attitude towards the Indians will persist until the Indians come to exercise power in the administration of their country.

Fiscal Autonomy

"There is yet another condition of the problem of the outstanding importance which demands attention, and that is the question of the fiscal autonomy. Mr Montagu. and Lord Chelmsford has noted the weakness of the India's economic position and also the keenness of the desire of the Indians to improve it. They have recognised that the economic, political and military considerations, all equally demand the industrial development of India. They truly say that they cannot measure the access of strength which an industrialised India would bring to the power of the Empire. They observe that after the War the need for industrial development will be all the greater unless India is to become a mere dumping ground for the manufactures of foreign nations which will then be competing for the markets on which their political strength so perceptibly depends. They note that the question of the Indian tariff is connected intimately with the matter of industries. We are grateful to them for having put forward the views of the educated Indians on this important subject. They have pointed out that the educated Indian opinion ardently desires a tariff ...That there is a real and the keen desire for the fiscal autonomy," that the educated Indian believes that as long as the Englishmen will continue to decide the question of the tariff for him, they will decide in the interests of England and not according to his wishes, as is shown by the debate on the cotton excise duty in the House of Commons. They have assumed with satisfaction that when the fiscal relations of all the parts of the Empire and the rest of the world come to be considered by an imperial conference, India will be adequately represented there. But how? By the nomination of an Indian by the Viceroy, as in the last two years? It is well known that the Indian public opinion is not satisfied with such nomination. And apart from that, whose views is such a nominee to represent at the conference, the Viceroy's or those of the Governor-General in Council or his own? If of the former, it will be a misuse of the language to say that the people of India are represented at the conference. If the latter, will the Government of India be willing to be bound in such an important matter as the question of tariffs by the independent opinion of their own nominee selected without the support of the Indian legislative council? The position will be quite anomalous. If the representation of India is to be a reality, the only course which should be followed is to ask the Indian members of the imperial legislative council (or of the imperial and Provincial legislative councils) to recommend a person for nomination by the Government of India as the India's representative at the conference. Such a representative will of course ascertain and voice the considered opinion of those to whom he will owe his appointment, to whom be will hold himself primarily responsible; and the Government of India must be prepared to accept such opinion as its own, or the idea of having India represented at the conference must be abandoned, and the experiment tried of subjecting her people to a policy laid down by the representatives of the United Kingdom and the Dominions without consulting the Indians. In view of the practice established during the last two years, it may be safely assumed that such a proposal will not be entertained for a moment. Power, then, must be given to the representatives of the people in the Central Government of India to direct the policy of the Indian Government in this matter, and the proposals of Mr Montagu and Lord Chelmsford must be expanded in this direction. All the proposals stand, they will not give any such power. As the authors themselves have observed: The changes which we propose in the Government of India will still leave the settlement of India's tariff in the hands of a government amenable to the parliament and the Secretary of State. This means that the policy of the Government of India will continue to be the policy of His Majesty's Government. For all the reasons which they have given, and which I have added, this will be wholly unsatisfactory. The development of the Indian industries is a matter of vital national importance to India. It will largely depend upon the Government of India having the power and the will to impose such tariffs as may be considered to be necessary either for revenue or for the protection of her industries from the powerful foreign competition. But what will the Government of India stand for in this all-important matter if it is not to express and carry out the will of the people of India, speaking through their elected representatives in the legislative council? The Government of India responsible to the Parliament and to the Secretary of State can only go so far as it is permitted by them and no farther. It is only a Government of India responsible to the people of India that can be expected to adopt the policy which their interests demand. In a matter of such vital concern to the people, where the disadvantages, temporary though they may be, of a policy of tariffs, will have to be borne by the people, the government cannot speak with even moral force unless it speaks in conformity with their ascertained wishes and opinions. If the view presented above is correct, then it follows that if the industrial development of India is to have a fair future, fiscal autonomy must be granted to India, and that if it is, power must be given to the representatives of the people in the central government to lay down the policy which the executive is to carry out.

"I have discussed the conditions of the problem at some length because it is obvious that the recommendations which Mr Montagu and Lord Chelmsford have made, have been determined and limited by the views they have taken of those conditions. They themselves have said: 'The considerations of which we took note in Chapter VI forbid us immediately to hand over the complete responsibility.' It is therefore that they decided to proceed by transferring responsibility for certain functions of the government; while reserving control over others. I hope I have shown that they have taken an exaggerated view of the difficulties of the problem, and have underestimated the value of the conditions which call for or favour the introduction of a substantial measure of the responsible government. I have also shown that they have not given due weight to the conditions created by the War the part which India has played in the War, and the needs of her situation in the immediate future as disclosed by the War. If in the light of these considerations their view of the conditions of the problem requires to be revised, it follows that the proposals which they have made needs to undergo large modifications and expansion. It is evident that the terms of the announcement of the 20th August last also imposed a severe constraint upon them. They seem to have convinced themselves early of the wisdom of the policy of that announcement, as they interpreted it and then unconsciously to have given special weight to the points which supported that policy. The distinguished authors appear to have been partly conscious of this. For after emphasising the difficulties of the problem, they proceed to justify their doing so. They say: 'Why have we tried to describe the complexities of the task before us, and in particular why have we laid stress upon the existence of the silent depths through which the cry of the press and the platform never rings? In the first place of course we wish to insist on the importance of these factors in considering the time necessary for the complete attainment of the responsible government in a country in which, in spite of the rapid processes of growth, so great a majority of the people do not ask for it and are not yet fitted for it. But our chief purpose is more important than this. We desired to test the wisdom of the announcement of August 20th. If we have conceded all that can fairly be said as to the difficulties of the task before us, then the policy which has been laid down can be judged in the light of all the facts....We believe that the announcement of the August 20 was right and wise, and that the policy which it embodies is the only possible policy for India.' 'If, as I have endeavored to show, the facts have not been correctly appreciated, the conclusions deduced from them cannot be right. We have no quarrel with the policy of the announcement so far as it lays down that complete responsible government should be established in India not at one bound but by stages. But I do not agree with the view that it necessarily demands that those stages shall be many and that they shall be reached in a long period of time. If that were the correct interpretation of the policy of the announcement, and if that announcement stood in the way of the needed measure of reform, the difficulty must be solved by a more liberal pronouncement. The people of India had no voice in determining the language of the announcement of August 20, and the cause of the Indian reform must not be prejudiced by it. But I maintain that there is nothing in that announcement which stands in the way of a substantial measure of the responsible government being introduced as the first step towards the goal. We have urged that the Congress-League scheme should be that first step. But if that is not to be, the proposals under consideration must yet be expanded and modified to become adequate to meet the requirements of the situation. I will indicate below the main directions in which, in my opinion, the proposals should be modified and expanded.

Suggestions for the Modification and Expansion

"(1) The many qualifying conditions contained in the pronouncement of the August 20, created a suspicion in the mind of the Indians that though His Majesty's Government had declared the responsible government to be the goal of the British Policy in India, the intention was that this goal should be reached only after a very long-time. The proposals of Mr Montagu and Lord Chelmsford based on that pronouncement tend to confirm that suspicion. They have proposed a very limited and qualified measure of the responsible government for the provinces to start with, and as regards the future development, they guard themselves by saying that their proposal for the appointment of a Commission ten years after the new Act, should not be taken as implying that there can be established by that time, the complete responsible government in the provinces. They say that the reasons that make the complete responsibility at present impossible are likely to continue operative in some degree even after a decade. As regards the Government of India, it is not prepared, without the experience of the results of their proposals relating to the provinces, to effect changes in it. I cannot reconcile myself to these views. I think the needs of the country demand that the provincial governments should be made autonomous at once, and that a period of time should be fixed within which the complete responsible government is to be established in the central government of India. Even if twenty years were fixed as the outside limit, we shall know where we stand. Among the Indians many will regard it too long a period; among the Europeans, many will consider it too short. But twenty years is in all conscience long enough time within which to prepare this country, with all the progress that stands behind it, and with all the advantages of a well-organised and well-established administration to bear the full burden of the new responsibility. The history of the other countries supports the view that in this period education can be made universal, industries can be developed, so as to make India self-sufficient both in respect of the ordinary needs of the people and also in respect of the military requirements, and the Indians can be trained in the sufficient numbers to officer the Indian army and to take their proper places alongside of their British fellow-subjects in the service of the country and the King-Emperor. The great advantage of the proposal would be that every one concerned will know that the journey to the goal has to be completed within the time specified, and the progress towards it will be better regulated and assured. If this suggestion is accepted, it should be stated in the statute which is being drafted in England, that it is intended that the full responsible government should be established in India within a period not exceeding twenty years. This will remove a lot of misapprehension and facilitate agreement on many matters.

"(2) My second suggestion is that, it being definitely settled that the responsible government is to be established within a specified time adequate provision should be made at once for training the Indians in India for admission to the extent of half the number, at present, of offices in every branch of the public service, military as well as civil, provided they pass the prescribed tests. These tests should of course be the same for them as for their English fellow-subjects. We should feel thankful to Mr Montagu and Lord Chelmsford for their recommendations on this subject. But the percentage of the recruitment in India which they have proposed for the Indian civil service is low; it should be raised to 50 per cent. As regards the military service, they have recommended that a considerable number of the Commissions should now be given to Indians? But it is high time that half the number of commissions should be thrown open to the Indians, subject of course to the essential condition that they pass the prescribed tests. This will at first sight seem to be a large order. But a little consideration will show that it is not so. This wicked War has taken a sadly heavy toll of the British officers. The Universities of the United Kingdom have covered themselves with undying glory by the contributions they have made to it. But their losses have been appalling; and in the years that lie before us they will be called upon to supply an increasing number of the captains to the various branches of the national activity which will be set up after the War. It is permissible to think therefore that the demand upon them for officers for the army will be greater than they will be able to meet. Besides owing to the tremendous wastage of the officers during the War and the greater demands of the army of the future, a much larger number of the youths will have to be put under training, than used to be before the War. These considerations enforce the claims of the Indian youths to be admitted in sufficient numbers for training as officers in the Indian army. It will be both unwise and unjust not to recognise and encourage these claims to the full. Let an equal number of the Indian and English youths be admitted into the colleges at Quetta and Wellington, and let them undergo the same training and tests together. The mutual confidence and friendships which will grow between them there will be assets of inestimable value to the cause of the empire. Similarly let it be provided that the Indians should be trained for and admitted to every other branch of the Navy and the Army, including the air service. These measures will furnish the most convincing proof to the Indians that England means to treat India in future as a partner and not as a dependency.

Provincial Government

"I have said that Mr Montagu and Lord Chelmsford have put an unduly strict interpretation on the terms of the pronouncement of the August 20th. It is due to them at the same time to say that, consistently with that interpretation, they have proposed to introduce an element of the real responsibility to the people in the provincial governments which they have recommended. They have proposed that the transferred subjects shall be in the charge of a minister or ministers to be nominated by the Governor from among the elected members of the Legislative Council; that such ministers shall be appointed for the term of the legislative councils; that the ministers, together with the Governor, should form the administration with regard to these subjects; that on such subjects the decisions of the ministers should be final, subject only to the Governor's advice and control. They have said that they expect the Governor to refuse assent to the proposals of his ministers only when the consequence of the acquiescence would clearly be serious, or when they are clearly seen to be the result of inexperience. They do not intend that the Governor should be in a position to refuse assent at discretion to all his minister's proposals. This is the best part of the proposals of Mr Montagu and Lord Chelmsford for which I offer thanks to them. It would give the ministers more power and responsibility with regard to the transferred subjects than they would have had under the Congress-League scheme. But it is weighed by the various conditions and it requires to be improved. In the first place it should be provided that the elected member or the members to be nominated by the Governor shall be selected from among the first few men who command the largest measure of confidence of their fellow-members. Appointment by the election having been negative, the best course to follow will probably be that the appointment should be made from among a panel of three or four recommended by the elected members. Though it will limit the field of selection, still it would leave the selection to the Governor. But it will at the same time ensure that the Governor shall not select a man, who, though he is an elected member, is not acceptable to the majority of the council.

"The second point is that the ministers should be the members of the executive council and not merely of the executive government. The distinction between the executive government and the executive council should be abolished. Dividing the government into what the authors themselves point out will, in effect, be two committees with the different responsibilities, will weaken the power and responsibility of the administration for promoting the welfare of the province. In fact the division of the subjects into transferred and reserved subjects requires to be reconsidered.

"Under the arrangements proposed, it would rest with the Governor to decide whether to call a meeting of his whole government or of the either part of it. The actual decision on a transferred subject would be taken by the Governor and his minister; the action to be taken on a reserved subject would be taken by the Governor and the other members of his executive council. At a meeting of the whole government, when it would be called, there would never be any question of voting, for the decision would be left to that part of the government which will be responsible for the particular subject involved. Under this arrangement the executive council will be practically relieved of all the responsibility relating to transferred subjects. The entire blame for the want of the adequate progress in the matter of the transferred subjects will be thrown upon the minister or ministers.

"Nor will the financial arrangements proposed under this system be satisfactory from the point of view of the transferred services. In the first place it is laid down as a postulate that so long as the Governor-in Council is responsible for the reserved subjects he must have power to decide what revenue he requires. It is proposed that the provincial budget should be framed by the executive government as a whole. The first charge on the provincial revenues will be the contribution to the Government of India; and after that the supply for the reserved subject will have priority. The remainder of the revenue will be at the disposal of the ministers for the purposes of the transferred subjects. If such residue is not sufficient for their needs, it will be open to the ministers to suggest extra taxation, either within the schedule of the permissible provincial taxation, or by obtaining the sanction of the Government of India to some tax not included in the schedule. It is said that the question of the new taxation will be decided by the Governor and the ministers. But it is clear that the responsibility for proposing the taxation will really lie upon the latter. The executive government as a whole will not be responsible for the proposal. The distinguished authors recognise that new taxation will be necessary for no conceivable economics, say they, can finance the new developments which are to be anticipated. Why then should the responsibility for the new taxation, to which certain odium attaches in the best of circumstances, be thrown upon the shoulders of the ministers alone and not upon the government of the province as a whole. The proposed arrangement is unfair. The responsibility for developing transferred subjects is to be placed upon the ministers. The power of deciding what part of the revenues shall be allotted for the discharge of the responsibility is to be retained in the hands of the Governor-in Council. Power is given to the ministers to propose additional taxation, but he is not to be supported in the exercise of that power by the collective responsibility of the executive government. Proposals for the new taxation are seldom popular. When such proposals will be put forward without the support of the government as a whole, the chances of their being accepted by the legislature will be seriously affected. It is proposed that the legislative council should have no option but to submit to the proposal of the Governor-in-Council with regard to the expenditure on reserved subjects. This is not related to promote a willingness in it to agree to the new proposals for taxation even for the transferred subjects. It is evident that the prospects of such subjects being properly financed are far from satisfactory. Nor are the prospects of the success of this part of the proposals as a whole more assuring. The position of the ministers will be unenviable. They must either bear the blame of failure to promote progress in their departments or they must expose themselves to the odium of proposing new taxation without having the power to deal with the revenue and expenditure as a whole.

"Under existing arrangements, it is the Government of India by whose authority allotments for the different subjects are made. Under the proposed arrangements, this power will be left to the Governor-in-Council. Under it both the ministers and the legislative councils will be liable to be compelled to accept allotments for the reserved subjects with which they do not agree, and they have no right of appeal even to the Government of India. Mr Montagu and Lord Chelmsford hold out the solace to the ministers as well as to the legislative council, that a periodic commission shall review the proceedings of the Governor-in-Council, and that there will be an opportunity of arguing before the Commission that the reserved subjects have been extravagantly administered. The Commission is too menace in the twelve years. An opportunity for arguing before it against the dead decisions of the Governor-in-Council can have little practical value. An arrangement more disadvantageous to the cause of the popular government could hardly be conceived. I am surprised that its obvious defects did not lead the distinguished authors to reject it.

"The entire question of a division between the transferred and the reserved subjects may be considered here. The *raison d'etre*, of such division, in the opinion of Mr Montagu and Lord Chelmsford, is that the complete responsibility for the government cannot be given immediately without inviting a breakdown, and some responsibility must be given at once if our scheme is to have any value. On this ground they have proposed that certain heads of the business should be regained under the official and certain others made over to the popular control. They have proposed that a committee should be appointed to decide what subjects should be transferred for the administration by the ministers. They have indicated the principle on which the list should be prepared, and they say that in pursuance of this principle we should not expect to find that departments primarily concerned with the maintenance of law and order were transferred. Nor should we expect the transfer of the matters which vitally affect the well being of the masses who may not be adequately represented in the new Councils, for example, as questions of land revenue or the tenant rights. They desire that the responsibility for such Subject should remain with the official government which is still responsible to the parliament. The responsibility to the parliament here means responsibility to the Secretary of State for India. We well know the meaning of this responsibility in Europe. It is high time that the responsibility to the Secretary of State were replaced by the responsibility to the properly constituted representative councils of the people. I have said before that the electorates which will be regarded as satisfactory by every reasonable man can be formed at once in the country, to secure the adequate representation of the masses in the councils. Let the right of returning a member to the provincial council be extended to every *tahsil* or *taluka*, or the groups of *tahsils* or *talukas*, which contain a certain minimum of population. It will be no argument against my proposal that the council will become a very large one. If the United Kingdom with population less than that of the United Provinces has a House of Commons consisting of 670 members, there is no reason why the United Provinces should not have an equally large legislative assembly. The difficulty about the different and possibly conflicting interests, will largely disappear if the representation is given to a sufficiently large number of units of the reasonable dimensions. If this is done, one may safely assume that the assembly will include representatives of the landholders, tenants, bankers, traders merchants, educationists, lawyers, doctors, engineers, etc. Is it reasonable to think that an executive council, consisting of the two European and one Indian members, can be more deeply interested in or be better qualified to form a judgment about the maintenance of the law and order in the province than the large body of the representatives of the people? Who can be more vitally interested in the maintenance of peace and tranquility, in the provinces than such representatives? Is it reasonable to apprehend that such a body will refuse to vote supplies which may be needed for the maintenance of the law and order? Again will not such an assembly, which will evidently include a large number of men of light and leading in the province, a most competent to consider the questions relating to the land revenue and tenants rights? Will it not be right to assume that their combined intelligence and sense of justice will lead such an assembly to advocate fair play between the government and the people and between one section of the people and another? Why then should these subjects be reserved to be specially dealt with both administratively and legislatively? The provision that if the legislative council should refuse to accept the budget proposals for the reserved subjects, the Governor-in-Council should have power to restore the whole or any part of the original allotment should be dropped. The legislative council should be trusted to rightly understand and discharge its obligations in a matter of such vital concern to the people as the maintenance of law and order. If there is an apprehension that the existing expenditure on departments primarily concerned with the maintenance of the law and order may be reduced, this may be guarded against by a special provision that this shall not be done unless it is assented to by the Governor.

"On the legislative side the proposal for a Grand

Committee should be dropped. It involves a serious and unwarrantable derogation from the power and dignity of the provincial legislative councils. All the provincial legislation is at present passed by the provincial legislative councils. This should continue to be so in the future. The Indian Statute book contains the over-abundant legislation for the maintenance of the law and order in the country. As a rule such legislation is the all-India legislation, and has with few exceptions been enacted in the past by the imperial legislative council. It may be safely assumed that it will continue to be so in the future. Few provincial councils have enacted any law affecting the maintenance of the law and order. The Bengal Council has between 1862 and 1914 enacted only the Calcutta Police Act, the Bengal Military Police Act, the Calcutta Sub-Police Act and the Village Chowkidari Act. And the Bombay Council has since 1867 enacted the Bombay Village Police Acts and the City of Bombay and District Police Acts. It will be a gratuitous affront to the provincial legislative councils, both present and future, to suggest that they will not deal in the right spirit with any legislation of that character that any provincial executive government may think fit to undertake. It is also difficult to understand what provincial legislation a Provincial Governor may require for the discharge of his responsibility for the 'reserved subjects. But assuming that he should, it passes my understanding why the provincial legislative council should not enact it. In view of the laws and regulations which already exist, the parliament should tell the executive governments in India that no legislation shall be passed in future unless it receives the support of the majority of the members of the legislative councils. It is evident that it is contemplated that the Grand Committees should be called into existence only occasionally. If then any occasion should arise when a provincial legislative council should refuse to pass any legislation which the executive government considers to be necessary, it will be better to ask the central government with the over-riding power of legislation which it is proposed to retain for it to enact it for the province. As regards legislation relating to land revenue and tenant rights, clearly it is the popular legislative council which must under a proper constitution include a large number of representative landholders and tenants, which would be the most appropriate body to deal with it.

"So far then as the provincial governments are concerned, I would recommend that there should be an executive council of four numbers, two of whom should be the Indians nominated by the Governor out of a panel elected by the elected members of the legislative council holding charge of and being specially responsible for the subjects of the most vital concern to the people, and that there should be no reserved subjects and no grand committee. I would agree that the resolutions of the Councils other than those relating to the budget should be treated as recommendations. Resolutions relating to the budget should be binding on the Executive and the budget should be modified to accord with them, subject to this limitation that the legislative council should not have the power to reduce existing expenditure on departments relating to law and order without the consent of the Governor-in-Council. No new expenditure should be incurred unless it is approved by the legislative council.

Burma

"I should not omit to say a few words about Burma. The reason given for setting aside the problem of Burma's political evolution for separate and future consideration are inadequate and unconvincing. Burma was annexed to the British India against the wish both of the Burmans and Indians. If it had been made a Crown Colony as the Indian National Congress had urged, it would not have had to bear the greater cost of the administration by the Indian civil service. But the proposal did not suit the service, for the emoluments and prizes of the Indian civil service are greater than those of a Crown Colony. However, as Burma has had to bear so long the disadvantages of having been made a province of India, it is nothing but fair that it should be allowed to share with the rest of India the advantages of a popular administration. It would appear that it has an even stronger claim to a measure of the self government than India. It was but yesterday that it was deprived of the self-rule and placed under foreign subjection. Those conditions upon which Mr Montagu and Lord Chelmsford have laid so much emphasis are much more favourable there than in India. Education is far more widespread among the people, there are no such religious differences as exist in India, and the claim of the upper classes to be in sympathy with the masses will perhaps be more readily conceded in their case than has been done in the case of the Indians. It is no fault of the Burmans that the provincial legislative council of Burma, as constituted under the Morley Minto scheme, has no Burman elected element. As regards the argument that the application to Burma of the general principles of throwing open the public services more widely to the Indians, would only mean the replacement of the one alien bureaucracy by another, the Indians do not desire to lord it over their brethren of Burma, and they will have no complaint to make if it will be laid down that the public services of Burma shall be recruited from the Burmese alone. If, however, as I fear, a good proportion of the services will be reserved for the recruitment from non-Burmans, it will not be violently unreasonable to expect that the Indians will be allowed to compete with the Canadians, Australians, New Zealanders and South Africans for admission to that portion of the services. But it is unnecessary to dilate further on this. I hope that the reforms which it may be decided to introduce into India will be extended to Burma, with any reservation which the Burmans themselves may desire to be made.

The Government of India

"But, as I have said before, no scheme of reform will meet the requirements of the India of today or satisfy her national sentiment, which will not admit the Indians to a reasonable share of power in her central government: and it is here that the proposals of Mr Montagu and Lord Chelmsford are sadly deficient. The Government of India is the centre of power in the Indian Empire and so it will largely remain even when the proposed reforms have been introduced. It will continue to deal with the most important questions which affect the country as a whole. It will still in a large measure lay down the principles and formulate policies. It will continue to deal with the great body of the adjective and substantive law which affects the peace and order, life, liberty and property, freedom of speech and of the press. Legislation affecting the various religions of the people will still continue to be its special care. It will continue to deal with the most important heads of taxation, the income-tax, the salt tax, customs, tariffs, stamps and court-fees; with currency and exchange, banking and credit, commerce and industry, with railways, posts and telegraphs, and other matters which closely touch the people throughout the country. Being in sole charge of the army and measures of defence, and of all the other imperial departments, it will continue to deal with the largest amount of the annual expenditure. In addition to all this, it is proposed by Mr Montagu and Lord Chelmsford that a general over-riding power of the legislation should be reserved to the Government of India for the discharge of all the functions which it will have to reform. It would be enabled under this power to intervene in any province for the protection and enforcement of the interests for which it should consider itself responsible; to legislate on any provincial matter in respect of which the uniformity of legislation is desirable, either for the whole of India or for any two or more provinces, and to pass legislation which may be adopted either simplicitor or with the modifications by any province which may wish to make use of it. Mr Montagu and Lord Chelmsford do not wish to admit the representatives of the people to any share in this vast power and responsibility which the Government of India wields. In their opinion pending the development of the responsible government in the provinces the Government of India must remain responsible only to the parliament. In other words in all the matters which it judges to be essential to the discharge of its responsibilities for peace, order and good government, it must, saving only for its accountability to the parliament, retain the indisputable power. I respectfully join the issue here. In the first place though it may not be difficult to understand the words responsibilities for peace and order, it will be impossible to define the responsibilities for good government. The expression is all-comprehensive, and may be used to include any measure which the executive government may set its heart upon. Past experience justifies apprehension. Whoever imagined that the words prejudicial to the public safety in the rules under the Defence of India Act, would be interpreted as they have been interpreted by the several executive governments? The words good government therefore ought in any event to be cut out of the formula for reserving power which Mr Montagu and Lord Chelmsford have suggested. In the second place even with this modification, I submit that it is essential that the Government of India should be made at least partly responsible to the people of India acting through their representatives in the legislative council. So far as the parliament is concerned, the distinguished authors themselves have observed that the interests shown by the parliament in the Indian affairs has not been well-sustained or well-informed. It has tended to concern itself chiefly with a few subjects, such as the methods of dealing with the political agitation, the opium trade, or the cotton excise duty, and they have rightly noted that in India such spasmodic interferences are apt to be attributed to the political exigencies at home. In another place they say: 'The parliamentary control cannot in fact be called a reality. Discussion is often out of date and ill-informed; it tends to be confined to a little knot of the members and to the stereotyped topics; audit is rarely followed by any decision. They no doubt recommend a remedy that the House of Commons should be asked to appoint a Select Committee for the Indian affairs at the beginning of the each session, which should exercise its powers by informing itself from time to time upon the Indian questions, and by reporting to the House before the annual debate on the Indian estimates. They also propose that the Secretary of State's salary should be placed on the English estimates and voted annually by the Parliament. This will no doubt enable some live questions of the Indian administration to be discussed by the House of Commons in the committee of Supply. But having regard to the other pre-occupations of the Parliament, which will greatly increase after the War, it is not reasonable to expect that the parliament will discharge its responsibilities for the welfare of India any better in the future than it has done in the past. The accountability of the Government of India to the parliament will, therefore, only mean its accountability to the Secretary of State for India who must generally be an uncertain factor. We know that this arrangement has not helped India very much in the past, and it is not likely to do so in the future. In the circumstances of the case, the parliament, will best discharge its responsibility to the millions of the Indias by telling the executive government of India, that subject to certain reservations in which the parliament, as represented by His Majesty's Government, must keep control to itself, for instance, matters relating to the defence, foreign and political relations, the Government of India should in future hold itself accountable to the people of India as they will be represented in the reconstituted legislative councils.

"Mr Montagu and Lord Chelmsford are opposed to this view. They say: 'We recommend no alteration at present in the responsibility of the Government of India to the parliament except in so far as the transfer of the subjects to the popular control in the provinces *ipso facto* removes them from the purview of the Government of India and the Secretary of State but we do provide greater opportunities for criticising and influencing the action of the Government of India. Such opportunities we have had in abundance in the past, in the press, on the platform, in our Congresses and conferences, and in the imperial and provincial legislative councils, and we have used them to the best extent we could. But we have found them of little avail because they were unsupported by power. It is therefore that we seek opportunity accompanied by responsibility and power. Mr Montagu and Lord Chelmsford propose to create an enlarged legislative assembly for India with an elective majority. But in their own words they do not offer responsibility to the elected members of the legislative assembly, nor even do they define the sphere in which the government will defer to the wishes of the elected members as they have done in the provinces. They say they do so by a general prescription, which they leave the government to interpret. Besides they have heavily discounted this proposal (of an enlarged legislative assembly with an elective majority) by their other proposal of treating a council of state, in which the government will command a majority. In their own words the council of state will be the supreme legislative authority upon all the Indian legislation. The council will not be a normal second chamber, but it will have greater power. It will take its part in the ordinary legislative business and shall be the final legislative authority in the matters which the government regards as essential to the interests of peace, order or good government. If the council of state should amend a bill which has been passed by the assembly in a manner which is unacceptable to the assembly, the assembly will not have the power to reject or modify such amendments, if the Governor-General-in Council should certify that the amendments introduced by the council are essential to the interests of peace and order or good government, including in this term the sound financial administration. If the assembly should refuse leave to introduce a government bill, or if the bill should be thrown out at any stage, the Governor-General-in Council will have the power, on certifying that the bill is within the formula cited above, to refer it *de novo* to the council of state. The Governor-General-in-Council will also have the power in the case of emergency so certified, to introduce the bill in the first instance and to pass it through the council of state, merely reporting it to the assembly. In the case of a private bill, if a bill should emerge from the assembly in a form which the government think prejudicial to the good administration, the Governor- General-in-Council will have the power to certify it in the terms already cited, and to submit or re-submit it to the council of state, and the bill will only become law in the form given it by the Council.

"Fiscal legislation will be subject to the same procedure which is recommended in respect of the government bills. The budget will be introduced into the legislative assembly, but the assembly will not verify it. Resolutions upon budget matters and upon all the other questions, whether moved in that assembly or in the council of state, will continue to be advisory in character.

"I doubt if it is worth while creating the legislative assembly if the council of states to overshadow it to the extent proposed and to reduce it to a non-entity under certain conditions. I recognise that its creation will give greater representation to the people and increased opportunity of criticism; but I do not want, more of it unaccompanied by responsibility. In summing up the result of the Morley-Minto Reforms of 1909, Mr Montagu and Lord Chelmsford said: 'Responsibility for the administration remained undivided, power remained with the government and the councils were left with no functions but criticism. The same criticism will apply to the proposals of Mr Montagu and Lord Chelmsford relating to the Government of India.

"Mr Montagu and Lord Chelmsford propose that this state of things should continue for ten years after the institution of the reforms proposed by them when it should be the duty of the commission, the appointment of which they have advocated, to examine and report upon the new constitution of the Government of India, and if they see fit to make the proposals for future changes in the light of the experience gained. This means that for fifteen years at least the Government of India should continue to exercise all its power as at present, and that the representatives of the people should have absolutely no share in it. Owing to the War, the next ten to fifteen years will be the most fateful years in the history of India. It oppresses my soul to think that during this period the Government of India, which, as I have shown above, has failed to build up the strength and prosperity of the people to the extent it should have done, should continue practically unchanged, and that the representatives of the people anxious to promote the good of their fellowmen, should still have to bear the pain and humiliation of having no determining voice in the government of their country. In the highest interests of humanity, as it is represented by the 320 millions of this land, and for the good name of England, I earnestly hope that this will not be so, and that the statesmen of England will see that the Government of India is brought to a reasonable extent under the control of the people whose affairs it administers. Mr Montagu and Lord Chelmsford have well-described the effects of the War on the Indian mind. Let the statesmen of England ponder whether it will be reasonable to expect the people of India to be satisfied with any scheme of reform which will still keep them out of all power in the central government of their country.

"The Congress-Muslim League did not suggest a Second Chamber because it was felt that the executive government, with its power of vetoing both resolutions and legislative proposals of the legislative councils, would really play the part of a Second Chamber. I still think that this is a sound view, for what is the main purpose of creating the council of state, but to give a legal form to the will of the executive government? Why then lets not the executive government exercise that will by means of the veto? It may be urged that that would not place in the hands of the Government the means of securing the affirmative power of legislation and of obtaining supplies. For the authors frankly say: 'What we seek is some means, for use on the special occasions, for placing on the statute book, after full publicity of discussion, permanent measure to which the majority of the members in the legislative assembly may be unwilling to assent. But either the government should give up such an idea, or they should abandon the idea of creating the legislative councils with elective majorities. Under the existing constitution, no existing enactment can be repealed without the consent of the head of the government. Let it be provided that no existing expenditure on the certain services, for instance, military charges for the defence of the counry, shall be decreased except with such consent. But with this reservation let that budget be voted upon by the council. It is nothing but fair that all the future increase in expenditure should depend upon the government being able to satisfy the elected representatives of the people, who will have to bear the burden of taxation, that every proposed increase, is needed in the interests of the country. So also with regard to all the new legislation. Let the government trust the council which it is going to create. The Indian members of the council have not on important occasions failed to stand by the government in the past, There is no justification for apprehending that the members of the reconstituted council, which will be much larger and more representative, will not lend similar support to the government in all the essential matters. Mr Montagu and Lord Chelmsford have been good enough to acknowledge the correctness of the attitude of the Indian members towards the government. They say: 'We desire however to pay a tribute to the sense of responsibility which has animated the members of the Indian legislative council in dealing with the government legislation. In the passage of very controversial measures, such as the Press Act, the government received a large amount of the solid support; from the non-officials; similarly it received assistance when the measures of real importance such for example as the Defence of India Act and the recent grant of the one hundred millions to the Imperial treasury, were under discussion. Again, good examples of the practical nature of the work done were afforded by the debates on the Factories Act and the Companies Act.'

"Having regard to all the considerations I have mentioned above, I would suggest that the proposal to create a council of state should be dropped. Any serious difference of opinion which may at any time arise between the executive government and the legislative council, would be got over by the means of the veto and the power of promulgating ordinances. But it should be provided, as was suggested by the Congress in 1886 that whenever the veto is exercised, a full exposition of the grounds on which this has been considered necessary, should be published and submitted to the Secretary of State; and in any such case on a representation made through the Government of India and the Secretary of State by the overruled majority, the proposed select committee of the House of Commons, should review the decision of the government. If however it is decided to create such a council, it is essential that its composition should be liberalised. So far back as 1886, the Indian National Congress urged that not less than one-half of the members of the imperial and provincial councils, which it recommended should be enlarged should be elected, not more than one-fourth should be officials holding seats ex-officio in the councils, and not more than one-fourth should be nominated by the government. During the thirty-two years that have since passed, the councils have been twice reformed, and as has been shown in the preceding paragraph, their work has been satisfactory. After this long lapse of time, and after the fresh proofs of fidelity and devotion which India has given during the last four years of the War, is it too much to ask that in the proposed council of state, which will really take the place of the present legislative council, the number of members selected by the electorates in which the Indians predominate, should not be less than half of the total number? Experience has proved that the elected representatives of the European community almost always side with the government. Therefore, though elected, they should be regarded as good as nominated by the government. If this is done, I think it will reconcile the Indian public opinion to the proposal of a council of state Mr Montagu and Lord Chelmsford propose that the regulations which the Governor-General-in-Council should make as to the qualifications of the candidates for the election to the council of state should be such as will ensure that their status and position and record of services will give to the council a senatorial character, and the qualities usually regarded as appropriate to a revising chamber. The government should find in this provision an assurance that the members of the council of state will be even more inclined by training and temperament to support it than the members of the present council have been, in matters essential to the interests of peace, order and good government. If this proposal is accepted, it will take away all the ungraciousness which at present surrounds the proposed council of state, and will enable the people to become familiar with and to form a fair estimate of the value of a normal second chamber.

Indians in the Executive Council

"There is only one more important change which I have to

suggest, and that is in the number of the Indian members in the executive council of the Government of India. The Congress-Muslim League scheme urged that half the number of the members in every executive council, imperial and provincial, should be the Indians. Mr Montagu and Lord Chelmsford have recommended that this principle should be adopted in the case of the provincial executive councils. But they have suggested the appointment of only one other Indian member in the executive council of the government of India. I submit that the principle which has been accepted in the case of the Provincial Executive Councils should be accepted in the case of the Government of India. Of course no one can say definitely at present how many members there will be in the Government of India when it has been reconstituted. But assuming, as it is not altogether unlikely, that there will be six such members, it is nothing but right and proper that three of them should be Indians. The filling up of half the appointments in the council with the Indians will not affect the decisions of the council so far as mere votes will be concerned. For, with the Viceroy, the European members will still form the majority. But it will provide for a much more satisfactory representation of the Indian public opinion to the executive council. It will be perhaps the most effective step towards training the Indians for full responsible government. In my opinion nothing will create a greater feeling of assurance about the intentions of the government regarding the establishment of the responsible government in this country than the step which I recommend. It will create widespread satisfaction.

To sum up, the proposals should be expanded and modified as follows:

(1) A definite assurance should be given that it is intended that the full responsible government shall be established in India within a period not exceeding twenty years.

(2) It should be laid down that the Indians shall be trained for and admitted, if they pass the prescribed tests, to the extent of at least a half of the appointments in every branch of the public service, civil and military.

(3) It should be provided that half the number of the members of the executive council of the Government of India shall be the Indians.

(4) If the proposed council of state is created, it should be provided that half of its members shall be those elected by the electorates in which the Indians predominate.

(5) It should be clearly laid down that the existing expenditure on certain services, in particular military charges for the defence of the country, shall not be reduced without the consent of the Governor-General-in-Council; but that, subject to this provision, the budget shall be voted by the legislative assembly.

(6) India should be given the same measure of fiscal autonomy which the self-governing Dominions of the Empire will enjoy.

Provincial Governments

(1) The provincial legislative councils should be enlarged as to permit of a member being returned from every *tahsil* or *taluqa*, or a group or groups thereof containing a certain minimum of population, and the franchise should be as broad as possible to ensure the adequate representation of every important interest, including that of the tenants, and

(2) It should be provided that the persona who are to be appointed the Ministers of the reconstituted councils, shall be those who command the confidence of the majority of the elected members.

(3) That though each ministers should hold special charge of certain subjects, they shall be the members of the executive council of the province.

(4) There should be no reserved subjects. If there is to be any reservation, it should be limited to this that existing expenditure on departments relating to law and order shall not be reduced without the consent of the Governor-in-Council.

(5) The proposal for the Grand Committee should be dropped.

(6) The principles of reform which may be finally laid down for the other provinces of India should be applied in Burma also, subject, if necessary, to any special reservation which the Burmans themselves may demand.

Conclusion

"I have done. At the conclusion of their very able and elaborate report, Mr Montagu and Lord Chelmsford invited reasoned criticism of their proposals. I have attempted to offer some. I hope that they may find it of some value, and that they may reconsider their opinions regarding the conditions of the problem and the recommendations which they have based upon those opinions. I hope also that the other members of His Majesty's Government, and generally other Englishmen who will have to deal with those recommendations, may find this criticism of some help. We are entitled to expect that they will examine the conditions of the problem in the light of well ascertained facts and the testimony of history, and above all with a broad-minded sympathy which India hopes she has deserved of England. The question of the adequacy of the reforms which are to be introduced is of the most vital concern to India. It is thirty-three years since educated Indians, having noted the defects of the existing system, first begged their English fellow-subjects to allow them a share in the administration of their country's affairs. Their proposals were rejected. The result is written large upon the country in the poverty and helplessness which pervade a land of abundant natural resources. A very unwelcome light has been thrown upon the situation by the fact that with a population of 320 millions, with every desire to do the best, and with a strenuous endeavor of eighteen months, we have been able to raise, by loan, barely half the amount of the hundred millions which we promised last year as a War gift to England. I have given reasons to justify my belief that if England had agreed to share with us power and opportunity for service, which we asked for in 1886, the country would have become so prosperous and so much more closely attached to England that we could have easily given away a thousand millions in cash, and a million or two more of men, as well equipped and trained as Englishmen, who would have long enough to turned the tide in favour of the Allies, and saved millions of bravo Englishmen and Frenchmen from death, We have reiterated the same request with greater unanimity and insistence since 1916. Let not England repeat the mistake of rejecting it again. The reforms which the Congress and the Muslim League have asked for, are as much needed to prepare India to defend herself and to be a source of greater strength and not of weakness to the Empire, as to promote the happiness and prosperity of her children. They have been long over-due. The War has only brought their need into greater prominence and relief, and lent unexpected and powerful support to the inherent justice of the demand. India has been faithful to England in the hour of her sorest trial. All that she asks is that is determining her future constitution. England should act upon the principles of justice and liberty, and of the right of every people to rule their own destinies, for which she has been fighting perhaps the most splendid fight known to history and in which she has been helped by India with her blood and treasure. Both England and India are on their trial. May God grant clarity of vision and courage to us Indians to press for ward and to the Englishmen, to consent to the full measure of reform which is needed in the vital interests of India and of the British Empire."

6

Speech on the Hindu University Bills

SPEECH ON THE INTRODUCTION OF BHU BILL

At the meeting of the imperial legislative council' held on the March 22, 1915, the Hon. Sir Harcourt Butler moved for leave to introduce the Banaras Hindu University Bill. Speaking on the motion Pandit Madan Mohan Malaviya said:

"My Lord, I should be wanting in my duty if I allowed this occasion to pass without expressing the deep gratitude that we feel towards Your Excellency for the broad-minded sympathy and large-hearted statesmanship with which Your Excellency has encouraged and supported the movement which has taken its first material shape in the Bill which is before us today. I should also be wanting in my duty if I did not express our sincere gratitude to the Hon'ble Sir Harcourt Butler for the generous sympathy with which he has supported and helped us.

"My Lord, I look forward to the day when the students professors, donors and the others interested in the Banaras Hindu University will meet on the banks of the Ganges to celebrate the Donors' Day; and I feel certain that the name that will stand at the head of the list on such a day will be the honoured name of Your Excellency, for there is no donor who has made a greater, a more generous gift to this new movement than Your Excellency has done. My Lord, generations of the Hindu students yet to come will recall with grateful reverence the name of Your Excellency for having given the start to this university. Nor will they ever forget the debt of gratitude they owe to Sir Harcourt Butler for the help he has given to it.

"I should not take up the time of the council today with a discussion of the provisions of the bill. The time for it is not yet. But some remarks which have been made point to the existence of the certain misapprehensions which might be removed.

"Two Hon'ble Members have taken exception to the proposed university on the ground that it will be a sectarian university. Both of my friends the Hon'ble Mr Ghuznavi and the Hon'ble Mr Setalvad have expressed an apprehension that being sectarian in its character, it may foster or strengthen the separatist tendencies. They have said that the existing universities have been exercising a unifying influence, in removing the sectarian differences between the Hindus and Mohammedans. My Lord, the university will be a denominational institution but not a sectarian one. It will not promote the narrow sectarianism but a broad liberation of mind and a religious spirit which will promote brotherly feeling between man and man. Unfortunately we are all aware that the absence of the sectarian religious universities, the absence of any compulsory religious education in our state universities, has not prevented the growth of the sectarian feeling in the country. I believe, my Lord, instruction in the truths of religion, whether it would be the Hindus or Mussalmans, whether it be imparted to the students of the Banaras Hindu University or of the Aligarh Moslem University, will tend to produce men who, if they are true to their religion, will be true to their God, their King and their country. And I look forward to the time when the students who will pass out of such universities, will meet each other in a closer embrace as sons of the same Motherland than they do at present.

"Objection has also been taken to the provision for the compulsory religious education in the proposed university. My Lord, to remove that provision would be like cutting the heart out of the scheme. Many people deplore the absence of a provision for the religious education in our existing institutions, and it seems that there would not be much reason for the establishment of a new university if it were not that we wish to make up for an acknowledged deficiency in the existing system. It is to be regretted that some people are afraid of the influence of religion. I regret I cannot share their views. That influence is ever ennobling. I believe, my Lord, that where the true religious spirit is inculcated, there must be an elevating feeling of humility. And where there is love of God, there will be a greater love and less hatred of man, and therefore I venture to say that if the religious instruction will be made compulsory, it will lead to nothing but good, not only for the Hindu students but for the other students as well, who will go to the new university.

"My Lord, it has also been said that if the sectarian universities must come into existence, we need not carry sectarianism to an extreme. The Hon'ble Mr Setalvad has referred to the provision in the Bill that in the university court, which will be the supreme governing body of the university, none but the Hindus are to be the members. The reason for it needs to be explained. The university has to teach the Vedas, the religious scriptures and to impart instruction even in the rituals and other religious ceremonies which are practised by the Hindus. The Bill provides that there shall be two bodies in the institution, the court and the senate. The court will be the administrative body, will deal mainly with the matters of finance and general administration, providing means for the establishment of chairs, hostels and other institution. The senate will be the academic body, having charge of instruction, examination and discipline of the students. Well, membership on the court has been confined to the Hindus in order that the Hindus who may make benefactions in favour of the institution should feel satisfied that their charities will be administered by men who will be in the religious sympathy with them and in a position to appreciate their motives and their desires. With that knowledge they will make larger endowments to support the university than they would make if the endowment was to be administered by men of different persuasions and faiths. There is nothing uncharitable in such an arrangement. Besides this, there is a second reason. When the Sanskrit College was first established in 1793, in the time of Lord Cornwalis, there was provision made for the teaching of the Vedas and other religious books in it. Later on, some missionary gentlemen took exception to the idea that a Christian Government should encourage the teaching of what they described as heathen religion; and for that reason the teaching of religion was stopped in that institution. In formulating proposals for the Banaras Hindu University, it was felt that, so far as possible, no room should be left for any apprehension which might prevent religious-minded Hindu donors from making large contributions to the university, and that the best means of giving them an assurance that instruction in Hindu religion shall always be an integral part of the education which the University will provide, and that their religious endowments will be administered in conformity with their wishes, was that the membership of the university Court should be confined to the Hindus. There is, however, no such restriction in regard to the membership of the Senate. In the Senate, which will be the soul of the university, we shall invite co-operation, we shall seek it and welcome it, fully one-fourth of the Senate may not be Hindus. There will be no disqualification on the ground of religion in the selection of professors. No restriction is placed upon the students of any creed or any class coming to the university. It will thus appear that while we confine membership on the administrative body of the university, the court, the members of the Hindu community, we keep open the Senate which, as I have said, is the soul of the university, to the teachers of every creed and race. That is a real provision. And we intended to get the very best teachers irrespective of any consideration of race or creed, from whichever part of the world we can, in order that our students should sit at their feet and learn the knowledge that they can impart.

"I should like to say one word more with regard to the provision that the religious instruction should be compulsory in the case of the Hindu students. It has been said that we should not make it compulsory even for the Hindu students, as it might keep some Hindu students who do not desire to receive religious instruction, from the benefit of education at the Banaras Hindu University. But, my Lord, in the first place, the general religious instruction which will be imparted will be such as will be acceptable to all the sections of the Hindu community. In the second place, a number of the Hindu students at present attend missionary institutions where the study of religion is compulsory. So I hope that even those Hindu students who may not appreciate the teaching of religion, will not be kept away from the proposed university on the ground that the religious instruction will be compulsory there.

"I do not think, my Lord, that I need take up more time at present. I beg again to express the gratitude that I am sure millions of the Hindus will feel towards Your Excellency's Government, and personally towards Your Excellency, and towards Sir Harcourt Butler, when they hear of the bill which has been introduced here today.

SPEECH WHILE PASSING BHU BILL BY THE LEGISLATIVE COUNCIL

At the meeting of the imperial legislative council held on the October 1, 1915, the Hon'ble Sir Harcourt Butler moved that the Report of the Select Committee on the Bill be taken into consideration. The Hon'ble Madan Mohan Malaviya in supporting the bill, spoke as follows:

"My Lord, it is my pleasing duty to offer my hearty thanks to your Excellency, to the Hon'ble Sir Harcourt Butler, and to the members of this Council for the very generous support extended to this measure for the establishment of a Hindu University. My Lord, that policy of which it is the product is the generous policy of trust in the people and of sympathy with them in, their hopes and aspirations, which has been the key-note of your Excellency's administration.

"The history of this movement hardly requires to be repeated here. But it may interest some of its friends to know that it was in 1904, that the first meeting was held at which, under the presidency of His Highness the Maharaja of Benares, the idea of such a university was promulgated. Owing, however, to a variety of causes into which it is not necessary to enter here, it was not until 1911 that the matter was taken up in the real earnest. From 1911 to 1915 was not too long a period for the birth of a University where we remember that the London University took seven years to be established from the time the idea was taken up.

"My Lord, in this connection, we must not overlook the work done by my Mohammedan friends. The idea of establishing a Muslim University was vigorously worked up early in the year 1911 when His Highness the Agha Khan made a tour in the country to enlist sympathy and support for it. Your Excellency was pleased to express your appreciation of the effort so made when replying to an address at Lahore. You were pleased to speak approvingly of the spirited response made by the Mohammedan community to the appeal for a Muslim University recently carried throughout the length and breadth of India under the brilliant leadership of His Highness the Agha Khan. We are thus indebted for a part of our success to our Mohammedan brethren, for the work which they did as pioneers in our common cause. We are indebted to His Highness the Agha Khan for having given practical shape to the question of a Muslim University at Aligarh; and to my friend, the Hon'ble the Raja of Mahmadabad for having carried on the first correspondence with the government which elicited the Secretary of State's approval to the idea of a denominational university in this country. My Lord, I confidently hope that it will not be long before a Muslim university will also come into existence, and that the two, the Hindu university and the Muslim university will work together in friendly co-operation on the good of the youth of India, Hindus and Mussalmans, that they will work as sister institutions to promote that real cordiality of feeling between them, the want of which so much hampers our progress and is regretted by all who desire the good of India.

"My Lord, I have carefully read the criticisms that have been levelled against the Bill before us, and it is only fair that I should explain the attitude and action of the promoters of the Hindu University. We are very thankful to the Secretary of State for according his sanction to the proposal to establish what have been described as denominational universities which marks a new and liberal departure in the educational policy of the government but our thanks are due, in a larger measure, to the Government of India who have from the beginning given to the movement their consistent and generous support. In the first proposals which we placed before the government, we desired that the Viceroy and Governor-General of India should be the Chancellor, ex-officio, of the university. That was unanimously supported by the Government of India, and our most sincere thanks are due to them for that support. But unfortunately for us the Secretary of State did not think it right that the Viceroy should be the ex-officio Chancellor of the university; he decided that the university should have the power of electing its own Chancellor; but he also decided, and we are very thankful to him for it, that the university should have the power to appoint its professors without reference to the government. The privilege of having the head of the government as head of the university was one that was naturally highly valued by us, and we submitted a representation asking that the decision of the Secretary of State on that point might be reconsidered. But on being given to understand that the decision was final, we reconciled ourselves to it, finding solace in the fact that the university would have the right instead to elect its own Chancellor. But subsequently the Secretary of State decided that even this privilege should be withheld from us, and that the Lieutenant-Governor of the United Provinces should be the Chancellor, ex-officio, and should exercise all the powers which the Governor-General was to have exercised. This new proposal met with strong disapproval both from the Mohammedan and the Hindu community. It was thought that we had arrived at an impasse, and that the scheme would have to be dropped.

"It was in that state of affairs that, with the generous sympathy of your Excellency's Government and of the very kind support which the Hon'ble Sir Harcourt Butler gave us, we were able to arrive at the compromise which is now embodied in the bill, under which the Lieutenant-Governor of the United Provinces has become the official visitor of the university, and the university has the right to elect its own

Chancellor. This conclusion has secured much of what the government wanted; but it has, at the same time, allotted to us a sufficiently large measure of independence and freedom in the internal affairs of the university, My Lord, we did not reconcile ourselves to this solution without reason. We felt that as the university is to have its home in the United Provinces, it will be an advantage that the head of the United Provinces government should have an official status in the university. We recognised that will be the best arrangement to ensure that the relations between him and the university should be cordial and friendly. I hope and trust that the fact of the Lieutenant-Governor being the official Visitor of the university will prove to be a guarantee and an assurance that such cordial relations will exist between the university and the government.

"My Lord, much objection has been taken to the large powers that have been reserved to the Governor-General under section 19 of the bill. We have accepted them, because, as the Hon'ble Sir Harcourt Butler has explained, they are only emergency powers, which may never be exercised, and can only rarely be exercised. I do hope they will seldom, if ever, be exercised. But assuming that the Governor-General in Council should at any time think that there is anything wrong with the university which requires an explanation, we shall neither be afraid nor reluctant to offer such explanation. The movement has from the start been worked in the conviction, the deliberate conviction, that it is essential for the success of the university that it should secure the goodwill and sympathy of the government, and that it should always retain that sympathy. The section in question provides that the Governor General in Council may, in certain circumstances, ask the university to submit an explanation in regard to the certain matters, and that if the explanation should not satisfy him, that he may offer such advice, as he may think fit to the university. I hope that the existence of this provision in the act will not be felt in the real working of the act, But even with the power which the government have thought it fit to reserve in their hands, it is only fair to say that no university existing in India enjoys so large a measure of freedom in the management of its affairs as your Excellency's Government has been pleased to secure to the Banaras Hindu University, and we feel very deeply grateful for it. The university will have full freedom in appointing its own professors and examiners. It is conceivable that among the Professors so appointed there may sometimes be a case I hope there will never be one in which the university did not know as much about the person appointed as the government. I have no doubt that if such a case should ever arise, it will be dealt with satisfactorily by the correspondence. I am sure that with the explanation and assurance given by the Hon'ble Sir Harcourt Butler that if it should become necessary that an explanation should be called for from any member of the staff engaged by the University, the person concerned will not be in a less favourable position than any one serving under the government. The provision in the Bill to that effect will not prevent any good man from offering his services to the university.

"My Lord, some of my countrymen, who are keenly interested in the proposed University and the educational movement which it represents, have somewhat misunderstood the position of the Hindu University Society and of the promoters of the university in respect of some of the powers vested in the Visitor. They seem to think that we have agreed to those powers without demur. That is not so. Sir Harcourt Butler knows that in regard to some of these powers, I have almost I should not say irritated him, but certainly gone beyond what he considered to be the proper limits in pressing for certain omissions. We have fully represented our views to the government whenever we thought it proper to do so. But having done our duty in that direction, we have agreed to accept; what the government but decided to give. I hope, my Lord, the future will prove that we have not acted wrongly.

"I am certain that as in the course of time experience will show that there are amendments needed in the Act which I hope will be passed today the government will receive representations for such amendments in a thoroughly sympathetic spirit, I take it, my Lord, that the object of the government! and the university is to create a great centre for education, where the education imparted should be the soundest and the best. And, in that view, I feel assured that there will be no difficulty in the government agreeing to any amendment which may be found necessary. As this Bill is being passed in very special circumstances, and we have agreed to avoid controversy at present, I fear some amendments will have to be made at no distant space; but it has perhaps that we should bring them forward when the university court and the senate have been constituted, and when we have found out by the actual experience where exactly the shoe pinches.

"My Lord, I thank God that this movement to provide further and proper facilities for high education for our young men has come to bear fruit in the course of these few years, It will not be out of place to mention here that one of the most fascinating ideas for which we are indebted to Lord Curzon, was the idea of a real residential and teaching university in India. I am tempted to quote the words in which his Lordship expressed his ideal of the university which he desired to see established in this country. What ought the ideal university to be in India as elsewhere? said Lord Curzon. 'As the name implies, it ought to be a place wher the knowledge is taught by the best teachers to all who seem to acquire it, where the knowledge is always turned to good purposes, and where its boundaries are receiving a constant extension.

"My Lord, I hope and pray that though we shall begin in a humble way in the fulness of time that the proposed university will fully answer this description.. His Lordship wanted to see in India a university which would really deserve the name, as he said:

"A university which shall gather round it collegiate institutions proud of affiliation, and worthy to enjoy it; whose students, housed in the residential quarters in close connection with the parent university, shall feel the inner meaning of a corporate life; where the governing body of the university shall be guided by the expert advice and the teachers shall have a real influence upon the teaching where the courses of study shall be framed for the development, not of the facial automation, but of the thoughtful mind; where the professors will draw near to the pupils and mould their characters for good; and where the pupils will begin to value knowledge for its own sake and as a means to an end I should like this spark of the sacred fire that has been brought across the seas lie in one or two places at least before I leave the country, and I would confidently leave others to keep alive the flame.

"My Lord, though this noble wish was not realised in the time of Lord Curzon, I am sure he will be pleased to hear that such a university has come into existence or rather is coming into existence through the generous support of your Excellency's Government.

"It is still more pleasing to think that the university that is coming to be will be better in one respect than the university outlined by Lord Curzon, because it will make religion an integral part of the education that will be provided. My Lord, I believe in the living power of religion, and it is a matter of great satisfaction to us to know that your Excellency is strongly in favour of the religious education. The want of such education in our schools and colleges has long been felt. I believe that the absence of any provision for the religious education in the otherwise excellent system which the government has introduced and worked for the last sixty years in this country, has been responsible for many unfortunate results. I do not wish to dwell upon them. I am thankful to think that this acknowledged deficiency is going to be removed as the proposed important centre of education, which is happily going to be established at a place which may well be described as the most important centre of the religion and learning of the Hindus. I venture to hope, my Lord, that the good influence of the Banaras Hindu University in the matter of religious instruction will be felt in the other institutions, far and near, and that in the course of a few years the religious instruction will become an integral part of the education imparted in the schools and colleges supported by the government and the people.

"My Lord, some well-meaning friends have been apprehensive lest we may not agree at the Hindu University as to what the religious education of our youths should be. This is due to a misapprehension. We have no doubt, many differences among us; we are divided by the many sects and forms of worship. Considering that we embrace a population of nearly 250 milions, it should not surprise any one that we have so many sects and divisions among us. But, my Lord, in spite of these differences, there is a body of truths and precepts which are accepted by all the denominations of our people. For sixteen years and more the religious instruction has been compulsory at the Central Hindu College at Banaras.

"There has been no complaint that the instruction so imparted has been found to be unacceptable to any Hindu boy who has gone to that institution. We have, no doubt, to adopt a compromise in these matters. If we do so, no difficulties will be found to be insuperable. I should like, in this connection, to remind those friends who are apprehensive that we may not be able to agree in regard to the matters relating to religion, to remember some wise words of Cardinal Newman. Speaking of the constitution of a Faculty of Theology in a university, and pointing out how incomplete a university would be which did not possess such a faculty, that great teacher has said: 'No two persons perhaps are to be found, however intimate, however congenial in tastes and judgments, however eager to have one heart and one soul, but must deny themselves for the sake of each other much which they like and desire, if they are to live together happily. Compromise in a large sense of the word, is the first principle of combination and every one who insists on enjoying his rights to the full, and his opinions without toleration for his neighbours, and his own way in all the things, will soon have all the things altogether to himself, and no one to share them with him.'

"In matters of the minor differences that there must be a compromise, I believe we have shown by sixteen years of work at the Central Hindu College, that we can drop minor differences, while we adhere to the substantial object which we have in view, and therefore, though the provision for the religious instruction has not been put in the Act in the form which I thought was best. I am thankful that it is there to give an assurance to the public that the religious instruction shall be a compulsory part of the education at the university. My Lord, I do not wish to dwell upon the amendment which I suggested in my note to the Report of the Select Committee, as I am convinced that no good purpose will be served by my doing so. I accept the provision for the religious instruction, as it stands, in the hope and faith than there will be no such differences in the University regarding the religious instruction as will defeat one of its basic principles, namely, that the religious instruction should form an integral part of the education imparted by it.

"I do not think, my Lord, that I should be justified in taking up the time of the council any further. I once more beg to offer my thanks to your Excellency, to Sir Harcourt Butler and to the Government of India, for helping this university to come into existence, and I conclude with the earnest hope and prayer, that this centre of light and life, which is coming into existence, will produce the students who will not only be intellectually equal to the best of their fellow-students in the other parts of the world, but will also be trained to live noble lives, to love God, to love their country and to be loyal to the Crown."

7

Convocation Address (1929) of BHU

PANDIT MADAN MOHAN MALAVIYA'S ADDRESS

"Ladies and Gentlemen, This is the twelfth Convocation of the Banaras Hindu University. It was in October 1917 that the university started its work. In the twelve years that have elapsed much progress has been recorded. The ideal of the university was an institution which should revive the best traditions of the ancient *gurukulas* of India—like those of the Takshasila and Nalanda, where the Hindu sages taught and fed ten thousand students at a time and which should combine with them the best traditions of the modern universities of the West where the highest instruction is imparted in Arts, Science and Technology.

The objects of the university were thus formulated:

(i) To promote the study of the Hindu *Shastras* and of the Sanskrit literature generally as a means of preserving and popularising for the benefit of the Hindus in particular and of the world at large in general, the best thought and culture of the Hindus, and all that was good and great in the ancient civilisation of India;

(ii) To promote learning and research generally in arts and science in all the branches;

(iii) To advance and diffuse such scientific, technical and professional knowledge, combined with the necessary practical training, as is best calculated to help in promoting the indigenous industries and in developing the material resources of the country; and

(iv) To promote the building up of the character in youth by making religion and ethics and the integral part of the education.

"It is hardly necessary for me to tell you, ladies and gentlemen, why the place of honour was given in the scheme to the first of these objects. We have had a proud lineage, and a proud heritage from our ancient forefathers. Of the various noble things we have inherited, the Sanskrit language and literature is the noblest. In it are preserved all our sacred literature, all our religious philosophy, all the records of our ancient civilisation and culture in all its rich and varied manifestations, containing a complete scheme of society, providing for the physical, intellectual, moral and spiritual welfare of the individuals and for their organisation into powerful communities. As a language Sanskrit is acknowledged, by those most competent to judge, to stand preeminent among the languages of the world. It has been the medium of expression of the most sublime thoughts conceived by man and uttered in the most elegant and majestic forms. It has been elaborated with such a keen sense of the laws of harmony that it stands unrivalled as the most economic means of recording, conveying and remembering knowledge. Its study, as remarked by Sir Monier Williams, 'Involves a mental discipline not to be surpassed.' We therefore conceived it to be our sacred duty to make satisfactory provision at the proposed new centre of learning of our race, for the study of this noble language and literature, as the most potent means of preserving the spiritual sense of the continuity of ages, of a fellowship with the past and present, by which our most cherished national treasure may yet be best utilised for the good of our people and of the world at large and handed down from generation to generation. It is for these reasons that in our scheme of studies, Hindu theology and Sanskrit learning occupied the first place. It is therefore that in conferring degrees at our convocations scholars who have studied theology and Sanskrit learning take precedence over all the other scholars.

"It is a matter of great satisfaction to us that we have secured the co-operation in the work of these faculties of the best pandits who are to be found in India. These revered repositories of the ancient learning help us in prescribing courses and examining the students, and a number of them are imparting regular instruction in our colleges of Theology and Oriental Learning in the Vedas, Vedangas, Darshanas, in literature, in Mathematics and Astronomy and in Ayurveda. We have been attracting students in increasing numbers. In conformity with our ancient national practice, we offer them free education, free accommodation, and free board, to the bulk of them in the shape of scholarships, so that they can carry on their studies here under the most favourable conditions on the lines of our ancient *gurukulas.*

"We encourage the students of Sanskrit to study English as a second language, and allow them to offer it as a subject by itself for the Intermediate and the degree examinations. We contemplate taking further steps to offer the greater facilities for study and research to the students of the Oriental department.

"Ever since the idea of the Hindu University was conceived it has been an article of faith with its promoters that the medium of instruction, even in the highest classes should be the mother-tongue of the people. But the use of English has become universal in our Anglo-vernacular middle and high schools, and Indian vernaculars have been too much neglected. The replacement of English by Hindi, or by any other of our vernaculars, must therefore necessarily take time. The work must begin in our schools. The Hindu University introduced this important change some years ago. In the schools affiliated to the university, instruction is imparted in all the subjects, except a language, by means of Hindi. The students appearing at the Admission Examination of the university—the final high school examination—are permitted to answer their papers in Hindi. It is a matter of satisfaction that this healthy change has been decided upon by the board of high school and intermediate education of the United Provinces also. I have every hope that it will be adopted before long by the other universities.

"A band of our scholars is now engaged in preparing textbooks in arts, science and medical subjects in Hindi for use in the Intermediate college classes of the university. It is expected that a sufficient number of them will be ready for use the next year. Our scholars will then take up the preparation of the text books for the BA classes.

"Hindi was made a distinct subject for examination for the MA degree several years ago, and it is becoming increasingly popular with the students. I hope the time is not very far when our scholars will be allowed to answer their question papers and offer their thesis for the M.A. degree also in Hindi. You will thus see that our progress in this direction, though slow, is full of hope.

"The second object which the University set before itself was to promote learning and research generally in all the arts and science subjects. Towards the fulfillment of this object, starting with the nucleus of the old Central Hindu College, we have provided teaching up to the MA and MSc standards in the Ancient Indian History and Culture, General History and Civics, Philosophy and Psychology, Economics and Political Science, English, Sanskrit, Arabic and Persian, Hindi, Urdu, Marathi, and Bengali, Mathematics and Astronomy, Physics, Chemistry, Botany, Zoology, and Geology. Our general and sectional libraries and laboratories are well-equipped both for practical instruction and research. We have also established a Teachers' Training College, a Law College, and an Ayurvedic College, to which a hospital of a hundred beds is attached, in which instruction up to the highest standard is imparted in Ayurveda—Hindu Medical Science combined with up-to-date instruction in Anatomy, Physiology and Surgery according to the modern allopathic system. A large dissection hall is nearing completion.

"We have also established a Women's College with a separate hostel in which a hundred women students can reside. The hostel is in charge of a Lady Superintendent. Students of the Intermediate classes study at this college with women teachers of whom we have four in number at present. Women preparing for the Bachelor's or Master's degree study with men students of the general classes of the university.

"The third object of the university was to advance and diffuse such scientific, technical and professional knowledge, combined with the necessary practical training, as is best calculated to help in promoting the indigenous industries and in developing the material resources of the country. Towards this end the university has established a College of Engineering in which instruction up to the standard of the degree of Bachelor of Science in Engineering is imparted in Mechanical Engineering, Electrical Engineering, Mining and Metallurgy. We have also established a department of Industrial Chemistry, in which instruction is imparted up to the MSc standard. There is no other college in India where such high class instruction for the degrees is offered in all these important branches of the Applied Science. There was a crying need in this country of such an institution, and the university has every reason to be proud of the privilege of having provided for this need. The College attracts students from all the provinces of India and from the Indian States. The competition for admission is very keen. Only those are admitted who have passed the intermediate examination in Science, with Physics, Chemistry and Mathematics, in the first or the second division. But because we are strict in selecting the students for admission and in turning out those who do not pass the first year's examination, we have had the satisfaction of passing as many as 92 and 94 per cent of our students at the last Examinations for the degree of Engineering.

"It is our constant endeavour that the instruction and training we impart in the Applied Science should be thorough and practical. Our students regularly go out at the prescribed periods for practical training in Railway and other workshops and mines, and I gratefully acknowledge that they receive every assistance and facility from the managers of these workshops and mines, and they come back to us after undergoing satisfactory practical training in them. This training is an integral part of the course we have prescribed. Unless a student puts in sufficient practical work, he cannot, according to the Regulations of the University, obtain the final degree of BSc in mechanical and electrical engineering of the university.

So also is the case with mining and metallurgy. A considerable amount of the practical field work is also demanded of a candidate for the BSc and MSc degrees in Geology. In courses for degrees in the Industrial Chemistry also we naturally insist upon much practical training. This insistence upon the sufficient practical training in all the branches of Applied Science, along with the high standard of theoretical knowledge which we impart, has given a high value to our degrees. I am glad to be able to say that the students who have obtained either diplomas or degrees in engineering in this university have found little difficulty in obtaining the situations. It is believed that 95 per cent of the young men who have gone out of this university with such a diploma or degree have obtained satisfactory appointments, and it is hoped that those who are waiting will also soon find work. This is a matter for great satisfaction and thankfulness. The demand for the practical engineers is likely to grow with the growth of time. Electrical installation are increasing in number. Thousands of miles of railways have been laid down and this mileage will go on increasing for a long time to come. For erecting and running the electrical stations, for carrying out the electrification of the railways and for serving railways in the other ways, the young men trained in mechanical and electrical engineering will be found to be the most suitable recruits.

"Another branch of instruction which will offer increasing opportunities of employment is Industrial Chemistry. Our Laboratory of Industrial Chemistry is well-equipped for imparting instruction and practical guidance to the students who take up ceramics or oils and soaps as one of their subjects. The governments of three provinces have appreciated this work and are co-operating with us by sending their scholars for study and training here, and we expect that an increasingly large number of students will be attracted to this department in the future, as the training given here will enable them to earn a respectable living without taking service either under government or in the private firms.

"We contemplate strengthening this department by providing instruction in several other branches of the applied chemistry. The problems of poverty and unemployment are staring us in the face. They are clamouring for solution. That solution will be found largely not in wishing that more lucrative appointments should be created in the public services, nor in seeking to earn a living wage in the professions which are already over-crowded, but in providing technical instruction and practical training to our youth in the various branches of the Applied Chemistry. We can thereby gradually reduce the quantity of imports of the finished goods which are pouring into our country in ever-increasing quantities years after year and also reduce the export of many raw materials. This is a field in which, with a suitable system of instruction and a reasonable measure of state aid to the industries, employment can be found for tens of thousands of Indians. If the government and the universities will co-operate in this matter, they can create only one effective means for the removal of the unemployment in this country. The Law College and the Teachers' Training College prepare men for the professions of law and pedagogy respectively, and the College of Ayurveda for the practice of medicine and surgery.

"The fourth object of the university was to promote the building up of character in youth by making religion and ethics an integral part of education. We have endeavoured to do much in this direction also. Lectures on religion are regularly given to the Hindu students. *Kathas* selected to inspire high religious and spiritual sentiments, are recited on every *Ekadashi* day which occurs every fortnight. Members of the staff and students are required to attend them. Discourses on religion take place on the other important occasions also, and an endeavour is made in the various ways to impress upon the minds of students in the broad fundamental teachings of religion and ethics. We believe religion to be the surest foundation of character and the truest source of human happiness. We believe patriotism to be a powerful elevating influences which inspires men to high-minded unselfish action. We therefore sedulously inculcate both upon our students.

"But we do not rely upon the teaching of religion alone for the building up of character in our youth. The whole life at the university is so happily moulded and regulated as to help a student to develop the best of which he is capable. Physical culture is greatly encouraged. It is practically compulsory. Out of 2,600 students 1,600 live in hostels built by the university on its own grounds. They live under the eye of the teacher, for residences for the teachers have been provided in the hostels themselves. The whole arrangement is such that the teachers and the taught come into close contact with each other, so also the students with students. Students have organised social and literary clubs, dramatic societies, and athletic associations and a university parliament where they have full freedom to discuss subjects of their own choice, political, social and educational. They organise games and sports, captain teams and administer their own funds. A certain number of them are members of the University Training Corps and undergo military training for which they have shown much keenness. The common life which makes the many one is pulsating more vigorously. The atmosphere is pure and elevating. Apart from the help which he receives from his teacher, each student is educating himself and educating his fellow-students at the university. A code of honour is silently growing among them—a good augury for the future.

"In the course of the twelve years that have elapsed since the university commenced work, it has instituted 32 departments of learning and gathered together over 150 members of the teaching staff, most of them residing on the university grounds, and over 2,600 students, 1,600 of them residing in the hostels built by the university. It has erected over 173 buildings, laid out on a magnificent site, healthy and extensive, two square miles in extent. It has collected nearly 60,000 books in its Library, provided 25 lakhs worth of equipment in its dozen laboratories and workshops, over 380 scholarships and over 400 free and half-free studentships for the poor but deserving students. It has also provided extensive playgrounds for cricket, football, hockey, and tennis, a stadium, an armoury for 300 rifles of the University Training Corps, a hospital which accommodates a hundred beds, a botanical garden and a pharmacy for the preparation of the Ayurvedic medicines. A huge hall for a college of physical culture is nearing completion.

"During this period the university has passed through its portals 2,954 graduates, of whom four are the doctors of science, 189 graduates in the faculty of Theology and the Oriental Learning, 1,763 in the faculty of arts, 740 in the faculty of science, and 262 in the faculty of law. Of these again 384 are the bachelors of teaching, 200 bachelors of teaching, 200 bachelors of science in mechanical and electrical engineering, and 14 in the mining and metallurgy.

"The University was established as an All-India Institution. It has proved in every sense of the word to be so. Contributions have been made to its funds by the Indian states and by the people of every province in India. It has on its staff representatives of all the major provinces. Its students also come from every province of India. It will be interesting perhaps to note the quota of each province during the current year. Assam has contributed 28 students, Bihar and Orissa 176, Bengal 243, Bombay 105, Burma 5, Central India (including Indore and Gwalior) 39, the Central Provinces 231, Berar 10, Madras 137, the North-West Frontier Province 28, the Punjab 143, Udaipur, Jodhpur, Jaipur, Bikaner, Alwar, Kotah, and other places in Rajputana and Patiala 105, Hyderabad (Deccan) 6, Nepal 6, Kashmir 15, Mysore, 3, the United Provinces 1,113, Travancore 17, Baluchistan 2, South Canara 1, Cochin 5, Andhra 31 and Delhi 3. There is also a student from Mauritius. These students represent altogether 222 districts of India.

"Ladies and gentlemen, most of you will probably remember that an appeal was initially made for a hundred lakhs to fund and maintain the university. I am happy to inform you that as a matter of fact a hundred and twenty-five lakhs has actually been collected up to this time. Of this a hundred and sixteen lakhs has been contributed by the Princes and people of India, and 9 lakhs by the Government of India. The Government of India also give us an annual grant of three lakhs, and the states a total annual grant of ₹ 80,000 a year. The rest of our recurring expenditure is met from fees and donations which we receive from the public. Our total income amounts to ten lakhs. Our expenditure is twelve lakhs. We have found the funds which we have collected and the income we have secured too insufficient for the purpose of building up and maintaining a first class university. An additional sum of rupees four crores will be required for the purpose. But for the present we have issued an appeal for another crore which should give us an additional income of at least three lakhs a year more for meeting our current expenditure, for strengthening the existing faculties of the Oriental learning and theology, and of arts and science both pure and applied, and of ayurveda and for establishing the faculties of technology, agriculture, commerce and music. The details of the objects for which more money is needed have been given in the appeal which has been widely published, and I will not therefore detain you by repeating them here. I am glad to be able to say that the appeal is receiving a good response, and I fervently hope that the second crore that we need will soon be granted to us.

"Ladies and gentlemen, I have detained you long by dwelling somewhat in detail over the development which the university has attained within the twelve years of its existence. I have done so because I felt that it is due to the university that its patrons and supporters and all who are interested in the University education in India should know what progress this young institution has so far achieved. I hope that what I have stated will enable you and them to feel that the University has rendered a good account of its work and activities and that it deserves the continued patronage and support of all the lovers of education. It has been given to the few institutions to achieve so much within so short a period. I am sure you will agree with me in thinking that God has blessed our endeavour, and join with me in sending up to Him our most humble prayers of thankfulness for it all.

"It is pleasing to note that this period of the growth of the Hindu University has also been an era of a general development of university education in India such as we never knew before. Twelve new universities have been re-organised or strengthened by the addition of staff and equipment to afford the facilities for higher education and research in both the arts and science subjects. This is a matter for profound satisfaction to all who love the higher education of Indians and desire to see our country rise and prosper. We have got a strong band of Indian scholars working in a dozen well-equipped laboratories, tackling different problems, carrying on research for new truth and extending the bounds of knowledge. An idea of the good work these scholars have been doing may be formed from the papers which are read by the Indians at the Indian Science Congress and other scientific and philosophical associations that have sprung up in this country. I am sure you will all join with me in offering cordial congratulations to all those who laboured to bring these new universities into existence or to strengthen the old ones, and in praying to God that these institutions may in ever-increasing measure become the sources of light and life to the people of our country and help it to re-establish its position among the nations of the world.

"It is a matter of special satisfaction that two of these universities have been established in Indian states, namely, in Mysore and Hyderabad. I am happy to think that other states regard the Hindu University as a part of the provision for the higher education of the youths of the state, and are sending their students in increasing numbers to the university. This, if I may say so, is a wise provision, for it is a pleasure to acknowledge that the states have contributed nearly half the amount which has so far been collected for the university, and the students of the states who come to us get the advantage of having the option of choosing their courses out of the large number of subjects in which instruction is offered by the university.

"Ladies and gentlemen, it has been a matter of great national gratification that during the period we have been surveying some of our countrymen have won world-wide distinction in learning and research and have thereby brought lustre to the name of the Motherland. We all know how Dr Sir Jagadish Chandra Bose has stirred the imagination of the Western scientists and elicited their admiration by his researches in the realm of science, and how Dr Sir C.V. Raman has won very high honour by the researches he has made in the field of Physics, and in particular by what is known as Raman Effects. And it gives me great pleasure to have in our midst today another scholar of eminence in the person of our esteemed friend Dr Saha. He is the third Indian who has been elected a Fellow of the Royal Society of Great Britain. He has won high honour at a comparatively early age, and we may be sure that he has many fresh laurels to win in the field of the scientific investigation and research which he is pursuing with infinite patience and cool enthusiasm.

"Gentlemen, time will not permit of my making mention of the achievements of the other scholars who have extended the bounds of knowledge. What I have said is enough to show that the Indian scholarship has won recognition in the world of science and is sure to win more of it in the future.

"I have said that the establishment of so many universities in the course of a few years is a matter of national gratification. But I regret to find that there is a tendency in some quarter to look askance at the development of the universities in India. There are some who think that they are growing too fast and that more is being spent on the university education in India than should be spent. This is a mistaken view. One has only to think of the large number of the universities in Great Britain, in Germany, in France, in Italy, not to speak of America, to understand that for the vast continent of India, which is equal to the whole of Europe minus Russia, 18 Universities are none too many, and I venture to think that this is the view which is taken a statement like view of this question. University education has come to be regarded in every civilised country as the most important part of a national system of education, and if the expense incurred on the university education in the West is compared with what we are expending on it here, it will be seen that we are far below the standard of the other civilised countries and have much lee-way to make up. Our universities are like so many power-houses needed to scatter the darkness of ignorance, poverty and cold misery which is hanging like a pall upon the country. The larger the number of the well-educated scholars the universities will send out, the greater will be the strength of the national army which is to combat ignorance and to spread knowledge. Every lover of India must therefore rejoice at the growth of the universities in India.

"But it is said that we do not get sufficient value for the money which is being spent on the universities, that they are not turning out work of the right type to justify the expense, that university standards in India are low, that the standard of admission is unsatisfactory, and that therefore efficiency is sacrificed and much educational power is wasted.

"I admit that this criticism is partly true. I unhesitatingly admit that, some brilliant exceptions apart, the Indian intellect cannot, under existing conditions, produce the best results of which it is capable. Indeed it is highly creditable to the Indian graduates that, despite the discouraging conditions under which they live and work, they have rendered so good an account of themselves in the competitions both in India and in England as they have done. To understand how we may get better value for the money and labour we spend on the universities, we must pass in review our whole system of education, we must note all its defects and deficiencies, and the obstacles which lie in the part of the Indian universities.

"It is an obvious truth that the standard of the university education depends directly upon the standard of the secondary education. If you wish to raise the former, you must raise the latter. But you can do this only when the primary education has been organised on a sufficiently sound and extensive basis. Bearing this in mind, let us recall what the state of education in India is and let us compare it with the systems which obtain in the other lands. Let us take the case of England. For sixty years England has sedulously promoted the universal education among its people. In 1870 the Elementary Education Act made elementary education compulsory. The Act of 1891 made it free. Since that time the elementary education has been both free and compulsory for all the boys and girls up to the age of 14. Compulsory education is split into three-grades: (1) Infant grade, 5 to 8 years; (2) elementary or primary grade, 8 to 11 years, (3) higher primary grade, which is sometimes called secondary education, 11 to 14 years. The secondary schools prepare the students for the university matriculation examination, and encourage them by the special grants to continue their studies for the special courses. There are 60 public schools which are regarded as of the first rank, which have a reputation for building up character and preparing young men for administrative appointments. There are over a thousand other secondary schools. Since the War a new type of schools called the Central School has come into existence. They take in boys and girls at the age of 11, on the result of a competitive examination, and impart free instruction. They are day schools. They divide their courses in groups, the commercial group, the technical group and the industrial group. The present-day tendency in England is to include the technical subjects in the scope of the general education and to obliterate the distinction between the primary, secondary and technical schools. But there is at present a net-work of part-time, whole time and evening schools and the technical schools, and there are technical colleges for the advanced technology. In these schools a variety of the technical and professional courses are offered to suit the particular bent of each student. In addition to these there are the polytechnics which prepare the lower middle and the working classes for the various industries and trade which require the skilled labour. They offer training in every industry which exists in the locality. There are also the technical institutes which offer teaching in specialised subjects. Polytechnics also provide teaching in ordinary arts and sciences for the university degrees. On the top of these institutions, stand the universities of which there are 16 in number. A large number of the scholarships is given in the secondary schools to encourage the promising pupils to prepare themselves to join the universities. It will be evident from this how much care is taken in England to see that every child receives the education for which he is naturally fitted. In all the important countries of the West similar steps have been taken, and the systems of primary and secondary education have been overhauled, enriched and put on a sound footing.

"Let me give you some idea of the provisions that have been made in the last ten years in those countries to help the youth and the cause of education. Having improved their respective systems of primary, secondary and technical education, they have introduced a system of the vocational guidance, which has been defined as the giving of information, experience and advice in regard to choosing an occupation, preparing for it, entering it, and progressing in it. They have created committees of the School masters and others, and juvenile employment exchanges ad bureaus to advise boys and girls after they leave the school as to the career they should enter upon. They do not think that they have discharged their duty to the child when they have passed him through the school. In all these countries the interest in the child has been extended to preparing him for occupational life and to securing him employment which may be suitable to him. Thus, in Austria, in 1922, an order of the State Education Office stated 'It is the duty of the School not only to provide suitable instruction and education for the children who attend it, but also to advise parents as to the future careers of their children and as to the choice of an occupation.' A French writer, F. Buisson, quoted by Prof. Shields in his book—*The Evolution of Industrial Organisations* wrote in 1921: 'The school is not made for the school, but for life. It must provide the society of the future with men. It is a cruel mockery suddenly to abandon its little pupils on the day they reach their thirteenth year, when they are flung unarmed into the battle of life. It is also the most foolish waste. What madness, having done so much for the school boy, to do nothing for the apprentice! From this has arisen the idea, which has rapidly spread, that the social functions of the school must be greatly extended. There are many new services which it must give. The first of these is the supervision of the transition from the school room to the workshop.' In England and Wales, vocational guidance has been provided for education (Choice of Employment) Act was passed in 1910 for giving advice to boys and girls under the age of 17 (extended to 18 by the Education Act, 1918) with respect to the choice of suitable employment. So also in the

Irish Free State, in France, in Belgium, in Germany, and in the United States, where probably the first systematic attempt to provide vocational guidance was undertaken in 1908.

"This will give you some idea of the amount of care which is bestowed in England and in the other civilised countries on the proper education of the child. Every civilised government regards it its duty to educate the child, and to educate him in such a manner that he should be able to earn a suitable living. During the ten years since the War, every civilised country has endeavoured to give a more practical bias to education. After six years of experiment Austria-Vienna in 1927 completely reorganised its school system. By 1928 Chile had reduced illiteracy to less than 30 per cent of the population of four and a half millions, and nearly one-seventh were at educational institutions of some kind. Vocational training has been introduced in the third year of the secondary school, and experimental schools and courses have been established and a system of model schools is to be created to determine the type best suited to Chile. In Hamburg schools are being turned into community centres, parents' co-operation enlisted, and self-government employed. The aim of the present Swedish Education is to fit young people for citizenship and to develop their whole personality. In 1918 a whole system of practical education for the young people was created and is vigorously at work. In Turkey since the War the old system of the religious schools has been discontinued, and a democratic, secular, modern and national system of education has been put into practice to fit the country's new conditions. The number of schools has been largely increased, all education made free, opportunity for self-government given everywhere, and the activity plan put in operation into the first three years of the elementary school. It is hardly necessary for me to remind you of the progress of education in France and Germany, America and Japan. The progress of their commerce and industries, the prosperity, power and happiness which they enjoy is in the largest measure due to the education which they have imparted to their sons and daughters during the last fifty years and more.

"Let us turn now to our own country. What do we find here? As has well been pointed out by a distinguished English scholar, there is no country where the love of learning had so early an origin or has exercised so powerful an influence as India. Yet after nearly a hundred and seventy years of British rule, India is still steeped in ignorance. According to the official reports the percentage of literates of both sexes and all the ages was only 7.2, in 1921. In 1927 only 6.91 per cent of the male population and only 1.46 per cent of the female population were at school. The total attendance in all the schools and colleges in India in 1921-22 was 7½ million. Of this about 5 million were in the first class of the primary schools, and the remaining one-third was distributed among the remaining three classes of the primary schools and among all the other educational institutions including the universities and colleges. The majority of the boys drop off in the first class and only 19 per cent of those who join the first class of the primary schools actually reach the fourth class. Children in the first class cannot read and write and the little they learn is soon forgotten. There is a loud wail in a recent official report that the wastage and stagnation which these figures reveal are appalling.

"Where provision for the primary education is so utterly inadequate it would be unwise to expect any system of night schools or continuation schools for the adult education.

"Secondary schools also are inadequate in number and poor in the quality of education they impart. The standard of general education they provide is much below that which obtains in the other countries and which is needed to give the education a practical value. They are also deficient in that they offer only a general and not vocational education. There are a few agricultural, commercial, technical and industrial schools. They are poor both in number and quality. We look in vain for the alternative groups of courses in agriculture, commerce and industry such as the central schools in England provide. The official report, to which I have referred, says with regard to secondary schools: The immense number of failures at the matriculation and in the university examination indicates a general waste of effort. Such attempts as have been made to provide vocational and industrial training have little contact with the educational system and are therefore largely in fructuous.

"Universities may be likened unto trees the roots of which lie deep in the primary schools, and which derive their sap and strength through the secondary schools. Where both are woefully deficient and defective, where there is no diverting of students to the vocational courses, where, speaking generally, every student is forced to adopt one general course which leaves him unfit for anything except the clerical service of a very poor kind, it is not surprising that the Universities have been hampered in their work by admitting the students who are not fitted by capacity for the university education, and of whom many would be far more likely to succeed in the other careers. In the circumstances that obtain at present, universities cannot be expected to secure and maintain such a general high standard as they would naturally desire to. Indeed, it is a wonder that with all the handicaps under which they have laboured they have been able to show such good results as they have shown. It is clear therefore that for bringing about the much-needed improvement in the university standards of admission, teaching and examination, a national system of the universal compulsory and free primary education and a sound system of the secondary education, with attractive vocational courses must be adopted. This way lies the remedy for the present unsatisfactory state of things and not in proposals for leaving out in the cold students who are not gifted or have not been fitted by proper school instruction for the university education.

"Ladies and gentlemen, another complaint against our universities and colleges is that they are turning out large numbers of graduates who cannot find employment. This is obviously due to the fact that our universities also do not provide a sufficient variety of courses to fit men for careers. As a rule those who take a degree in arts or in pure science are fit only for a teacher's work or for an administrative appointment. But schools and colleges and the public services can absorb only a small proportion of the graduates who are turned out year after year. The provision for medical relief in the country's administration is scanty, and medicine therefore can absorb only a few at present. Want of the alternative courses for professional or vocational training compels many students to take to law, only to find that the bar is overcrowded and to chew the bitter cud of disappointment. The remedy lies in providing education on an adequate scale and of the right type in commerce, in agriculture, in technology, in engineering and in applied chemistry. It is no answer to say that agriculture and commerce do not demand the services of a large number at present. The education has to be made so practical that there shall be a demand for it and the demand has to be sedulously increased. The government and the universities have to co-operate to give the right kind of education to the youth of the country and to find careers for them. No one branch of the national activity can absorb an unlimited number of the trained men. But many branches can find work for a few each, and all together can accommodate quite a large number.

"It has often been cast as a reproach against our students that too many of them take to law. But it ought to be remembered that it is not their fault but their misfortune that they do so. What is the alternative open to them?

"At one time in Japan an unduly large number of young men used to take to the profession of law. The bar was soon overcrowded. Subsequently A Faculty of commerce was started. Commerce was encouraged. Banks were started and many of the young lawyers left the bar and took up commercial careers and thus served both themselves and their country.

"It is the greatest condemnation of the present system—it is tragic that after twenty years of school and university education, an Indian youth should not be able to earn a decent living to support himself, his wife, and children and his poor parents. The system is radically wrong and requires to be greatly altered. The whole atmosphere has to be changed. The education of the child has to begin from the time when he comes into the womb of his mother. For this young men and young women have to be educated before they become parents. Look at England again. There the mother is educated, the father is educated, the neighbours are educated. Almost every one has received the benefit of schooling. Educational institutions and activities greet one in every direction. The newspaper and books are in everybody's hand. The desire to learn, to read, to know is stimulated in every conceivable way. It has become ingrained in the minds of the people. Education has become a necessity of life. An attempt has been made, and it has largely succeeded, to provide it for all the stages from the cradle to the grave. It is in such an atmosphere that an English child is born and brought up. He is carefully looked after in the nursery school, the primary school, the secondary school and the technical school. When he leaves the school finally, he is fit for and is helped to get a suitable job. If he enters the university, he enters it well prepared to pursue the higher studies at the university, buoyant with hope and ambition. Place the Indian student under similar conditions, give him a fair chance, and he will not be beaten by the youth of any country on earth.

"There is no end to the difficulties which beset the path of an Indian student at present. But if I may say so, the greatest of them all is education cannot therefore be raised to the right level of excellence until the vernacular of the people is restored to its proper place as the medium of education and of public business.

" 'I do not underestimate the value of the English language. I frankly acknowledge that its knowledge has been of great use to us. It has helped the unification of the public administration in all parts of India. It has also helped to strengthen the national sentiment. I concede that it is or is on the road to become a world-language. I would advise the every educated Indian who wishes to proceed to a university, or to go abroad for the higher education, to acquire a knowledge of this language and also of German or French. But we should encourage the study of English only as a second language, as a language of commerce with men, or practical business usefulness. We should not allow it to continue to occupy the supreme position which it occupies today in the system of our education and our public administration and in the business world. It is impossible to calculate the full extent of the loss which the disregard of our vernaculars has inflicted upon our people. We should take early steps to check it. If there be anyone who thinks that our present vernacular should not be used as the medium of the higher education and public business because it is not as highly developed today as English is, let me remind them that this very English language, which now possesses a literature of which every Englishman is justly proud, was neglected and condemned in England itself, until a few centuries ago. Up to the middle of the fourteenth century French was taught in England to the exclusion of English. It was only towards the end of the 14th century that the people of England began to use the English tongue in their schools, courts and public offices,' says Green in his *Short History of the English People*.

"In the middle of the fourteenth century the great movement towards freedom and unity which had began under the last of the Norman Kings seemed to have reached its end, and the perfect fusion of the conquered and conquerors into an English people was marked by the misuse, even amongst the nobler classes, of the French tongue. In spite of the efforts of the grammer schools, and of the strength of fashion, English was winning its way throughout the reign of Edward III to its final triumph in that of his grandson. 'Children in School', says a writer of the earlier reign, 'against the usage and manner of all the other nations, be compelled for to leave their own language, and for to construe their lessons and their things in French, and so they have since the Normans first came into England. Also gentlemen's children be taught to speak French from the time that they be rocked in their cradle, and know how to speak and play with a child's toy; and uplandish (or country) men will liken themselves to gentlemen, and fondell (or delight) with great business for to speak French to be told of.' 'This manner', adds a translator of Richard's time, 'was much used before the first murrain (the plague of 1349) and is since somewhat changed; for John Cornewaile, a master of grammar, changed the lore in grammar school, and construing from French into English; and Richard Penchriche learned this manner of teaching of him, as others did of Penchriche. So that now, the year of our Lord, 1385, and of the second King Richard after the conquest nine, in all the grammar schools of England, children leaveth French, and construeth and learneth in English.' A more formal note of the change thus indicated is found in the Statute of 1362, which orders English to be used in the pleadings of courts of law, because the French tongue is much unknown.

"Ladies and gentlemen, the result of this simple natural change was that within about two centuries of it, Shakespeare, Milton, and a host of poets and writers built up a glorious literature, the most important monument of which is the English version of the Bible, the noblest store-house of the English tongue. Imagine what the loss of the English- speaking world would have been if English had continued to be neglected as it was till 1382. Similarly who can calculate the loss which India has suffered because Hindi and the other Indian vernaculars have not received the attention they deserved and their literatures have not been developed to the extent they could have been developed as the media of national education and communication? English can never become the *lingua franca* of India. After nearly three quarters of a century of education, only 0.89 per cent of the total population of India knows English. It must therefore yield the place of honour in India to the principal Indian vernacular to Hindi or Hindustani the language of Hindustan. So long as English will occupy its present prominent place in India in the courts of law, in public offices and bodies, in schools and colleges and universities, the language of Hindustan cannot acquire its rightful position in the economy of national life, and a national system of education cannot be developed.

"Ladies and gentlemen, I have described to you some of the disadvantages under which university education labours in India. I have pointed out its defects and deficiencies, and the obstacles which obstruct its progress. Let me now invite attention to the remedy. What is all this enormous difference between education in England and education in India due to? Both countries are under the same sovereign. The affairs of both have been controlled by the same parliament. A hundred and fifty years ago the Parliament of Great Britain and Ireland assumed direct responsibility for guiding the destinies of India. It has during this period repeatedly avowed that it is responsible for the moral and material progress of the people of India. It has of course also been responsible for the welfare of the people of England. It has discharged its responsibility to the people of England by introducing a most excellent system of the national education. Sixty years ago it made elementary education compulsory throughout the Great Britain and Ireland. In 1891 it made that education free. During this half a century it has organised and reorganised its system of education, general and technical, to meet varying national needs and requirements and by means thereof, it has enabled the Britishers to hold their own in the keen competition with the other advanced nations of the world in the various directions. The prosperity and power which England enjoys today in the world is due in large measure to its system of education. Turn now to India. In spite of the repeated professions of solicitude for the welfare of the masses of India the, parliament has not been able to secure to them the blessings even of the elementary education. The need for such education has repeatedly been pointed out and admitted. Only a few years after the Act of 1870 was passed in England, an Education Commission was appointed by the Government of India. It reported in 1883 and recommended the universal extension of the elementary education. Several commissions and committees have since then made similar recommendations. The last to do so was the Royal Commission on Agriculture which reported only a year ago. Besides, for forty-five years we Indians have been asking that elementary education should be made universal, and that a system of the technical, agricultural, industrial and commercial education should be introduced. But this has not been done. In 1910 Mr Gopal Krishna Gokhale introduced a bill to initiate a system of the permissive compulsory education, but his bill was opposed by the government and defeated. Since the reforms were introduced in 1920, the representatives of the people have tried to introduce an element of compulsion in certain areas in some provinces. But the total progress of the elementary education brought about in India under the administration for which the Parliament of England has been responsible for a century and a half, is attested by the fact that only 6.91 per cent, of the total male population and only 1.46 of the female population was at school in 1927. This is truly appalling. The conclusion to which we educationists in India are driven is that the difference is due to the fact that in England the parliament has been responsible to the people, but the government in India has not been so, and that no foreign government can serve the interests of the people over whom it has acquired sway as a government of their own can.

"The question of the national education is the most vital problem in the administration of a country. It can be dealt with in all its varying phases effectively and well only by a national government. When a national government is established, as I hope it will be established the next year, one of the first things it will have to do is to call a conference of the eminent educationists to discuss and recommend a national educational policy to be pursued in India. Such a conference will of course take note of the experience which has been gained by the other nations in the matter of public education and will recommend a comprehensive programme of the education suited to the needs of all the classes of the people of the country. When such a policy and programme have been adopted by the future government of this country, and have been put into operation, then and then only will the universities of India be able to produce the highest results of which the Indian intellect is capable.

"That the education system which is in vogue in India is unsuitable to our national and cultural needs hardly needs saying. We have been blindly imitating a system which was framed for another people and which was discarded by them long ago. Nowhere is this more forcibly illustrated than in the education of our women. We are asking our girls to pursue the same courses which are prescribed for our young men without defining to ourselves the results which we desire to follow from their education.

"The education of our women is a matter of even greater importance than the education of our men. They are the mothers of the future generations of India. They will be the first and most influential educators of the future statesmen, scholars, philosophers, captains of commerce and industry and other leaders of men. Their education will profoundly affect the education of the future citizen of India. *The Mahabharata* says: 'There is no teacher like the mother.' We must therefore define the goal of their education and take counsel together and obtain the best advice as to what courses will most suit them, how we shall secure to them a good knowledge of our ancient literature and culture and combine with it a knowledge of the modern literature and science, particularly biological science, of art and painting, and of music, how we shall secure the physical, intellectual, moral and spiritual building up of the womanhood of the country. Do we want to rear up women of the type of Savitri and Arundhati, Maitreyi and Gargi, Lilavati and Sulabha of old, or of the type of administrators like Ahalyabai, or of the type of the brave fighter Lakshmi Bai of Jhansi, or women who will combine the best characteristics of the women of the past and of the present, but who will be qualified by their education and training to play their full part in building up the new India of the future? These and similar questions will demand consideration before a national programme for the education of our women will be settled. Statesmen and scholars shall have to sit together to discuss and recommend such a programme.

"It has been said that the backwardness of India in education constitutes a great obstacle in the way of the establishment of the responsible self-government in India, and yet we have seen that in the establishment of such government only lies the hope of removing that backwardness. It has also been said that as the masses of India are illiterate they are incapable of exercising an intelligent vote. But, it is forgotten that though the masses are illiterate, they are not wanting in natural intelligence and can be educated in no time. It is also said that there is too much of religious fanaticism and communal feeling in this country to permit of Indians becoming a united self-governing nation. Let us have charge of the education of the country with the sufficient funds at our disposal, and on behalf of all my fellow-educationists in India, I promise that in the course of a few short years we shall banish illiteracy from the land, and spread education and ideas of citizenship among our people to such an extent that the fogs of comunalism will vanish before the sun of nationalism, which it will be our earnest and proud endeavour to install in the hearts of our people.

"Let no one think that I am claiming too much for the school-master. I am not. The school master is recognised now in every civilised country as a very strong factor in the national advance of a country. He is indisputably the most important servant of the State. It lies largely in his hand to mould the mind of the child who is father of the man. If he is patriotic and devoted to the national cause and realises his responsibility, he can produce a race of the patriotic men and women who would religiously place the country above the community and national gain above communal advantage. Germany and France, America and Japan, and the other civilised countries have built up national strength and solidarity by the direct teaching of patriotism in their schools. England herself has been doing it, particularly since the War. But Japan perhaps affords the best example for us in this matter. The great Revolution which laid the foundation of the modern Japan took place in 1868. The national government of Japan soon introduced a national system of education, which included the direct teaching of patriotism. An Imperial rescript on education was issued in 1890 in which the Mikado, the Emperor of Japan, exhorted his subjects to loyalty, filial piety, patriotism and the pursuit of learning, as a means to perfect morality and civic behaviour. This rescript is hung up in every school in Japan and is held in great reverence by every teacher and pupil. This teaching has produced excellent results. Patriotism has become the religion of Japan. It has taught the Japanese to sacrifice themselves in the cause of the country. Japan was divided and weak sixty years ago. By introducing a system of the elementary, secondary, and higher schools, universities, technical and special schools, by compelling the attendance at the elementary schools of boys and girls between the ages of 6 and 14, Japan in a few years educated the rank and file of the whole nation. It is the education and the compulsory universal military training which was introduced along with it, that have been the principal cause of the wonderful rise of Japan. Educated and made doubly efficient by patriotism, the Japanese defeated China in 1895 and Russia in 1905. Japan has now long enjoyed the high position of being one of the big five powers of the world. This is all the result of education, of national patriotic education. Let India be permitted to adopt a similar system of national education and let it be expected with confidence that the similar gratifying results will follow.

"Ladies and gentlemen, I have detained you long. But I hope you will bear with me just a little longer while I say a few words to the graduates who have obtained their diplomas today and who are going out to enter life. I will be as brief as possible.

"I ask you young men and young women to remember the promises you have made to me and through me to you *alma mater* before you obtained your Diplomas. Remember those promises. Remember also the advice which our esteemed Pro-Vice-Chancellor has given to you in the words of the revered *Rishis* of old. Speak the truth, live truth, think truth. Continue your studies throughout your life. Be just and fear none. Fear only to do that which is ill or ignoble. Stand up for right. Love to serve your fellow-men. Love the motherland. Promote public weal. Do good where ever you get a chance for it. Love to give whatever you can spare.

"Remember the great fundamental truth which you have repeatedly been taught in this university. Remember that the whole creation is one existence, regulated and upheld by the one eternal, all-pervading intelligent power, or energy, one supreme life without which no life can exist. Remember that this universe is the manifestation of such a power, of the one without a second, as says the *Upanishadas*, the creator and sustainer of all that is visible and of a vast deal which is invisible to the human eye. Remember that such a power call him *Brahma*, call him God, is both imminent and transcendent, and has existed throughout all the stages of evolution. He constitutes the life in all the living creation. He constitutes the life in all the living creation. Should a doubt arise in your mind about the existence of this power, turn your gaze to the heavens, wonderfully lit with stars and planets, that have been moving for unimaginable ages in the majestic order. Think of the light that travels with marvellous rapidity from the far distance Sun to foster and sustain life on earth. Turn your eyes and mind to the most excellent machine—your own body which you have been blessed with, and ponder over its wonderful mechanism and vitality. Look around you and see the beautiful beasts and birds, the lovely trees, with their charming flowers and delicious fruits. Remember that One Supreme Life which we call *Brahma* or God dwells in all this living creating in the same way as it does in you and me. This is the essence of all the religious instructions:

स्मर्तव्यः सततं विष्णुर्विस्मर्तव्यो न जातुचित्।
सर्वे विधि-निषेधाः स्युरेतयोरेव किंङ्कराः।।

'Ever to remember God, never to forget Him' All religious injunctions and prohibitions subserve these two alone. If you will remember that God exists and that He exists in all the living creatures, if you will remember these two fundamental facts, you will ever be able to stand in correct relation with God and with all your fellow creatures. From the belief that God exists in all the sentient beings has flowed the fundamental teaching which sums up the entire body of moral injunctions of all the religions, namely—

आत्मनः प्रतिकूलानि परेषां न समाचरेत्।

That is, one should not do unto others that which he would dislike if it were done to him. And

यद्यदात्मनि चेच्छेत तत्परस्यापि चिन्तयेत्।

i.e., whatever one desires for himself, that he should desire for others also. These two ancient injunctions lay down a complete code of conduct for all the mankind.

"If anybody should steal your watch or any other of your possessions you would be pained. Therefore cause not such pain to another by stealing his watch or any article. When you are ill or thirsty you desire that some one should give you medicine or relieve your thirst. Therefore if there be any sister or brother who stands in need of the similar relief from you, consider it your duty to render it. Remember these two grand negative and positive injunctions; they embody the Golden Rule of conduct which has been applauded by all the religions of the world. It is the very soul of religion and ethics. Christianity claims it to be its own special contribution. But in reality it is a much older teaching and found a place of honour in the *Mahabharat* thousands of years before the advent of Christ. I say this not in any narrow spirit, but only to impress upon you that this ancient teaching has come down to us as a noble heritage, and that it is one of the most precious possessions not only of the Hindus but of the whole human race. Treasure it in your hearts, and I am sure your relations will be right and loveable both with God and man.

"You must at the same time also remember that this is the country of your birth. It is a noble country. All things considered there is no country like it in the world. You should be grateful and proud that it pleased God to cast your lot here. You owe it a special duty. You have been born in this mother's lap. It has fed you, clothed you, brought you up. It is the source of all your comfort, happiness, gain and honour. It has been your play-ground, it will be the scene of all your activities in life, the centre of all your hopes and ambitions. It has been the scene of the activities of your forefathers, of the greatest and the humblest of your nation. It should be for you the dearest and the most revered place on the surface of the earth. You must therefore always be prepared to do the duty that your country may demand of you. Love your countrymen and promote unity among them. A large spirit of toleration and forbearance, and a larger spirit of loving service is demanded of you. We expect you to devote as much of your time and energy as you can spare to the upliftment of your humble brethren. We expect you to work in their midst, to share their sorrows and their joys, to strive to make their lives happier in every way you can. And here I have a definite advice to offer you. We all deplore that there is immense ignorance in our country. We should not wait for its removal till we get *Swaraj*. I call upon every one of you, young men and young women, to take a vow that you will start a crusade against illiteracy, a campaign to spread knowledge and enlightenment among the teeming millions of India. Organise your strength. During the period of your leisure or vacation, make it a point to go to the villages and work among your countrymen. Be determined to dispel the darkness which envelopes our masses. Open schools. Instruct the masses in the three R's. i.e., reading, writing, and arithmetic. To which add one more, viz. religion, the religion of which I have spoken, the religion of love and service, of toleration and mutual regard. Teach these four R's to every boy and girl, every man and woman, old or young. Do not discard religion. Properly understood and taught, it will contribute in rich measure to promote harmony and happiness among all mankind. Promote education by the simplest means. Help our people by your instruction to advance sanitation, health and hygiene in their villages by their own co-operative organisations. I exhort you all, those who are going out of the university now and those who will still he here, to form a People's Education League, and start the campaign against illiteracy and ignorance, which to our shame has to long been delayed. Invite all the educated youth of our country to joint in undertaking this grand endeavour. We have only to combine and work. Success is certain to crown our efforts.

"Throughout the period of your work, take care to keep alive the sense of your duty towards God and towards your country. It will sustain you in the most difficult situations and help you to avoid the many obstacles which beset your path. A remembrance of what you owe to God will help you to cherish feelings of brotherliness, of kindness and compassion, not only towards men but towards all innocent creatures of God. It will save you from causing hurt to any one except in the right of private self-defence or the defence of your country. A remembrance of your duty to your country, will help you always to be prepared to offer any sacrifice which may be demanded of you for the protection of its interests of honour. You want freedom, you want self-government in your country. You must be prepared to make every sacrifice which may be needed for it. You have in the course of your education studied the inspiring history—past and present of the struggles to establish or maintain freedom, which have taken place in our own country and in the other lands. You have read of the spirit of valour and self-sacrifice which breathes through the best part of the Sanskrit literature and of the modern Indian literatures. You have read and re-read and admired many growing passages in the glorious literature of England which sing in high strain of liberty and of daring and self-sacrifice in its cause. You have learnt how in the recent Great War, the youths of England and France voluntarily exposed themselves to death in the defence of their own freedom or the freedom of other countries; with what valour and courage and tenacity French and English lads continued to fight until victory crowned their efforts, and thus won imperishable glory for their motherland. I exhort you to cultivate the same love of freedom and the same spirit of self-sacrifice for the glory of your motherland. Thus only shall we again become a great nation.

"The education you have received would have been lost upon you if it did not plant an ardent desire in your minds to see your country free and self-governing. I wish you to cherish that desire, and to prepare yourselves to discharge every obligation which may be cast upon you for the early fulfillment of it. You know that the highest duty of a citizen is to offer the final sacrifice of his life when the honour of the motherland requires it. I desire you at the same time to remember that duty also demands that life shall be preserved for service and not lightly thrown away under wrong inspiration. I therefore wish you to act with a full sense of responsibility and to work in the right spirit and under proper guidance for the freedom of the country."

8

Other Important Speeches

GAYA PRESIDENTIAL ADDRESS HINDU MAHASABHA: 1923

Pandit Madan Mohan Malaviya began his address with Veda path (recitation of Vedic mantras) and heartily thanked the audience for electing him the president. He laid emphasis on the greatness of the hoary Hindu civilisation, the four *varnas* (castes) and four *ashramas* (stages) of the Hindu society. Paying respect to the Buddha he said: Lord Buddha, the third greatest benefactor of mankind, is worshipped by the Hindus as one of the ten incarnations of Vishnu. The ten Buddhistic commandments tally exactly with Manu's rules about *achar* and there is no difference between the Hindus and Buddhists. He said that the *ashrama* system of the Hindu society was unparalleled in its perfection, which divided life into four parts of *brahmacharya, grehastha, vanaprastha* and *sanyasa*. The ancient great men and sages, Rama and Krishna, Bhishma, Drona, Yudhistira, Arjuna, Vashishta, Gautama and others were the seers of the Hindu civilisation. Tolerance and forgiveness were the characteristics of the Hindu society and even in the earlier age Prithvi Raj captured Mohammad Ghori and set him free. The Hindu ideal is never to hurt or be aggressive to anybody, but at the same time the Hindus wished that they should not also be hurt or attacked by the others.

"The Hindu religion sustained many attacks. The Hindus never cared so much for *rajya* as for dharma. We had fallen down and before the British advent anarchy and chaos reigned supreme in India. The Hindus and Mohammedans both had fallen down and were fighting one another. The British came to India and ruled over India, of course with a selfish motive and interest, but some common advantages have been derived by us. People of different and farthest corners have been brought nearer and together due to railways and telegraphs and on account of a common language and common laws, mutual relations have increased and they have ample facility for coming together. From 1885 to 1915 the Congress strove its utmost and worked hard for India's upliftment, although the Mohammedans as a community kept themselves aloof, except a few liberal-minded statesmen. In 1916 all of us joined and drew up a scheme for reform. Something was given, but it was insufficient and incomplete. Since then our condition has been worse. The greatest of the Indians and the saint of the world, Mahatma Gandhi was most unjustly imprisoned by the government and we have not yet been able to get him released—our weakness and helplessness cannot be greater than this, that we have not yet been able to effect his release. The heart of India is most pained at this government attitude and explosives are collecting which may one day prove very dangerous. Besides this, our trade and commerce are destroyed. The traders and merchants are impoverished. The government is increasing taxation and our condition and status are pitiable. Formerly the government had some fear of us, but since Mahatma Gandhi's reachings of non-violence the government's attitude hads completely changed. We have now to consider what is our duty in the present circumstances, what relations we have to maintain towards the government, Mohammedans, Parsis and the other Indian communities.

Hindu-Muslim Problems

Referring to the relations with Mohammedans Pandit Madan Mohan Malaviya said that it was an unhappy, a painful episode. The relations between the Hindus and Mohammedans have not been as happy and cordial as they ought to be. During the Bengal Partition days the government was inciting the Mohammedans to attack Hindus. In 1916 in Eastern Bengal inhuman, brutal, and unparalleled atrocities were perpetrated on the Hindus. The Hindu women were outraged by fanatic Mohammedans and many Hindu women had to take shelter in rivers and tanks to protect their honour. Then came the Great War in 1914. In 1914 in the frontier districts, particularly Muzaffarnagar the Hindu houses were regularly looted and the Hindu women dishonoured, but the Indian patriots preached not to heed them. As adviced by Mahatma Gandhi The Hindus worked with Mohammedans and helped them in the Khilafat cause, not because the former wanted something in return, but because they were for the liberty and freedom of every nation and also because of their sympathy for the fellow-Muslim brothers. The speaker emphasised that he did not attribute such inhuman attacks to the good and gentle Mohammedans but to the rogues, vagabonds and the bad elements of the Muslim society. Again in 1920 the brutal and inhuman atrocities were perpetrated on the Hindus by the Moplahs in Malabar. The Hindu houses were looted, women were outraged, male and female butchered with the greatest cruelty for refusing to embrace Islam and many were forced into Islam at the point of the sword. The speaker pathetically and movingly said that it is better to die than to be beaten and oppressed anywhere and everywhere, than to see women's modesty outraged, temples attacked and burnt and the idols broken. The whole of India was severely pained and afflicted at these horrible inhumanities. Due to tolerance we patiently bore all this and drank the bitter dose simply with anxiety and desire that no ill-feeling and differences be created between the two sister communities. The Amritsar episode is not out of memory. At Multan temples were burnt down and women's chastity was outraged and later on Geeta and Granth Sahib were burnt. In the temples the broken idols were found. Next an appeal was issued to maintain unity and peace on the *Bakrid* day, but riots occurred at several places, although not so many as were expected. Our ladies do not consider they are as safe as 50 years ago. Amritsar Hindu women do not come out of houses so frequently and abruptly as they used to do formerly. Every moment they fear of being dishonoured. Everybody knows what happened at Panipat and at Ajmer. Temples were broken and burnt and the idols destroyed.

"In such circumstances it is our individual and social duty to increase our strength and be on terms of love and goodwill with the Muslims. It is most deplorable that the Hindus are so fallen that a handful of the foreigners can be ruling over us. It is on the Hindus who live to see the breaking of the temples and the outrage of women. Miss Ellis was kidnapped and the vibration pervaded the whole of British Empire. Behind English girls and women there is national strength which protects them wherever they go. So also with the Mohammedan women. There was a time when the Hindu ladies had also such national backings behind them. Unless we have such strength, we cannot match pace with the strong nations of the world. Whatever steps we adopt, we should see that we may not harm the others and put hindrance to the national unity. The main reason of the present disunity is that the Hindus are comparatively weak and cannot protect their religion and women. Unity and goodwill can exist only between two equally strong parties. When the irresponsible element of the Muslims will realise that we can react to the policy of tit for tat they would never venture to attack us.

Malaviya continued, "I solemnly affirm before God I never mean to hurt Muslims or have the supremacy of the Hindus over Muslims. If that be the sentiment in me, God may give me the greatest punishment, but I wish that my Hindu brethren be wiped off this earth if they cannot protect their sisters, daughters and others, cannot save the honour of our religion. We are responsible for our weakness. We have forgotten our duty. We should not fight shy of being called the Hindus. When the Hindus are oppressed we should approach the Muslim leaders to devise means to settle disputes. In case riots occur we should settle matters in consultation with the leaders of both communities.

Pandit Madan Mohan Malaviya then emphasised on girls' education. He laid great emphasis on the importance and necessity of *brahmacharya*, physical strength and exercise and urged the establishment of the wrestling places (*Akharas*) in every quarter, every town and village. He next urged economy in social functions such as marriages, *upanayan* and others. He denounced dowry and urged its abolishment. Regarding untouchability Pandit Madan Mohan Malviya spoke very feelingly and tears were trickling down his cheeks when he referred to the untouchables. He said the Hindu Sabha comprises all the sects of Hindus. The untouchables too follow the Hindu religion, worship Rama, Krishna and the other Hindu gods, take their meal after bath, and if wealthy, even build temples. Swami Shraddhanand interrupted to express his views: "But then they are not allowed to enter those temples and worship there." With tears in his eyes Malaviya then took off the turban from his head and said: "Why should I not place my turban at the feet of my untouchables brother who follows the Hindu religion? Why should I not allow my untouchable brother to have darshan in temples? Full of sins as I am, what right have I to stop my untouchable brother from entering tempes?

Addressing the orthodox pandits, he then said with folded hands: "Oh, the learned Pandits, for God's sake do not prevent these brothers from having darshan in the temples.

Referring to permission to the untouchables for drawing water from the wells the president said that the Christians and Mohammedans are asking the untouchables to embrace their religion, for so long as they remain Hindu they are not allowed to draw water from wells and if they accept their faith, they will not be so outcasted, insulted, and disallowed. This exactly happened at Panipat. But this is to be remembered that these untouchables who are so outcasted by the high caste people were the first to come to defend the Hindu temple at Panipat when it was attacked by the Mohammedans. Quoting the story of Raja Rantideva, Pandit Madan Mohan Malaviya said that this Raja after starvation for 48 days got something to eat. A Brahman beggar went to him and he fed him with that food and then successively came two untouchable beggars with dogs to whom Rantideva gave all that he had with the greatest respect and affection. Pertinently remarked Pandit Mandan Mohan Malaviya: "An untouchable comes under the hottest sun from your labour and is extremely thirsty. I ask what true Hindu is there who will so cruelly prevent these untouchables from drawing water from wells while they do not object the untouchables' entry in houses when their services are required. Teach them to be clean. When they travel with us in trains, when they sit with us in schools, we do not object because this has been forced upon us by the Government.

Re-conversion

Referring to the *Shuddhi* movement Pandit Madan Mohan Malaviya said there are forty-eight crores of the Muslims in India of whom not more than fifty lakhs are those who might have come from outside. The rest were converted from Hinduism. Theirs is a proselytising religion while our religion has closed the doors for those who wish to come in our fold. *Mullas* have recently prepared an expansive scheme for reconversion of the Hindus on a grand scale in their private and confidential meeting and have scrupulously given no publication to this resolution and they have also collected fifty lakhs, but you will be surprised to know that it has not been scrupulously kept secret. Hindus are converted by dupes. In Gujarat some Mussalmans with notices bearing prints of, 'Om preach Kalauki incarnation is H.H. Agha Khan' say that they should join that sect. Within three years one lakh of the Hindus have been converted by the Khojas. He asked: "Is there no *prayashchitta* for those who unknowingly took anything touched by the non-Hindus. Malkanas ought to be taken into Hinduism. He further questioned: "What Hindu is there who has this right to say that some particular man has no right to offer prayers after coming into the Hindu fold?

The President then referred to a verse in *Dharmshastra Mahaprabandha* which lays down that those who had been converted to the other religion either by force or willingly can be taken back to the Hindu religion if they so desire. He asked the audience to decide this question. Replying to those who say that we should not care for our numerical strength and that those who have already been converted should not be taken into Hinduism, Malaviya said: "When now we are so badly treated with a numerical strength of the 22 crores, what would be our condition in future with a much reduced Hindu population, if we allow this rate of conversion from Hinduism and do not allow reconversion into Hinduism?"

Malaviyaji's Last Message (Excerpts) November 1, 1946

Backgournd

The last Message of Pandit Madan Mohan Malaviya on (Nov 1, 1946) is talked off in a hushed voice as if it contained some secret and unprofane message only for the Hindus. Here is the background and the brief details about the last message as per his biographer Paramanand: "These last few months were a period of torture; as news of communal conflicts and killings came pouring in grief overpowered him and hastened his end....We have the testimony of many persons who visited him as to the weak state of his health, the feebleness of his voice, his fading memory and, at the same time, of his grave anxiety regarding the future of the country and particularly of the Hindu community.....In the city of Calcutta alone the riot, which lasted for four days (Aug 16-19, 1946), caused five thousand deaths and fifteen thousand other casualities. The mass killing, forced conversion and the other excesses that perpetrated in the Noakhali district of East Bengal in October caused Malaviya intense suffering. At last he must have agreed with his younger brother Gandhiji, who siad: "I do believe that, where there is only a choice between cowardice and violence, I would advise violence."

The excerpts from Pandit Madan Mohan Malaviya's message are as follows:

"For years Hindus have been trying fully from their side to realise the true Hindu-Muslim unity... But it saddens me to see that their tolerance is mistaken for weakness and their co-operation has been rejected mostly by the Muslims. I am making this statement, not from any feeling of intolerance but out of patience and after careful thinking. Because it is certain that as long as the Hindus as a community do not get ready, the Hindu-Muslim problem with all its fearfullness will persist to live.

"...It is absolutely necessary that the Hindus unite together, work closely as one, build up a unit of selfless and patriotic workers, whose sole purpose would be only service. Forget the caste and creeds and sacrifice more and more for the protection of the Hindu community, own ideals and culture....

"...Conversion should definitely be stopped... Those who have been forcibly converted and those who would like to be back as the Hindus should be given special facility... The Hindus should be free from fear and become brave and strong... A central self-help sena should be built up for the self protection...Hindus should raise up their head against oppression...

"...The bell of challenge should be sounded. But having united and got prepared, built the self-help group or setup or by giving it a look of an army, they should not show any inclination for violence (or intention of inflicting pain/torture) against any one. Self-protection and self-survival should be its purpose. To live and let others live should be its aim.

"The Hindu do not like to see the death of their *Dharma*, the erasing of its culture, the dwindling of its number...

"I think it is my duty to inspire you like this because now humanity is under threat, the Hindu culture and *Dharma* is in danger..."

Index

Acland, A.H. Dyke 344
Adamson, Sir Harvey 52, 54
adult education 450
Afghanistan 392
Africa 194, 263
Ahalyabai 458
Ahimsa 5
Aiyar, S. Subramania 358
Ajmer 467
Ajmer-Merwara, Reform in 226
Akbar 258
Alexander 257
and Co. 321
Ali Brothers, Release of 231
Ali, Ameer 146
Ali, Barkat 231
Ali, Mohammad 179
Ali, Shaukat 179
Aligarh school 113
Aligarh Muslim University 422, 426
Alliance Bank of Simla Limited 323
All-India Muslim League 174, 206
Alsace-Lorraine 198
America 142, 169, 193, 196, 199, 315, 329, 342, 449, 459
ideals of 199
Amritsar Bank 324
Amritsar episode 467
Amritsar Hindu women 467
anarchical crimes 37-8, 149
ancient custom 383
Ancient Indian History and Culture 437
Andreades 321
Andrews 19-23, 29
Anglo-Indian bureaucracy 112, 123
Anglo-Indian officials 113
Anglo-Indian Press 112
Anglo-vernacular middle and high schools 436
Arbuthnot, Sir George 76, 323
Arjuna 465
Arkwright 267
Arnold, Sir Edwin 272
Arundale 179
Arundhati 458
Aryans 6
Asanga 5
Asia 194
Asiatic country 82
Asiatic subjects 264

Asquith 210, 214, 290
Assam 96, 119, 123, 127, 257, 442
Astronomy 436
Australia-Hungary 211
Australians 408
Austria 44, 194, 282, 289, 374
Austria-Hungary 198
Austria-Vienna 449
Ayurveda 436, 443

Bactrians 6
Baker, Sir Edward 52, 119
Balfour, Lord of Burleigh 292
Ball 273
Banaras Hindu University 2-3, 10, 421-2, 424, 429, 431, 433
Banerjee, Surendranath 109-10
Banerji, Sir Gurudas 127
Bank of Bengal 322
Bank of Burma 323
Bank of England 320
Bank of Madras 322
Bank of Upper India 323
Bayer 282
beggar and rasad 386
Behar 55
Belgium 193, 300, 304, 449
Bengal 96, 119-20, 128, 133, 152-3, 209, 269, 323
Bengal Government 65
Bengal Military Police Act 406
Bengal National Bank 324
Bengal, partition of 324
Benthall 236-37
Besant, Annie 174, 179
Bhandarkar 127
Bhargava, Rajeev 6
Bhishma 465
Bigge, Selby 344
Bihar 214, 442
Bill, Ilbert 111
Birmingham 315
Boer War 130
Boer-British Government 148
Bombay 55, 77, 97, 102, 117, 119, 128, 139, 170, 209, 300, 315, 323
Bombay Council 131, 406
Bombay Merchant Bank 324
Bombay Presidency 132
Bombay Village Police Acts 406
Bonar Law 210, 214
Borneo 263
Bose, Ananda Mohan 109
Bose, Jagadish Chandra 212, 444
Brad, Charles 90
Bradlaugh, Charles 90, 113, 172, 358
Brahma 461
Brahmans 161
Brahmin 214
Bright, John 75, 79, 106, 362
British Army 393
British Colonies 14, 388
British Crown 183, 212, 214
British Empire 16, 157, 172, 388, 468
British Firms in India 270
British Government 64, 68, 80, 148, 153, 155, 158, 183, 213, 240, 387
  in India 385
British Guiana 15, 24-5, 27, 30
British India 380, 407
British Indian Empire 145
British Indians 229
British Parliament 167, 238, 240
British Policy in India 398
British Rajputana 226
British rule 55, 57, 136, 155, 215, 383
British Sovereign and Parliament 388
British treasury 145

British weavers 260
Brown, J.A.C. 21
Bruce, Sir Charles 25, 374
Brunyate 327
Buck, Sir Edward 15
Buddhistic commandments 465
Buisson, F. 448
bureaucracy 88-9, 112, 117, 137, 383-84, 219, 387
 and Parliament 373
 and the Educated India 382
 measure 385
bureaucratic system 220
Burma 55, 123, 194, 407
Burmans 408, 419
Burns, John 130
Burton, J.W. 28
Bussell 304
Butler, Sir Harcourt 66-7, 73, 421, 425, 427, 429

Calcutta 55, 59, 77, 90, 110, 181-2, 233-4, 244, 246, 281, 321, 327
Calcutta Police Act 406
Calcutta Sub-Police Act 406
Calcutta University 310
Camilla and Jamalpur riots 380
Campbell-Bannerman, Henry 216
Canada 201, 300, 375, 382
Canadians 408
Cannons 257
Canton 263
Cardinal Newman 432
Cartwright 268
Caste Hindus 250
caste panchayats 375
castes and numerous creeds 64
Catholic Emancipation Bill 381
Catholics 381
Central Bank in India 324, 328
Central Hindu College 432, 437
Central Provinces 55, 96, 104, 214
Central State Bank 326
Challey, M. 202
Chamberlain, Austen 203, 290
Chariar, C. Vijiaraghava 231
Charter Act of 1833 75, 77, 322
Chesney, General George 121
Chile 449
China 292
Chinese labour 31
Chinese people 32
Chinese workmen 277
Chintamani, C.Y. 1
Chitnavis, Sir Gangadhar Rao 63
Christ 258
Christian Government 424
Christians 112, 127, 149, 160-61, 164, 187, 202, 213, 240
 and Mohammedans 469
City of Bombay 406
Civil Disobedience Movement 236, 238
Civil Disobedience Programme 241
Clark, William 252-3
Clarke, Sir George 132
classes and creeds 213
Clive 259, 268
Colonies of England 270
colossal poverty and illiteracy 373
Colvin, Sir Auckland 94
Commercial Education 314-5
Communal Award 8, 9
communal vs Hindu politics 7
communalism 7
conflict vs harmony 7
Congress 8, 105, 113, 115, 118, 132, 155, 157, 159, 162, 172, 199, 201, 203, 206, 218, 225, 228-9, 237, 241, 244, 247, 280, 357, 385, 420
 agitation 162

and the Political Reforms 164
movement 356
Congress Nationalist Party 9
Congress-League scheme 188, 203, 205-6, 213, 368-9, 370, 371, 401
Congress-Muslim League 414
Cornewaile, John 454
Coromandel Coast Indians 263
Cotten, Sir Henry 221, 259
Craigh, James 382
Credit Bank of India 324
criminal law 43
Criminal Law Amendment Act 227
Criminal Procedure Code 38, 40-1, 59
Crown 75, 119, 146, 215
Crown Colonies 15, 229
Cunningham, W. 266-7
Curzon-Wyllie, Lady 150

Dadabhoy 45
Damascus blades 257
Darshanas 436
Das, C.R. 231
Decentralisation Commission 122
Defence of India 227
Act 179
Dehradun Forest Research Institute 336
Delhi 234, 335, 381
Reform in 226
Denmark 300
depressed classes 383
Devi Dass 246
Dharma 4
dharmic universalism 7
Dicey 239
Digby 264, 268-9, 275
Disraeli 374
District Police Acts 406
Drona 465
Dudley, Dodo 267
Durham's recommendation 375
Dutch 259
Dutch Guiana 25-8, 30
Dutt, Romesh Chandra 106-7, 260, 262, 265
Duty demands 160
Dyer, Henry 313

East African coast 265
East India Company 169, 259, 262, 264, 269, 321
Act 74
Eastern Bengal 53, 55, 59, 96, 119, 123, 127, 153
economic and social reforms 11
educated class 117-8, 383
Education Commission 72
of 1884 384
educational backwardness 372
educational system 1, 68
Edward III 454
Egypt 153, 194
Egyptian law of deportation 153
Electoral Reform Bill 180
Elementary Education Act 374, 446
Elementary Education Bill 9, 62, 184, 374
Elphinstone 257
Emigration Act of 1908 18
Emigration Acts 15
England 75-6, 78, 102, 115, 129, 142, 145, 186, 193-5, 257, 259, 265, 270, 304, 306, 315, 347-8, 371, 374-6, 392, 413, 448, 454-5
English 195, 382
fellow subjects 185
iron industry 268
language 453
power 261

trade and commerce with India 272
equal felicity 9
Eurasians 82
Europe 79, 169, 194, 295, 303, 313, 387, 388
Europe Britain 388
Europe, industrial development of 279
European Agency 216
European cities 379
European community in India 186
European labour 32
European world 194
Europeans 2, 82, 214, 244
and Anglo-Indians 111
Excise 9

Fakir Chand 247
Famine Commission 219
Famine Commissioners 297
Famine Insurance Fund 93
Fawcett 77
Fazl-ul-Haq 231, 233
Fiji 24, 26, 28, 30
first class world-power 387
forced labour and supplies 386
Forster 375
Fort Saint George, Bombay, and Agra 102
France 193, 195, 199, 267, 304, 374, 449, 459
France and Flanders 194
French 195, 198, 382
brains 306
technical skill 306
Fundamental Rights 242

Gaekwar 107
Gandhi, Mahatma 1, 6, 11-2, 16, 147, 212, 229, 236-7, 248, 466-7
Fast 242
Gandhian programme of Non-Cooperation 9
Gandhi-Irwin Pact 236
Gargi 458
Gautama 465
Geeta 467
Genoa 258-9
George, Lloyd 35, 84, 200, 210-1, 214, 227
German militarism 193, 389
Germans 195
Germany 142, 193-4, 199, 282, 289, 295, 304-5, 315, 341-2, 374, 449, 459
Ghadr Conspiracy 215
Ghadr Movement 215
ghazis 151
Ghori, Mohammad 465
Ghose, Lalmohan 106
Ghosh, Rash Behari 127
Ghuznavi 422
Gibbs, H.P. 342
Gladstone, William Ewart 42-3, 50, 110, 357, 360, 376
Reform Bill 374
Gokhale, Gopal Krishna 1, 3, 9, 11, 17, 30, 60, 66-7, 71, 82, 115, 130, 132, 165, 172, 184, 212, 219, 456
Education Bill 62
Government of India 17-8, 26, 32, 49, 51, 55, 67-8, 78, 92, 97-8, 100-01, 117, 121, 131, 142, 171, 239, 289, 335, 338, 340, 350, 360-2, 367, 394-5, 402, 408, 411, 413, 415, 417-8, 433, 442
Government of Lord Lansdowne 94
Governor-General-in Council 412, 416, 418
Governor-in-Council 96, 402-3, 405, 407

Grant, Sir Charles 75
Granth Sahib 467
Great Britain 199, 341, 388
Great War in 1914 467
Green, John Richard 266
Guiana 28
Gujarat 470
Gupta, Nellie Sen 243

Hafliday 357
Haldane 210
Hamilton, C.J. 254
Hayden, H.H. 349
Higher Technological Training 311
Himalaya Bank Limited 323
Hindi 455
Hindi and Urdu languages 63
Hindu University 444
  growth of the 443
  idea of the 436
Hinduism 470
Hindu-Mohammedan riots 380
Hindu-Muslim problems 466
Hindu-Muslim unity 471
Hindus 5, 7, 112, 120, 127, 149, 160-2, 164, 169, 187, 202, 211, 213, 237, 240, 256, 364, 370, 377, 380, 382, 422-3, 426, 431, 468
  civilisation 6, 465
  community 4
  culture 472
  Delhi 381
  dharma 6
  donors 424
  houses 467
  Mahasabha Movement 3
  minorities 127
  religion 424, 469
  right 7
  sages 434
  Shastras 434
  society 465
  students 424
  women 466-7
Hindustan Bank 321
Hindustani 455
Hindutva 6
Holyoake, George Jacob 7
Home Rule League 174, 182
Horniman, B.G. 231
Houghton, Bernard 88
Humanity and patriotism 160
Hume, Allan Octavian 107, 221
Huns 6
Hunter, Sir William 82, 100, 271-2, 352
Hyderabad 444

Ilbert 15-6
illiterate masses 383, 387
Imam, Syed Hasan 229, 231
impartial justice 89
Imperial Engineering Colleges 312
Imperial Industrial Service 339, 343
Imperial Legislative Council 3
Imperial Polytechnic Institute 312, 339, 348
indentured labourers, financial prosperity of the 30
India 21, 25, 67, 257, 279, 282, 342, 385, 387, 428, 458
  agricultural conditions 295
  agricultural problems of 300
  Anglo-Indian bodies in 214
  and Europe, navigation between 264
  and the Peace Conference 200
  backwardness of 1
  banking in 321

blood and treasure 389
economic stability 293
educated class in 109, 373
Loyalty 225
people of 202
public opinion in 205
recruiting depots in 15
safety in the future 392
universities in 445
youth of 426
Indian administration 102, 410
Indian and English youths 400
Indian Army 393, 400
Indian Bank of Madras 324
Indian banks 323, 326
Indian Budget in 1907 117
Indian bureaucracy 113
Indian capacity for the joint-stock banking 320
Indian Chemical Service 339, 346
Indian Civil Service 74, 76, 79-80, 87, 89, 102, 122, 146, 184, 186, 217, 220-01, 226, 368, 407
Indian Civil Service Association 220
Indian communities 466
Indian cotton manufactures 261
Indian cottons 269
Indian Councils 32
Indian Councils Act 124, 129, 356, 359
Indian culture 5
Indian demands 168
Indian electorate 372
Indian Emigration Bill 16
Indian Empire 408
Indian Expeditionary Force 193
Indian Famine Commission 281
Indian fellow-subjects 148
Indian freedom and nation building 11
Indian Government 395
Indian graduates 446
Indian immigrants 15
poverty of the 25
Indian Industrial Commission 2, 3, 325
Indian Industrial Conference 280, 313, 315
Indian industrial development 293
Indian industries 265, 274, 286
and handicrafts 258
Indian Judges 80
Indian manufacturers 260
Indian National Congress 9, 34, 90, 104, 107, 112, 157, 170, 174, 203, 221, 233-4, 242, 279, 281, 301, 313, 356, 407, 415
Indian Penal Code 40
Indian people 152
Indian public 279
Indian public opinion 394
Indian reform 397
Indian Science Congress 444
Indian shipping 265
Indian society 7, 372, 390
Indian Specie Bank 324
Indian states 444
Indian Statute 406
Indian tariff 394
Indian trade 185, 259
Indian troops 225
Indian universities 348, 446
Indian vernaculars 436
Indian village 30
Indian youths 310
Indians in South Africa 147
Indians, educated 386, 389
Indians, higher education of 444
indigenous agency 145
Indo-British Association 214
Industrial Chemistry 439
Industrial Development 3

industrial revolution 268
Industrial Commission 229
Irish Free State 449
Irish Nationalists 290
Italian 195
Italy 198
Ito, Hirobumi 329
Ito, Marqais 313
Iyengar, Bhashyam 212
Iyer, C.P. Ramaswamy 233
Iyer, Sir Subramania 127

Jackson, C. 150, 322
Jamaica 24, 28, 30
Japan 86, 142, 158, 166, 169, 184, 282-3, 291-2, 312, 315, 341, 392, 449, 459
    banking in 329
    contrast progress in 387
Japanese 313, 387
    defeated China in 1895 and Russia in 1905 460
Java 263
Jayakar 237
Jenkins, M.H. 51, 299
Jinnah 63
joint-stock banks 320
Jung, Salar 212
justice and freedom 187
Justice Telang 358
justice, civil and criminal 383

Kabir Panthis 20
Kahimtoola, Ibrahim 251
Kama 4
Karnatik 269
Kathiawar 265
    and Ahmedabad Banking Corporation 324
Kaye 357
Kelkar, N.C. 131-2, 231
Khaddar 241
Khan, Agha 426, 470
Khan, Hakim Ajmal 231
Khaparde, G.S. 231
Kher, L.G. 248
Khilafat cause 467
Khojas 470
King Richard 455
King-Emperor George V 55, 86
Kobe 316
Krishna 469
Kunzru, Hirday Nath 82, 184

Labour Party 290
Lahore 66, 104
Lakshmi Bai of Jhansi 458
Lal, Chimman 17
Lal, Lala Harkishan 231
Lalkaka 150
Lancashire 268, 290
Lancashire party in England 35
Land Acquisition Act 317
land revenue 386
landed aristocracy 112-3
landholders 364
Lands Clauses Acts 318
Lawley, Sir Arthur 129
League of Nations 200
Lee, William 267
Lees-Smith 315
legislative council 92-3, 113
    reform of the 90
Lely, Frederick 79
liberal government 124
liberty and despotism 388
Lilavati 458
Limited Liability Law 321
Local self-Government 111, 128
London 77, 80, 82, 236, 268
London University 426
Lord Buddha 465
Lord Canning 363
Lord Chelmsford 205-6, 209, 213,

215, 368-9, 371-2, 377-8, 388-90, 392-3, 395-6, 398, 400-01, 403-4, 408-11, 413-7, 419
Lord Cornwalis 423
Lord Crewe 15-6, 286, 288
Lord Curzon 46, 110, 114-5, 124, 210, 430-31
Lord Dalhousie 271-2
Lord Durham 382
Lord Hardinge 191, 221, 271, 289, 293, 388
Lord Lytton 88, 110-11, 115
Lord Mayo 97, 100, 220
Lord Minto 108, 115-6, 118-9, 124, 136, 150, 356-7, 359
Lord John Morley 108, 115, 117-9, 123-5, 128, 131-3, 136, 138, 143, 145-6, 159, 286, 288-9, 355-7, 359-60, 362, 364-5
Lord Ripon 19, 68, 94, 107, 111, 128
Lord Salisbury 88
Lord Stanley 75
low caste Hindu 20

Macaulay 75, 80, 111, 183, 216, 378
Macdonald, Ramsay 9
MacDonnell, Antony 102, 122, 124, 275, 361
Mackarness 61, 153
MacKenna, James 294, 296-8
Macnaughten 76
Madan, T.N. 6-7
Madge 59
Madras 29, 55, 77-8, 97, 102, 117, 119, 128, 139, 209, 214, 315, 356
government 65
Magna Carta of British Liberties 376
Mahabharata 151, 458, 462
Mahajana Sabha 37
Maharaja of Benares 133, 425
Maharaja of Bikaner 201
Maitreyi 458
Malabar 467
Malaviya, Madan Mohan 1-4, 6-10, 13, 32, 62, 74, 87-8, 164, 168, 187, 189, 230, 233, 237, 242, 248, 251, 355-6, 365, 421, 425, 465-71
colossal personality 11
Malay Peninsula 265
Manchester 315
Mangles 76
Mann, Harold 350
Manu 150
Marco Polo 258
Marey-Oyens, M. 299
marriage law 29
Marwari Association 22
Mathematics 436
and Astronomy 437
Maujilal 247
Mauritius 15
Maynard 72
McNeill 17
Medicine, Indigenous System of 231
Meerut 244
Megasthenes 257
Mehta, Sir Pherozeshah 90, 105, 212
Meyer, Sir William 231
middle class 113, 116
military expenditure 145
Mill, Hugh Robert 338
Milton 455
Mineral Wealth of India 273
Misra, G.N. 233
Misra, Gokaran Nath 231
Mohammedan community 426
Mohammedan fellow-subjects 125-7, 134, 137

Mohammedan graduates 127
Mohammedans 8, 64, 112-3, 116-7, 120, 136, 149, 160-62, 164, 169, 192, 211, 215, 364, 370-71, 377, 380-82, 465-7
Mohammedan students 63
Montagu 85, 205-6, 209, 213, 215, 368-9, 371-2, 375, 377-8, 388-90, 392-3, 395-6, 398-401, 403-4, 408-11, 413-7, 419
Montagu-Chelmsford Reforms 365
Montford 235
Morley Minto scheme 408
Morley-Minto Reforms 108, 173, 182, 413
Morocco 194
most backward classes 64
Moulvi Abdul Latif of Lucknow 246
Mughal Empire 257-8
Mukerjee, Radhakumud 263
Multan temples 467
Mundella 305-6
Munshi, K.M. 231
Murray 259
Muslim 5, 202, 468
and Hindus 377
Muslim League 34, 126, 160-62, 172, 174, 177, 182, 201, 203, 213, 369, 371, 420
Muslim society 467
Mussalmans 187, 213, 240, 422, 426, 470
Mutiny 75, 217
dark days of the 44
Mysore 444

Nagasake 316
Nagpur 59
Nalanda 434
Nandy, Ashis 6-7
Naoroji, Dadabhai 76, 78, 82-3, 114-5, 130, 146, 171-2, 181-3, 185, 212, 217, 358
Napoleon 267
Natal 15
National finance and economy 329
National Flag 244
nationalism 57
Native Princes 40
natural birth-right 75
natural intelligence 376
Nawab Abdul Majid 63
Nawab of Rampur 133
New Zealand 300, 379
New Zealanders 408
Newspapers Offences Act 42
in 1908 47
Nicholson, Sir Frederick 253, 299, 341
Noakhali 471
North-West Frontier 300
North-West Frontier Province 55
North-Western Provinces 94-5, 102, 110, 120
Norton, Bardley 358
Nottingham, riots of 379

Oldham 349
Olive Day 292
Open schools 463
Oriental learning and theology 443
Orissa 214, 442
Osaka 316
Oudh 94-5, 120
Oudh Commercial Bank 324

Pal, Kristo Das 18
Paliwal, Jwaran 244
panch mukhtar 376
Pandit Ajodhya Nath 358

Pandit Balak Ram Pandya 324
Pandit Jay Dev Shastri 246
Pandit Kapil Dev Pande 246
Pandit Lakshmi Narayan Dhar 110
Pandit Om Prakash Tiwari 246
Pandit Satya Narayan Datt 246
Pandit Shiva Datta Pande 246
Pandit Shiva Prasad Shukla 246
Panipat 467, 469
Parekh, Gokuldas 209
Paris 303
Park Brothers and Company 342
Parsis 8, 127, 149, 112, 160, 164, 187, 202, 213, 240, 466
partition of Bengal 153
Patel, V.J. 231, 233
patriotism and brotherliness 164
patriotism and public spirit 377
Patro 237
Patwari Cess 94-5
Paul, Herbert 78
Peace Conference 200-01
    Representation at the 229
Pearson 19-21, 29
peasant and labouring population 383
Penchriche, Richard 454
People's Bank of India 324
Perry, Sir E. 76
Persia 392
Persian merchants 257
Persians 6
Phipps, Henry 296
Pillai, P. Xesava 233
Plague Administration 222
politically-minded clashes 383
Post-War Reforms 34
poverty 11, 219
Prasad, Mata 247
Prasad, Sukhdev 247
Presidencies of Fort St. George, Bombay 120
    and Agra 120
Presidencies of Fort William in Bengal 102, 120
Presidencies of Madras and Bombay 96, 123
Presidency Banks 326, 328
    Act 323
Presidency of Agra 102
Press Act of 1878 43, 61
Press Bill 36
Press prosecutions 42
Prithvi Raj 465
Protestants and Catholics 380
Provinces of Bengal 46, 121
Provinces of Bombay 121
Provinces of Madras 121
Provincial Civil Service 79
Provincial Councils 129, 130
Provincial Executive Councils 417
Provincial Governments 96
    Constitution of the 101
Punjab 53, 55, 99, 119, 123, 127, 135, 154, 163, 300, 324
Punjab Banking Co. 323
Punjab Hindu Sammelan 5
Punjab Land Alienation Act 154
Punjab National Bank 325-6
Punjab Provincial Industries Committee 325
Punjab, Reform in the 226

Queen Elizabeth 259
Queen Victoria 111
Quinton 94

Rai Gangaram Bahadur 300
Rai Jogendra Ghose Bahadur 281
Rai, Lala Lajpat 131, 152
Raja of Mahmadabad 426
Raja of Tehri 133

Raja Sir T. Mohave Rio 357
Ram Saroop 247
Rama 469
Rama and Krishna 465
Raman, C.V. 445
Ranade, Mahadev Govind 212, 270
Rao, Subba 78
Reform Bill of 1832 376
Reform Bill of 1867 374
Reform of the legislative councils 112
Regulation of 1818 152
religion and ethics 462
religion and politics 6
religion and women 468
religions, races and castes 377
religious and patriotic workers 161
religious animosities 378
religious ceremonies 423
religious differences 377
religious dissensions 377
religious extremism 6
religious injunctions and prohibitions 461
religious marriages 29
religious scriptures 423
religious toleration among the Protestants of England 381
religious tradition 7
Resolutions, re-Affirmation of the 225
Rislay, Sir Herbert 45
rituals 423
Row, T. Madhava 212
Rowlatt and the Bundelkhand Land Alienation Bills 9
Rowlett Committee 214-5, 221, 227
Roy, P.C. 348
Royal Commission 78, 122, 143, 327, 349, 351
Royal Commission on Agriculture 456
Royal Commission on the public services in India 348
Royal Highness the Prince of Wales 102
rural classes 373
Russell, J. Scott 301, 303
Russia 166, 194, 199, 313, 445
Russian 195
ryots 389

Sadh, Virendra Kumar 246
Salt Tax 95
salvation (moksha) 4
Samuelson 304, 306, 308
Sanatan Dharma 5, 7
Sanatan Dharma Mahasabha 9
Sanderson Committee 14-5, 21, 24-6, 28
Sanskrit language and literature 435
Sapru 237
Sastri 34
Savitri 458
scholarships and fellowships 311
Scientific and Technical Education 4
Scythians 6
secular and the religious 6
secularism 7
    in India 6
seditious meetings 51
Seditious Meetings Act 51, 61-2
Self-determination 227
Self-Governing Dominions 229
Self-Government 70, 115, 118, 166, 172-4, 178, 180, 182-3, 185, 187-8, 203, 213, 216, 220, 222, 225, 239, 368, 391
    for India 187

in India 372
Setalvad 422-3
Shahjahan 258
Shakespeare 455
Shand, Alexander Allan 330
Sharp, W.H. 313
Shields 448
Shimla 335
Shuddhi movement 470
Sikhs 8, 240
Singh, Naroang 247
Singh, Puran 336
Singh, Ram Palak 247
Singh, Thakur Munshi 247
Sinha, Satyendra Prasad 119, 200, 388
Sir Charles Wood 363-4
Sir Edward Baker 133
Sir Harold Stuart 38, 116, 136, 138
Sir J. Willoughby 76
Sir John Hewett 122, 124, 133-4
Sir Profulla Chandra Roy 2
Sir William Curzon Wyllie 149
slave labour 14
Smith, Adam 378-9
South Africa 149
South Africa Republics 194
South Africans 408
Spain 194
Stead 111
Strabo 257
Strachey, John 380
Sudan 194
suicide rate among indentured labourer 30
Sumatra 263
Surat 155
Swadeshi banking and industry 325
Swaraj 187
Swaraj Leagues 182
Sweden 268
Switzerland 300

tahsil or taluka 404
Takshasila 434
Talukdars 94
Tata Hydro-Electric Works 282
Tata Industrial Bank 319
Tata Iron and Steel Works 282, 342
Tata, J.N. 212
Taylor 263
Teachers' Training College 437
Technical and Industrial Education 142
technical schools 309
terrorism 55
terrorists and anarchists 56
Thakur Kamal Singh 246
Tilak, Bal Gangadhar 11, 229
Tisserand, M. 299
Tiwari, Sampuran 247
Tokyo 329
Tower, Charles 341
Toynbee, Arnold 265
Trinidad 24-5, 30
trivarga 4
Tucker, Henry St. George 262
Turkey 192, 195, 198, 392
Turkish rule 199
Turks 6

U.P. 244, 247
United Kingdom 82, 99, 170, 214, 224, 283, 300, 321, 342, 366, 374, 376, 395, 404
Universities and University College 311, 399
United Provinces 29, 64, 96, 99, 119, 122-3, 133, 208, 214, 300, 373, 404, 436
United Provinces Congress Committee 37
United States 282-3, 292, 306, 312,

342, 374
universal education 64
Universities of Tokyo and Kyoto 338
University of Leeds 315
University of London 310
University Training Corps 441
Upper India 365
Urdu language 63

Vaccination Act 65
Vande Mataram 241
Vashistha 138, 465
Veda Vyasa 161
Vedangas 436
Vedas 423, 436
Venice 258-9
Vernacular Press Act 36, 43-4, 50
of 1878 42, 48
Vijiaraghavachariar 189
Village Chowkidari Act 406
Vishnu 465
Vishvamitra 137, 138
Voelcker 300

Wacha 33
Wadia 179
Wales 374, 380, 448
War 200, 388, 391, 396, 447
War for Cadetships 393
War in Europe 219
War, Eastern theatres of 392
War, effects of the 388
Waseda University 316
wasteful military expenditure 93
Watt 267, 268
Wedderburn, Sir William 107, 221, 301
Western Bengal 153
Western concept 6
white paper 240, 241
Williams, Monier 435
Wilson, H.H. 197, 199, 227, 262
women's franchise 227

Yamaguchi 316
Yorkshire 380
Yudhistira 465
Yule, George 358

zamindars 94, 154